Mark Twain:
A Bibliography of the Collections of The Mark Twain Memorial & The Stowe-Day Foundation.

One of a series of autochrome photographs taken by Alvin Langdon Coburn at Stormfield, about 1908

MarkTwain

A Bibliography of
the Collections of the
Mark Twain Memorial and the
Stowe-Day Foundation

Compiled by William M. McBride

A Publication of
McBride/Publisher
Hartford, Connecticut

Copyright (c) 1984 by
McBride/Publisher.

ISBN 0-930313-00-3

First edition.

Except for brief quotations in critical reviews, no part of this book may be reproduced or used in any form or by any means electronic or mechanical including photocopying, recording or by an information storage and retrieval system without permission in writing from the publisher.

Printed in U.S.A.

Gramercy!

This book is better because these people helped: **Deidre Whitlock** (patience), **Diana Royce** (knowledge, perception, advice, resourcefulness), **Margaret Cheney and Wynn Lee** (consent to the whole project and cooperation at every turn), **Dudley Whittelsey** (steadfast enthusiam), **Bob Doherty** (encouragement at all the right times) and, fundamentally and always, **Dad,** whose part in this began with the phrase "Go look it up!" during almost every evening meal from the time I was five.

Special thanks to **Fred Bentley, Sr.,** of Marietta, Georgia, whose innocent question in 1981 started all this in motion.

This book is in your hands because a few people I have not yet met face-to-face trusted in it. Like many projects undertaken by humans, this one was championed most by those closest to it, encouraged by those closest to those closest to it, and brought to reality, in the end, by comparative strangers. Well-wishers were plentiful, but type and paper and ink cost more than "good luck" will buy. Sometimes, the way to get what you want is to just ask. When we did, enough of the right people answered. Jim Burch, an occasional yet steady buyer of first editions from our book lists, happened to own a printing establishment. We presented our case: a book ready to print, the type all set and in place, the photographs all taken, but not quite enough money to pay for it all at once. Jim agreed to print it anyway and to handle the mail orders and to send out the books and to generally become one of those closest to the project.

Mason Carter, a subscriber and a Mark Twain collector, is substantially responsible for overcoming the well-known inertia small publishers face every day. Shirley Schneider, another mail order customer, contributed more than a few hard-earned ergs as well. And John Zubal, Bob Doherty and Esther Doherty added theirs, too, and before long, we had a book going to press.

When this book was first announced in the fall of 1982, some 281 people and organizations placed their orders, fully believing, as we did, that the book was mere months from their shelves. Through the intervening two years (!), less than a dozen have given up hope. The remaining faithful are to be thanked and thanked again. We hope your patience will be well rewarded by what you are about to read.

Photographic Credits

The photographs of Mark Twain included in this book are all in the collection of the Mark Twain Memorial and are used with their permission. Specific acknowledgement is made to the following individuals and organizations that donated various of these photographs to the Memorial: The Wadsworth Atheneum, Olivia Loomis Lada-Mocalski, Mrs. John Arnold, The Library of Congress, Ida Langdon, Talcott Mountain Science Center, Olivia Jensen, The Keystone View Company, Yale University, The Reader's Digest et al.

An Introduction.

Mark Twain's place in American literature is secure. And the place of his books in the libraries of scholars, collectors and just plain readers is likewise secure. This sustaining interest is evidenced, in part, by the content of this book. The multiplicity of reprints, many with new introductions, comments and so forth, show that Mark Twain's books continually move people to put words on paper for one reason or another. The many children's editions and adaptations confirm the simplicity and power of his characters and their adventures. The many foreign editions attest to the universality of his works. The endless stream of scholarly investigation of Mark Twain, his contemporaries and his writings prove the depth and complexity of the man and his creations. While other major figures in American literature are often grouped into schools or styles, Mark Twain stands alone, atop them all.

Merle Johnson compiled the first Mark Twain Bibliography in 1910. It was revised in 1935 by Jacob Blanck, who went on to produce the monumental and indispensable *Bibliography of American Literature* in 1957. Blanck's three sections on Mark Twain in BAL, together with Johnson's two editions, have stood for decades as the basic reference on Mark Twain. Tom Tenney contributed greatly to Mark Twain scholarship with the publication of *Mark Twain: A Reference Guide* (G.K. Hall & Co., Boston) in 1977 and the issuing of two updates since then. Even with all the fine work available, there was no single volume that covered the full breadth of Mark Twain's writings.

This Bibliography of the Mark Twain Collections of the Mark Twain Memorial and the Stowe-Day Foundation, both of Hartford, Connecticut, does not list every book ever published by or about Mark Twain; it does list every book by or about him in the possession of the two organizations.

To produce a book at once useful to the collector and the book dealer, the librarian and the scholar, is the aim here. To satisfy the collector and the dealer, photographs of each cover, title page and points of issue (where they occur) are shown; this aids in quick identification of first editions. To assist the librarian and scholar, primary and secondary works of Mark Twain are organized chronologically and a full section devoted to works of criticism and biography are included. This section is keyed by Tenney reference numbers and a fuller summary of content may be found in his book and supplements. Every letter from Mark Twain that the Stowe-Day Foundation and Mark Twain Memorial own are here summarized. Samples of first pages of letters are shown photographically; these were selected at five year intervals from about 1865 to 1909. Complete indexes of names, titles, publishers and illustrators follow the main text.

The organization of the book is chronological and structured around the American first editions, even in cases where the English or Canadian editions precede them. The order of listing is:
First American Edition(s)
First English Edition(s)
First Canadian Edition(s)
First editions in English other than the above
All later English-language editions, arranged
  chronologically
Foreign-language editions arranged alphabetically
  by language, then chronologically within
  the language grouping.

Within the listing of each title, ordinary editions are listed first (in the order of issue where points of issue occur), copies inscribed by Clemens next, and copies of importance inscribed by others last. All inscriptions noted are by Clemens unless otherwise indicated.

Sets are broken up by title for the main text of the book. Many later editions change the content from the first edition, but no attempt is made to describe the page-by-page content of every reprint. Abridged or otherwise altered editions are listed under the main title from which they were taken.

A supplementary list of primary Mark Twain items which are not owned by either collection follows the indexes; this section is solely for the sake of completeness and full bibliographic descriptions of these items are to be found in the *Bibliography of American Literature*.

The photographs of Mark Twain throughout the text are from the Mark Twain Memorial collection. Placement of the photographs is intended to be contemporaneous with the books being described on adjoining pages wherever possible.

In sum, this book serves two purposes: it provides access to the two collections on which the book is based; and it provides a working checklist for anyone interested in Mark Twain and his works, for whatever reason.

The plan is to issue supplements to this book as additions to the collections warrant.

The Contents.

- 1-361 **Books by Mark Twain**
- 363-412 **Letters by Mark Twain**
- 413-418 **Contributions by Mark Twain to Collections and Anthologies**
- 419-426 **Ephemeral Material by and about Mark Twain**
- 427-460 **Biographical and Critical Works about Mark Twain**
- 461-467 **Primary Mark Twain material not in our Collections**
- 469 **Indexes**

[front cover (with dust-jacket if so issued)]

[title page]

[point of issue *or* inscription by Clemens]

Author (if other than Clemens).
Title of Book.
City of publication, date: publisher.
    Other information about the book such as edition, issue, etc.
    Other named authors (such as editors, translator, etc.)
    Illustrator, if any.
    Binding.
    Inscription, if any:
    Quotation/line by line/with slash/ indicating new line./All inscriptions are
BAL Number *by Clemens/unless otherwise indicated.*

The books.

Under each title, the first book listed is the first American edition, unless otherwise stated. Each first edition is described and the front cover and title page is shown. Where a dustjacket is present, it is also shown. Covers which bear no title or decoration are not shown and the title page illustration is moved to the position usually occupied by the front cover illustration.

BAL numbers are given for each first edition where it first appears. Additional listings (such as inscribed copies) that bear the same date as the first listing do not have the BAL number repeated. Points of issue noted are based on BAL but for the sake of clarity, the first issue of a given point is designated A, the second issue B, etc. Charts of multiple copies with points of issue often accompany listings and each point is described beneath the chart.

For the sake of economy, "etc." in roman type, may occur in a listing other than the first. This abbreviation is used to (1) shorten a title (Example: *Adventures of Huckleberry Finn Tom Sawyer's Comrade*. In second listings of the title, "etc." replaces "Tom Sawyer's Comrade".) and (2) shorten a list of publishers (Example: *Roughing It* lists multiple publishers for the first edition; "etc." is used where the following listing of publishers is exactly the same as the immediately previous one.).

Books by Mark Twain.

Mark Twain in the Quarry Farm study, Elmira, New York, 1903.

The Celebrated Jumping Frog of Calaveras County and Other Sketches.
New York, 1867: C.H. Webb, Publisher, 119 & 121 Nassau St. American News Co., Agents.
Edited by John Paul (actually Charles Henry Webb).
First issue with leaf of ads before title page; 66: last line: *life* unbroken; and 198: last line: *this* unbroken
Copy 1: blue cloth
Copy 2: red cloth

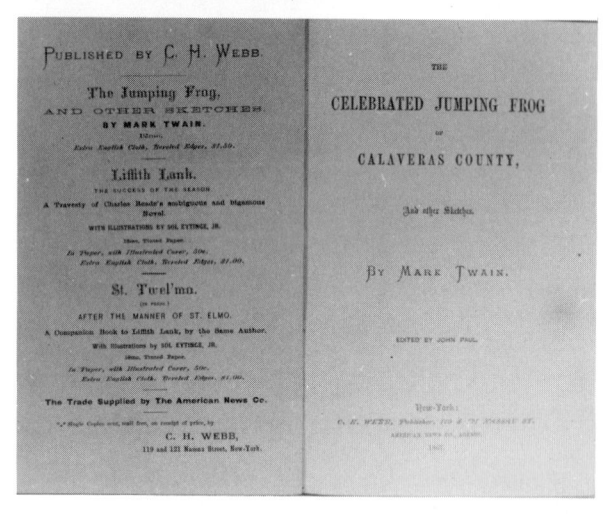

BAL 3310

The Celebrated Jumping Frog of Calaveras County and Other Sketches.
New York, 1867: C.H. Webb, Publisher, 119 & 121 Nassau St. American News Co., Agents.
Second issue lacking ads before title page.
Brown cloth.

Mark Twain, about 1864, was a reporter on the Virginia City (California) Territorial Enterprise.

The Celebrated Jumping Frog of Calaveras County and Other Sketches.
New York, 1868: C.H. Webb, Publisher, 119 & 121 Nassau St. American News Co., Agents.
Plum cloth.

The Celebrated Jumping Frog of Calaveras County and Other Sketches.
New York, 1869: C.H. Webb, Publisher.
Copy 1: terra-cotta cloth.
Copy 2: brown cloth.

The Celebrated Jumping Frog of Calaveras County and Other Sketches.
n.p., 1959: West Virginia Pulp and Paper Company.
Designed by Bradbury Thompson.
Paper over boards with leather shelfback.(Slipcase absent).

The Celebrated Jumping Frog of Calaveras County.
Palmer Lake, Colorado, 1965: Filter Press.
Centennial edition.
Illustrated.
Paper wrappers.

The Celebrated Jumping Frog of Calaveras County and The Man That Corrupted Hadleyburg.
New York, (1968): Franklin Watts, Inc.
Illustrated by Harold Berson.
Printed cloth library binding.

The Notorious Jumping Frog & Other Stories.
Avon, Connecticut, (1970): The Heritage Press.
Selected and introduced by Edward Wagenknecht.
Illustrated by Joseph Low.

The Jumping Frog and Other Stories and Sketches from the Exquisite Pen of Mr. Samuel L. Clemens.
Mount Vernon, N.Y., n.d.: The Peter Pauper Press.
Illustrated by Donald McKay.
Pictorial paper over boards.
Slipcase.

(The Celebrated Jumping Frog.)
n.p., n.d.: The Eihosha Ltd.
In English with Chinese footnotes.
Edited with notes by Sakae Morioka in Chinese.

La célèbre grenouille sauteuse et autres contes.
n.p., (1979): Mercure de France.
        In French.
            Translated by Gabriel deLautrec.
            Illustrated by Roger Blachon.
            Paper wrappers.

Il Ranocchio Saltatore E Altri Racconti
(Milan, 1950): Rizzoli Editore.
        In Italian.
            Paper wrappers.

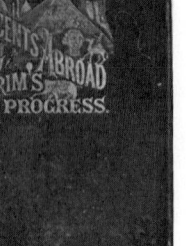

The Innocents Abroad, or The New Pilgrims' Progress.
Hartford, 1869: American Publishing Company. Bliss & Co., Newark, N.J.; R.W. Bliss & Co., Toledo, Ohio. F.G. Gilman & Co., Chicago, Ill.; Nettleton & Co., Cincinnati, Ohio. F.A. Hutchinson & Co., St Louis, Mo. H.H. Bancroft and Company, San Francisco.
First issue with page reference numbers lacking on xvii-xviii; last entry on xviii: *Valedictory*; 129: no illustration; 643: *Chapter XLI;* and 654: *Personal History.*
Brown cloth: three copies.
Full leather: one copy.
BAL 3316   Three-quarter morocco: one copy.

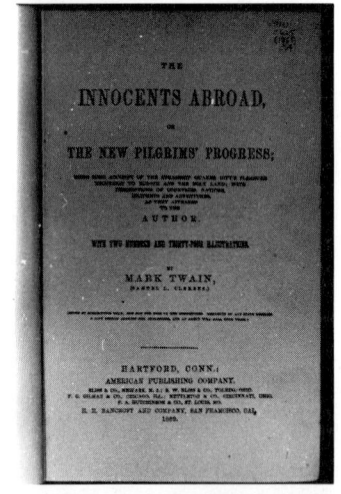

The Innocents Abroad, or The New Pilgrims' Progress.
Hartford, 1869: American Publishing Company. etc.
First issue.
New endpapers.
Tipped in:
1: Original prospectus for *Excursion to the Holy Land,* etc. 2: Original passenger list from the "Quaker City" showing *"Sml. Clemens . . . . . San Francisco, Cal."* with handwritten notes in an unknown hand.
3: ANS by Merle Johnson on the publication of this title.
4: Autograph poem by "Bloodgood Cutter", *("The Farmer Poet, who was aboard, & referred to constantly in the book(. . . .) Merle Johnson")*
Brown cloth.

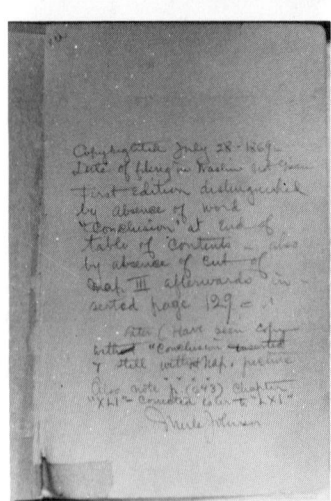

The Innocents Abroad, or The New Pilgrims' Progress.
San Francisco, Cal. 1869: H.H. Bancroft and Company.
Hartford: American Publishing Company.
First issue.
Variant title page with above imprints.
Brown cloth.

The Innocents Abroad, or The New Pilgrims' Progress.
Hartford, 1869:   American Publishing Company. etc.
First issue.
Brown cloth.
Inscribed copy:
Miss Ida Clark./August 1869/ Compliments of The Author

The Innocents Abroad, or The New Pilgrims' Progress.
Hartford, 1869:   American Publishing Company. Bliss & Co., Newark, N.J.; R.W. Bliss & Co., Toledo, Ohio. F.G. Gilman & Co., Chicago, Ill.; Nettleton & Co., Cincinnati, Ohio. F.A. Hutchinson & Co., St. Louis, Mo. H.H. Bancroft and Company, San Francisco.
Publisher's prospectus. Brown cloth. Probably the second issue, since the page reference numbers are present on xvii-xviii and the last entry on xviii ends *Conclusion*.

The Innocents Abroad, or The New Pilgrims' Progress.
Hartford, 1869: American Publishing Company. etc.
Second issue with page reference numbers present on xvii-xviii; last entry on xviii: Conclusion; 129: portrait of Napoleon III; 643: Chapter XLI; and 654: Personal History.
Brown cloth: one copy.
Full leather: one copy.
Red library leather: one copy.
One copy rebound.

The Innocents Abroad, or The New Pilgrims' Progress.
Hartford, 1869: American Publishing Company. etc.
Third issue with the same points as the second except 654: *History of the Bible*.
Brown cloth: three copies.
Three-quarter morocco: one copy.
One copy rebound.

The Innocents Abroad, or The New Pilgrims' Progress.
Hartford, 1869: American Publishing Company. etc.
Third issue.
Full leather.
Inscribed copy:
To Sir John Bennett/With the warm regards of/The Author.—/Saml. L. Clemens/Mark Twain./Nov. 7, 1872.

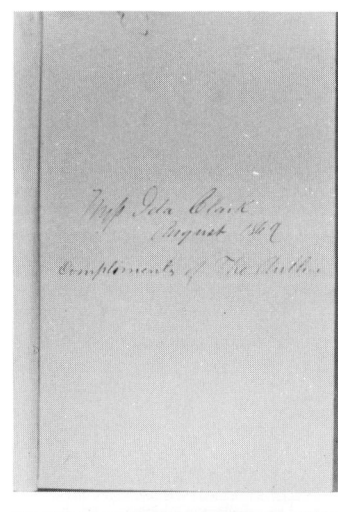

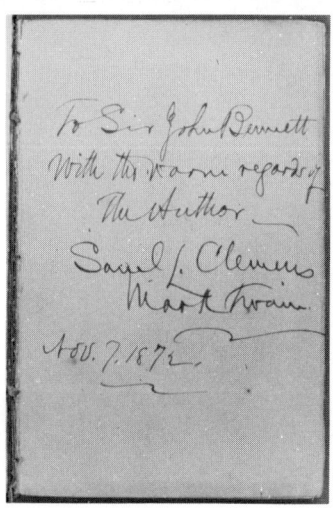

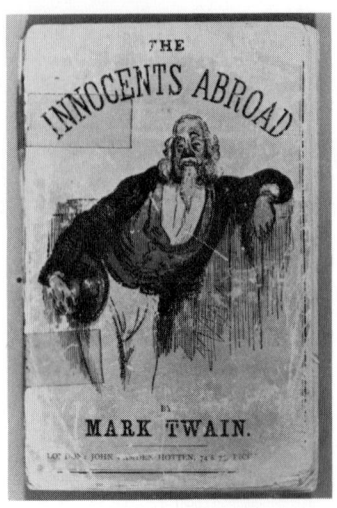

The Innocents Abroad.
London, n.d. (1870): John Camden Hotten, Piccadilly. First English edition, unauthorized by Clemens. Introduction by Edward P. Hingston.
BAL 3590   Printed paper wrappers.

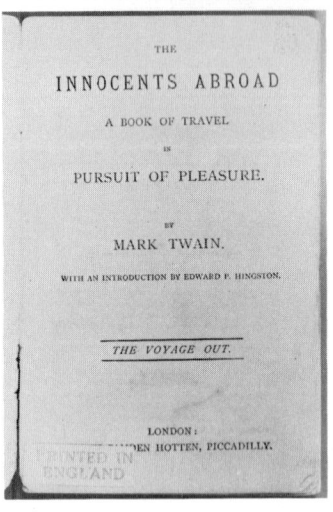

The Innocents Abroad, or The New Pilgrims' Progress.
Hartford, 1870:   American Publishing Company. etc. Seven copies in various bindings: black cloth, leather, assorted rebindings.

The Innocents Abroad, or The New Pilgrims' Progress.
Hartford, 1871:   American Publishing Company. F.G. Gilman & Co., Chicago, Ill.; Nettleton & Co., Cincinnati, Ohio. H.H. Bancroft & Co., San Francisco, Cal. Black cloth: two copies.

The Innocents Abroad, or The New Pilgrims' Progress.
Hartford, 1872:   American Publishing Company. etc. Black cloth.

The Innocents Abroad, or The New Pilgrims' Progress.
Hartford, 1873:   American Publishing Company, F.G. Gilman & Co., Chicago, Ill., W.E. Bliss, Toledo, Ohio.; Nettleton & Co., Cincinnati, Ohio.; D. Ashmead, Philadelphia, Penn. J.W. Goodspeed, New Orleans, La.; A. Roman & Co., San Francisco, Cal. Black cloth: two copies.

The Innocents Abroad, or The New Pilgrims' Progress.
Hartford, 1875:   American Publishing Company. Black cloth.

The Innocents Abroad, or The New Pilgrims' Progress.
Hartford, 1876: American Publishing Company.
Black cloth.

The Innocents Abroad, or The New Pilgrims' Progress.
Hartford, 1876: American Publishing Company. etc.
Black cloth.
Inscribed copy:
To Mr. Bartlett, who has/robbed the historical/command "Away/with him to the Tower!"/of all its terrors — this,/with the grateful acknowledgements of/Mark Twain/Hartford, Oct. 1877."

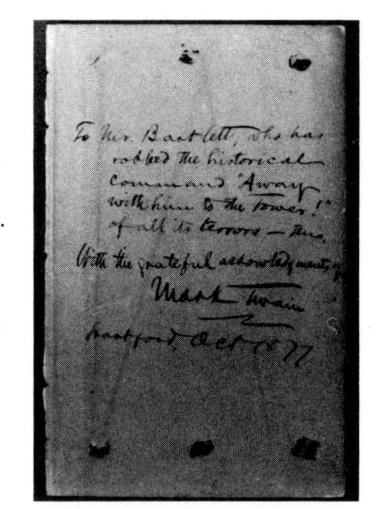

The Innocents Abroad, or The New Pilgrims' Progress.
Hartford, 1877: American Publishing Company.
Black cloth.

The Innocents Abroad, or The New Pilgrims' Progress.
Hartford, 1879: American Publishing Company.
Black cloth: two copies.

The Innocents Abroad, or The New Pilgrims' Progress.
Leipzig, 1879*: Bernhard Tauchnitz.
Authorized edition.
Two volumes.
* — A Note about Tauchnitz editions: The date on the title page of Tauchnitz editions is misleading. Frequently, the list of books "By the same Author" opposite the title page will list later titles than the title page date would allow.
This edition printed a 1½ page note "To the Reader" by Clemens dated March, 1879 and specifically for this reprint.
Set 1: last title opposite title page: *Capt. Stormfield, etc.* (1909).
Set 2: last title: *More Tramps Abroad* (1897).

BAL 3381

The Innocents Abroad, or The New Pilgrims' Progress.
London, 1882: Chatto & Windus, Piccadilly.
Rebound.

The Innocents Abroad, or The New Pilgrims' Progress.
Hartford, 1891: American Publishing Company. Black cloth: two copies

The Innocents Abroad, or The New Pilgrims' Progress.
Hartford, 1895: American Publishing Company. Black cloth.

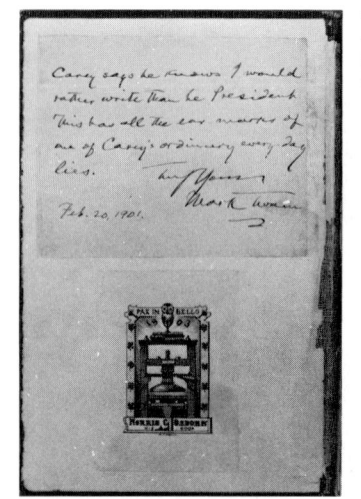

The Innocents Abroad, or The New Pilgrims' Progress.
Hartford, 1899: The American Publishing Company.
Volume I (only) of
The Writings of Mark Twain.
Edition de Luxe.
Set #252 of 1000.
Green cloth.
Tipped in:
ANS by Clemens:
Carey says he knows I would/rather write than be President./This has all the ear-marks of/one of Carey's or-/dinary every-day/lies./Truly yrs/Mark Twain/Feb. 20, 1901.
Also tipped in:
Letter front dated Feb. 20 2:30 PM, New York Sta(tion) 0/1901, inscribed by Clemens in upper left corner:
"I hear, & I obey!"
and addressed in his hand to:
Wm. Carey, Esq./University Club/City

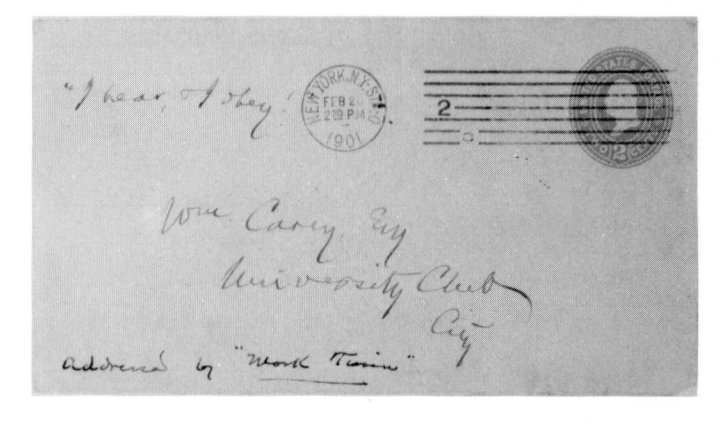

The Innocents Abroad, or The New Pilgrims' Progress.
Hartford, 1899: The American Publishing Company. Contains a two-page preface by Clemens "to the Uniform Edition" dated at Vienna, January, 1899. Cloth.

The Innocents Abroad, or The New Pilgrims' Progress.
Hartford, 1899: The American Publishing Company. Volumes I & II of The Writings of Mark Twain. Autograph Edition of the Edition de Luxe.
One of 512 sets on paper watermarked CLEMENS; this set not numbered.
Three-quarter morocco.
Biographical criticism by Brander Matthews.
Bound into Volume I:
ALS by Clemens to (Frank E.) Bliss, 4 pp., 1899 March 31 (& April 2).
Bound into Volume II:
ALS by Clemens to Bliss, 2 pp., 1900 September 18.
Volume I is inscribed on back of half-title:
Truly yours/Mark Twain/Oct. 23/03.

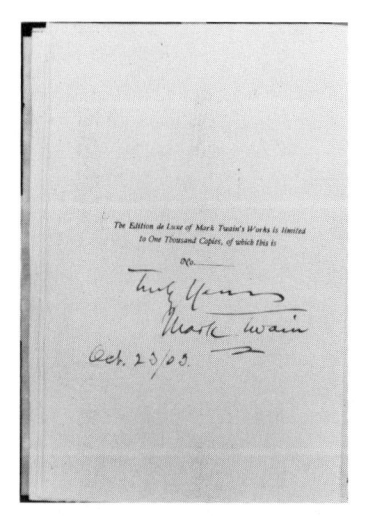

The Innocents Abroad, or The New Pilgrims' Progress.
Hartford, 1899: The American Publishing Company. Volumes I & II of The Writings of Mark Twain. Edition de Luxe.
Set #54 of 1000 on paper watermarked MARK TWAIN.
Uses the same plates as the Autograph Edition.
Green cloth.

The Innocents Abroad, or The New Pilgrims' Progress.
Hartford, 1901: The American Publishing Company.
New York: H.G. Newbegin Company.
Volume I of the Riverdale Edition.
Set #550 of 625.
Three-quarter morocco.
Bound into Volume I:
Page 1411 of Clemens' manuscript of *The Gilded Age* (page 555 of the text), and Page 1445 of Charles Dudley Warner's manuscript of the same book (pp. 568-69 of the text).

The Innocents Abroad, or The New Pilgrims' Progress.
Hartford, 1901: The American Publishing Company.
Maroon cloth.

The Innocents Abroad, or The New Pilgrims' Progress.
Hartford, 1902: The American Publishing Company.
Leather.

The Innocents Abroad. etc.
New York, 1904: Harper & Brothers Publishers.
Volumes I & II of The Writings of Mark Twain.
Hillcrest Edition.
Three-quarter morocco.
Volume I inscribed:
To/Jean Lampton Clemens/THESE BOOKS/with the love of her father/ The Author./November 27, 1904/ Circumstances make man,/not man circumstances./Mark Twain.
(Quote from *Mark Twain's Notebook*, p. 379).
Volume II inscribed:
Thou shalt not pay a person/a compliment & then/disembowel it with a/criticism./Mark Twain.
(*Notebook*, p. 379, but a variant.)

The Innocents Abroad, or The New Pilgrims' Progress.
New York and London, 1905: Harper & Brothers Publishers.
Two volumes in one.
Red cloth.

The Innocents Abroad, or The New Pilgrims' Progress.
New York and London, (1915): Harper & Brothers Publishers.
Volumes I & II of
the Author's National Edition.
Red cloth.

The Innocents Abroad, or The New Pilgrims' Progress.
New York and London, (1918): Harper & Brothers Publishers.
Volumes I & II of
the Author's National Edition.
Green cloth.

The Innocents Abroad, or The New Pilgrims' Progress.
New York and London, (1919): Harper & Brothers Publishers.
Two volumes in one.
Blue cloth.

The Innocents Abroad, or The New Pilgrims' Progress.
New York and London, (1927): Harper & Brothers Publishers.
Two volumes in one.
Blue cloth.

The Innocents Abroad, or The New Pilgrims' Progress.
New York, 1929: Harper & Brothers.
Volumes 1 & 2 of
The Stormfield Edition of
The Writings of Mark Twain.
Set #212 of 1024.
Appreciation by E.V. Lucas.
Introduction by Albert Bigelow Paine.
Blue cloth stamped in gold.

The Innocents Abroad, or The New Pilgrims' Progress.
New York, 1964: Bantam Books.
    First Bantam Classic edition,
    January 1964.
    Introduction by Alfred Kazin.
    Pictorial paper wrappers.

(The Innocents Abroad (or The New Pilgrims' Progress).)
n.p., n.d.: The Eihosha Ltd.
    In English with Chinese footnotes.
    Introduction in Chinese.
    Paper wrappers.

(The Innocents Abroad or The New Pilgrims' Progress.)
Zagreb, 1964: Matica Hrvatska.
    In Yugoslav.
    Translated by Leonardo Spalatin.
    Two volumes with dustjackets.
    Tan cloth.

Mark Twain, about 1872.

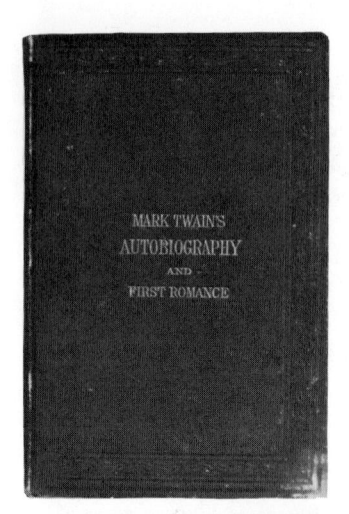

Mark Twain's (Burlesque) Autobiography and First Romance.
New York, (1871): Sheldon & Company, 677 Broadway, Under the Grand Central Hotel.
First issue with the copyright page lacking the ad for Ball, Black & Co.
Copy 1: paper wrappers.
Copy 2: terra-cotta cloth.
BAL 3326   Copy 3: green cloth.

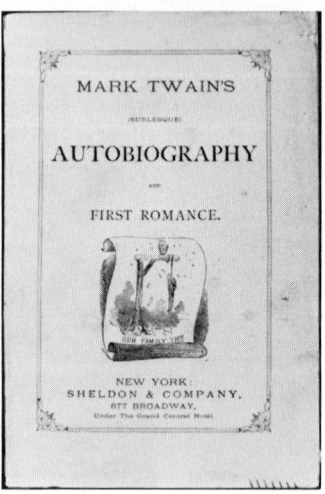

Mark Twain's (Burlesque) Autobiography and First Romance.
New York, (1871): Sheldon & Company. etc.
Second issue with the ad for Ball & Black on the copyright page.
Copy 1: terra-cotta cloth.
Copy 2: plum cloth.
Copies 3, 4 & 5: green cloth.
Copies 6 & 7: paper wrappers.

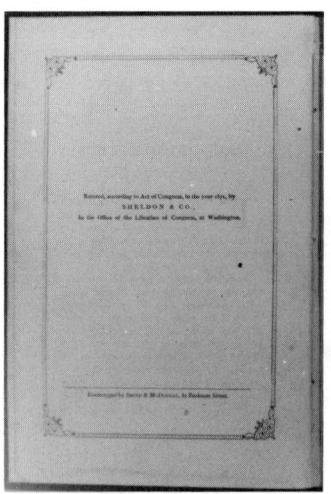

First issue. 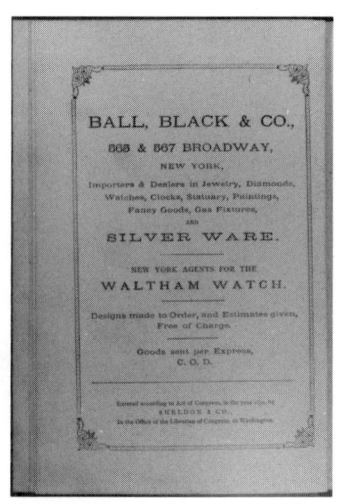   *Second issue.*

16

Mark Twain's (Burlesque) Autobiography and First Romance.
New York, (1871): Sheldon & Company. etc.
    Second issue.
    Paper wrappers bound in leather.
    Original cover inscribed:
    Sincerely yours/Mark Twain.

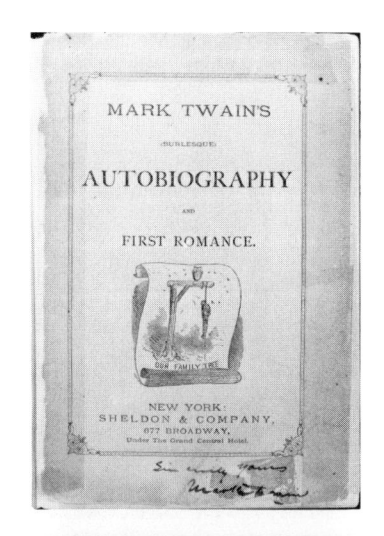

Autobiography, (Burlesque) First Romance, and Memoranda.
Toronto, n.d.(c. 1871): James Campbell & Son.
    Purple cloth.
BAL 3334   First Canadian edition.

Mark Twain's Burlesque Autobiography.
Larchmont, N.Y., 1930: Peter Pauper Press.
    Illustrated by Herb Roth.
    One of 525 copies.
    Green cloth.

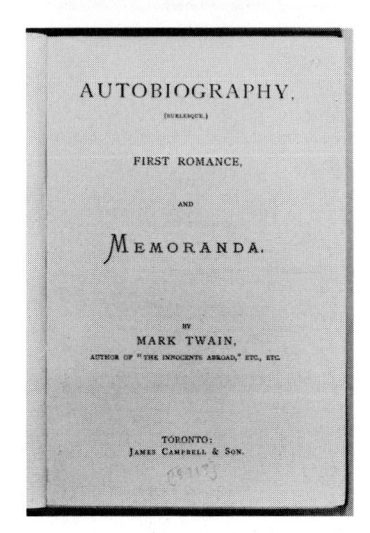

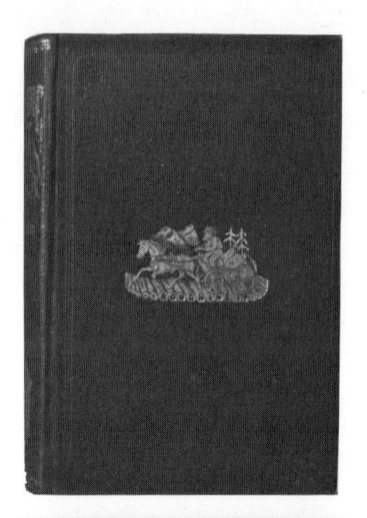

Roughing It.
Hartford, 1872: American Publishing Company. F.G. Gilman & Co., Chicago, Ill.; W.E. Bliss, Toledo, Ohio; Nettleton & Co., Cincinnati, Ohio; D. Ashmead, Philadelphia, Penn,; George M. Smith & Co., Boston, Mass.; A. Roman & Company, San Francisco, Cal.
Publisher's prospectus.
Black cloth.

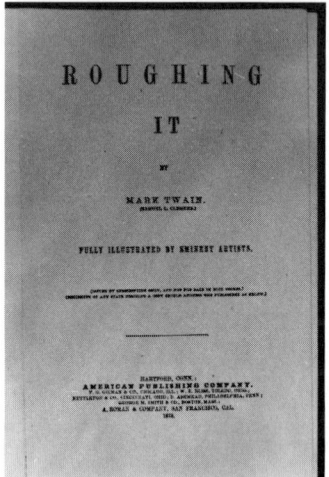

Roughing It.
Hartford, 1872: American Publishing Company. F.G. Gilman & Co., Chicago, Ill.; W.E. Bliss, Toledo, Ohio; Nettleton & Co., Cincinnati, Ohio; D. Ashmead, Philadelphia, Penn.; George M. Smith & Co., Boston, Mass.; A. Roman & Company, San Francisco, Cal.
First issue with an advertisement on page (592) and 242:20-21: *premises — said he/was occupying his*
Black cloth: eight copies.
BAL 3337 Three-quarter morocco: one copy.

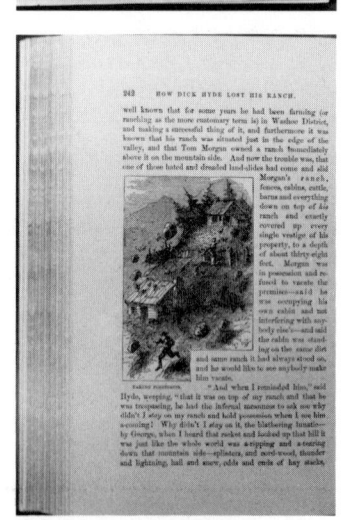

First issue of p. 242.

Mark Twain in 1874.

Roughing It.
Hartford, 1872: American Publishing Company. etc. Second issue with an advertisement on page (592) and letters and words missing from 242: 20-21. Black cloth: six copies.

Roughing It.
Hartford, 1872: American Publishing Company. etc. Third issue with no ad on page (592) and letters or words missing from 242: 20-21.
This is a rebound copy and the ad from (592) may have been deleted during binding.

Roughing It.
London, n.d.(1872): George Routledge and Sons, The Broadway, Ludgate.
First English edition.
BAL 3335   Pictorial yellow boards.

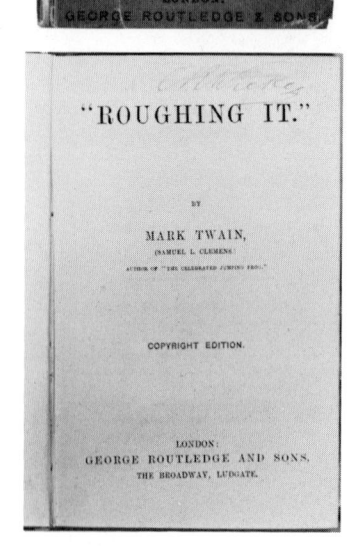

Roughing It.
Hartford, 1873: American Publishing Company.
F.G. Gilman & Co., Chicago, Ill.; W.E. Bliss, Toledo, Ohio; Nettleton & Co., Cincinnati, Ohio; D. Ashmead, Philadelphia, Penn.; J.W. Goodspeed, New Orleans, La.; A. Roman & Company, San Francisco, Cal.
"Eighty-fifth thousand."
Black cloth.

Roughing It.
Hartford, 1874: American Publishing Company. etc. as in first edition.
Leather.

Roughing It.
Hartford, 1876: American Publishing Company.
"Eighty-fifth thousand."
Obviously the 1873 or this edition is in error as to what thousand this copy belongs.
Black cloth.

Roughing It.
Hartford, 1879: American Publishing Company.
Black cloth.

Roughing It.
Hartford, 1880: American Publishing Company.
Black cloth.

Roughing It.
London, 1883: George Routledge and Sons, Ludgate Hill. New York: 9 Lafayette Place.
Illustrated by F.A. Fraser.
Rebound.

Roughing It.
Hartford, 1884: American Publishing Company.
Black cloth.

Roughing It.
London, n.d. (c. 1885): George Routledge and Sons, Limited.
Pictorial paper wrappers.

Roughing It.
Hartford, 1897: The American Publishing Company.
Black cloth.

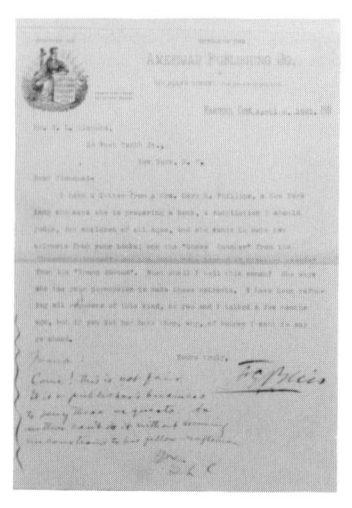

Roughing It.
Hartford, 1899: The American Publishing Company.
Volumes VII & VIII of
The Writings of Mark Twain.
Autograph edition of
the Edition deLuxe.
Three-quarter morocco.
Bound into Volume VII:
TLS from F(rank) E. Bliss to
Clemens, 1 p., 1901 April 4 with a
return note on the same sheet by
Clemens.

Roughing It.
Hartford, 1899: The American Publishing Company.
Volumes VII & VIII of
The Writings of Mark Twain.
Edition de Luxe.
Set #54 of 1000.
Green cloth.
Uses the same plates as the
Autograph edition.

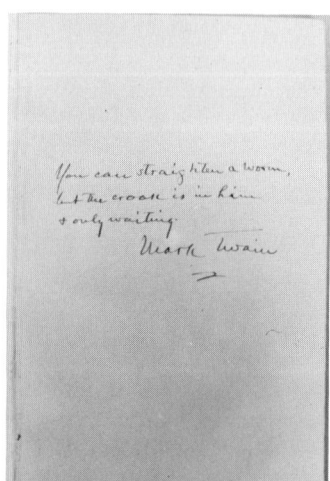

Roughing It.
Hartford, 1900: The American Publishing Company.
Black cloth.

Roughing It.
New York and London, 1904: Harper and Brothers
Publishers.
Two volumes.
Red cloth.

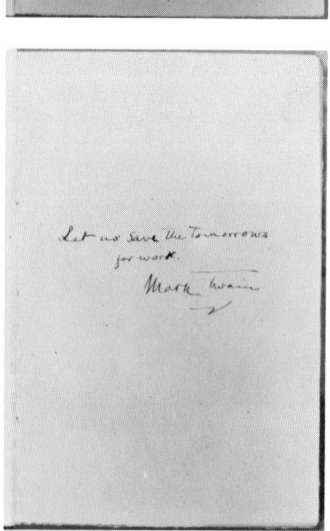

Roughing It.
New York, 1904: Harper & Brothers Publishers.
Volumes VII & VIII of
The Writings of Mark Twain.
Hillcrest Edition.
Three-quarter morocco.
Volume VII inscribed:
You can straighten a worm,/but the crook is in him/& only waiting./Mark Twain.
(*More Maxims of Mark*, p. 4)
Volume VIII inscribed:
Let us save the tomorrows/for work./Mark Twain.
(*More Maxims of Mark*, p. 10)

Roughing It.
New York and London, (1915): Harper & Brothers
           Publishers.
           Volumes VII & VIII of
           The Writings of Mark Twain.
           Author's National Edition.
           Red cloth.

Roughing It.
New York and London, (1917, 1918): Harper &
           Brothers Publishers.
           Two volumes.
           Limp leather edition, one volume
           with dustjacket.
           Red leather.

Roughing It.
New York and London, (1918): Harper & Brothers
           Publishers.
           Volumes VII & VIII of The Writings
           of Mark Twain.
           Author's National Edition.
           Green cloth.

Roughing It.
New York and London, (1923): Harper & Brothers
           Publishers.
           Two volumes in one.
           Blue cloth.

Roughing It.
New York and London, (1926): Harper and Brothers
           Publishers.
           Two volumes in one.
           Blue cloth.

Roughing It.
New York, 1929: Harper & Brothers.
           Volumes 3 & 4 of
           The Stormfield Edition of
           The Writings of Mark Twain.
           Set #212 of 1024.
           Appreciation by E.V. Lucas.
           Introduction by Albert
           Bigelow Paine.
           Blue cloth stamped in gold.

Roughing It.
New York, 1959: Rinehart & Co., Inc.
           Introduction by Rodman W. Paul.
           Fourth printing, November 1959.
           (The first printing was 1953.)
           Paper wrappers.

23

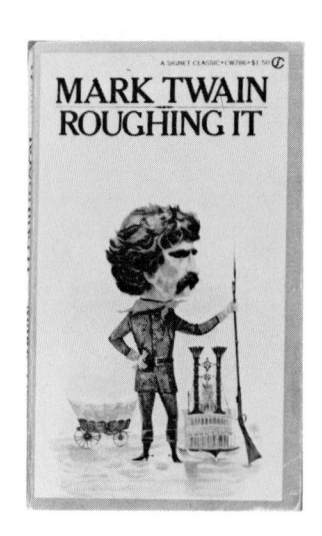

Roughing It.
New York, (1962): New American Library.
    Foreword by Leonard Kriegel.
    Signet Classic #CW786, price $1.50.
    9th printing of this edition, about 1975.
    Pictorial paper wrappers.

Roughing It.
Berkeley, Los Angeles, London, (1972): University of California Press for the Iowa Center for Textual Studies.
    Introduction and explanatory notes by Franklin R. Rogers.
    Text established by Paul Baender.
    "First paperback edition, 1973."
    Paper wrappers.

Mark Twain, about 1878.

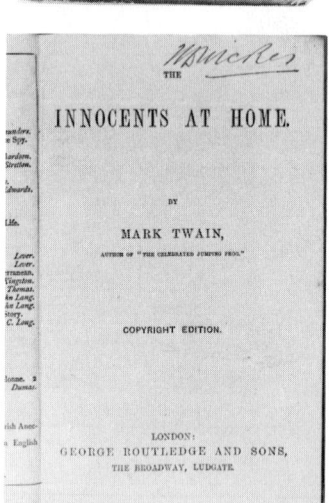

The Innocents at Home.

London, n.d. (1872): George Routledge and Sons, The Broadway, Ludgate.
"Copyright edition."
Pictorial yellow boards.

BAL 3336*   * — A state of the binding not listed in BAL: to wit, back cover lists seven numbered book titles and two unnumbered titles under the heading *Routledge's American Library.* This copy meets all other BAL points, but BAL calls for five titles (state A) or eleven titles (state B).

A Curious Dream; and Other Sketches.
London, n.d.(1872): George Routledge and Sons, The Broadway.
"Selected and revised by the author."
BAL 3340 Pictorial yellow boards.

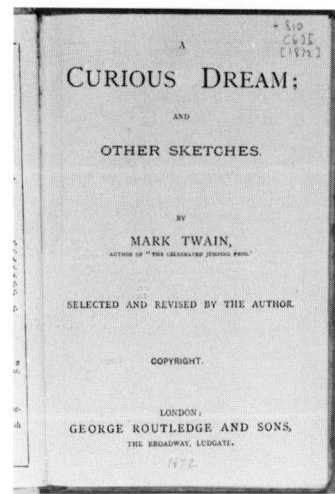

The Gilded Age. A Tale of Today.

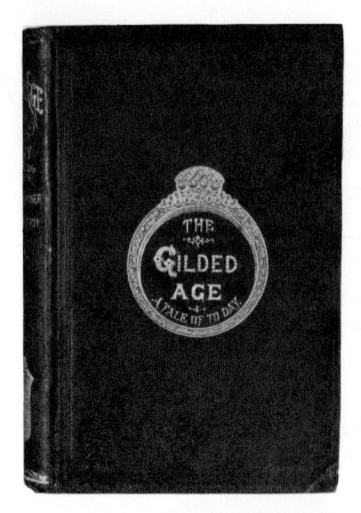

Hartford, 1873: American Publishing Company. Chicago, Ill.: F.G. Gilman & Co.
BAL 3357   Written with Charles Dudley Warner.

BAL point:	1	2	3	4	5	6	7	8	9	Binding
Copy 1:	*	A	A	A	A	A	A	A	A	black cloth
Copy 2:	*	A	A	A	A	A	A	A	A	leather
Copy 3:	A	A	A	A	A	A	B	B	A	black cloth
Copy 4:	B	B	A	B	A	B	B	B	B	leather

Point 1: A: *Everybody's Friend* described as a *truex inde* in ads at end of book
B: *true index*
*: ads not present
Point 2: A: artist *White* present on title page
B: *White* absent
Point 3: A: (vii): *Eschol* under Chapter V
B: (vii): *Beriah*
Point 4: A: xvi: final illustration numbered *211*
B: xvi: *212*
Point 5: A: 246: 5 up: *Halleluiah*
B: 246: 5 up: *Hallelujah,*
Point 6: A: 280:18: *Dr. Jackson.*
B: 280:18: *Dr. Jackson*
Point 7: A: 351:last: *would kill me if she could, thought the Colonel; but he*
B: 351: last: above line absent
Point 8: A: 353:1-2: *let him keep it. She looked down into his face, with a pitia-/ble tenderness, and said in a weak voice,*
B: above lines absent
Point 9: A: 403: no illustration
B: illustration present

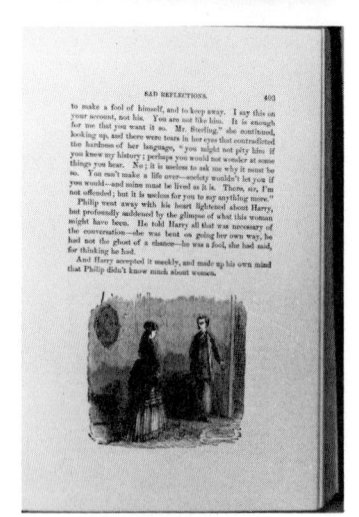

Second issue of p. 403.

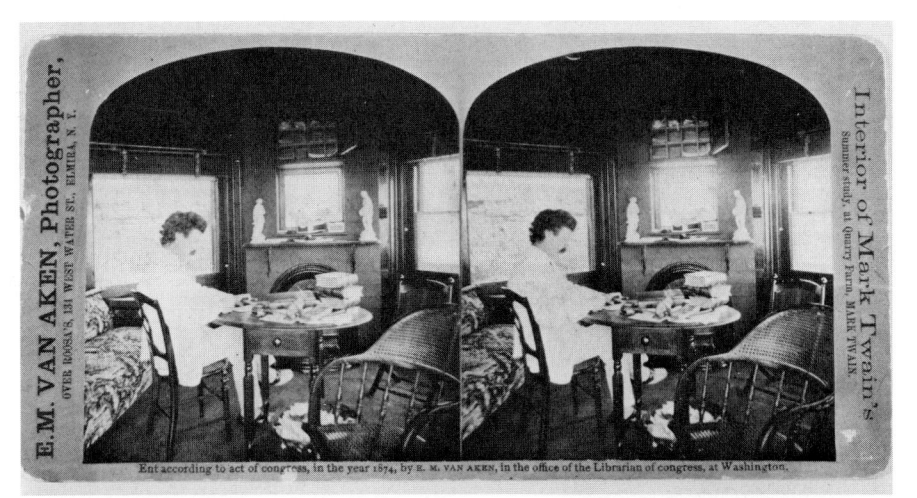

Mark Twain in the Quarry Farm study, about 1874.

The Jacksons and Livy and Mark Twain, on the verandah at 351 Farmington Avenue, Hartford, about 1875.

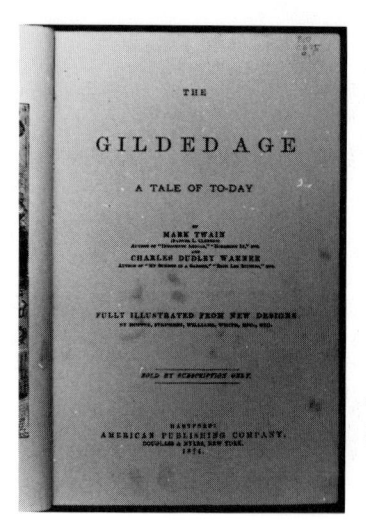

The Gilded Age. A Tale of Today.
Hartford, 1874: American Publishing Company.
Chicago, Ill.: F.G. Gilman & Co.
Publisher's prospectus.
Brown cloth.
Samples of cloth and leather bindings on inside covers.

The Gilded Age. A Tale of Today.
Hartford, 1874: American Publishing Company.
Black cloth: seven copies.
Leather: three copies.
Three-quarter morocco: one copy.

The Gilded Age. A Tale of Today.
Hartford, 1874: American Publishing Company.
Chicago, Ill.: F.G. Gilman & Co.
Black cloth.

The Gilded Age. A Tale of Today.
Hartford, 1874: American Publishing Company.
New York: Douglass & Myers.
Black cloth: two copies.
Leather: one copy.

The Gilded Age. A Tale of Today.
Hartford, 1879: American Publishing Company.
Black cloth.

The Gilded Age. A Tale of Today.
Hartford, 1880: American Publishing Company.
Black cloth.

The Gilded Age. A Tale of Today.
Hartford, 1887: American Publishing Company.
Black cloth.
Inscribed in an anonymous hand:
From/The Am. Pub. Co./To/H.C. Burton/Christmas/1887.

The Gilded Age. A Tale of Today.
Hartford, 1899: The American Publishing Company.
Volumes X & XI of
The Writings of Mark Twain.
Autograph Edition of
the Edition de Luxe.
Bound into Volume X:
Pages 670-672 of Clemens' manuscript of *The Gilded Age* (page 315 of the text).
Bound into Volume XI:
Pages 1337-1338 of Clemens' manuscript of *The Gilded Age* (pages 299-300 of the text).
Three-quarter morocco.

The Gilded Age.
New York, 1904: Harper & Brothers Publishers.
    Volumes X & XI of
    The Writings of Mark Twain.
    Hillcrest Edition.
    Three-quarter morocco.
    Volume X inscribed:
    The human race consists/of the violently insane/& such as are not./Mark Twain.
    (Notebook, p. 381)
    Volume XI inscribed:
    We often feel sad in the/presence of music without/words; & often more than that/in the presence of music/without music./Mark Twain.
    (More Maxims of Mark, p. 14.)

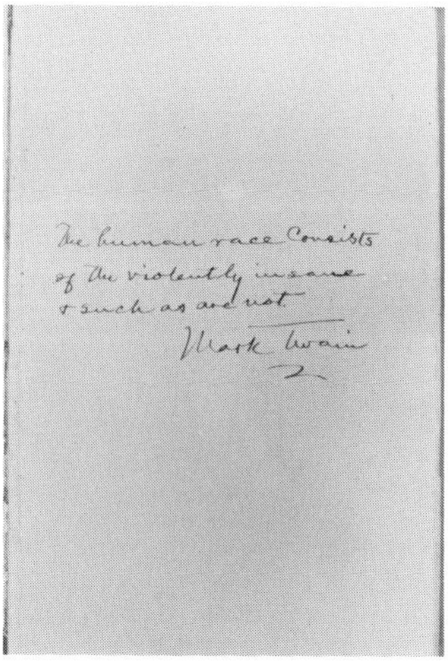

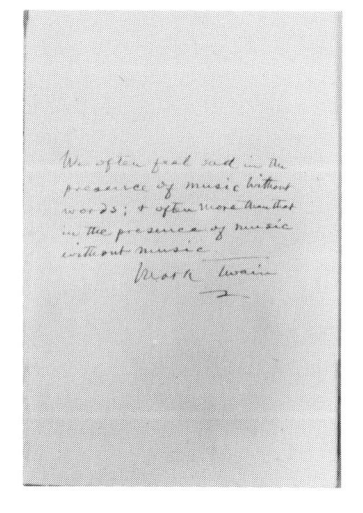

The Gilded Age. A Tale of To-day.
Hartford, 1899: American Publishing Company.
    Volumes X & XI of
    The Writings of Mark Twain.
    Edition de Luxe.
    Set #54 of 1000.
    Uses the same plates as the Autograph edition.
    Green cloth.

The Gilded Age. A Tale of To-day.
New York and London, (1915): Harper & Brothers Publishers.
    Volumes X & XI of
    The Writings of Mark Twain.
    Author's National Edition.
    Red cloth.

The Gilded Age. A Tale of Today.
New York and London, (1915): Harper & Brothers Publishers.
    Two volumes in one.
    Green cloth.

The Gilded Age. A Tale of To-day.
New York and London, (1917): Harper & Brothers Publishers.
    Two volumes
    Limp leather edition.
    Red leather.

The Gilded Age. A Tale of To-day.
New York and London, (1918): Harper & Brothers Publishers.
    Volumes X & XI of
    The Writings of Mark Twain.
    Author's National Edition.
    Green cloth.

The Gilded Age. A Tale of To-day.
New York and London, (1918): Harper & Brothers
        Publishers.
        Two volumes.
        Limp leather edition.
        Red leather.

The Gilded Age. A Tale of To-day.
New York and London, (1927): Harper & Brothers
        Publishers.
        Two volumes in one.
        Blue cloth: two copies.

The Gilded Age.
New York, 1929: Harper & Brothers.
        Volumes 5 & 6 of
        The Stormfield Edition of
        The Writings of Mark Twain.
        Set #212 of 1024.
        Appreciation by E.V. Lucas.
        Introduction by Albert
        Bigelow Paine.
        Blue cloth stamped in gold.

The Gilded Age. A Tale of To-day.
New York, 1964: Trident Press.
        Introduction by Justin Kaplan.
        First edition thus.
        Cloth with dustjacket.

The Gilded Age.
n.p., (1979): no publisher.
        In Chinese.
        Paper wrappers.

John T. Raymond, who played Col. Sellers in the stage adaptation of "The Gilded Age," and Mark Twain, January 11, 1875.

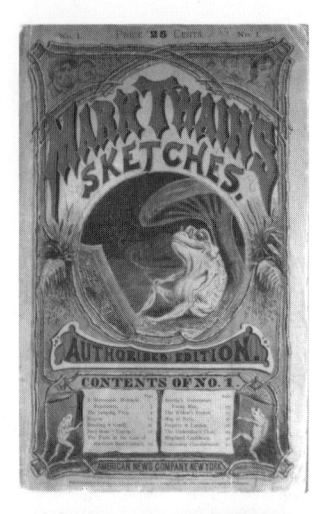

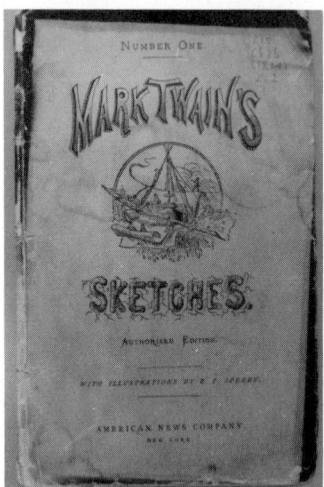

Mark Twain's Sketches.
New York, (1874): American News Company.
"Authorised edition."
Illustrated by R.T. Sperry.
Pale blue pictorial wrappers:
BAL 3360 two copies.

Mark Twain's Sketches, New and Old.
Hartford and Chicago, 1875: The American Publishing Company.
Publisher's prospectus.
Blue cloth: two copies.

Mark Twain's Sketches, New and Old.
Hartford and Chicago, 1875: The American Publishing Company.
First issue with footnote present on page 119, footnote repeated on page 120, and an eleven-line skit *"From Hospital Days"* on page 299. Two copies, both with an erratum slip bound in at page 299.
Copy 1: blue cloth.
Copy 2: three-quarter green morocco.

BAL 3364

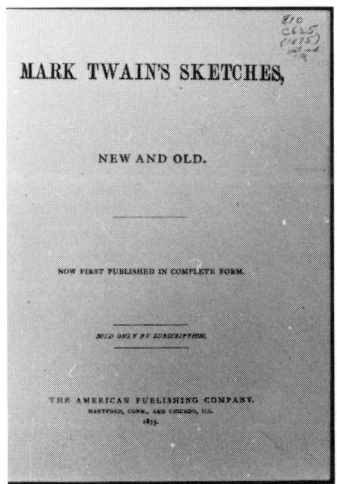

Mark Twain's Sketches, New and Old.
Hartford and Chicago: The American Publishing Company.
Second issue with footnote present on page 119, not repeated on 120, and *"From Hospital Days"* absent from 299.
Blue cloth: seven copies.

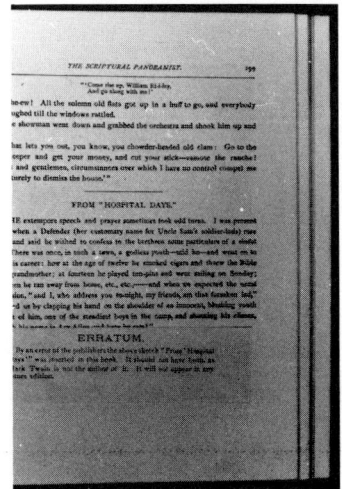

First issue of p. 299; erratum slip overlaid.

35

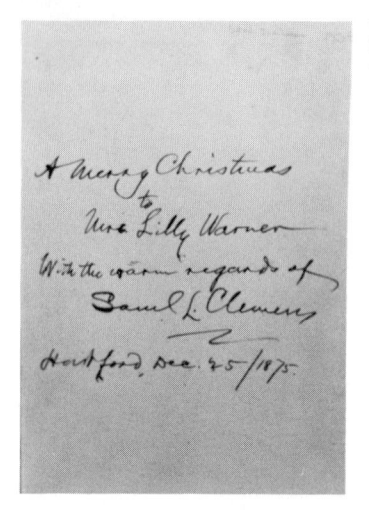

Mark Twain's Sketches, New and Old.
Hartford and Chicago, 1875: The American
    Publishing Company.
    Second issue.
    Three-quarter green morocco.
    Inscribed copy:
    A Merry Christmas/to/Mrs. Lilly Warner/With warm regards of/Sml L. Clemens/Hartford, Dec. 25/1875.

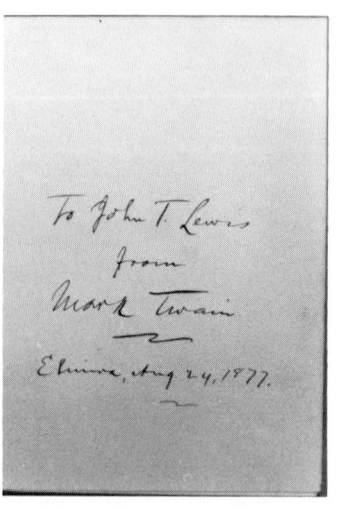

Mark Twain's Sketches, New and Old.
New York and Chicago, 1875: The American
    Publishing Company.
    Second issue.
    Blue cloth.
    Inscribed copy:
    To John T. Lewis/from/Mark Twain/Elmira, Aug. 24, 1877.

Mark Twain's Sketches, New and Old.
Hartford and Chicago, 1880: The American
    Publishing Company. Blue cloth.

Sketches.
n.p., (Toronto), 1880: Slemin & Higgins.
    Reprints selections from the American first and the Canadian first
BAL 3624   (BAL 3384). Green cloth.

Mark Twain's Sketches, New and Old.
Hartford and Chicago, 1884: The American
    Publishing Company. Blue cloth.

Mark Twain's Sketches, New and Old.
Hartford and Chicago, 1886: The American
    Publishing Co.
    Blue cloth.

Mark Twain's Sketches, New and Old.
Hartford and Chicago, 1888: The American
           Publishing Co. Blue cloth.

Mark Twain's Sketches, New and Old.
Hartford and Chicago, 1890: The American
           Publishing Company
           Blue cloth.

Sketches, New and Old.
Hartford, 1893: American Publishing Company.
                Syracuse, N.Y.: Watson Gill.
                Reprints selected pieces from the
                first edition.
                "Mr. Bloke's Item" (pp. 170-174)
                appears here in the index for the first
                time in the printing history of this
                title. It appeared in all earlier
                American editions (pp. 167-170)
                but not in their indexes.
BAL 3651   Tan pictorial cloth.

Sketches, New and Old.
Hartford, 1899: The American Publishing Company.
                Volume XIX of
                The Writings of Mark Twain.
                Autograph Edition of
                the Edition de Luxe.
                Bound in:
                Facsimile ALS from Clemens to
                (T.F. Frisbie), 1 1/2 pp., 1897 October 25, and ALS by Frederick Burr
                Opper to Mr. Bliss, 1 p., 1899 April 4.
                Three-quarter morocco.

Sketches, New and Old.
Hartford, 1899: American Publishing Company.
                Volume XIX of
                The Writings of Mark Twain.
                Edition de Luxe.
                Set #54 of 1000.
                Uses the same plates as the
                Autograph edition.
                Green cloth.

Sketches New and Old.
New York, 1904: Harper & Brothers Publishers
                Volume XX of
                The Writings of Mark Twain.
                Hillcrest Edition.
                Three-quarter morocco.
                Inscribed copy:
                If you had your choice/between riches
                & righteousness,/which would you
                take?/(A chromo goes with this
                one.)/Mark Twain.
                (Source not located elsewhere.)

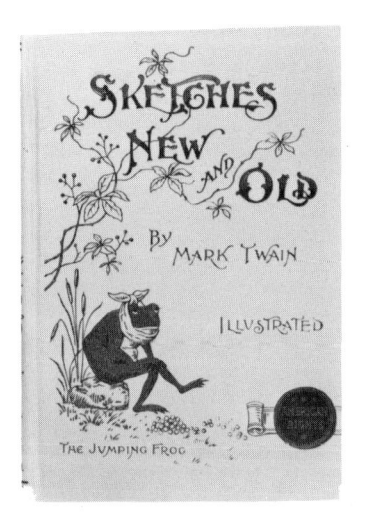

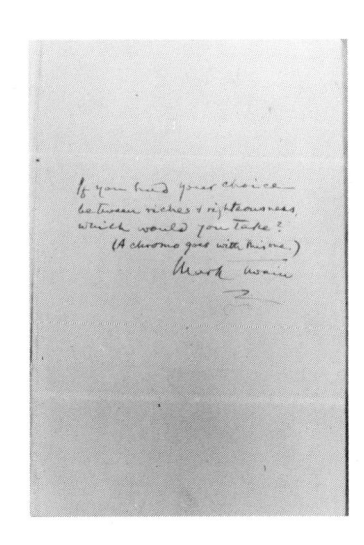

Sketches, New and Old.
New York and London, (1915): Harper & Brothers
        Publishers.
        Volume XIX of
        The Writings of Mark Twain.
        Author's National Edition.
        Red cloth.

Sketches, New and Old.
New York and London, (1918): Harper & Brothers
        Publishers.
        Volume XIX of
        The Writings of Mark Twain.
        Author's National Edition.
        Green cloth.

Sketches, New and Old.
New York and London, (1924): Harper & Brothers
        Publishers.
        Mississippi Edition.
        Green cloth.

Sketches, New and Old.
New York and London, (1927): Harper & Brothers
        Publishers.
        Blue cloth with dustjacket.

Sketches New and Old.
New York, 1929: Harper & Brothers.
        Volume 7 of
        The Stormfield Edition of
        The Writings of Mark Twain.
        Set #212 of 1024.
        Appreciation by E.V. Lucas.
        Introduction by Albert
        Bigelow Paine.
        Blue cloth stamped in gold.

Lost og Sast.
Copenhagen, 1884: J.H. Schubothes Boghandels
        Forlag.
        In Danish.
        Cloth.

Nuevos Cuentos.
Buenos Aires, (1947): Espasa-Calpe Argentina, S.A.
        In Spanish.
        Paper wrappers.

Esquisses Americaines de Mark Twain.
Paris, 1881: P. Ollendorff, Libraire-Editeur.
        In French.
        Translated by Emile Blemont.
        Cloth.

Mark Twain, about 1867.

The Adventures of Tom Sawyer.

Hartford, 1876: The American Publishing Company. Chicago, Ill.: Cincinnati, Ohio. A. Roman & Co., San Francisco, Cal.

BAL 3369* *:First issue, pagination of front matter as stated in BAL. However, this copy has the entire text printed on laid paper with wove paper triple flyleaves; BAL calls for the opposite use of paper.
Blue cloth, all edges gilt (an option).

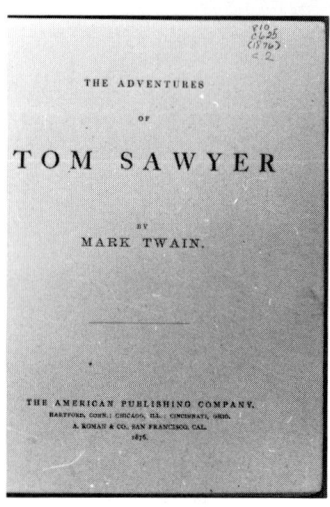

Mark Twain, about 1875.

The Adventures of Tom Sawyer.
Hartford, 1876: The American Publishing Company. etc.
First issue.
Laid in:
ALS from Jacob Blanck 1938 October 14 to Mr. T.A. Jones valuing this copy at "$1,000."

The Adventures of Tom Sawyer.
Hartford, 1876: The American Publishing Company. etc.
Second issue A, according to BAL pagination.
Three-quarter morocco.

Petroleum V. Nasby, Mark Twain and Josh Billings, about 1874.

The Adventures of Tom Sawyer.
London, 1876: Chatto & Windus, Piccadilly.
        First English edition which precedes the American first by six months.
        Red cloth stamped in black and gold: two copies.
        Copy one bears the bookplate of
BAL 3367   Harry Bacon Collamore.

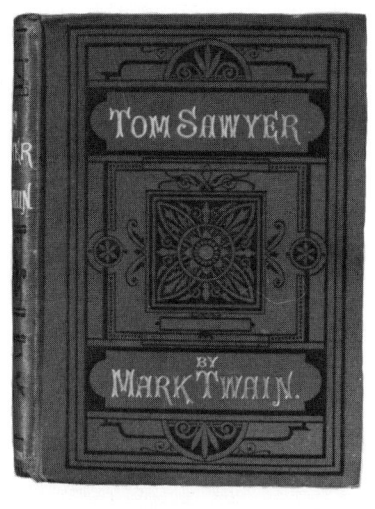

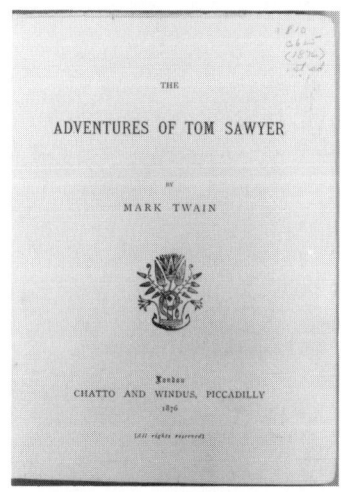

The Adventures of Tom Sawyer.
London, 1876: Chatto & Windus, Piccadilly.
        First English edition.
        Red cloth stamped in black and gold.
        Inscribed copy:
        S.L. Clemens/Hartford 1876
        Additional notations on inside front cover, possibly by Clemens.

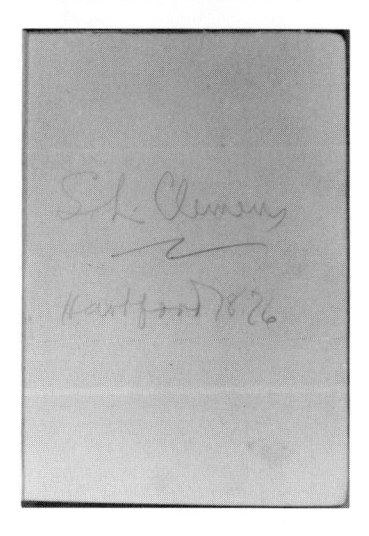

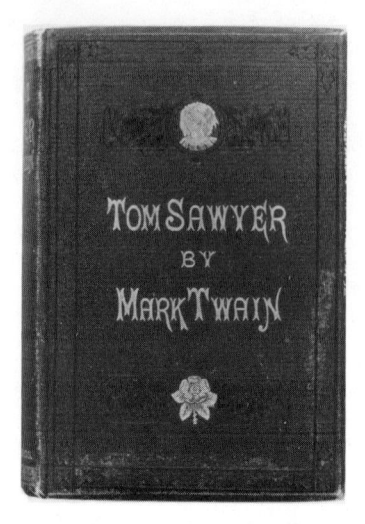

The Adventures of Tom Sawyer.
Toronto, 1876: Belford Brothers, Publishers.
                First Canadian edition.
BAL 3609   Maroon cloth.

The Adventures of Tom Sawyer.
Toronto, 1877: Belford Brothers.
                Terra-cotta cloth.

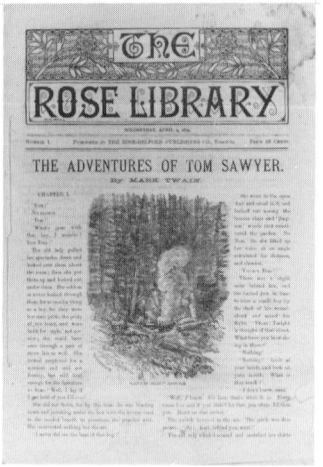

The Adventures of Tom Sawyer.
Toronto, 1879: The Rose-Belford Publishing Co.
                The Rose Library, number 1,
                Wednesday, April 2, 1879
                Paper wrappers.

The Adventures of Tom Sawyer.
Hartford, 1883:   The American Publishing Company.
                Chicago, Ill., Cincinnati, Ohio.
                Blue cloth.

The Adventures of Tom Sawyer.
Hartford, 1890:   American Publishing Company.
                Blue cloth: two copies.

The Adventures of Tom Sawyer.
Hartford, 1892:   American Publishing Company.
                Syracuse, N.Y.: Watson Gill
                Pictorial brown cloth.

The Adventures of Tom Sawyer.
Hartford, 1899: The American Publishing Company.
　　　　　　　　Volume XII of
　　　　　　　　The Writings of Mark Twain.
　　　　　　　　Autograph edition.
　　　　　　　　Three-quarter morocco.
　　　　　　　　Bound in:
　　　　　　　　DS by J(ohn) G. Brown, 1899
　　　　　　　　March 6, for receipt of $1000. for
　　　　　　　　four paintings for *Tom Sawyer.*

The Adventures of Tom Sawyer.
Hartford, 1899: The American Publishing Company.
　　　　　　　　Volume XII of
　　　　　　　　The Writings of Mark Twain.
　　　　　　　　Edition de Luxe.
　　　　　　　　Set #54 of 1000.
　　　　　　　　Uses the same plates as the
　　　　　　　　Autograph edition.
　　　　　　　　Green cloth.

The Adventures of Tom Sawyer.
New York, 1904: Harper & Brothers Publishers.
　　　　　　　　Volume XII of
　　　　　　　　The Writings of Mark Twain.
　　　　　　　　Hillcrest Edition.
　　　　　　　　Three-quarter morocco.
　　　　　　　　Inscribed copy:
　　　　　　　　On the whole it is better/to deserve
　　　　　　　　honors and/not have them/than
　　　　　　　　have them & not/deserve them./
　　　　　　　　Mark Twain.
　　　　　　　　(Notebook, p. 380)

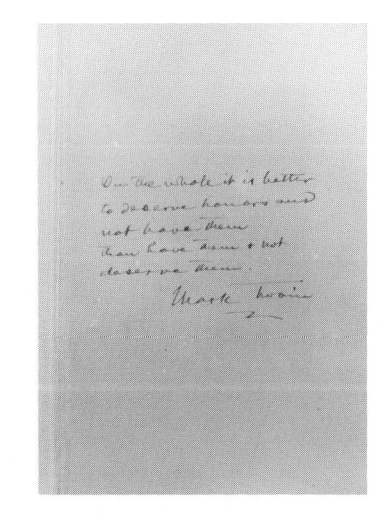

The Adventures of Tom Sawyer.
New York and London, (1903): Harper & Brothers Publishers.
Red cloth: two copies.

The Adventures of Tom Sawyer.
New York and London, 1904: Harper & Brothers.
Red cloth.

The Adventures of Tom Sawyer.
New York and London, (1915): Harper & Brothers Publishers.
Volume XII of
The Writings of Mark Twain.
Author's National Edition.
Red cloth.

The Adventures of Tom Sawyer.
New York and London, (1917): Harper & Brothers Publishers.
Limp leather edition.
Red leather with dustjacket.

The Adventures of Tom Sawyer.
New York and London, (1919): Harper & Brothers Publishers.
Volume XII of
The Writings of Mark Twain.
Author's National Edition.
Green cloth.

The Adventures of Tom Sawyer.
New York and London, (1927): Harper & Brothers Publishers.
Blue cloth.

The Adventures of Tom Sawyer.
New York, 1929: Harper & Brothers.
Volume 8 of
The Stormfield Edition of
The Writings of Mark Twain.
Set #212 of 1024.
Introduction by Albert Bigelow Paine.
Blue cloth stamped in gold.

The Adventures of Tom Sawyer.
New York, (1929): Grosset & Dunlap.
  Reprinted from Harper & Brothers plates including the copyright page plate; this makes the establishment of exact printing date almost impossible. The date used here is from the Harper's date code on the copyright page so this reprint is no earlier than 1929.
  Green cloth.

The Adventures of Tom Sawyer.
New York and London, (1930): Harper & Brothers.
  Illustrated by Worth Brehm.
  Black cloth with color plate on front cover: two copies.

The Adventures of Tom Sawyer.
Chicago, (1931): John C. Winston Co.
  Illustrated by Peter Hurd.
  Red cloth with color plate on front cover.

The Adventures of Tom Sawyer.
New York, (1933): Three Sirens Press.
  Illustrated by Richard Rogers.
  Purple cloth.

The Adventures of Tom Sawyer.
New York, (1936): The Heritage Press.
  Illustrated by Norman Rockwell.
  Tan cloth in slipcase.

The Adventures of Tom Sawyer.
Chicago, 1938: Rand McNally & Company.
"Abridged edition."
Illustrated by True Williams.
Cover illustrated by Milo Winter.
Pictorial paper over boards.

The Adventures of Tom Sawyer.
Cambridge, 1939: Limited Editions Club.
Edited and with an introduction by
Bernard DeVoto.
Prologue and *"Boy's Manuscript"*
printed for the first time.
Illustrated by Thomas Hart Benton.
#562 of 1500.
Signed by Benton on the colophon
BAL 3562   page.

The Complete Story of Tom Sawyer.
New York, 1942: Dell Publishing Company.
Number 2 of
A Famous Stories Book series.
Paper over boards.

The Adventures of Tom Sawyer.
New York, (1946): Grosset & Dunlap.
Illustrated by Donald McKay.
Red cloth.

The Adventures of Tom Sawyer.
New York, August 1948: Gilberton Company, Inc.
The Classics Illustrated edition.
Number 50 in the series; price 15¢
Pictorial paper wrappers.

The Adventures of Tom Sawyer.
New York, (August 1959): Signet Classic.
Afterword by George P. Elliott.
#CD2; price 50¢
Pictorial paper wrappers.

Tom Sawyer: A Drama.
(Washington, D.C., 1940): no publisher
Inscribed on back:
*This is One of Twenty-five Copies
printed in Addition To a Small Paper
Edition of One Hundred Unnumbered
Copies. December — MCMXL No.
One for Frank J. Hogan — Jacob*
BAL 3565   *Blanck.*

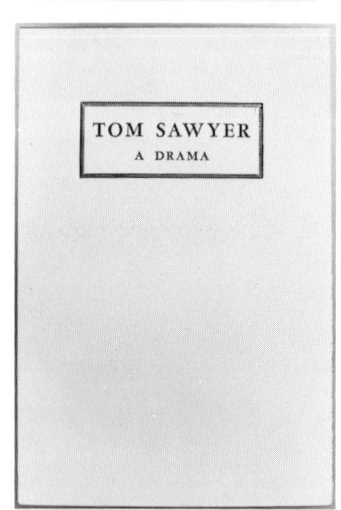

48

Tom Sawyer to Read Aloud.
New York, (1961): Wonder Books.
  Adapted and abridged by Edmund Collier.
  Illustrated by Jon Nielsen.
  #2027 in the Wonder Read Aloud Books series.
  Pictorial wrappers.

The Adventures of Tom Sawyer.
Boston, (1962): Houghton Mifflin Company.
  Riverside Literature Series edition.
  Introduction by Walter Blair.
  Suggestions for reading and discussion by Frank H. Townsend.
  Fifth printing of this edition.
  Yellow decorated cloth.

The Adventures of Tom Sawyer.
(Harmondsworth, 1958): Penguin Books Ltd.
  The Puffin Books edition, third printing (first was 1950).
  Editorial note by Eleanor Graham.
  #PS62 in the series.
  Pictorial paper wrappers.

Tom Sawyer.
New York, 1976: Marvel Classics Comics.
  Adapted by Irwin Shapiro.
  Illustrated by E.R. Cruz.
  #702556; price 50¢.
  Pictorial paper wrappers.

The Adventures of Tom Sawyer.
Chicago, n.d.: The Goldsmith Publishing Company.
  Two copies, neither dated, yet both state "Complete new edition" on the title page.
  Copy 1: red cloth; copy 2: brown cloth.

(The Adventures of Tom Sawyer.)
n.p., n.d.: no publisher.
    In Chinese and English.
    Illustrated by Harold Minton.
    Paper wrappers.

(The Adventures of Tom Sawyer.)
n.p., (1961): no publisher.
    In English with Chinese footnotes.
    Paper wrappers.

Pustolovine Toma Sojera.
Sarajevo, 1965:   Veselin Maslesa.
    In Croatian.
    Translated by Nika Milicevic.
    Illustrated by Husnija Balic.
    Paper over boards.

Toms Evetyr.
(Copenhagen, c. 1960s): Gyldendal.
    In Danish.
    Translated by Poul Steenstrup.
    Illustrated by Bernhard Petersen.
    Cover illustrated by Robert Viby.
    Pictorial cloth.

de Avonturen van Tom Sawyer.
's-Gravenhage & Djakarta, n.d.: G.B. Van
    Goorzonen's
    Uitgeversmaatschappij.
    In Dutch.
    Translated by P. DeZeeuw.
    Illustrated by Roothciv.
    Paper over boards.

De avonturen van Tom Sawyer.
(The Hague), n.d.: uitheverij V.A. Kramers-'s-
>Gravenhage.
>In Dutch.
>Cover illustrated by Coby C.M.
>Krouwel.
>Paper wrappers.

Tom Sawyer.
(Paris, 1938): Hachette.
>In French.
>Translated by P.F. Caille.
>Illustrated by G. Barret.
>Green cloth with dustjacket.

Les Aventures de Tom Sawyer.
(Paris, 1961): Lucien Mazenod, Édition D'Art.
>In French.
>Translated by William-L. Hugues.
>#846/5000.

Les Aventures de Tom Sawyer.
(Paris, 1973): Gallimard.
>In French.
>Translated by Francois de Gail.
>Illustrated by Jean Oliver Heron.
>Dustjacket illustrated by Claude
>LaPointe.
>Blue paper over boards.
>Pictorial dustjacket.

Tom Sawyers Abenteuer.
Gottingen, (1971): W. Fischer-Verlag.
>In German.
>Translated by Gisela Eppe.
>Illustrated by Kurt Schmischke.
>Pictorial cloth over boards.

o Tom Solier Astynomikos.
Athens, n.d.: Exdoseis L.S. Blessa Odos Miltiadou.
>In Greek.
>Translated by K.A. Sphaellou.
>Illustrated by Bur. Aptosliou.
>Pictorial paper over boards.
>Dustjacket.

Oi Peripeteies tou Tom Soler.
Athens, 1960: Al. and E. Papademetriou.
    In Greek.
    Illustrated by Marlaritas Dalmate.
    Translated by Th. Andreoposlos.
    Pictorial paper over boards: two copies.

Tom Sawyer.
Tel Aviv, (1970): Izreel Publishing House Ltd.
    In Hebrew.
    Translated by A. Akabia.
    Illustrated by Walter Trier.
    Pictorial paper over boards.

Tom Sawyer Anak Amerika.
Djakarta, 1957: Dinas Penerbitan Balai Pustaka.
    In bahassa Indonesia.
    Translated by Abdoel Moeis.
    Pictorial wrappers: two copies.

Le Avventure di Tom Sawyer.
Firenze, (1954): Casa Editrice Marzocco.
    In Italian.
    Translated by T. Orsi and B.C. Ranolle.
    Illustrated by Roberto Lemmi.
    Color plates by F. Faorzi.
    17th printing. Pictorial red cloth.

(The Adventures of Tom Sawyer.)
(Tokyo, c. 1975): no publisher.
    In Japanese.
    Contains two Norman Rockwell illustrations from the Heritage Press edition (1936), copied here in black and white.
    Two volumes: paper wrappers.

(The Adventures of Tom Sawyer.)
n.p., n.d.: Obunsha Library.
    In Japanese.
    #B96 of the series.
    Paper wrappers.

The Adventures of Tom Sawyer.
Petersburg and Moscow, n.d.: M.O. Wolfe.
    In Russian.
    Translated by M. Nikolaev.
    Illustrated.
    Third edition.
    Paper over boards.

Tom Sawyer.
(Madrid, 1963): Aguilar.
In Spanish.
Translated by Maria Alfaro.
Fifth edition.
Leather cover with dustjacket.

Las Aventuras de Tom Sawyer.
n.p., 1970: Salvat Editores, S.A.
In Spanish.
Translated by Ramon Strack.
Introduction by Julio Manegat.
#42 in the series Biblioteca Basica Salvat de Libros RTV.
Paper wrappers.

Las Aventuras de Tom Sawyer.
Barcelona, 1974: A.G. Ponsa.
In Spanish.
Translated by Maria Teresa Quintana.
Illustrated by Walter Trier.
Third edition.
Pictorial paper over boards.

Las Aventuras de Tom Sawyer.
(Havana, November 1974): Editorial Gente Nueva.
In Spanish.
Introduction by Francisco M. Mota.
Illustrated by Miriam Gonzalez Gimenez.
Cover illustrated by Jose Gonzalez Rodriguez.
Paper wrappers.

Tom Sawyer En Skolpjkhistoria.
Stockholm, (1877): Jos. Seligman Forlag.
In Swedish.
Translated by L. Lipmanson.
Three-quarter leather.

(The Adventures of Tom Sawyer.)
n.p., n.d.: no publisher.
In Thai.
Simplified by W.J. Hoggett.
Illustrated.
Pictorial paper wrappers.

Tom Sawyer.
Istanbul, 1970: Nesrivat Anonim Siketi.
In Turkish.
Translated by Vahdet Gultekin.
Red cloth with pictorial dustjacket.

Information Wanted and Other Sketches.
London, (1876): George Routledge and Sons.
Second edition, containing
"Honored as a Curiosity."
BAL 3608   Yellow pictorial paper over boards.

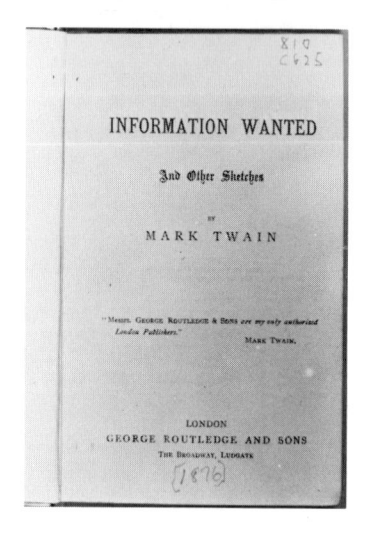

Old Times on the Mississippi.
Toronto, 1876: Belford Brothers, Publishers.
                BAL reprint B with (158) blank, (159) with *Pausanias the Spartan* and (160) with *New and Popular Books*.
                Two copies.
                Copy 1: green cloth.
BAL 3368   Copy 2: purple cloth.

Old Times on the Mississippi.
Toronto, 1876: Belford Brothers, Publishers.
                BAL reprint C with (158) & (159) as in reprint B and with (160) with *Norman MacLeod's Works*

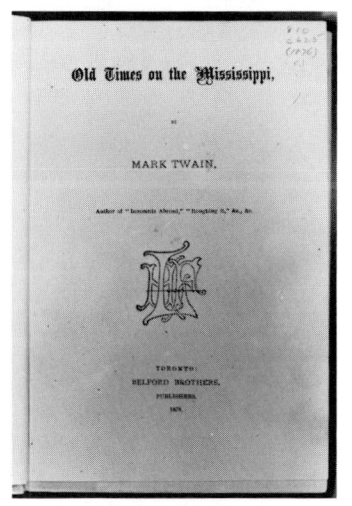

Als Lotse auf dem Mississippi.
Wien, 1973: Verlag: Carl Ueberreuter.
                In German.
                Translated by Otto Wilck.
                Illustrated by von F.J. Tripp.
                Pictorial cloth over boards.

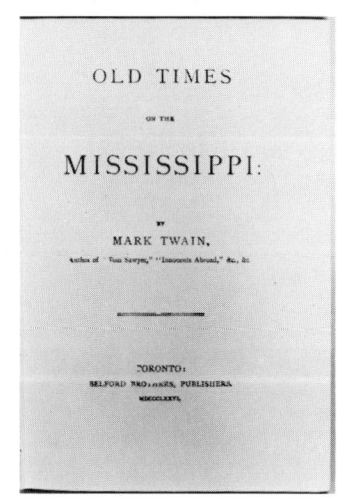

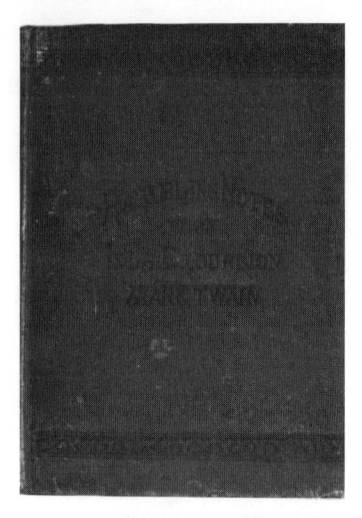

An Idle Excursion.
Toronto, 1878: Rose-Belford Publishing Company. Stamped on rear flyleaf: "Railroad Edition".
BAL 3377 Brown cloth.

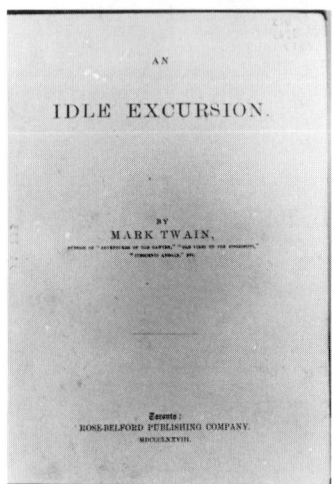

An Idle Excursion.
Girard, Kansas, n.d.:Haldeman-Julius Company. Little Blue Book No. 930. Edited by E. Haldeman-Julius. Yellow wrappers.

Mark Twain's Nightmare. A Story of Haunting Horror with Tales, Sketches, and Poetry by Mark Twain, F.C. Burnand, H.S. Leigh, etc., etc.
London, (c. 1878): Ward, Lock, & Co.
                Illustrated by Linley Sambourne,
                A.B. Frost and others.
                First printing.
BAL 3618   Printed paper wrappers.

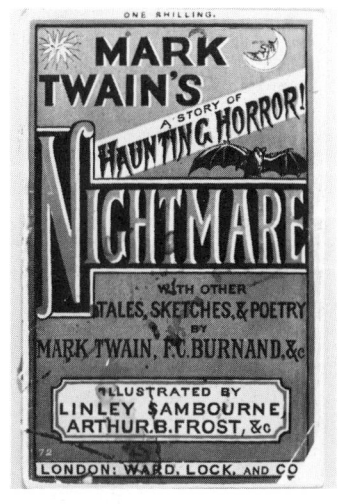

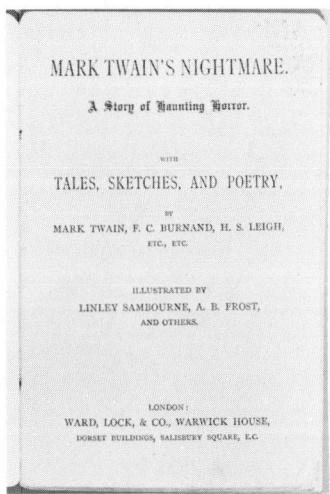

A True Story of the Recent Carnival of Crime.
Boston, 1877: James R. Osgood and Company,
Late Ticknor and Fields, and Fields, Osgood & Co.
First issue binding with *JRO&Co* monogram on cover.
Terra-cotta cloth.

BAL 3373

Punch, Brothers, Punch! and Other Sketches.
New York, (1878): Slote, Woodman & Co.

                First issue with author's name on title-page in roman type, 91:4 up: *health offi....... could* and 101 with thirteen lines of text.

BAL 3378   Red printed wrappers.

Punch, Brothers, Punch! and Other Sketches.
New York, (1878): Slote, Woodman & Co.

                Second issue with the author's name in facsimile autograph, 91:4 up: *health officer's funeral* and 101 with thirteen lines of text and a three-line postscript.
                Wrappers (covers missing).

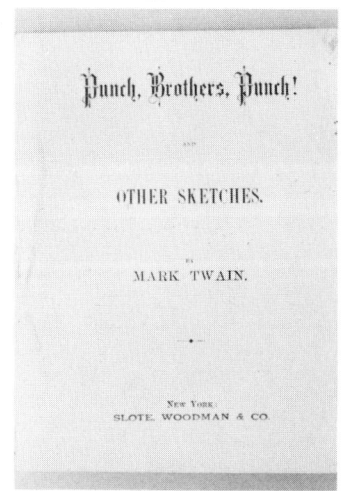

First issue.

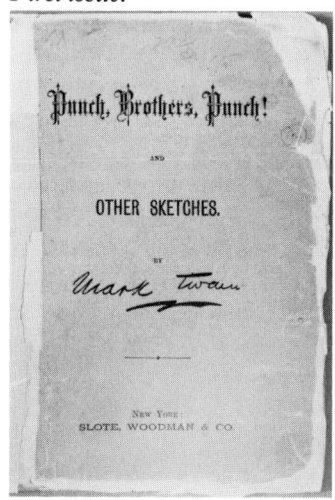

Second issue.

A Tramp Abroad.

Hartford, 1879: American Publishing Company, San Francisco, Cal: A.L. Bancroft & Co. Publisher's prospectus.
Text consists of random pages of the text, bound out of sequence. Spine samples in leather and black cloth on inside covers.
Brown cloth: two copies.

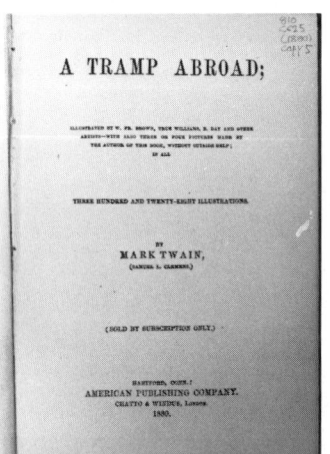

A Tramp Abroad.

Hartford, 1880: American Publishing Company. London: Chatto & Windus.

BAL 3386

BAL point:	1	2	3	Binding
Copy 1:	B	B	B	black cloth
Copy 2:	B	B	B	brown cloth
Copy 3:	B	B	B	black cloth*
Copy 4:	C	B	A	black cloth
Copy 5:	B	B	B	black cloth**
Copy 6:	B	B	B	black cloth
Copy 7:	B	A	A	black cloth***
Copy 8:	B	B	B	black cloth
Copy 9:	B	B	—	¾ morocco
Copy 10:	B	B	B	brown cloth
Copy 11:	B	A	B	black cloth
Copy 12:	B	B	—	¾ morocco
Copy 13:	C	B	B	black cloth

* — under embossed device on back cover is stamped *88*
** — under embossed device on back cover is stamped *7*
*** — under embossed device on back cover is stamped *0*

Point 1: A: In Portrait frontispiece, underlying lines in lapel at left almost vertical; engraver's imprint at lower left.
B: Lines definitely slanted; imprint at lower left.
C: Lines slanted; imprint barely present.

Point 2: A: Frontispiece *Moses*
B: Frontispiece *Titian's Moses*

Point 3: A: blindstamped border on cover is about square at inner corners.
B: border definitely curved at inner corners.

First issue of frontispiece.

A Tramp Abroad.
Hartford, 1880:   American Publishing Company.
London: Chatto & Windus.
Publisher's prospectus.
Pages selected for this prospectus
are not the same as those in the 1879
prospectus (above).
Black cloth.

A Tramp Abroad.
Hartford, 1880:   American Publishing Company. etc.
Point 1: issue B
Point 2: issue A
Point 3: not applicable
Bookplate of Harriet Whitmore.
Cover stamped in gold: *Mrs. F.G. Whitmore*
Leather.
Inscribed copy:
To Mrs. F.G. Whitmore/With kindest regards of/The Author./Hartford, April 11, 1880.

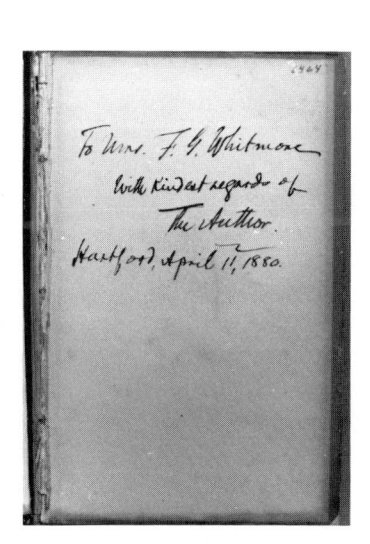

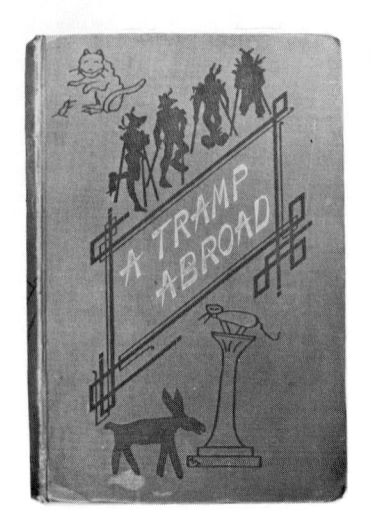

A Tramp Abroad.
London, 1880: Chatto & Windus.
First English edition in one volume.
Red cloth stamped in black and gold.

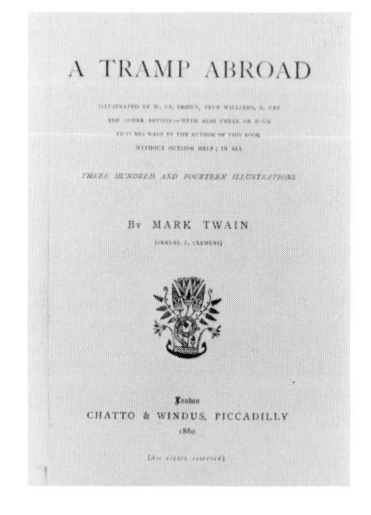

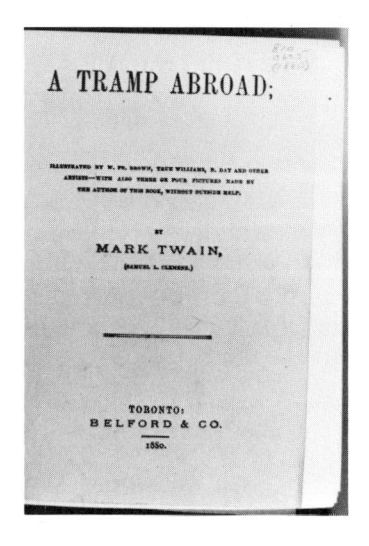

A Tramp Abroad.
Toronto, 1880: Belford & Co.
                First Canadian edition.
BAL 3626   Green cloth.

A Tramp Abroad.
Toronto, 1880: Belford & Co.
                First Canadian edition.
                Printed paper wrappers (back cover missing).
                Not in BAL with this binding.

A Tramp Abroad.
Leipzig, 1880: Bernhard Tauchnitz.
Collection of British Authors, Volumes 1899-1900.
See note on Tauchnitz editions under *The Innocents Abroad* (page 9).
Two volumes: two sets.
Set 1, Volume 1: last title opposite title page is *A Double-Barrelled Detective Story* (1902).
Set 2, Volume 1: last title is *Extract from Captain Stormfield,* etc. (1909).
BAL 3622   Paper wrappers.

A Tramp Abroad.
London, 1884: Chatto & Windus.
"A new edition."
Illustrated paper over boards.
Spine missing.

A Tramp Abroad.
Hartford, 1886: American Publishing Company. etc.
Black cloth.

A Tramp Abroad.
Hartford, 1899: The American Publishing Company.
Volumes III & IV of
The Writings of Mark Twain.
Autograph Edition of the Edition de Luxe.
Three-quarter morocco.
Bound into Volume III:
Two cancelled checks 1874
March 14 and April 1, payable to Clemens from Elisha Bliss and Frank Bliss.

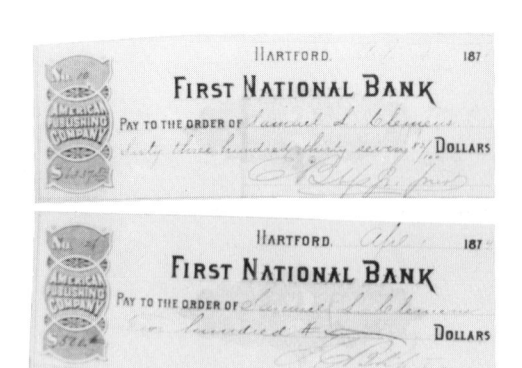

64

A Tramp Abroad.
New York, 1904: Harper & Brothers Publishers.
   Volumes III & IV of
   The Writings of Mark Twain.
   Hillcrest Edition.
   Three-quarter morocco.
   Volume III inscribed:
   To create man was a/quaint & original idea;/but to add the sheep was tautology./Mark Twain.
   (Notebook, p. 379)
   Volume IV inscribed:
   One fly makes a summer./Mark Twain.
   (*Pudd'nhead Wilson's Calendar*)

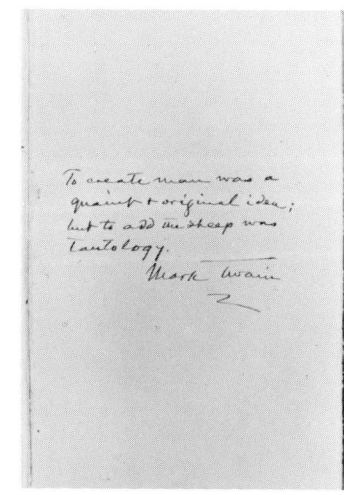

A Tramp Abroad.
Hartford, 1899: The American Publishing Company.
   Volumes III & IV of
   The Writings of Mark Twain.
   Edition de Luxe.
   Set #54 of 1000.
   Uses the same plates as the
   Autograph edition.
   Green cloth.

A Tramp Abroad.
New York and London, (1906): Harper & Brothers
   Publishers.
   Volume (III missing) & IV of
   The Writings of Mark Twain.
   Hillcrest Edition.
   Green cloth.

A Tramp Abroad.
New York and London, (1915): Harper & Brothers
   Publishers.
   Volumes III & IV of
   The Writings of Mark Twain.
   Author's National Edition.
   Red cloth.

A Tramp Abroad.
New York and London, (1918): Harper & Brothers
   Volumes III & IV of
   The Writings of Mark Twain.
   Author's National Edition.
   Green cloth.

A Tramp Abroad.
New York and London, (1926): Harper & Brothers
   Publishers.
   Two volumes in one. Blue cloth.

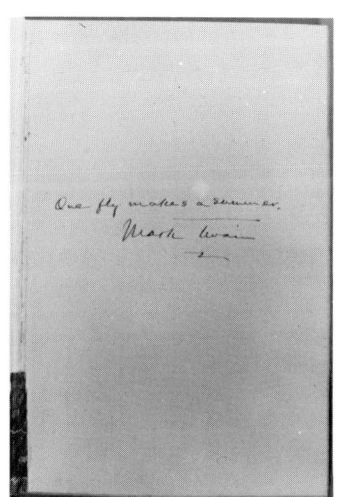

A Tramp Abroad.
London, 1909: Chatto & Windus.
"A New Impression."
Blue cloth.

A Tramp Abroad.
New York, 1929: Harper & Brothers.
Volumes 9 & 10 of
The Stormfield Edition of
The Writings of Mark Twain.
Set #212 of 1024.
Appreciation by E.V. Lucas.
Introduction by Albert
Bigelow Paine.
Blue cloth stamped in gold.

A Tramp Abroad.
New York, (1966): The Heritage Press.
With an introduction by Edward
Wagenknecht.
Illustrated by David Knight
"including several pictures made by the author of this book without outside help"
Blue leatherette in slipcase.

A Tramp Abroad.
Leipzig, 1903: Berlag von G. Freytag.
Excerpts from the original.
Text in English with introduction
and footnotes in German.
Translated by Max Mann.
Green cloth.
Inscribed copy:
S.L. Clemens/Stormfield/Oct. 30/09.

Rafting Down the Neckar.
Heidelberg, 1966: Edition European Places of Culture.
"From Heilbronn to Heidelberg."
Excerpts from *A Tramp Abroad*.
Edited by Wolfgang Boehler.
Two copies: one in English, one in
German (1967).
Pictorial paper wrappers.

A Tramp Abroad.
Frankfort, 1971: Verlag Ullstein GmbH.
In German.
Translated by Ulrich Steindorff
Carrington.
Pictorial paper wrappers.

Ur En Lanstrykares Anteckningar. Valda stycken ur.
Stockholm, (1882): Jos. Seligman & Chs. Forlag.
In Swedish.
Translated by Anna Grete.
Paper wrappers.

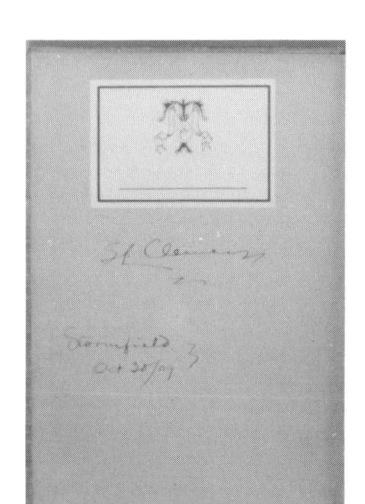

Mark Twain, about 1870.

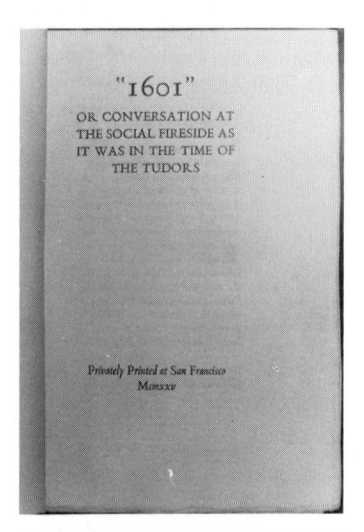

"1601" or Conversation at the Social Fireside As It Was in the Time of the Tudors.
San Francisco, 1925: Grabhorn Press.
    Foreword by Charles Erskine Scott Wood.
    One of 100 copies.
    Leather.

Note:
None of these is the first published edition:
(The first printing was 1880.)

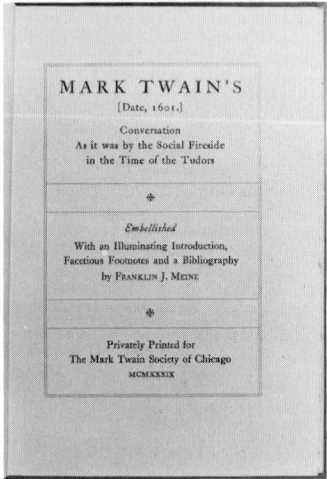

Mark Twain's 1601.
Chicago, 1939: Privately printed for the
    Mark Twain Society.
    "Embellished with an illuminating introduction, facetious footnotes and a bibliography by Franklin J. Meine."
    Frontispiece by H.H. Winkler.
    #M-25 of 550 copies.
    Contains a 44-item bibliography of "1601."
    Cloth over boards with gold-stamped leather panel on cover and spine.

Mark Twain's 1601.
Chicago, 1939: Privately printed for the
    Mark Twain Society.
    Red cloth.
    One of 1000, this copy not numbered.

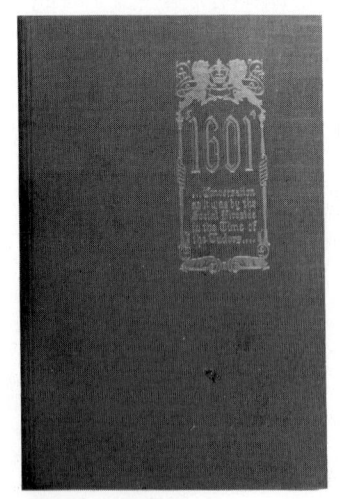

1601: A fireside chatte in ye time of ye Tudors.
n.p., 1941: Privately printed by ye Three Asterisks
    at ye Sign of ye Gaye Goose.
    Paper over boards.

1601.
n.p., (1955): Earth Publishing Company.
    Illustrated by Richard Roth.
    Pictorial paper wrappers.
    Three copies, one rubber stamped $1.50

Mark Twain's Date-1601. Conversation As It Was By The Social Fireside in the Time of the Tudors.
n.p., n.d.,: Privately printed.
    Blue leather stamped in gold.
    #19 of 110. With an anonymous foreword.

Chicago, 1939.

Mark Twain's (Date 1601.).
New York, n.d. (c. 1961): Privately printed for
    Lyle Stuart.
    Introduction, footnotes and a
    bibliography by Franklin J. Meine.
    A reprint of the 1939 edition (above).
    Red cloth with printed slipcase and
    yellow paper band stating a special
    pre-publication price of $4.95.

1601.
Chicago, 1962: The Black Cat Press.
    "With Notes on Mark Twain's 1601
    and a Check-list of Various Editions
    and Reprints Compiled by Irvin Haas."
    Accompanied by a prospectus of The
    Black Cat Press and its publications.
    Miniature book.
    Full leather stamped in gold.

1601.
n.p., (Northampton, Mass.), 1978: Lazarus Edition.
    Wood engraved portrait frontispiece
    by Barry Moser, signed by the artist.
    One of 200 assembled from "newly
    discovered sheets of a 1920 privately
    printed edition on Old Town Book
    paper."
    Cloth over boards.

"1601" or Conversation As It Was By the Social Fireside in the Time of the Tudors.
n.p., n.d.: no publisher.
    Green paper self-wrappers.

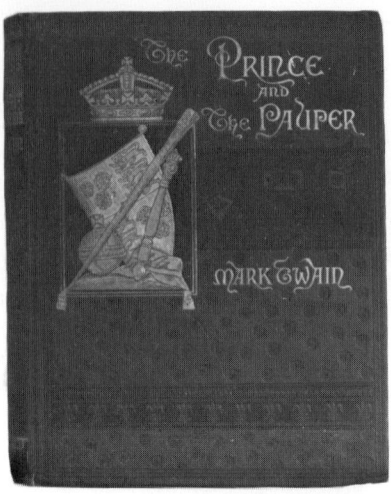

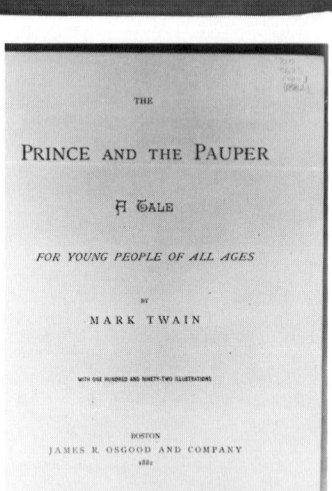

(The Prince and the Pauper.)
(title page missing)
> Publisher's prospectus.
> Cloth spine sample on inside front cover.
> Five pages clipped out of front matter.

The Prince and the Pauper. A Tale for Young People of All Ages.
Boston, 1882: James R. Osgood and Company.
> First issue with spine rosette 1/8″ below fillet and Franklin Press imprint on copyright page.

BAL 3402   Green cloth.

The Prince and the Pauper. etc.
Boston, 1882: James R. Osgood and Company.
> Second issue with spine rosette 1/16″ scant below fillet and Franklin Press imprint on copyright page.
> Green cloth: four copies.
> Copy 1 bears the signature of Abbott Lawrence Lowell (1856-1943, and President of Harvard University 1909-33); this signature is dated 1883.

Left: first issue; right: second issue.

The Prince and the Pauper. etc.
Boston, 1882: James R. Osgood and Company.
    First issue.
    Green cloth.
    Inscribed copy:
    To/Robert J. Burdette,/Burlington, Iowa,/With the Kindest regards of/The Author./Hartford Dec. 20, 1881.
    This title was deposited for copyright Dec. 12, 1881 and first advertised in *Publisher's Weekly* January 2, 1882, according to BAL. Thus this is quite possibly the earliest known copy inscribed by Clemens.

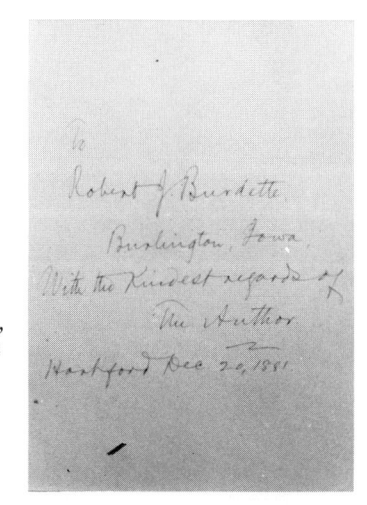

The Prince and the Pauper. etc.
Boston, 1882: James R. Osgood and Company.
    First issue.
    Green cloth.
    Inscribed copy:
    This is the book which I had/intended to give my friend Mrs./Taft, but the book agent arrived first./S.L. Clemens/(Mark Twain)/Hartford July 1882.

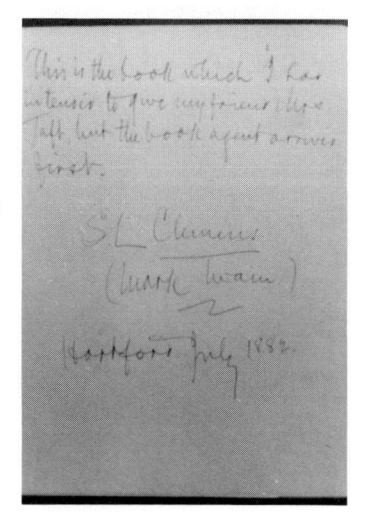

The Prince and the Pauper. etc.
Boston, 1882: James R. Osgood and Company.
    First issue copyright page (Franklin Press).
    Three-quarter morocco.
    Inscribed copy:
    Lyman Beecher Stowe/1 Beekman Place/New York; To/Mrs. Harriet Beecher Stowe —/with the reverence + admiration/of/The Author, Self-appointed instructor of the public/ under the name of/Mark Twain/ Hartford, March 26, 1887.
    In another hand:
    For Lyman Beecher Stowe/With the love of/His affectionate Grandmama/Harriet Beecher Stowe

The Prince and the Pauper. etc.
Boston, 1882: James R. Osgood and Company.
        Second issue.
        Green cloth.
        Inscribed copy (not by Clemens):
March 10, 1882/Everlovingly your mother/Eliza S. W. Jones./and Sister, Julia J. Beecher/Here in Bridgeport/We have read it/together and enjoyed/it very much/E.S.W.P./JJB.?D.J.D.

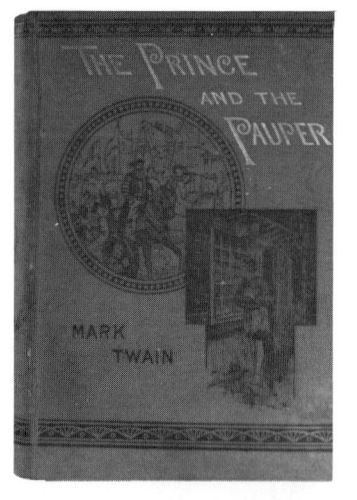

The Prince and the Pauper. etc.
London, 1881: Chatto & Windus, Piccadilly.
        First English edition.
BAL 3396   Red cloth.

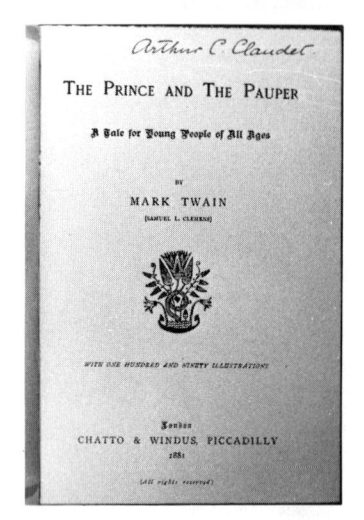

The Prince and the Pauper. etc.
Montreal, 1881: Dawson Brothers.
First Canadian edition.
Paper wrappers.
* — This binding not noted in BAL.
Cover wrapper with the imprint
BAL 3397*   *Toronto: Albert Britnell, Bookseller.*

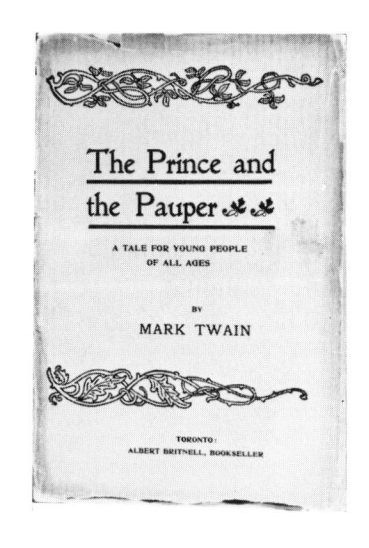

The Prince and the Pauper. etc.
Toronto, 1882: Rose-Belford Publishing Co.
BAL 3629   Red cloth stamped in gold.

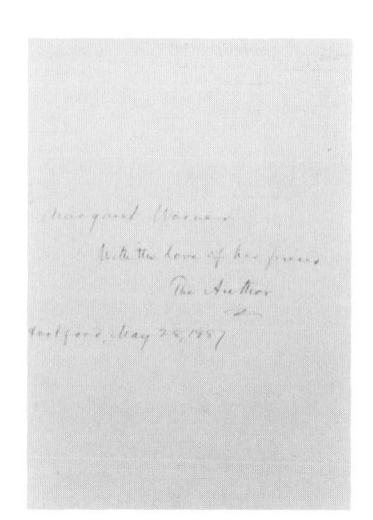

The Prince and the Pauper. etc.
New York, 1887: Charles L. Webster and Company.
               Full leather.
               Inscribed copy:
               To/Margaret Warner/With the love of her friend/The Author./Hartford, May 28, 1887.

The Prince and the Pauper. etc.
New York, 1889: Charles L. Webster and Company.
               Green pictorial cloth.

The Prince and the Pauper. etc.
New York, 1892: Charles L. Webster & Company.
               Tan pictorial cloth: three copies.

The Prince and the Pauper. etc.
New York, 1893: Charles L. Webster & Co.
               Tan pictorial cloth.

The Prince and the Pauper. etc.
Hartford, 1899:   The American Publishing Company.
               Volume XV of
               The Writings of Mark Twain.
               Autograph edition of
               the Edition de Luxe.
               Three-quarter morocco.

The Prince and the Pauper. etc.
Hartford, 1899:   American Publishing Company.
               Volume XV of
               The Writings of Mark Twain.
               Edition de Luxe.
               Set #54 of 1000.
               Uses the same plates as the
               Autograph edition.
               Green cloth.

The Prince and the Pauper.
New York, 1904: Harper & Brothers Publishers.
>Volume XV of
>The Writings of Mark Twain.
>Hillcrest Edition.
>Three-quarter morocco.
>Inscribed copy:
>*Twelve or fifteen years ago,/Andrew Carnegie gave me/this advice:/Put all your eggs in one basket-and watch that basket. Mark Twain/I was willing to try it, and offered/to borrow his basket, but* — (Pudd'nhead Wilson, p. 145: a variation on:
>*Behold, the fool saith, "Put not all thine eggs in one basket" — which is but a manner of saying, "Scatter your money and your attention; but the wise man saith, "Put all your eggs in the one basket and — WATCH THAT BASKET.")*

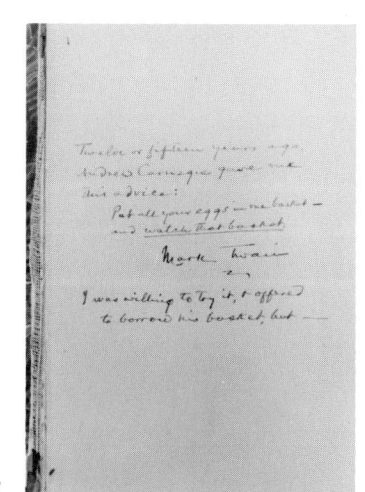

The Prince and the Pauper. etc.
New York and London, 1906: Harper & Brothers
>Publishers.
>Volume XV of
>The Writings of Mark Twain.
>Hillcrest Edition.
>Green cloth.

The Prince and the Pauper. etc.
New York and London, (1909): Harper & Brothers
>Publishers.
>Red cloth.

The Prince and the Pauper. etc.
New York and London, (1915): Harper & Brothers
>Publishers.
>Volume XV of
>The Writings of Mark Twain.
>Author's National Edition.
>Red cloth.

The Prince and the Pauper. etc.
New York and London, (1918): Harper & Brothers
>Publishers.
>Volume XV of
>The Writings of Mark Twain.
>Author's National Edition.
>Green cloth.

The Prince and the Pauper. etc.
New York and London, (1919): Harper & Brothers
>Publishers.
>Limp leather edition.

The Prince and the Pauper. etc.
New York and London, (1927): Harper & Brothers
        Publishers.
        Blue cloth: two copies.

The Prince and the Pauper.
New York, 1929: Harper & Brothers.
        Volume 11 of
        The Stormfield Edition of
        The Writings of Mark Twain.
        Set #212 of 1024.
        Blue cloth stamped in gold.

The Prince and the Pauper. etc.
New York, (1931): Harper & Brothers
        Publishers.
        Harper's Modern Classics edition
        published October, 1956 (from
        Harper's date code).
        Edited by Emily Fanning Barry and
        Herbert B. Bruner. Red cloth.

The Prince and the Pauper.
New York, (1958): TAB Books.
        Illustrated by Charles Beck.
        #T92 in the series.
        Pictorial paper wrappers.

The Prince and the Pauper.
New York, (1964): Airmont Publishing Co., Inc.
        Classics series #CL32.
        Introduction by Lucy Mabry
        Fitzpatrick.
        Pictorial paper wrappers.

The Prince and the Pauper.
New York, 1964: Gilberton Company, Inc.
        Classics Illustrated edition.
        No. 29 in the series; price 15¢
        (Original copyright 1946).
        Pictorial paper wrappers.

The Prince and the Pauper.
New York, (n.d.): Books, Inc.
        Giant Junior Classics edition #77.
        Pictorial paper wrappers.

The Prince and the Pauper.
New York, (1967): Collier Books.
        New introduction by DeLancey
        Ferguson.
        Illustrated by Kevin McIntyre.
        Pictorial paper wrappers.

The Prince and the Pauper.
New York, 1970: Gilberton Company, Inc.
        Classics Illustrated edition.
        No. 29 in the series; price 25¢
        (Original copyright 1946).
        Pictorial paper wrappers.

Mark Twain on the "Wake Robin" piazza, Onteora Club, Tannersville, New York, August, 1890.

(The Prince and the Pauper.)
U.S.A., 1930: no publisher.
    In Armenian.
    Uses many illustrations from the original edition.
    Purple cloth.

(The Prince and the Pauper.)
n.p., n.d. (1900s): no publisher.
    In Chinese.
    Illustrated.
    Pictorial paper wrappers.

Kraljevic I Prosjak.
Zagreb, (1964):   Izdavako Knjizarske Produzece mladost.
    In Croatian.
    Translated by Slobodan A. Jovanovic.
    Illustrated by Josip Vanista.
    Pictorial paper wrappers with dustjacket.

Princas Ir Elgeta.
Leidinys, 1951:   Vokietijos Krasto Valdybos.
    In Czech.
    Uses illustrations from the original edition.
    Paper over boards with dustjacket: two copies.

Le Prince et Le Pauvre.
(Paris, 1980): Editions Gallimard.
    In French.
    Translated by Marie-Madeleine Fayet.
    Dustjacket illustrated by Patrick Couratin.
    Blue paper over boards with dustjacket.

O Prigkipas kia O Phtochos.
Athens, (1962):   Apollon Papademetriou & Siou.
    In Greek.
    Translated by Poulas Chatzopolou.
    Illustrated by N. Koukake.
    Pictorial boards.

Basilopoulo kai Zetianopoulo.
n.p., n.d.: To Biblio Tou Paidiou, Ekdotikos Oikos.
    In Greek.
    Translated by Georgias Tarsoule.
    Illustrated by P. Paulide.
    Pictorial boards.

The Prince and the Pauper.
Tel Aviv, (1972): Izreel Publishing House Ltd.
        In Hebrew.
        Translated by A. Akabia.
        Illustrated.
        Paper over boards.

Il Principe e il Povero.
Bologna, (1959): Edizioni Capitol.
        In Italian.
        Translated by Brunella Cocchi.
        Illustrated by F. Baldi and R. Lemmi.
        Padded pictorial covers.

Il Principe e il Povero.
Milan, (1962): Editrice Boschi.
        In Italian.
        Translated by T. Malinverni.
        Illustrated by G. Toffolo.
        Paper over boards.

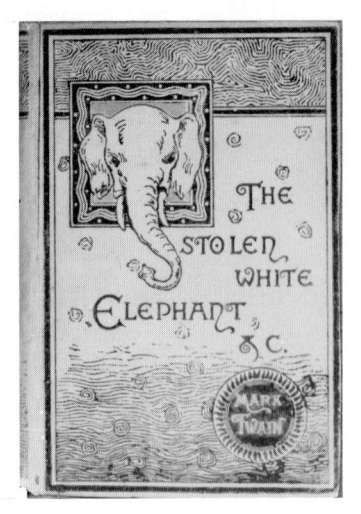

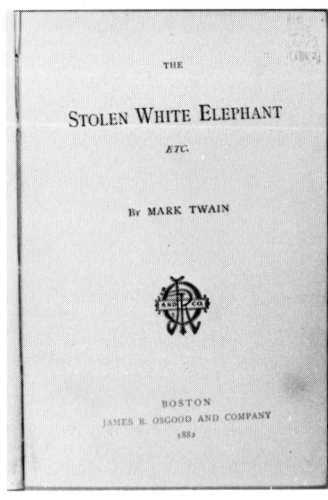

The Stolen White Elephant. Etc.
Boston, 1882: James R. Osgood and Company.
BAL 3404   Tan cloth: five copies.

The Stolen White Elephant. Etc.
Boston, 1882: James R. Osgood and Company.
    Three-quarter morocco.
    Bookplate of Harriet Whitmore.
    Inscribed copy:
    Dear Mrs. Whitmore: If the/dog had waited, he could have got this copy, which is much superior to the other. An/impatient dog, a dog that —/is always in a hurry, is/his own worst enemy./The waiting dog is the suc-/cessful dog./With the kindest regards of/The Author./Hartford, Nov. 18/82.

The Stolen White Elephant. Etc.
Boston, 1882: James R. Osgood and Company
    Tan cloth.
    Inscribed copy:
    Mrs. F.G. Whitmore/With the friendliest/regards of/The Author./July 1882.
    A well-chewed example, as described above.

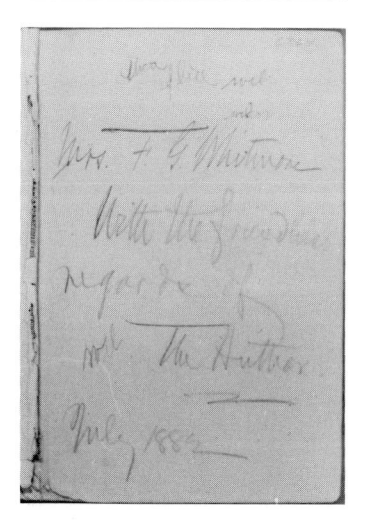

The Stolen White Elephant. Etc.
London, 1882: Chatto & Windus, Piccadilly.
                First English edition.
                Red cloth stamped in black and gold.
BAL 3403   Two copies.

The Stolen White Elephant. Etc.
Boston, 1883: James R. Osgood and Company.
                Tan cloth.
                Inscribed copy:
                To/Miss Laura Taft/With the
                kindest/regards of/The
                Author./Hartford, New Year's 1883.

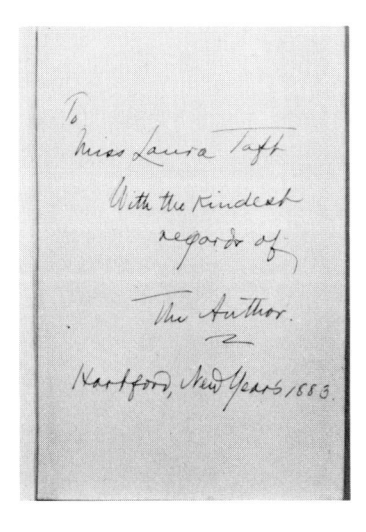

The Stolen White Elephant. Etc.
Boston, 1883: James R. Osgood and Company.
                Tan cloth.

The Stolen White Elephant.
New York, 1891: Charles L. Webster and Co.
                Green cloth.

The Stolen White Elephant And Other Stories.
Girard, Kansas, n.d.: Haldeman-Julius Company.
                Little Blue Book No. 931.
BAL 3696   Green paper wrappers.

The Stolen White Elephant.
n.p., n.d.: no publisher.
                In Arabic.
                Paper wrappers.

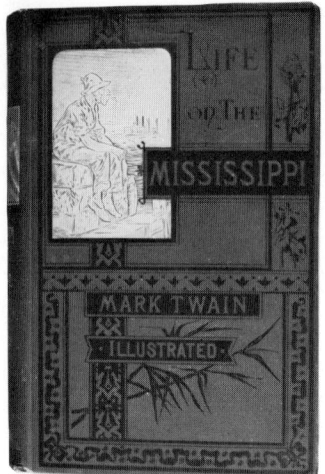

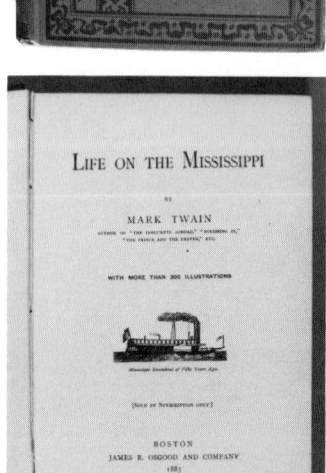

Life on the Mississippi.
Boston, 1883: James R. Osgood and Company.
First issue with 441: illustration of Mark Twain in flames; 443: *The St. Louis Hotel.*
BAL 3411 Brown cloth.

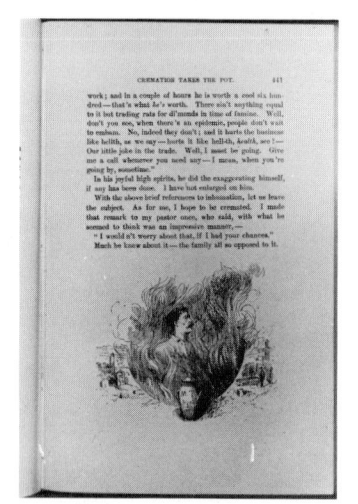

First issue of p. 441.

Life on the Mississippi.
Boston, 1883: James R. Osgood and Company.
>Second intermediate issue with 441:
no illustration; 443: *The St. Louis
Hotel.*
Brown cloth: four copies.

Life on the Mississippi.
Boston, 1883: James R. Osgood and Company.
>Second intermediate issue.
Brown cloth.
Inscribed copy:
With kindest regards of/The Author.

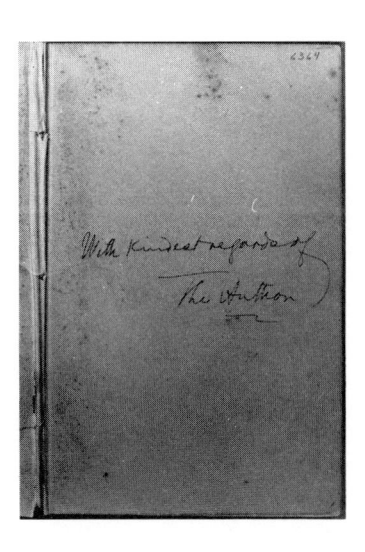

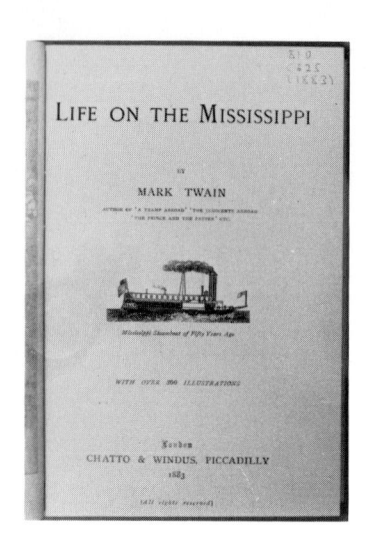

Life on the Mississippi.
London, 1883: Chatto & Windus.
First English edition.
Rebound in three-quarter leather; the publisher's catalog at the rear is absent, probably deleted for binding.

BAL 3410

Life on the Mississippi.
Montreal, 1883:　Dawson Brothers.
　　　　　　　　First Canadian edition.
　　　　　　　　Red leather.
　　　　　　　　Inscribed copy:
　　　　　　　　Truly yrs/S L Clemens/Mark Twain/May 13 '83.

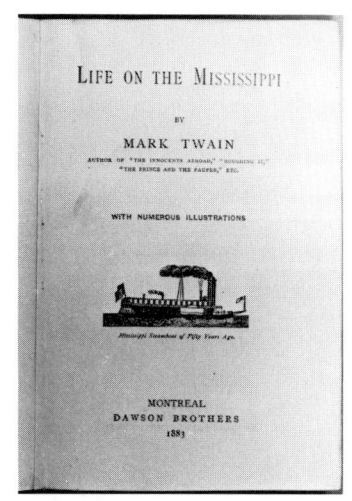

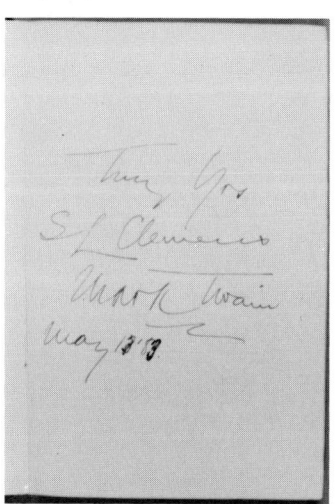

Life on the Mississippi.
Hartford, 1899:　The American Publishing Company.
　　　　　　　　Volume IX of
　　　　　　　　The Writings of Mark Twain.
　　　　　　　　Autograph Edition of
　　　　　　　　the Edition de Luxe.
　　　　　　　　Three-quarter morocco.
　　　　　　　　Bound in:
　　　　　　　　ALS by Edmund H. Garrett to the
　　　　　　　　American Publishing Company, 1 p.,
　　　　　　　　1899 May 8.

Life on the Mississippi.
Hartford, 1899: American Publishing Company.
    Volume IX of
    The Writings of Mark Twain.
    Edition de Luxe.
    Set #54 of 1000.
    Uses the same plates as the
    Autograph edition.
    Green cloth.

Life on the Mississippi.
New York and London, 1899: Harper & Brothers
    Publishers.
    Biographical edition.
    Bluegreen cloth.

Life on the Mississippi.
New York and London, 1900: Harper & Brothers.
    Red cloth.

Life on the Mississippi.
New York and London, (1903): Harper & Brothers
    Publishers.
    Red cloth.
    Inscribed copy:
    Very Truly yours/Mark Twain/to
    Commander Dow, R.N.R./June 17/08.

Life on the Mississippi.
New York and London, (1906): Harper & Brothers
    Publishers.
    Harper's Library Edition.
    Purple cloth.

Life on the Mississippi.
New York, 1904: Harper & Brothers Publishers.
    Volume IX of
    The Writings of Mark Twain.
    Hillcrest Edition.
    Three-quarter morocco.
    Inscribed copy:
    The man who is a pessimist/before 48
    knows too much;/if he is an optimist
    after it,/he knows too little./Mark
    Twain.
    (Notebook, p. 381)

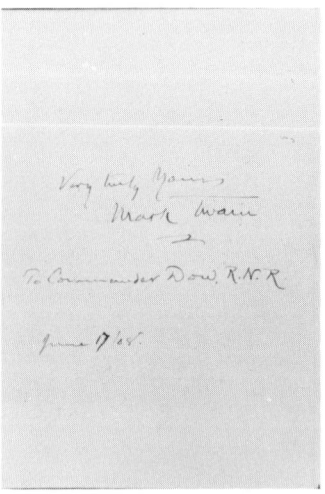

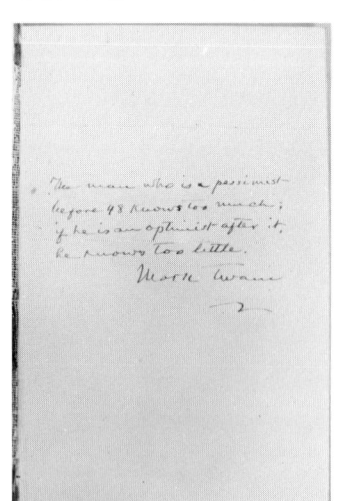

Life on the Mississippi.
New York and London, (1915): Harper & Brothers
                Publishers.
                Volume IX of
                The Writings of Mark Twain.
                Author's National Edition.
                Red cloth.

Life on the Mississippi.
New York and London, (1917): Harper & Brothers
                Publishers.   Green cloth.

Life on the Mississippi.
New York and London, (1919): Harper & Brothers
                Publishers.
                Volume IX of
                The Writings of Mark Twain.
                Author's National Edition.
                Green cloth.

Life on the Mississippi.
New York, (1929): Harper & Brothers.
                The Authorized Edition of
                The Complete Works of Mark
                Twain.
                Green cloth.

Life on the Mississippi.
New York, 1929: Harper & Brothers.
                Volume 12 of
                The Stormfield Edition of
                The Writings of Mark Twain.
                Set #212 of 1024.
                Appreciation by E.V. Lucas.
                Introduction by Albert
                Bigelow Paine.
                Blue cloth stamped in gold.

Life on the Mississippi.
New York, 1944: The Limited Editions Club.
                Introduction by Edward
                Wagenknecht.
                Edited and with a note by Willis
                Wager.
                Stated to contain *"a Number of*
                Previously Suppressed Passages, Now
                Printed for the First Time."
                Illustrated by Thomas Hart Benton.
                #562/1200.
                Printed by William E. Rudge's Sons.
                Signed by the illustrator on the
                colophon page.
                Pictorial cloth with leather
                shelfback, tissue wrapper and
BAL 3571   folding box.

Life on the Mississippi.
New York, (1944): The Heritage Press.
    Introduction by Edward Wagenknecht. Content the same as the Limited Editions Club edition (above).
    Green cloth with slipcase.
    Copy 1: inscribed by Thomas Hart Benton *"To the Mark Twain Memorial/from/Thomas H. Benton.*
    Copy 2: unsigned.

Life on the Mississippi.
New York, 1946: Bantam Books.
    Second printing, January, 1946.
    Stiff paper wrappers.

Life on the Mississippi.
New York, 1956: Bantam Books, Inc.
    Bantam Fifty #F1445, price 50¢.
    "5th printing (new edition), March, 1956."
    Pictorial paper wrappers.

Life on the Mississippi.
New York, 1961: New American Library.
    Afterword by Leonard Kriegel.
    Signet Classic #CT614, price 75¢.
    Eighth printing of this edition, about 1975.
    Pictorial paper wrappers.

Life on the Mississippi.
(New York, 1963): New American Library.
    Afterword by Leonard Kriegel.
    Signet Classic #CD111, price 50¢.
    "Second printing, January 1963"
    Pictorial paper wrappers.

Life on the Mississippi.
New York, (1965): Airmont Publishing Company, Inc.
    Introduction by John Willoughby.
    Classics Series #CL55, price 50¢.
    Pictorial paper wrappers.

Life on the Mississippi.
New York, (1968): Lancer Books, Inc.
    Magnum Easy Eye Edition #59, Catalog #14-623, price 75¢.
    Pictorial paper wrappers.

Zycie Na Mississippi.
(Warsaw), 1967: Czytelnik.
    In Polish.
    Translated by Zofia Siwicka.
    Silkscreened cloth with dustjacket.

Mark Twain, about 1883.

Adventures of Huckleberry Finn (Tom Sawyer's Comrade).
New York, 1885: Charles L. Webster and Company.
                Copyright page dated 1884.
                Publisher's prospectus.
                Green cloth.
                Samples of library leather and morocco spines on inside front cover.

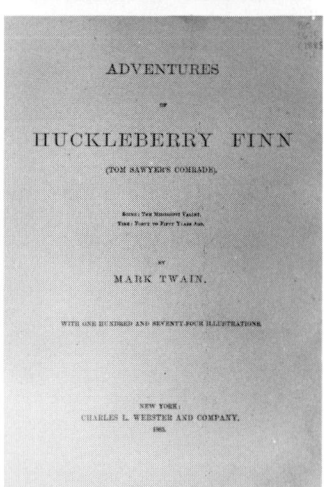

Adventures of Huckleberry Finn (Tom Sawyer's Comrade).
New York, 1885: Charles L. Webster and Company.
BAL 3415

BAL point	1	2	3	4	5	6	7	Binding	New point
Copy 1	C	A	A	A	A	C	B	blue cloth	A
Copy 2	B	A	A	C	A	C	A	green cloth	A
Copy 3	B	A	A	A	A	C	A	blue cloth	A
Copy 4	B	A	A	C	A	C	A	green cloth	A
Copy 5	B	A	A	A	A	C	B	blue cloth	A
Copy 6	B	B	B	C	A	D	C	green cloth	C
Copy 7	C	B	B	C	A	D	C	blue cloth	C
Copy 8	C	B	B	C	A	D	C	green cloth	C
Copy 9	C	B	B	C	A	D	C	green cloth	C
Copy 10	B	A	A	A	A	C	B	blue cloth	A*
Copy 11	C	A	A	A	A	A	B	morocco	A
Copy 12	C	A	A	A	A	D	B	morocco	A*
Copy 13	B	A	A	A	A	C	A	green cloth	A
Copy 14	B	A	A	C	A	C	A	green cloth	A*
Copy 15	C	A	A	A	A	C	B	morocco	A
Montreal ed.	—	A	A	C	B	C	—	red cloth	B

Copy 10 is inscribed by the author to F.G. Whitmore (see below).
Copy 12 is the Walter P. Chrysler copy, with his bookplate (see below).
Copy 13 is the Smillie copy, dated by him 19 February 1885, the earliest known dated copy (earlier than any copy noted in BAL).
Copy 14 is inscribed by the author to Rev. E.P. Parker (see below).
Copy 15 is inscribed by the author to his nephew, Jervis (see below).
The Montreal edition is further described below.

Point 1: A: Copyright notice dated 1885
         B: Copyright notice dated 1884, leaf tipped in.
         C: Copyright notice dated 1884, leaf bound in.
Point 2: A: Page (13): *Him and Another Man* listed at *p.88*
         B: Page (13): *Him and Another Man* listed at *p.87*
Point 3: A: 57:11 up: *with the was*
         B: 57:11 up: *with the saw*
Point 4: A: 155, folio: final 5 absent
         B: 155, final 5 present, same font, above the line
         C: 155, final 5 present, wrong font
Point 5: A: 161, signature mark *11* absent
         B: 161, signature mark *11* present
Point 6: A: 283, fly-line of trousers a definite curve; leaf bound in
         B: 283, engraving defaced, priapically; leaf bound in
         C: 283, engraving redone, leaf tipped in
         D: 283, engraving redone, leaf bound in
Point 7: A: Portrait frontispiece: cloth under bust visible; *Heliotype* imprint
         B: Cloth not visible; *Heliotype* imprint; sculptor's name on shoulder of bust
         C: Cloth not visible; *Photo-Gravure* imprint

New Point: A: Page 143: *l* missing in *Col.* that is part of the illustration; *b* in *body,* line 7, broken
         B: Page 143: period and bottom of *l* in *Col.* missing; *body* perfect
         C: Page 143: *l* in *Col.* replaced; *body* perfect

Copies with an A and an asterisk* have a faint tip of the top of *l* still visible but since wear could have have obliterated that residue at any time, it is not convincing as a point of issue.

93

The debate over the first issue of *Huck Finn* is now almost a century old. Among those writing about it are Merle Johnson (1910, 1935), Irving S. Underhill (1931, 1932, 1933, 1935), John K. Potter (1932), Jacob Blanck (1939, 1942, 1950, 1957), Norman Clarke (1941), Lucille Adams (1950), Walter Blair (1960) and Franklin Meine (1960). The intent always was to decide, once and for all, which issue of *Huck Finn* was the earliest; but each writer, in effect, only added to the confusion. The intent here is to explain the mechanical facts of the printing art in 1884, to bring those facts to bear on *Huck Finn* and on the arguments raised by the various writers above. In the great tradition of the bibliography of *Huck Finn,* a new point of issue will be introduced here, not to get collectors, dealers and librarians to throw up their arms in frustration, but instead to reinforce a portion of this explication.

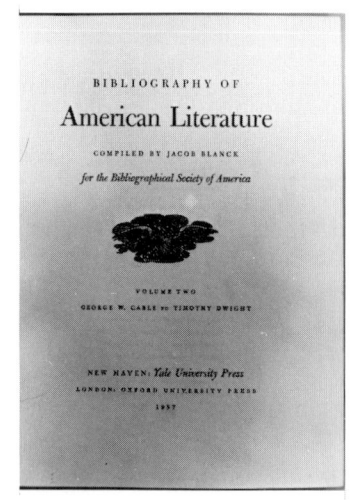

In the discussion that follows, each writer will be identified by last name and the statements of position of each will be gathered from all that each wrote on the subject.
Here is a list of sources (those with an asterisk(*) are in our collection):

JOHNSON
A Bibliography of the Works of Mark Twain. (New York, 1910).
*A Bibliography of the Works of Mark Twain. Revised Edition. (New York, 1935).

UNDERHILL
*"An Inquiry into Huckleberry Finn." (Colophon, Part VI, 1931).
"Two Interesting Letters Pertaining to Huckleberry Finn." (American Book Collector, November, 1932).
"Tempest in a Teapot or Notes on Huckleberry Finn." (American Book Collector, September-October, 1933).
*"The Haunted Book: A Further Exploration Concerning Huckleberry Finn." (Colophon, Autumn, 1935).

POTTER
*Samuel L. Clemens. First Editions and Values. (Chicago, 1932).

BLANCK
*A Supplement to "A Bibliography of Mark Twain". (New York, 1939).
*American First Editions. (by Merle Johnson, revised by Blanck, New York, 1942).
"In Re Huckleberry Finn." (The New Colophon, 1950).
*Bibliography of American Literature. (New Haven, 1957).

CLARKE
*Huckleberry Finn Again. (Detroit, 1941).

ADAMS
*Huckleberry Finn: A Descriptive Bibliography of the . . . Collection at the Buffalo Public Library. (Buffalo, 1950). *Note: The cornerstones of the Buffalo collection are those copies owned once by Irving S. Underhill.*

BLAIR
*Mark Twain & Huck Finn. (Berkeley and Los Angeles, 1960).

MEINE
*"Some Notes on the First Editions of Huck Finn." (American Book Collector, June, 1960).

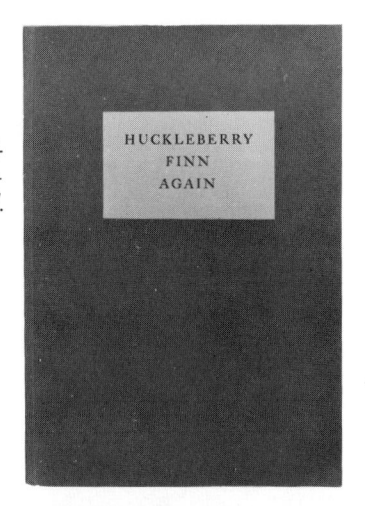

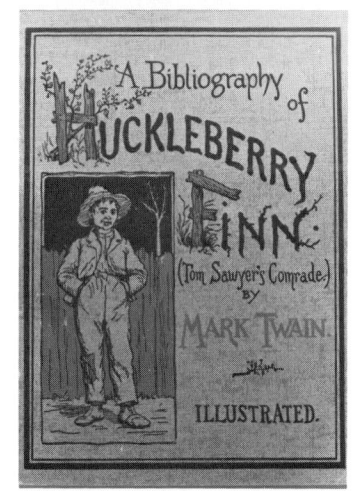

Summary
Here, in chronological order, are the collective opinions of each author as to what points of issue the earliest copies of *Huck Finn* should have:

(Based on the points of issue in the chart accompanying the first edition)

Point	1	2	3	4	5	6	7
Johnson	B or C	A	A	B	A	A or B	A or B
Underhill	—	A	A	B	—	B	B
Potter	—	A	A	B	—	C	—
Clarke	—	A	A	—	A	A*	A or B
Adams	—	—	—	—	A	—	—
Blanck	A	A	A	A or B	A	A	A
Blair	—	—	—	C	A	C or D	—
Meine	—	—	—	C	—	C or D	—

* — bound in or tipped in

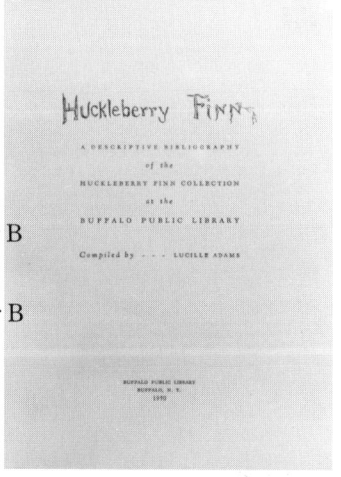

Copyright Page/Title Page
When prospectuses were first prepared, the date of publication was contingent on the scale of, to quote Clemens, "a large edition," no matter how long it took. The estimate was that it would not be until 1885. But sales exceeded expectations and the publication date was moved up to late 1884, thus necessitating a change in the date of the copyright notice. The title date was left intact, probably because the book, while ready for copyright by late 1884, would not be formally issued until 1885.

Johnson:
Copyright page dated 1884, tipped in or bound in; no preference.

Underhill, Clarke, Blair and *Meine* do not discuss the point. *Potter* expresses no preference.

Adams:
Copyright page dated 1884: four copies (one blue cloth, three green cloth) with leaf tipped in; five copies (one leather, four green cloth) with leaf bound in. No preference. A prospectus, owned previously by Underhill, bears a copyright date of 1885.

Blanck:
A: Copyright page dated 1885. "Noted only in the prospectus and in a set of the advance sheets."
B: Copyright page dated 1884; leaf tipped in.
C: Copyright page dated 1884; leaf bound in.

Mark Twain and George Washington Cable, in 1884.

Page (13)
Part of the list of illustrations.

Johnson:
A: *Him and Another Man* listed as at *p.88*
B: *Him and Another Man* listed as at *p.87*

Underhill, Potter, Clarke and *Blanck* agree with Johnson. *Blair* and *Meine* do not discuss the point.

Adams:
Johnson A: six copies (one leather, one blue cloth, four green cloth)
Johnson B: three copies (all green cloth)

Page 57, Line 23

Johnson:
A: *with the was*
B: *with the saw*

Potter, Underhill, Clarke and *Blanck* agree with Johnson. *Blair* and *Meine* do not discuss the point. *Adams* lists six copies (one leather, one blue cloth, four green cloth) with Johnson A; and three copies (all in green cloth) with Johnson B.

Page 155, folio

Johnson:
A: Final 5 is in "various 'off-balance' positions." Same typeface.
B: Final 5 is missing.
C: Final 5 is of a different font (typeface) and extends slightly below the base line of the other two numerals.

Potter and *Underhill* agree with Johnson.

Clarke:
Not discussed.

Adams:
Johnson A: three copies (one leather, two green cloth)
Johnson B: no copies
Johnson C: six copies (one blue cloth, five green cloth)
No preference.

Blanck:
A (B?): Johnson A
B (A?): Johnson B
C: Johnson C

Page 161, signature mark (11)

Johnson:
Signature mark missing. "I have never seen a copy with the numeral present."

Underhill, Potter and *Meine* do not mention this point.

Clarke agrees with Johnson.

Adams notes all nine copies lack the signature mark.

Blanck states "Thus far no copy of the New York, 1885, edition has been seen with the signature mark . . . present."

Blair mentions only the Montreal edition and states that "the Canadian printers had reason to insert (the signature mark) and could have done so."

Montreal edition, with signature mark.

BAL state A.

BAL state C and D.

One of the Merle Johnson copies of the "priapic" plate.

Page 283, illustration
The illustration captioned *Who could it be?* was prepared by E.W. Kemble. When sent to the engraver, it was innocent; but somewhere between the sending and the putting of ink to the plate which resulted, mischief or accident intervened. The illustration became defaced in such a way as to render Silas Phelps naughtily priapic. The so besmirched illustration found its way into prospectuses of the book and, it is suggested by some, into copies of the finished book. Corrections on the part of Charles L. Webster & Co. were undertaken; salesmen with copies of the prospectus containing the error were commanded to return the page and they dutifully did so. Copies of the book were corrected by the adding of a leaf printed from a newly-engraved plate; some copies had the leaf tipped in, some had it bound in. Thus, at the time of publication, no copies of the book bore the erroneous engraving.

The difficulty here is that there also exist two distinct states of an apparently innocent illustration, one with the fly-line on the trousers curved or bulged, and one with the fly-line about straight. Some writers on the subject, including cataloguers of Mark Twain collections, have mistaken the "curved fly plate" for the "priapic" one, thus adding to the confusion about the earliest state. In addition, discussions have gone on about the earliest state of the illustration and, simultaneously, about the earliest state of the book itself. Yet, in the nearly 100 years since the book was issued, no copy of the finished book has surfaced bearing the "priapic" illustration. In fact, about the only evidence we have that the "priapic" plate existed at all is the result of Merle Johnson finding an unbound copy of the original leaf in the collection of Willard S. Morse of Santa Monica, California, and convincing Morse to allow Johnson to make a photographic copy of it. This he did, probably for his own records, and he printed 100 copies of it, which have found their way into various public and private collections.

Johnson (1935):
A: corrected plate; page bound in (or tipped in.)
B: corrected plate; page tipped in (or bound in.)
C: corrected plate bound in.
Supporting A, he quotes "the popularly accepted theory" that earliest copies had pages printed from the defective plate and were corrected by tipping in a page run from the corrected plate.
Supporting B, he suggests that "it is equally possible that the damage occurred after copies had been run (and) the first state would be printèd from a perfect plate and the page . . . bound in."

Underhill
A: corrected plate; page bound in. ("California copies")
Underhill suggests that 250 copies, containing the

naughty engraving, were already in California (or on their way such a distance that they could not be practically recalled to New York for correction) when the error was detected; and that those copies were dismantled, corrected and rebound by "a San Francisco binder." During this process, various signatures from cloth copies (plain edges) and leather (sheep) copies (sprinkled edges) were mixed on re-assembly, thus creating a way of identifying "California" copies by the existence in them of signatures both plain-edged and sprinkled.

However, all this "California theory" is called into question by a letter from Clemens to Webster, 12 April 1884:
"The book is to be issued when a big edition has been sold. It must wait until they *are* sold, if it is seven years." By December, ten copies had been prepared for copyright purposes. "One of the first three copies bound, in green cloth, was given by Charles L. Webster to his father for Christmas, 1884" (Meine). If these were the first copies *bound,* it seems unlikely that other copies with the defaced 283 ever saw the inside of the bindery, let alone go through the disassembly and reassembly described by Underhill. It seems indisputable that no copies of any sort left New York for California or anywhere else before the error was detected and corrected. Granted, the New York *Herald* of 29 November 1884 quotes Webster as saying "But 250 copies left the office, *I believe,* before the mistake was discovered." (Italics added). But consider the state of newspaper reporting in 1884 and observe the qualifying *I believe* in Webster's statement before using this report as the basis for ironclad conclusions.

Further, even if copies of the book had been gathered and sewn (but not *bound*) before the error was discovered, and were indeed disassembled for corrections, any accidental mixing of signatures intended for sheep and cloth copies could have occurred at any time during the process, that is, when they were disassembled, when they were stacked and stored awaiting new sheets, or when they were being reassembled, prior to binding.

He also differentiates two "first New York issues":
A: corrected plate; page tipped in
B: corrected plate; page bound in
He also suggests that the earliest state of the engraving for A was doctored "with pen and ink (to remove) the details of the offensive original." This is disputed by Clarke: ". . . careful examination shows the plate was re-engraved."

Potter
A: leaf on a stub; not further described.

Clarke
A: Same as Blanck A (see below); bound in or tipped in.
B: Same as Blanck C (see below); bound in or tipped in.
He uses the California argument as well: copies were corrected out there, either by tipping in or binding in (see Blair, below).

Adams
Six copies (one leather, one blue cloth, four green cloth) with leaf tipped in; no further description.
Three copies (all green cloth) with page bound in; no further description.
No preference. Adams notes that the prospectus in the Buffalo Public Library collection has the suppressed leaf; in fact, the copy has the reprinted Johnson facsimile laid in.

Blanck:
A: "The line indicating the fly on Silas Phelps's trousers is a quite definite curve." Seen only in prospectuses and leatherbound copies. Page bound in.
B: "The engraving is in the original state but defaced . . . such that the engraving is ribald." Seen only as an excised leaf, in a prospectus and in the set of advance sheets owned by Barrett. Page bound in.
C: "The engraving has been redone and the line indicating the fly . . . is, with slight variation, a straight vertical line."

Blair:
A: corrected plate; page bound in or tipped in.
"I see no way to determine certainly, on the basis of evidence I have seen, which (of these) procedure(s) (of correction) was followed:"
1. Reengraved plate made; pages run; tipped in on a stub.
2. Reengraved plate made; entire signature run; bound as usual.
He suggests that the English and Canadian publishers detected the naughty defacement in advance sheets sent them about September 19, 1884, and each publisher corrected the plate independently.

Meine:
A: Blanck C, page tipped in
B: Blanck B
C: Blanck A
He bases his argument on the existence of two early presentation copies of the book, both with the illustration as described by Blanck as his state C; the two copies were: a copy, one of the first three bound, given by the publisher, Charles L. Webster, to his father for Christmas, 1884; and, a copy, one of three, sent to William Dean Howells.

Portrait Frontispiece
A bust of Mark Twain by Karl Gerhardt. The leaf is printed on different paper than the book and is inserted by tipping in between the frontispiece illustration of Huck Finn and the title page.

Johnson:
A: printed by the *Heliotype Printing Company*
B: printed by the *Photo-Gravure Co.*

Underhill:
Describes nine variations in his nine copies; seems to perfer the *Heliotype* bust, measuring 3 3/16 x 3 7/8 " and 3/8" from the "shoulder of the bust to the left edge of the plate," lacking the cloth beneath the bust, with *Karl Gerhardt, Sc.* on the edge of the sculpture.

Potter:
No preference.

Clarke:
A: *Heliotype*
B: *Photo-Gravure*
"There are no supporting facts to allow using small changes (in A) to date priority. This type of plates was run off in sheets and minute to more evident alterations certainly could be present in the various individual plates of the same sheet. Furthermore, these sheets were run in quantities, cut and naturally would not be kept separate according to sequence but set aside in more or less confusion as they were not part of the book but only inserted at the time of assembling and binding. These evident circumstances rob them of value as accurate guides for point of issue but they do serve as a marker of broad periods of issue and leave the question of accurate early dating to more positive proof."

Adams:
No preference.
Copies in Blanck A: three (one blue cloth, two green cloth)
Copies in Blanck B: three (one leather, two green cloth)
Copies in Blanck C: three (all green cloth)

Blanck:
A: *Heliotype* "with scarf on which the bust rests . . . clearly visible; (plate) printed in black.
B: *Heliotype* "with scarf . . . not visible. The statement *Karl Gerhardt, Sc.* has been added to the finish edge of the shoulder. (Plate) printed in black."
C: *Photo-Gravure*

Blair and *Meine* do not discuss this point.

Johnson state A, Blanck state B

Another point of issue.
John S. Van E. Kohn, one of the proprietors of the Seven Gables Bookshop in New York City, wrote in a three-quarter morocco copy (BAL first issue) of *Huck Finn* about a possible point on page 143.

Page 143 bears a chapter-head illustration captioned "COL. GRANGERFORD." The illustration was meant to include the first word of the chapter: *Col.* But in examined New York copies, the final *l* and the period following it are either completely absent or in a few copies, the faint tip of the top of the *l* is visible. Because the sentence ("GRANGERFORD was a gentleman, you/see.") is not made confusing by this absence, the point of issue has gone unnoticed. In Montreal copies, the upper three-fifths of the *l* is present, but the period is absent. The final *l* with the period finally reappears in copies clearly of a later New York issue, that is, with the common typographical errors corrected (pages 13 and 57), with the corrected state of 283 bound in, and with the Photo-Gravure portrait frontispiece and the title page bound in.

In the first paragraph of the text on page 143, the word *nobody* is hyphenated on lines 6-7. In line 7, *body* has a broken *b* until the corrected state of *Col.* reappears in indisputably later copies as described above. In the Montreal edition, the *b* in *body* is not broken. Both these errors, the missing *l.* and the broken *b* could be the result of careless routing.

The impact of this new point is that it reinforces the validity of the errors on pages 13 and 57, supports the argument that the book was printed from plates, and suggests that the original type was *not* distributed by the typesetter immediately after the first sets of plates (U.S. and Canadian) were made. This conclusion is based on the correction of 143 *involving an illustration* and the presence of identical final 5's in very early and very late copies of the book. The so-called "replaced" 5 is seen in copies as late as 1888. It is likely that the original type was retained so that new plates might be made as they were required for anticipated reprints. Remember, one of the major expenses in a book is the typesetting; electrotyping was a way of protecting that original type from the wear and tear of a long press run. Instead, the type was set once, plates were made, and the type kept its sharpness. If damage during printing occurred, the plates could be inexpensively replaced.

First issue of page 143.

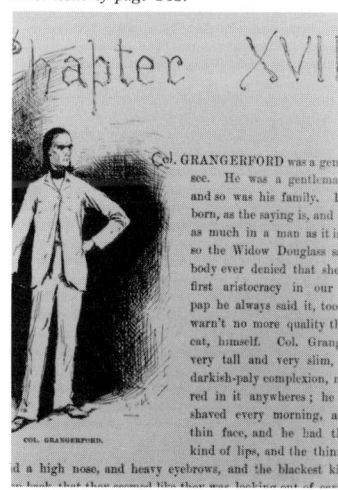

First issue, Canadian edition.

Later issue of page 143.

What conclusions can be drawn from all this disputation are left to the reader. The key points of argument are about just three points: *the portrait frontispiece, the illustration on page 283* and *the final folio on page 155.* On the other points, everyone agrees.

The portrait frontispiece was an added item, tipped into the book, and cannot be considered as an absolute guide to priority of issue. Here, Clarke seems to have the best logic.

The illustration on page 283 has never been found in its defaced state in any issued copy of the book. The argument then comes down to which of the corrected states is earliest and whether it should be bound in or tipped in. But since all corrections, however they were accomplished, were completed before the book was issued, it is almost impossible to judge on the published evidence which copies were corrected first or how they were corrected.

To properly explain the final *5* on *155,* this historical digression is necessary.

The Printing Art in 1884.

In the early 1800s, type was still set primarily by hand, even though Otmar Mergenthaler's first Linotype machine was on the verge of becoming essential equipment in any printing establishment. His invention was first used in the United States in 1886. But few books in the 1880s were actually printed from the original type. They were instead printed from electrotype plates, a process first used about 1840 to duplicate type for printing. Steroetyping, the forerunner of electrotyping, was commonplace from the beginning of the 18th century. Electrotyping consists of several steps: making a mold of wax or lead, pressing the original type into the molding material, placing the mold in a bath of copper-sulphate dissolved in water and sulphuric acid, and passing an electric current through the solution to deposit the copper portion of the solution on the mold, thus forming a shell reproducing the type. When the disposition is complete, the mold is removed, backed with an alloy of lead, tin and antimony to strengthen it, and then readied for mounting on metal or wood. Two of the preparations for mounting are beveling of the edges of the plate and routing the "blanks," the negative areas of the plate, including the margins and the areas around the illustrations (cuts). Routing was done to cut away the non-printing areas of the plate to prevent accidental inking; this was necessary since the distance between the printing surface and the non-printing "body" of the plate was a smaller distance than in the original type. Routing was not infrequently more workmanlike than craftsmanlike and minor damage to the text and the illustrations did occur, particularly at the ends of lines and the edges of illustrations.

With this brief summary of the state of the printing art in 1884 in mind, let us examine *Huck Finn* and its "points of issue." To begin with, it seems clear that the book was printed from electrotype plates, not from the original type. Charles L. Webster, in a letter to Clemens (19 September 1884) states, "(We are) getting up a set of plates *the same as ours* . . . for Dawson." (italics added). Dawson is the Canadian publisher of *Huck Finn.* The New York *World,* 27 November 1884, in a discussion of the faulty page 283, "When the plate was sent to the electrotyper . . . ." It has been argued that some of the traditional points of issue resulted from loose or missing type. However, such arguments about "loose" type or individual numbers or letters "on the way out" cannot be supported by the mechanical facts of printing from plates. No single letter or number can be "loose" or fall out because the plate is of a piece. Letters and numbers can, however, be damaged by the accidental dropping of a tool or other object on the printing surface. The damage can be anything from the slight bending of a part of a letter to the complete excision of an entire word. Damage can also result from careless routing.

The Montreal edition seems to be the obvious source of a fair solution to the priority of the first New York edition. Since it is clearly established that the Canadian publisher (Dawson) received a "set of plates the same as ours" (the New York edition), then it follows that both sets of plates were made from the same original type. Since the errors on page 13 and 57 are present in both editions, and are corrected in later editions of the New York issue (Canadian later issue not seen), it follows that those errors were present in the original type. The explanation that the original final 5 in the folio of page 155 was wrong before the plates were made is not improbable to anyone who ever worked with handset type. Typically the type is stored in cases (drawers) containing compartments for each letter and number. After the plates are made for a given job, the original type is distributed so that another can be set. The patent advantage of electrotyping was that it allowed the type to be reused immediately rather than being held for possible reprints; any subsequent editions could be done from the plates. But the distribution of the type into the cases was handwork and subject to human error, especially since the job usually fell to the rankest printer's devil. The likelihood that a 5 from one font landed in another's case, and was then picked to be in the folio of *155,* is very high. Further, the act of setting type by hand does not involve the inspection of the face of every letter, so the error could easily pass unnoticed until proofing.

It then could go unnoticed because the font was nearly correct and the important proofing was that of the text, not the page numbers. Another equally logical possibility is that the original final 5 was set in the correct font, but was defective or broken; the defect was noticed during the reading of the foundry proofs (the original type) and then corrected using an incorrect font *before the plates were made.*

As to the missing final 5 in many copies of the first edition, consider this possibility: an errant tool, dropped by a pressman, could have knocked it away. Or it could have been partially broken, then removed completely when the accident was discovered. Two copies with the final 5 broken have been reported in recent years, but it is not within the scope of this bibliography to discuss them since we do not own them, nor have we been able to examine them fully. However, if there is evidence of an intermediate state of *155,* that is with the final 5 broken, the resolution of the question of priority will depend a great deal on whether the broken 5 is of the correct original font or the wrong font.

Further, if one examines the folios of the right-hand pages of the book, one finds repeated damage to final numerals in many of them (pages 65, 175, 201, 215, 231, 233, etc.). A physical anomaly of the press itself could account for such damage.

The final state of *155* is that with the final 5 of the same font but in varying positions slightly above the line. Underhill recounts the acquisition on April 30, 1931, of a copy that had the final 5 "stamped in" *by hand* with a 5 matching the original font. Is it possible that *all* copies bearing the final 5 of the correct font were similarly done, varying in position because they were manually inserted and varying in precision for the same reason? Some could be almost perfect with full inking, others could be more askew and less completely inked. This possibility would leave only two actual states of *155* as it was published: with the final 5 of the wrong font or with the bobtail *15.*

In summary, the best advice to collectors is to look for copies that have the most first issue points since it is obvious that no copy (yet!) has all of them.

Adventures of Huckleberry Finn. etc.
New York, 1885: Charles L. Webster and Company.
Green cloth.
At the top margin of the title page is written:
Charles F. Smillie 19th Febry. '85
This is the earliest known dated inscription of this book. The Boston Atheneum copy was received March 9, 1885; BAL notes a copy dated March 10, 1885.

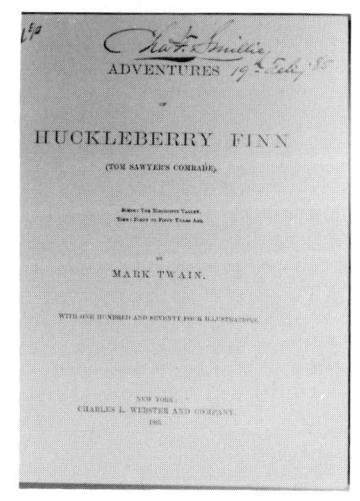

Adventures of Huckleberry Finn. etc.
New York, 1885: Charles L. Webster and Company.
Green cloth.
Inscribed copy:
To Rev. E.P. Parker/with the warmest/ regards of/The Author./Hartford, March 16, 1885.
In another hand:
This book given to me by/the Author, with his autograph on the first leaf. 2nd given/to my grandson, Louis P. Parker, hoping he will carefully keep/it —/Edwin P. Parker/ Hartford Sept. 21, 1910.

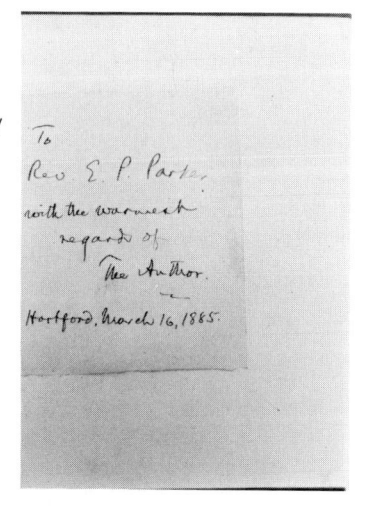

Adventures of Huckleberry Finn. etc.
New York, 1885: Charles L. Webster and Company.
Three-quarter morocco.
Inscribed copy:
To My Nephew Jervis/with the love of his uncle/The Author./New York, March 21, 1885.
The initials of Clemens, cut from a letter, are also taped in.

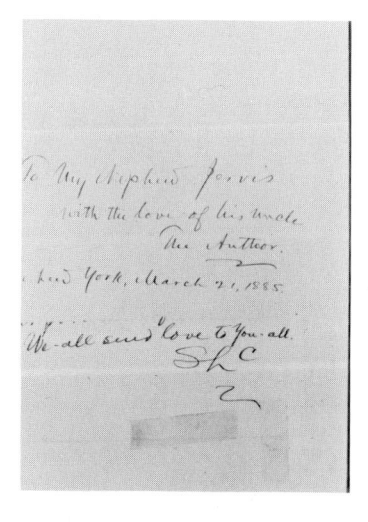

111

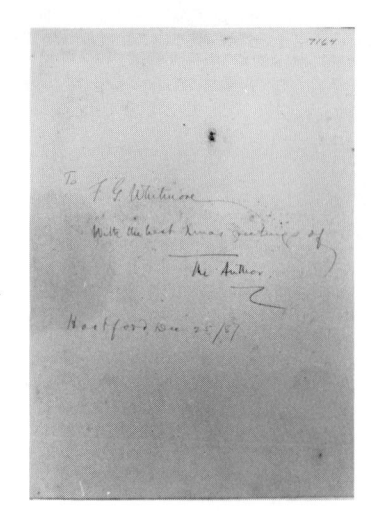

Adventures of Huckleberry Finn. etc.
New York, 1885: Charles L. Webster and Company.
>Blue cloth.
>Inscribed copy:
>*To/F.G. Whitmore/with the best Xmas greetings of/The Author,/ Hartford, Dec. 25/87.*

Adventures of Huckleberry Finn. etc.
New York, 1885: Charles L. Webster and Company.
>Three-quarter morocco.
>With the bookplate of Walter P. Chrysler.

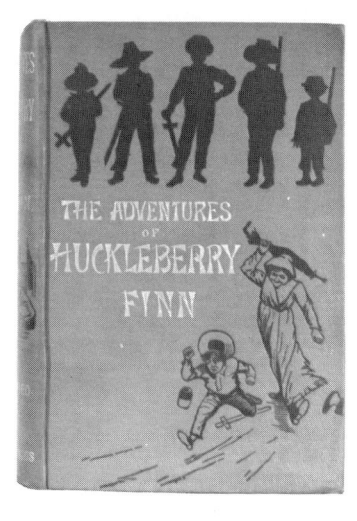

The Adventures of Huckleberry Finn (Tom Sawyer's Comrade).
London, 1884: Chatto & Windus, Piccadilly.
Red cloth stamped in black and gold: four copies.
First English edition.
Two copies:
Copy 1: Binding A (gatherings sewn).
Copy 2: Binding B (gatherings saddle-stitched).

BAL 3414

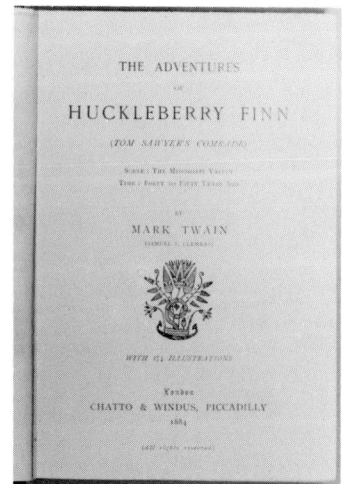

Adventures of Huckleberry Finn (Tom Sawyer's Comrade).
Montreal, 1885: Dawson Brothers.
First Canadian edition.
Red cloth.
Listed in BAL under the British first even though this edition uses a set of the American plates. (See above).

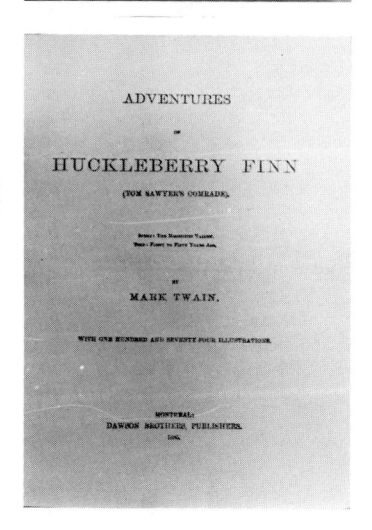

113

The Adventures of Huckleberry Finn.
Leipzig, 1885: Bernhard Tauchnitz.
    Collection of British Authors.
    Two Volumes: paper wrappers.
    See note on Tauchnitz editions under
    The Innocents Abroad (page 9).
    Last listed title opposite title page:
    Extracts from Captain Stormfield, etc.
    (1909).

Adventures of Huckleberry Finn.
New York, 1888: Charles L. Webster and Company.
    Green cloth.

Adventures of Huckleberry Finn.
New York, 1889: Charles L. Webster & Co.
    Tan pictorial cloth.

The Adventures of Huckleberry Finn (Tom Sawyer's Comrade).
Hartford, 1899:   The American Publishing Company.
    Volume XIII of
    The Writings of Mark Twain.
    Autograph Edition of
    the Edition de Luxe.
    Bound in:
    ALS from Edward (Windsor)
    Kemble to Mr. Bliss, 1p., 1899
    September 14.

The Adventures of Huckleberry Finn. etc.
Hartford, 1899:   The American Publishing Company.
    Volume XIII of
    The Writings of Mark Twain.
    Edition de Luxe.
    Set #54 of 1000.
    Uses the same plates as the
    Autograph Edition. Green cloth.

The Adventures of Huckleberry Finn.
New York, 1904: Harper & Brothers Publishers.
    Volume XIII of
    The Writings of Mark Twain.
    Hillcrest Edition.
    Three-quarter morocco.
    Inscribed copy:
    It is not likely that any/completed life has ever/been lived which was not/a failure in the secret judgment of the person/who lived it./Mark Twain.
    (*More Maxims of Mark*, p. 9)

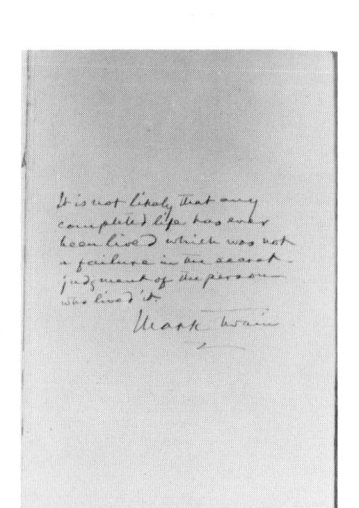

The Adventures of Huckleberry Finn. etc.
New York and London, 1906: Harper & Brothers
            Publishers.
            Volume XIII of
            The Writings of Mark Twain.
            Hillcrest Edition.
            Green cloth.

The Adventures of Huckleberry Finn. etc.
New York and London, (1915): Harper & Brothers
            Publishers.
            Volume XIII of
            The Writings of Mark Twain.
            Author's National Edition.
            Red cloth.

The Adventures of Huckleberry Finn. etc.
New York and London, (1918): Harper & Brothers
            Publishers.
            Volume XIII of
            The Writings of Mark Twain.
            Author's National Edition.
            Green cloth.

The Adventures of Huckleberry Finn. etc.
New York and London, (1919): Harper & Brothers
            Publishers.
            Limp leather edition.
            Red leather.

The Adventures of Huckleberry Finn. etc.
New York and London, 1923: Harper & Brothers.
            First illustrated edition thus.
            Illustrated by Worth Brehm.
            Harper's date code for September,
            1923 (I-X) on copyright page.
            Black with color plate on front cover.

The Adventures of Huckleberry Finn. etc.
New York and London, (1927): Harper & Brothers
        Publishers.
        Illustrated by Worth Brehm.
        Black cloth with color plate on front
        cover; matching dustjacket.

The Adventures of Huckleberry Finn. etc.
New York and London, (1927): Harper & Brothers
        Publishers.
        Blue cloth: two copies.

The Adventures of Huckleberry Finn. etc.
New York, 1929: Harper & Brothers.
        Volume 13 of
        The Stormfield Edition of
        The Writings of Mark Twain.
        Set #212 of 1024.
        Appreciation by William A. White.
        Introduction by
        Albert Bigelow Paine.
        Blue cloth stamped in gold.

The Adventures of Huckleberry Finn.
New York (1940): The Heritage Press.
        The Heritage Illustrated Bookshelf
        edition.
        Illustrated by Norman Rockwell.
        Green cloth.

The Adventures of Huckleberry Finn.
London, 1950: The Cresset Press.
        First edition thus.
        Introduction by T.S. Eliot.
        Grey cloth with dustjacket.

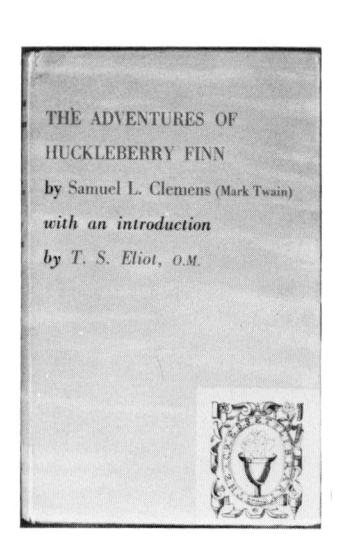

The Adventures of Huckleberry Finn.
New York, 1950: Pocket Books.
        Pocket Book, Jr. #J-42
        "1st printing March 1950"
        Illustrated by Harold Minton.
        Pictorial paper wrappers.

The Adventures of Huckleberry Finn.
New York, 1953: Pocket Books.
        Cardinal edition #C-139
        "1st printing December 1953"
        Illustrated by Harold Minton.
        Pictorial paper wrappers.

The Adventures of Huckleberry Finn (Tom Sawyer's Comrade)
Garden City, N.Y., n.d. (about 1955): Dolphin Books,
        Doubleday & Company, Inc.
        Doubleday Dolphin Book #C98;
        price 95¢.
        Illustrated by Edward W. Kemble.
        Paper wrappers.

Adventures of Huckleberry Finn.
Boston, (1958):   Houghton Mifflin Co.
        Riverside Edition #A15.
        Edited with an introduction and
        notes by Henry Nash Smith.
        Paper wrappers.

The Adventures of Huckleberry Finn.
New York, (1962): S/R Books, Farrar. Straus and
         Cudahy and Scholastic Roto.
         Introduction and study aids by
         Edward J. Gordon.
         Pictorial paper wrappers.

The Adventures of Huckleberry Finn.
San Francisco, (1962): Chandler Publishing Company.
         Introduction and bibliography by
         Hamlin Hill.
         "A Facsimile of the First Edition"
         Pictorial paper wrappers.

Adventures of Huckleberry Finn.
New York, (1962): W.W. Norton & Company, Inc.
         Norton Critical Edition.
         "An Annotated Text.
         Backgrounds and Sources.
         Essays and Criticism."
         Edited by Sculley Bradley,
         Richmond Croom Beatty and E.
         Hudson Long.
         Seventh printing.
         Paper wrappers.

Huckleberry Finn.
New York, 1965: Gilberton Company, Inc.
         Classics Illustrated edition.
         No. 19 of the series; price 15¢.
         Pictorial paper wrappers.

The Adventures of Huckleberry Finn.
Avon, Conn., (1968): The Heritage Press.
         Illustrated by Norman Rockwell.
         A Reprint of the 1940 Heritage
         edition (above).
         Green cloth with slipcase.

The Adventures of Huckleberry Finn.
Franklin Center, Penn., (1979): The Franklin Library.
         Illustrated by Edward Windsor
         Kemble.
         "from the 1885 first edition."
         Quarter leather: two copies.
         Copy 1: probable first thus
         Copy 2: probable eighth printing
         thus: a sequence of eight diamonds
         appears beneath the copyright
         notice; these are absent from Copy 1.

Adventures of Huckleberry Finn (Tom Sawyer's Comrade).
(Birmingham, Alabama, 1982): (Oxmoor House.)
"A Facsimile of the 1885 edition. Published exclusively for Members of the Southern Classics Library."
Uses an original of Copy 4 of this collection's first editions with regard to textual, but not collation, points of issue.
Full leather.
Accompanied by a 28-page booklet describing the edition and reprinting an essay on the book by Cleanth Brooks, R.W.B. Lewis and Robert Penn Warren adapted from *American Literature: The Makers and The Making* (St. Martin's Press, 1973).

(The Adventures of Huckleberry Finn.)
n.p., (1979): no publisher.
In Chinese.
Paper wrappers.

(The Adventures of Huckleberry Finn.)
n.p., n.d.: no publisher.
In Chinese.
Paper wrappers.

Pustolovine Haklberi Fina.
Sarajevo, 1965:   Izdavacko Preduzece veselin Maslesa.
In Croatian.
Translated by Nika Milicevic.
Illustrated by Anica Kovac.
Paper over boards.

Dozivljajai Haklberi Fina (Drugara Toma Sajera).
Boegrad, 1968: Sportska Knjiga.
In Croatian.
Translated by Jelisaveta Markovic.
Illustrated by Mirko Stojnic.
Pictorial paper over boards.

Les Aventures de Huck Finn.
(Paris, 1950): Hachette.
>In French.
>Translated by Yolande and Rene Surleau.
>Illustrated by Rene-Georges Gautier.
>Two copies:
>Copy 1: Pictorial paper over boards.
>Copy 2: Green cloth with dustjacket.

Les Aventures D'Huckleberry Finn.
(Paris, 1973): Gallimard.
>In French.
>Translated by Suzanne Netillard.
>Dustjacket illustrated by Claude Lapointe.
>Blue paper over boards with dustjacket.

Huckleberry Finn.
Reutlingen, (1949): Ensslin & Laiblin Verlag.
>In German.
>>"158th-167th thousand"
>Blue cloth with pictorial dustjacket.

Huckleberry Finn.
Tel Aviv, 1968: Izreel Publishing House Ltd.
>In Hebrew.
>Translated by A. Fishkin and
>A. Halperich.
>Paper over boards.

(The Adventures of Huckleberry Finn.)
n.p., n.d. (c. 1960): no publisher.
>In Japanese.
>Paper wrappers.

Przygody Huck'a.
n.p., (1912): no publisher.
>In Polish.
>Red cloth.

Aventuras de Huck Finn.
Buenos Aires, (1962): Editorial Atlantida, S.A.
>In Spanish.
>Translated by Celso Cruz.
>Illustrated by Lisa.
>Fifth edition.
>Pictorial paper over boards.

Las Aventuras de Huckleberry Finn.
Madrid, 1962: Aguilar.
>In Spanish.
>Translated and with an introduction
>by Amando Lazaro Ros.
>Third edition.
>Red cloth.

Huckleberry Finns Aventyr.
Stockholm, (1957): Svensk Lararetidnings Forlag.
>In Swedish.
>Translated by Herald Johnsson.
>Illustrated by Per Silfverhjelm.
>"14th-21st thousand"
>Pictorial paper over boards with
>cloth spine.

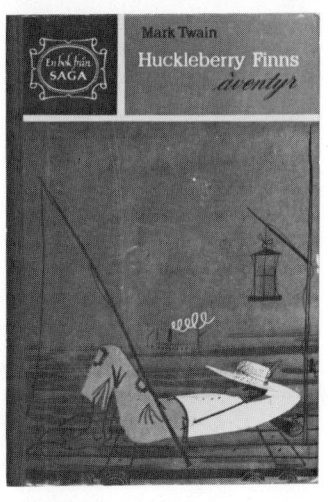

Mark Twain's Library of Humor.
New York, 1887: Charles L. Webster & Company.
    Publisher's prospectus.
    Anonymously edited by William Dean Howells.
    Illustrated by E.W. Kemble.
    Brown cloth.
    Samples of three-quarter morocco, "fine red seal" bindings on inside covers.

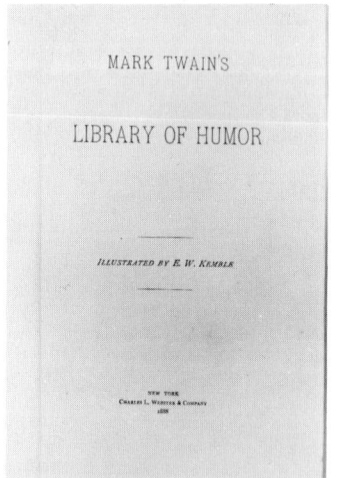

Mark Twain's Library of Humor.
New York, 1888: Charles L. Webster & Company.
    Anonymously edited by William Dean Howells.
    Illustrated by E.W. Kemble.
    Brown cloth: nine copies.

BAL 3425   Three-quarter morocco: one copy.

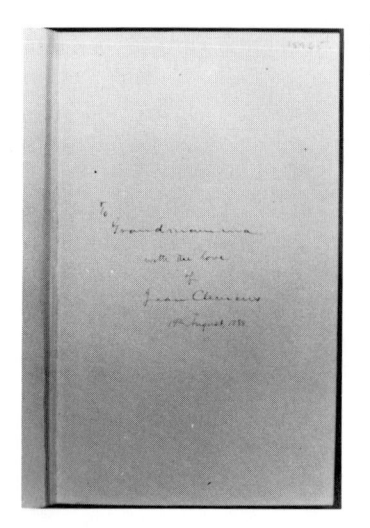

Mark Twain's Library of Humor.
New York, 1888: Charles L. Webster & Company.
    Brown cloth.
    Inscribed copy.
    To Grandmamma/with the love/of/ Jean Clemens/19th August, 1888.
    Inscription in Clemens' hand.

Mark Twain's Library of Humor.
New York, 1889: Charles L. Webster & Company.
        Publisher's prospectus.
        Brown cloth.

Mark Twain's Library of Humor.
London, 1888: Chatto & Windus Piccadilly.
        First English edition.
        Illustrated by E.W. Kemble.
        Rebound.
        Not in BAL.

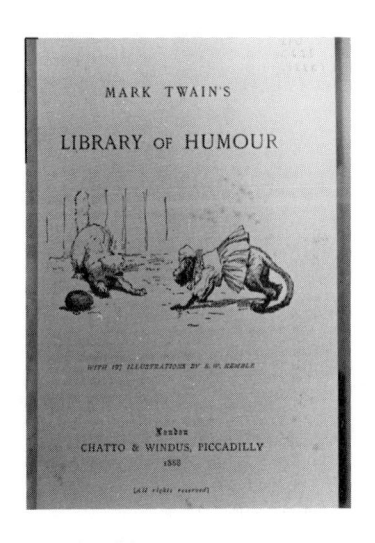

Mark Twain's Library of Humor.
New York, (1975): Hart Publishing Company, Inc.
        Illustrated by E.W. Kemble.
        First edition thus.
        Yellow cloth over boards.
        Dustjacket.

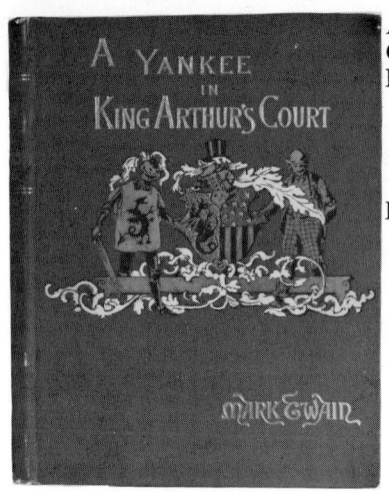

A Connecticut Yankee in King Arthur's Court.
New York, 1889: Charles L. Webster & Company.
First issue with the S-like ornament between the words THE KING on page (59).
Illustrated by Dan Beard.

BAL 3429   Green cloth: two copies.

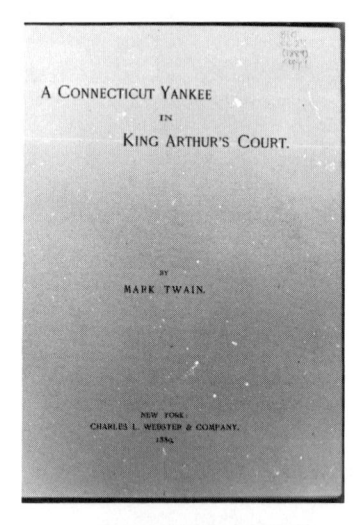

First issue of p. (59).

A Connecticut Yankee in King Arthur's Court.
New York, 1889: Charles L. Webster & Company.
    Second issue with the space blank between the words THE KING on page (59).
    Green cloth: three copies.
    Leather: one copy.

Second issue of p. (59).

A Connecticut Yankee in King Arthur's Court.
New York, 1889: Charles L. Webster & Company.
    First issue.
    Green cloth.
    Publisher's control stamp *#B/4210* on r.f.e.p.
    Inscribed copy:
    To/My Dear Miss Annie Trumbull/with the best wishes of/The Author./1889.

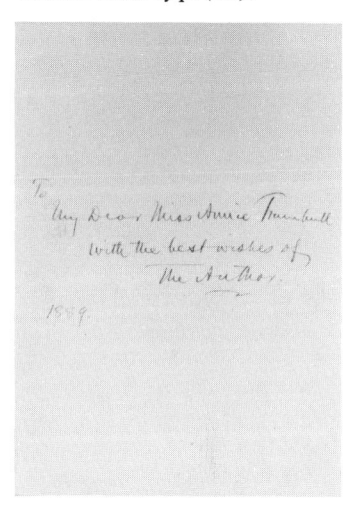

A Connecticut Yankee in King Arthur's Court.
New York, 1889: Charles L. Webster & Company.
    Second issue.
    Green cloth.
    No publisher's control stamp on r.f.e.p.
    Inscribed copy:
    Mrs. F.G. Whitmore/with the affectionate regards of/The Author./Xmas, 1889.

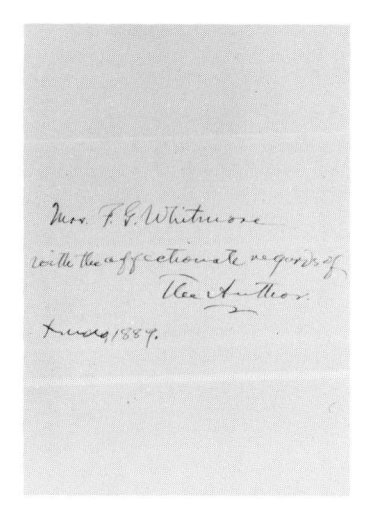

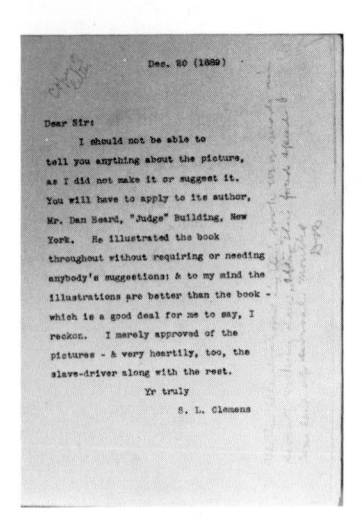

A Connecticut Yankee in King Arthur's Court.
New York, 1889: Charles L. Webster & Company.
  Second issue.
  Publisher's control stamp B/3396.
  Green cloth.
  Bookplates of Paul Hyde Bonner and David Lane Billings.
  Laid in:
  Copy of a TL by Clemens, (1889) Dec. 20, to (C.P. Everitt) with regard to the source of the illustrations in the book. The letter is inscribed by Beard:
  All the illustrations in this book were made in/seventy working days, after this forced speed I/was laid up several months/DB
  Flyleaf inscribed by Beard:
  Illustrations identified/for my friend C.P. Everitt/May 1915/by/Dan Beard/
  (ff. by arrow pointing upward).
  The entire book is annotated by Beard on the illustration pages.

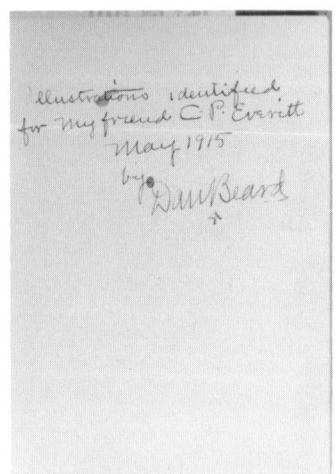

A Connecticut Yankee in King Arthur's Court.
New York, 1889: Charles L. Webster & Company.
  Second issue.
  Publisher's control stamp C/758.
  Green cloth.
  Inscribed by Beard on the frontispiece:
  Mark Twain said 'Dan the grin on the/helmet is a source of/(unidentified word) joy to me' Dan Beard.

Dan Beard's notation on the frontispiece of A Connecticut Yankee in King Arthur's Court.

Dan Beard's notation: "I used Anna Russell's photograph as my motif for Sandy."

Dan Beard's notation: "For Merlin I used photographs of Alfred Tennyson, the magic I got from ancient books on that subject."

127

A Yankee at the Court of King Arthur.
London, 1889: Chatto & Windus, Piccadilly.
>First English edition.
>"220 illustrations by Dan Beard."
>Red cloth.

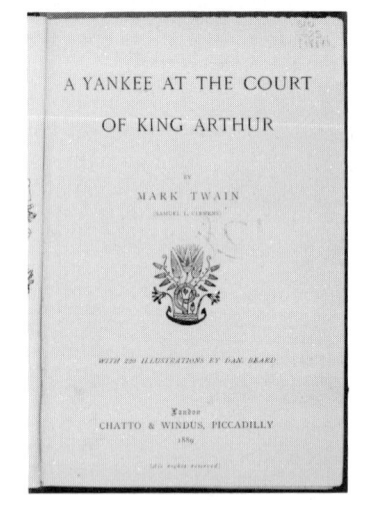

A Connecticut Yankee in King Arthur's Court.
Toronto, (1889): G.M. Rose & Sons.
                First Canadian edition.
                Olive green cloth.

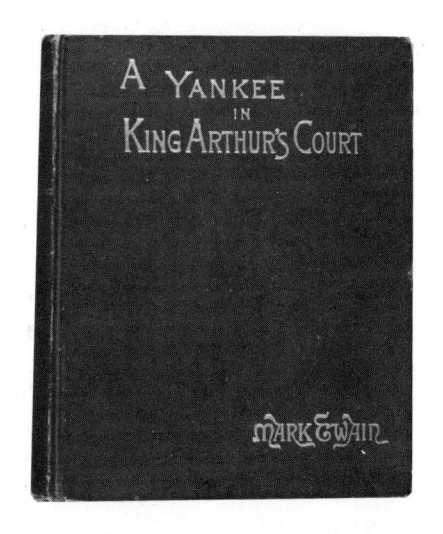

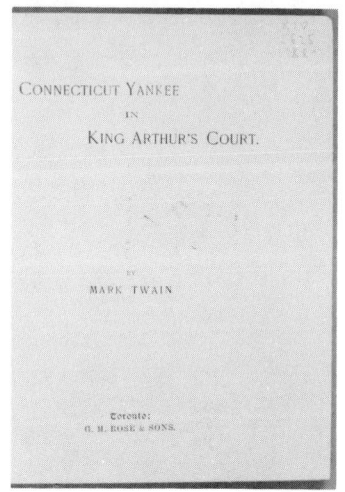

A Connecticut Yankee in King Arthur's Court.
New York, 1890: Charles L. Webster & Company.
                Green cloth: two copies.

A Connecticut Yankee in King Arthur's Court.
Hartford, 1899:   The American Publishing Company.
                Volume XVI of
                The Writings of Mark Twain.
                Autograph Edition of
                the Edition de Luxe.
                Three-quarter morocco.

A Connecticut Yankee in King Arthur's Court.
Hartford, 1899: American Publishing Company.
Volume XVI of
The Writings of Mark Twain.
Edition de Luxe.
Set #54 of 1000.
Uses the same plates as the
Autograph Edition.
Green cloth.

A Connecticut Yankee in King Arthur's Court.
New York and London, 1906: Harper & Brothers Publishers.
Volume XVI of
The Writings of Mark Twain.
Hillcrest Edition. Green cloth.

A Connecticut Yankee in King Arthur's Court.
New York, 1904: Harper & Brothers Publishers.
Volume XVI of
The Writings of Mark Twain.
Hillcrest Edition.
Three-quarter morocco.
Inscribed copy:
Few things are harder to/bear than the annoyance/of a good example./Mark Twain.
(*Pudd'nhead Wilson*, p. 182, variant)

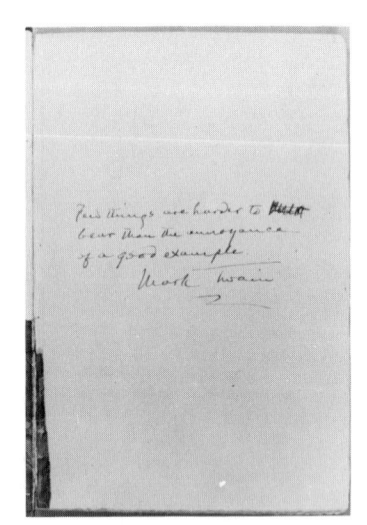

A Connecticut Yankee in King Arthur's Court.
New York and London, (1915): Harper & Brothers Publishers.
Volume XVI of
The Writings of Mark Twain.
Author's National Edition.
Red cloth.

A Connecticut Yankee in King Arthur's Court.
New York and London, (1918): Harper & Brothers Publishers.
Volume XVI of
The Writings of Mark Twain.
Author's National Edition.
Green cloth.

A Connecticut Yankee in King Arthur's Court.
New York and London, (1920): Harper & Brothers
Publishers.
Limp leather edition.
Red leather with dustjacket.

A Connecticut Yankee in King Arthur's Court.
New York and London, (1926): Harper & Brothers.
Illustrated by Henry Pitz.
Black cloth with color plate on front cover.

A Connecticut Yankee in King Arthur's Court.
New York and London, (1927): Harper & Brothers.
Blue cloth with dustjacket.

A Connecticut Yankee in King Arthur's Court.
New York, 1929: Harper & Brothers.
Volume 14 of
The Stormfield Edition of
The Writings of Mark Twain.
Set #212 of 1024.
Appreciation by Stephen Leacock.
Introduction by Albert Bigelow Paine.
Blue cloth stamped in gold.

A Connecticut Yankee in King Arthur's Court.
New York, (1948): The Heritage Press.
Introduction by Carl Van Doren.
Illustrations by Honore Guilbeau.
Paper over boards with cloth spine and slipcase.

A Connecticut Yankee in King Arthur's Court.
New York, (1953): Pocket Books, Inc.
Cardinal Edition.
"2nd printing November, 1953."
Pictorial paper wrappers.

A Connecticut Yankee in King Arthur's Court.
New York and London, (1959): Harper & Brothers
Publishers.
Illustrated by Henry Pitz.
Black cloth with pictorial dustjacket.

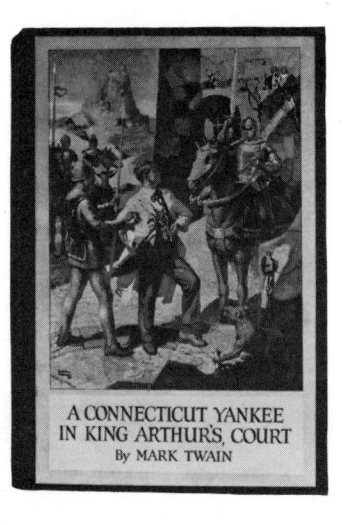

A Connecticut Yankee in King Arthur's Court.
New York, (1960): Hill and Wang.
    Introduction by Charles Neider.
    "First American Century Series Edition May 1960"
    Pictorial paper wrappers.

A Connecticut Yankee in King Arthur's Court.
San Francisco, (1963): Chandler Publishing Co.
    "A reproduction of the first edition"
    Introduction by Hamlin Hill.
    Paper wrappers: two copies.

A Connecticut Yankee in King Arthur's Court.
New York, (1964): Airmont Publishing Company, Inc.
    Introduction by Lucy Mabry Fitzpatrick.
    Classics Series CL29, price 60¢.
    Pictorial paper wrappers.

A Connecticut Yankee in King Arthur's Court.
New York, 1966: Gilberton Company, Inc.
    Classics Illustrated edition.
    #24 in the series; price 15¢.
    Pictorial paper wrappers.

A Connecticut Yankee in King Arthur's Court.
New York, (1977): I. Waldman & Son, Inc.
    Adapted by Lucia Monfried.
    Cover illustrated by Al Leiner.
    Pictorial paper wrappers.

A Connecticut Yankee in King Arthur's Court.
Berkeley, Los Angeles, London, 1979: University of California Press for the Iowa Center for Textual Studies.
    Edited by Bernard L. Stein.
    Introduction by Henry Nash Smith.
    Orange cloth with dustjacket.

(A Connecticut Yankee in King Arthur's Court.)
n.p., (1961): no publisher.
    In Hebrew.
    Paper over boards with pictorial dustjacket.

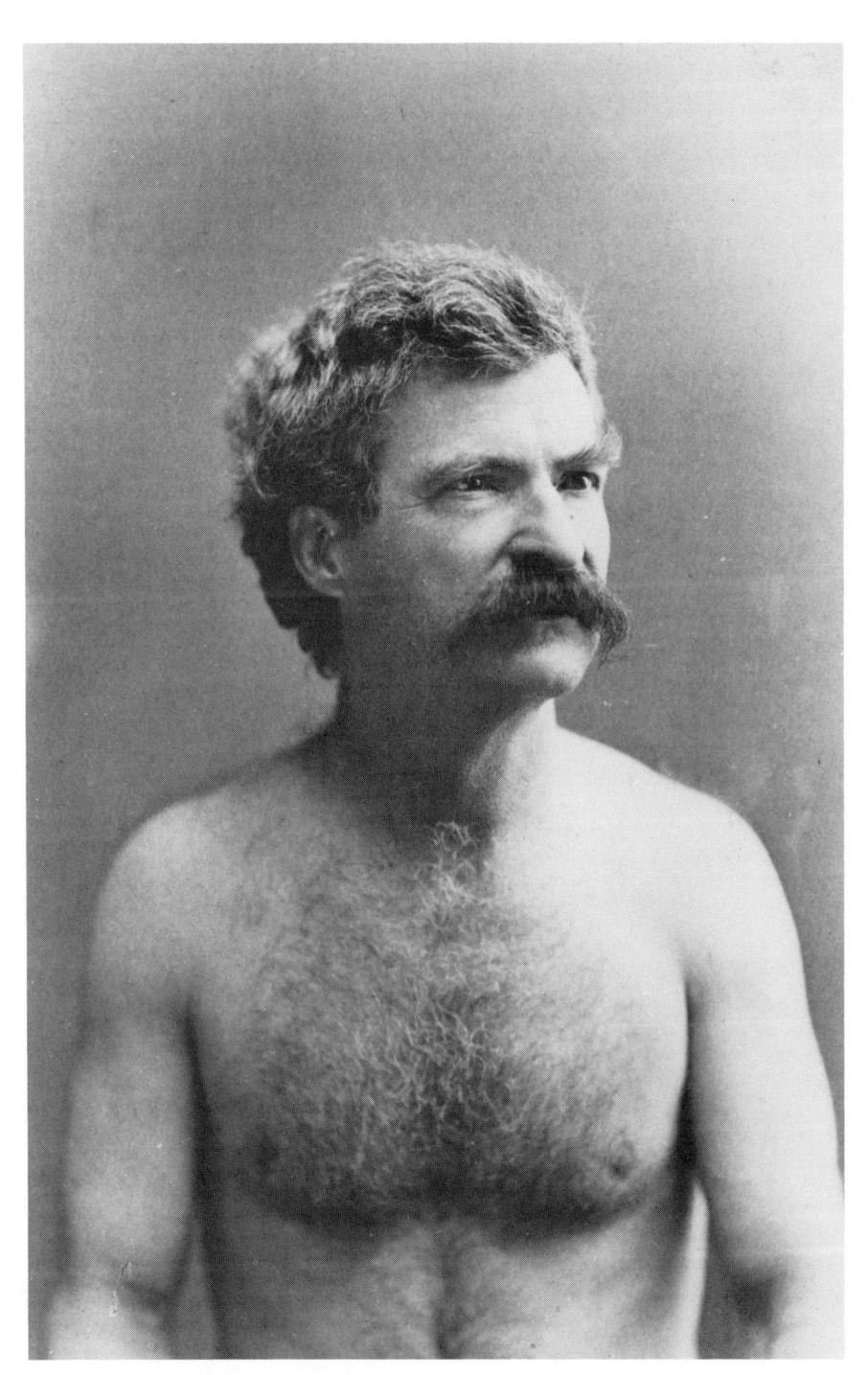

Mark Twain's 50th birthday photograph, 1885.

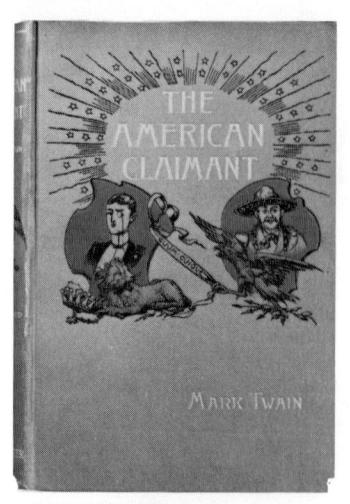

The American Claimant.
New York, 1892: Charles L. Webster & Co.
  Illustrated by Dan Beard.
  Grey-green cloth: two copies.
BAL 3434 Olive-green cloth: three copies.

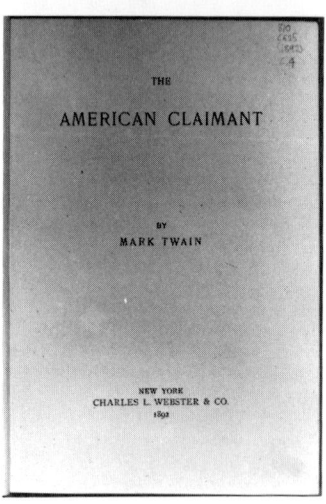

The American Claimant.
New York, 1892: Charles L. Webster & Co.
  Olive-green cloth.
  Inscribed copy:
  S.L. Clemens/(Mark Twain.)

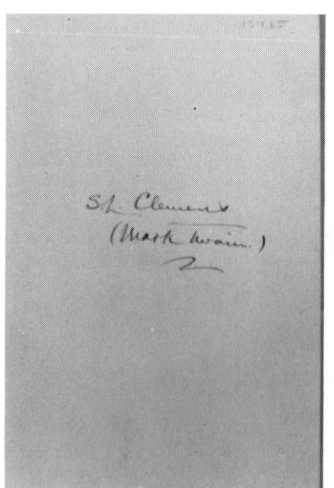

The American Claimant.
London, 1892: Chatto & Windus, Piccadilly.
               First English edition.
               81 Illustrations by Dan Beard and
               Hal Hurst.
               Red cloth stamped in black and gold.

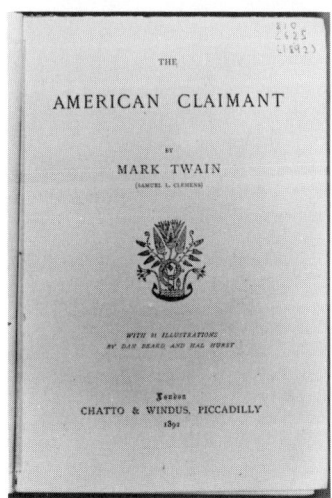

The American Claimant and Other Stories and Sketches.
Hartford, 1899:   The American Publishing Company.
                   Volume XXI of
                   The Writings of Mark Twain.
                   Autograph Edition of the Edition
                   de Luxe. Three-quarter morocco.

The American Claimant and Other Stories and Sketches.
Hartford, 1899:   American Publishing Company.
                   Volume XXI of
                   The Writings of Mark Twain.
                   Edition de Luxe.
                   Set #54 of 1000.
                   Uses the same plates as the
                   Autograph Edition.
                   Green cloth.

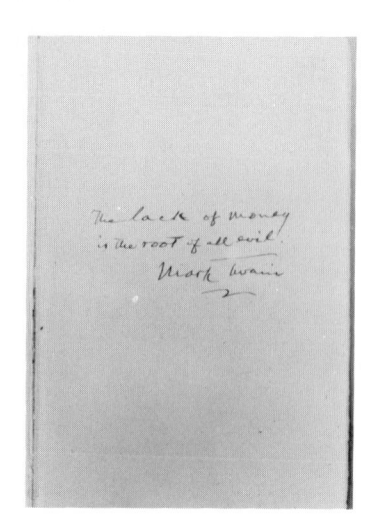

The American Claimant & Other Stories & Sketches.
New York, 1904: Harper & Brothers Publishers.
  Volume XXI of
  The Writings of Mark Twain.
  Hillcrest Edition.
  Three-quarter morocco.
  Inscribed copy:
  The lack of money/is the root of all evil.
  Mark Twain.
  (*More Maxims of Mark*, p. 10)

The American Claimant and Other Stories and Sketches.
New York and London, (1899, actually a later reprint of the 1906 Hillcrest Edition.): Harper & Brothers Publishers.
  Volume XXI of
  The Writings of Mark Twain.
  Hillcrest Edition.
  Green cloth.

The American Claimant and Other Stories and Sketches.
New York and London, (1915): Harper & Brothers Publishers.
  Volume XXI of
  The Writings of Mark Twain.
  Author's National Edition.
  Red cloth.

The American Claimant and Other Stories and Sketches.
New York and London, (1917): Harper & Brothers Publishers.
  Volume XXI of
  The Writings of Mark Twain.
  Author's National Edition.
  Green cloth.

The American Claimant and Other Stories and Sketches.
New York and London, (1918): Harper & Brothers Publishers.
  Volume XXI of
  The Writings of Mark Twain.
  Author's National Edition.
  Green cloth.

The American Claimant and Other Stories and Sketches.
New York and London, (1919): Harper & Brothers
	Publishers.
	Blue cloth: two copies.

The American Claimant and Other Stories and Sketches.
New York and London, (1927): Harper & Brothers
	Publishers.
	Blue cloth.

The American Claimant and other stories and sketches.
New York, 1929: Harper & Brothers.
	Volume 15 of
	The Stormfield Edition of
	The Writings of Mark Twain.
	Set #212 of 1024.
	Introduction by Albert Bigelow Paine.
	Blue cloth stamped in gold.

Laurence Hutton, Mark Twain and J.M. Dodge on the "Wake Robin" piazza, Onteora Club, Tannersville, New York, 1890.

This color section reproduces the front covers of selected first American editions, one first English edition and two sets of the works of Mark Twain. Each cover has been reproduced as large as the page format will allow. Actual sizes for each cover are given below.

Plate	Title
1.	**The Celebrated Jumping Frog of Calaveras County.** 6 5/8" x 4 1/2"
2.	**Mark Twain's Sketches, New and Old.** 8 1/2" x 6 9/16"
3.	**The Adventures of Tom Sawyer.** 8 7/16" x 6 9/16"
4.	**The Prince and the Pauper.** 8 5/16" x 6 9/16"
5.	**The Stolen White Elephant, Etc.** 6 5/8" x 4 7/16"
6.	**Life on the Mississippi.** 8 3/4" x 5 3/4"
7.	**A Connecticut Yankee in King Arthur's Court.** 8 5/16" x 6 9/16"
8.	**Adventures of Huckleberry Finn.** *Green cloth binding.* 8 7/16" x 6 9/16"
9.	**Adventures of Huckleberry Finn.** *Blue cloth binding.* 8 7/16" x 6 9/16"
10.	**The American Claimant.** 8" x 5 1/2"
11.	**The £1,000,000 Bank Note.** 7 5/8" x 5 3/8"
12.	**The Tragedy of Pudd'nhead Wilson and The Comedy of Those Extraordinary Twins.** 8 3/4" x 5 3/4"
13.	**The Man That Corrupted Hadleyburg.** *First English edition.* 5 1/8" × 7 11/16"
14.	**The Mysterious Stranger.** 9 1/4" x 7"
15.	*Top:* **The Autograph Edition of the Edition deLuxe.** (1899-1907). *Bottom:* **The Author's National Edition.** (1915).
16.	**First Editions of Mark Twain, 1867-1910.**

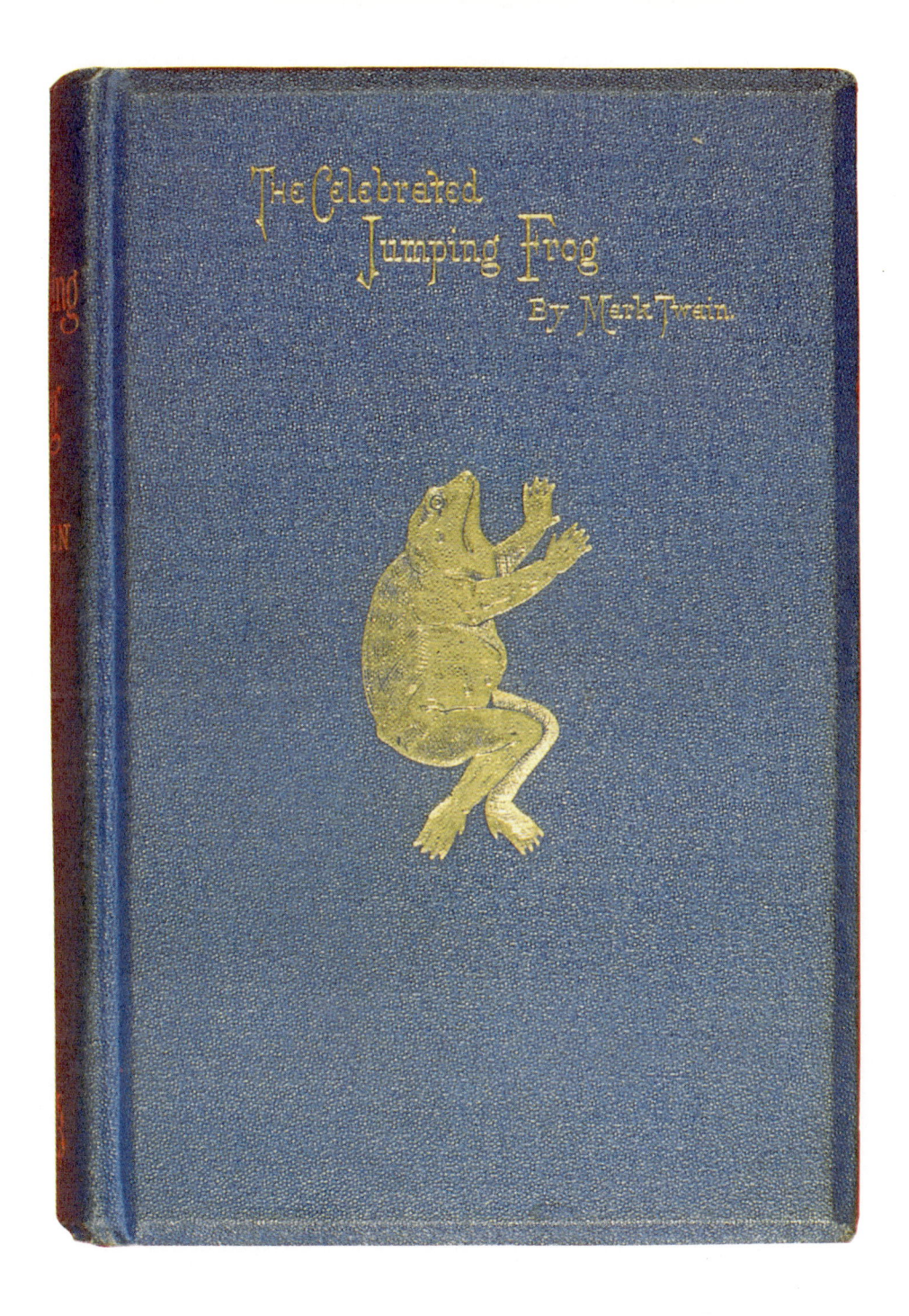

Plate 1. The Celebrated Jumping Frog of Calaveras County.

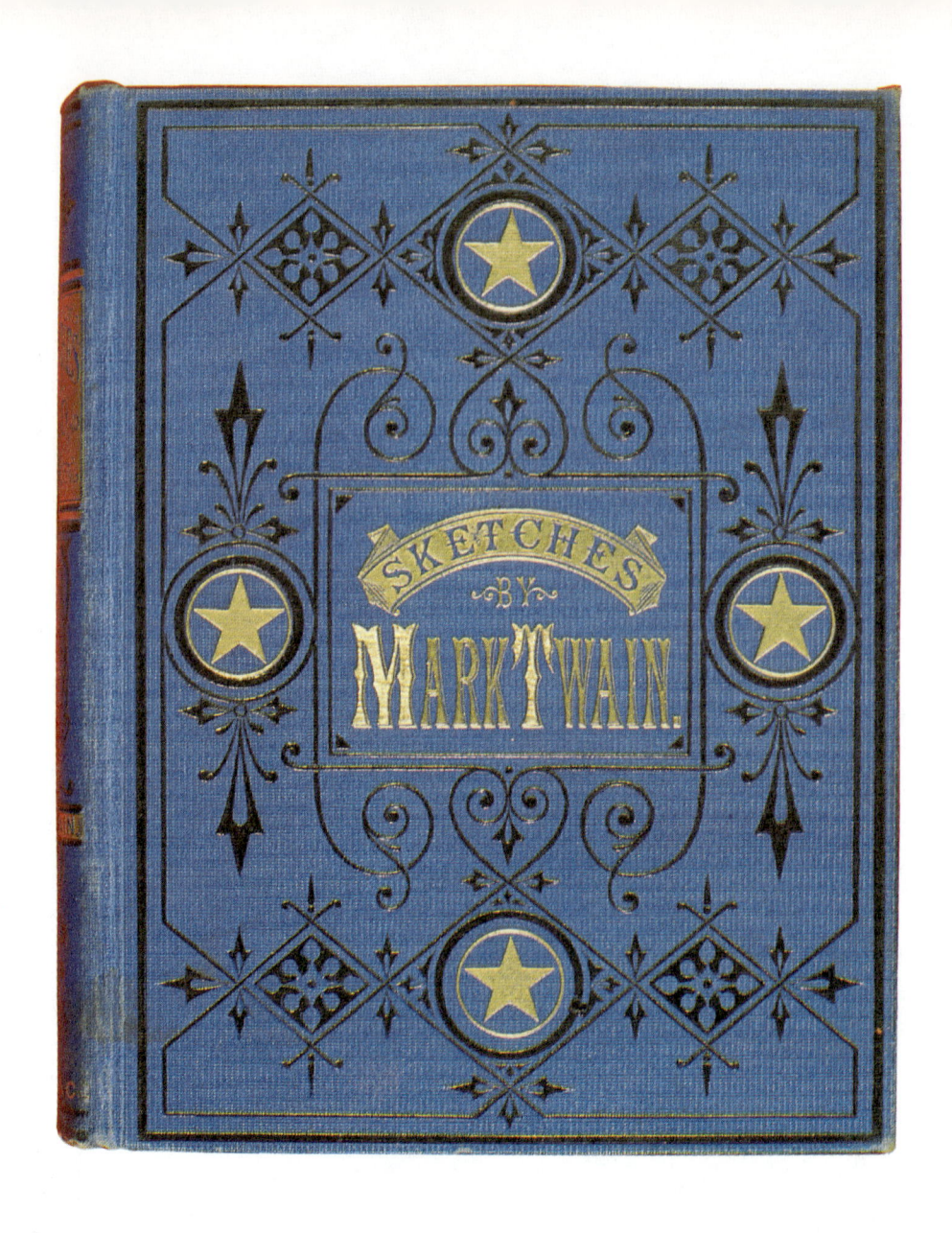

Plate 2. Mark Twain's Sketches, New and Old.

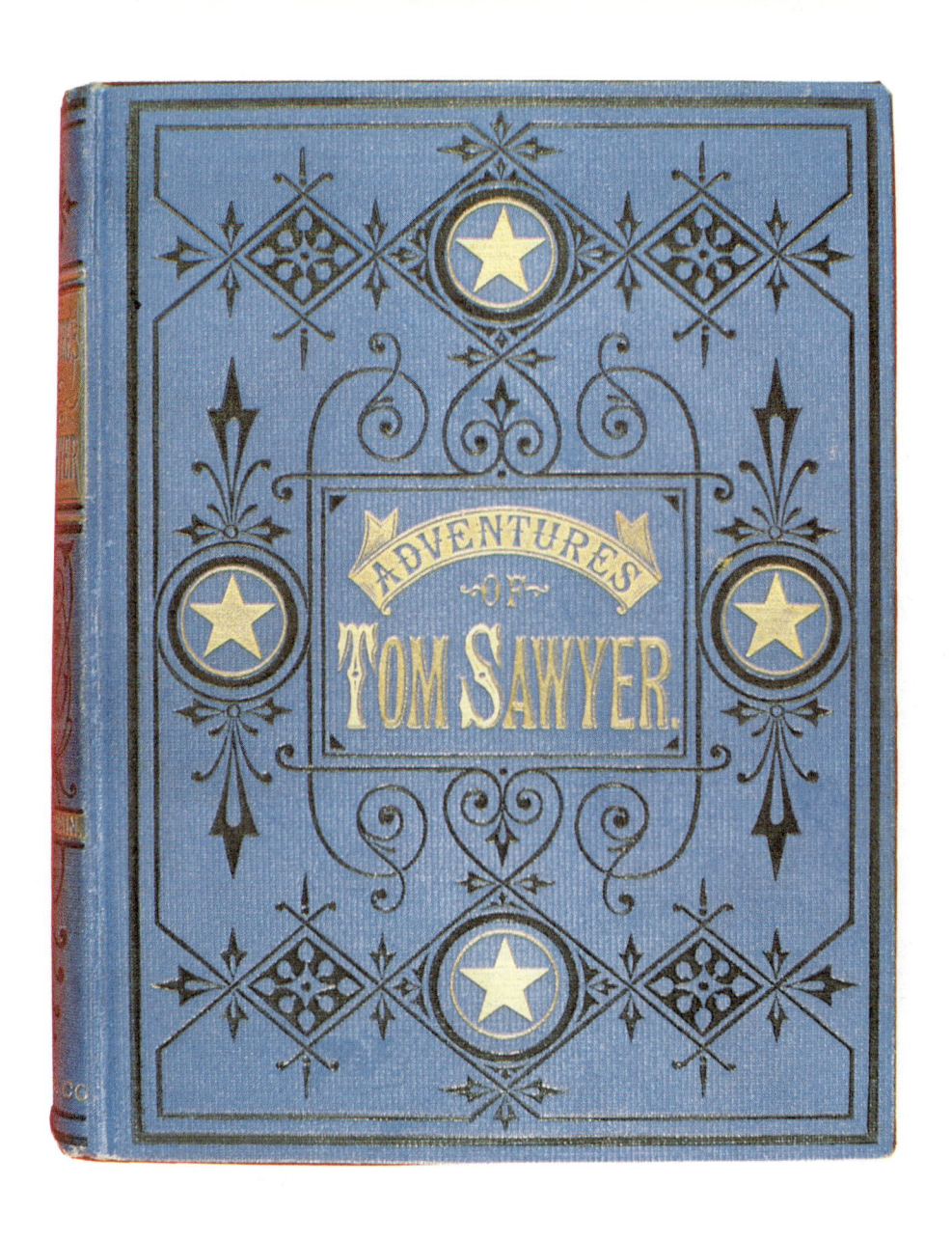

Plate 3. The Adventures of Tom Sawyer.

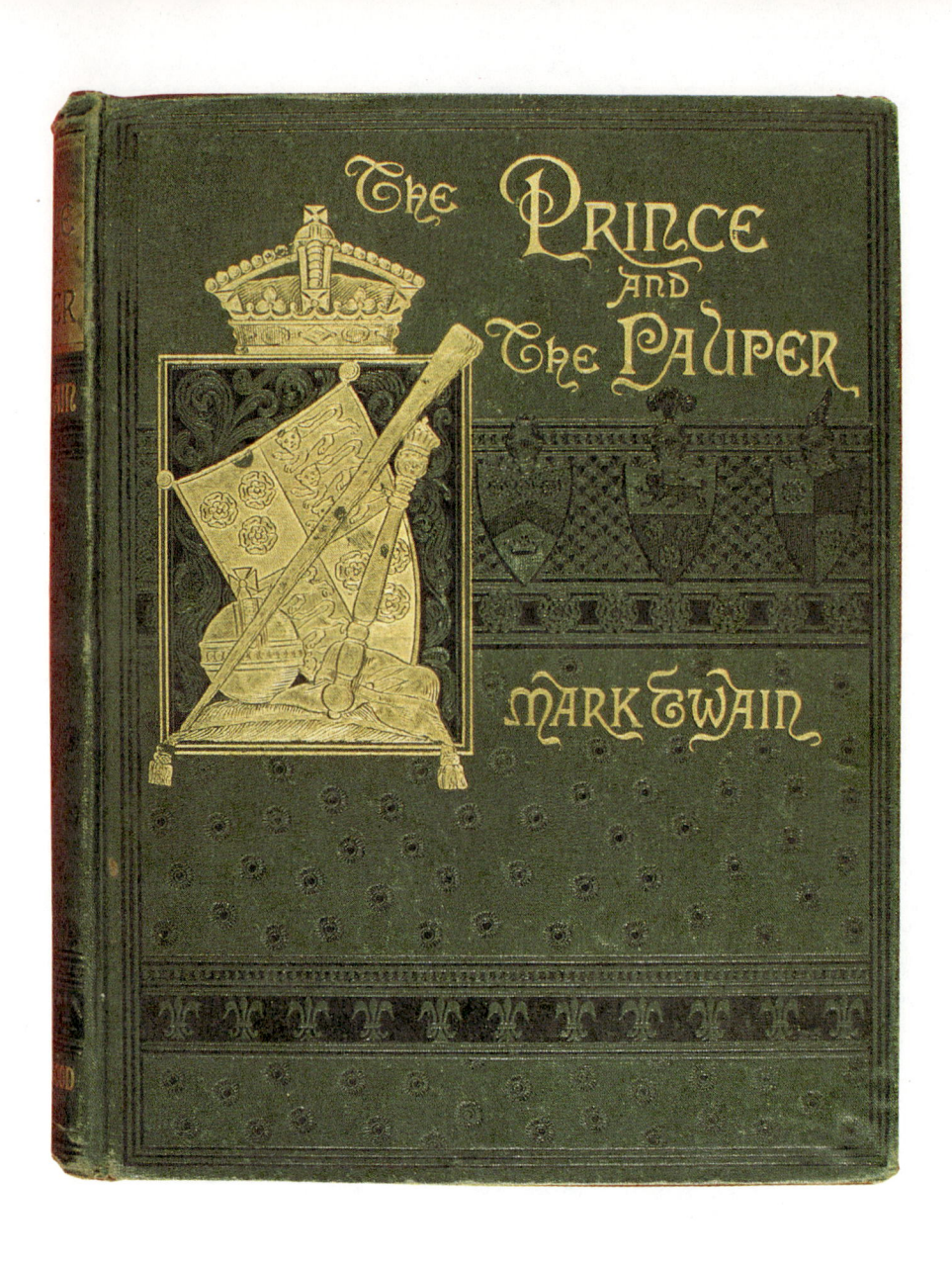

Plate 4. The Prince and the Pauper.

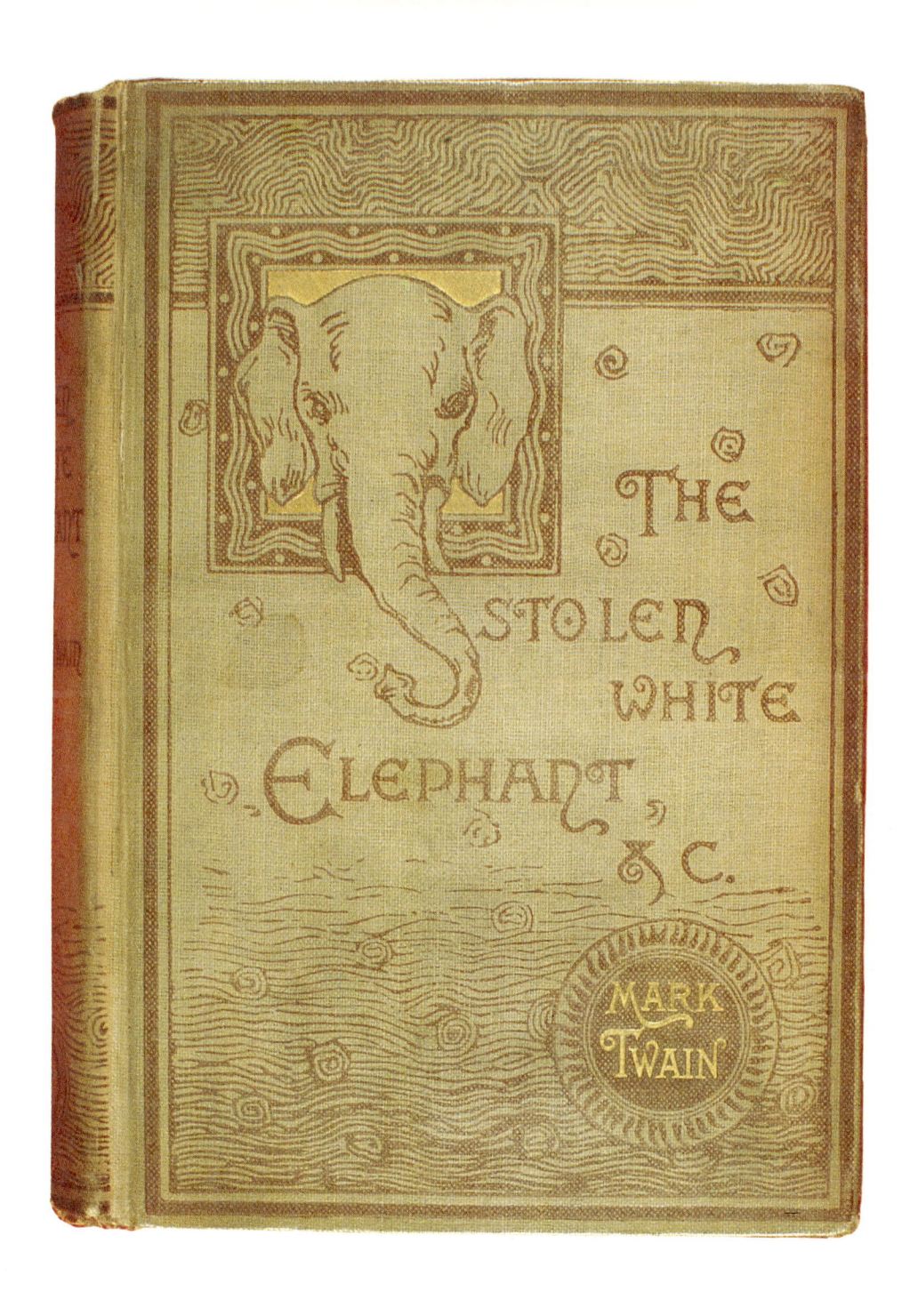

Plate 5. The Stolen White Elephant.

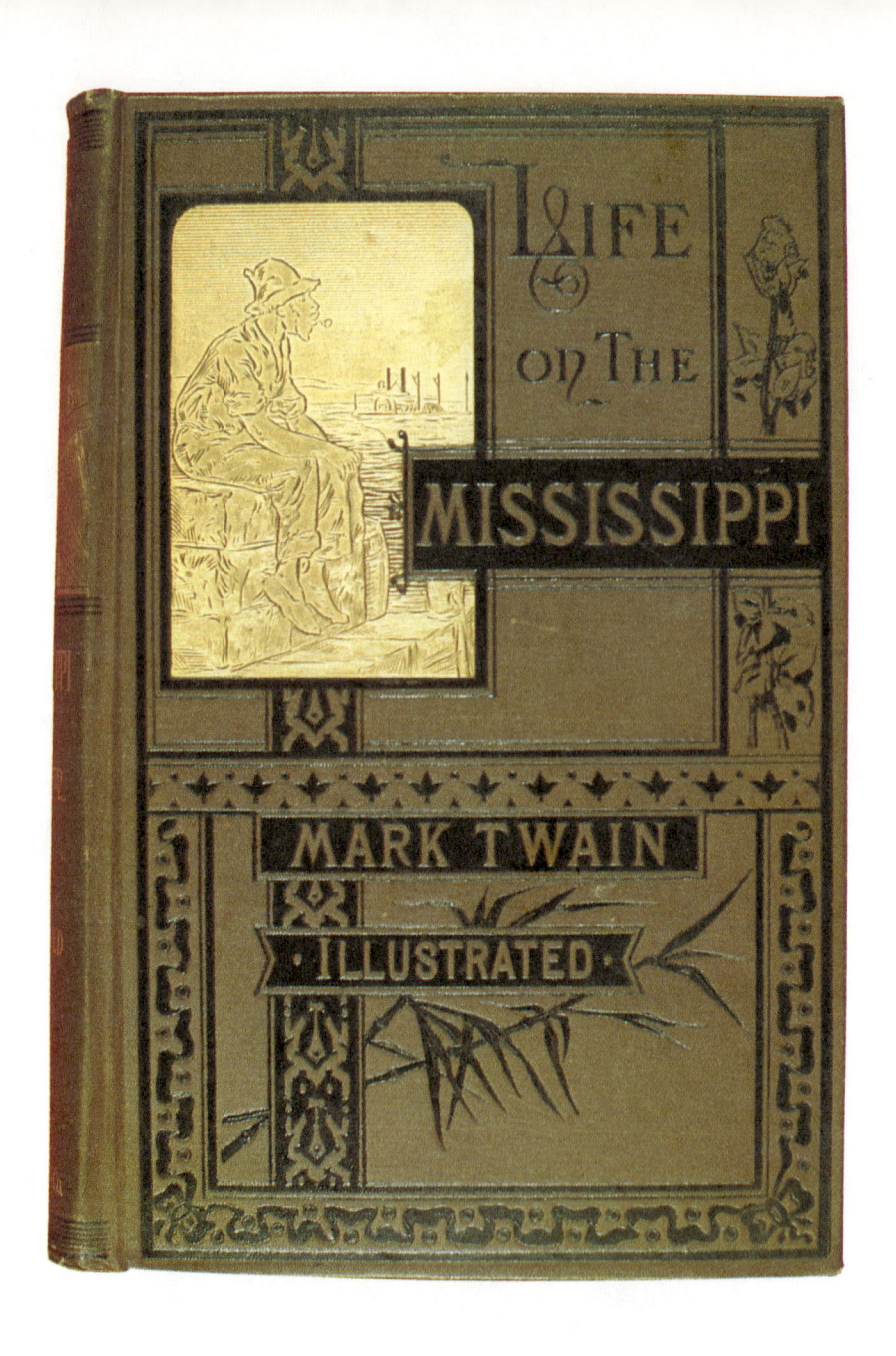

Plate 6. Life on the Mississippi.

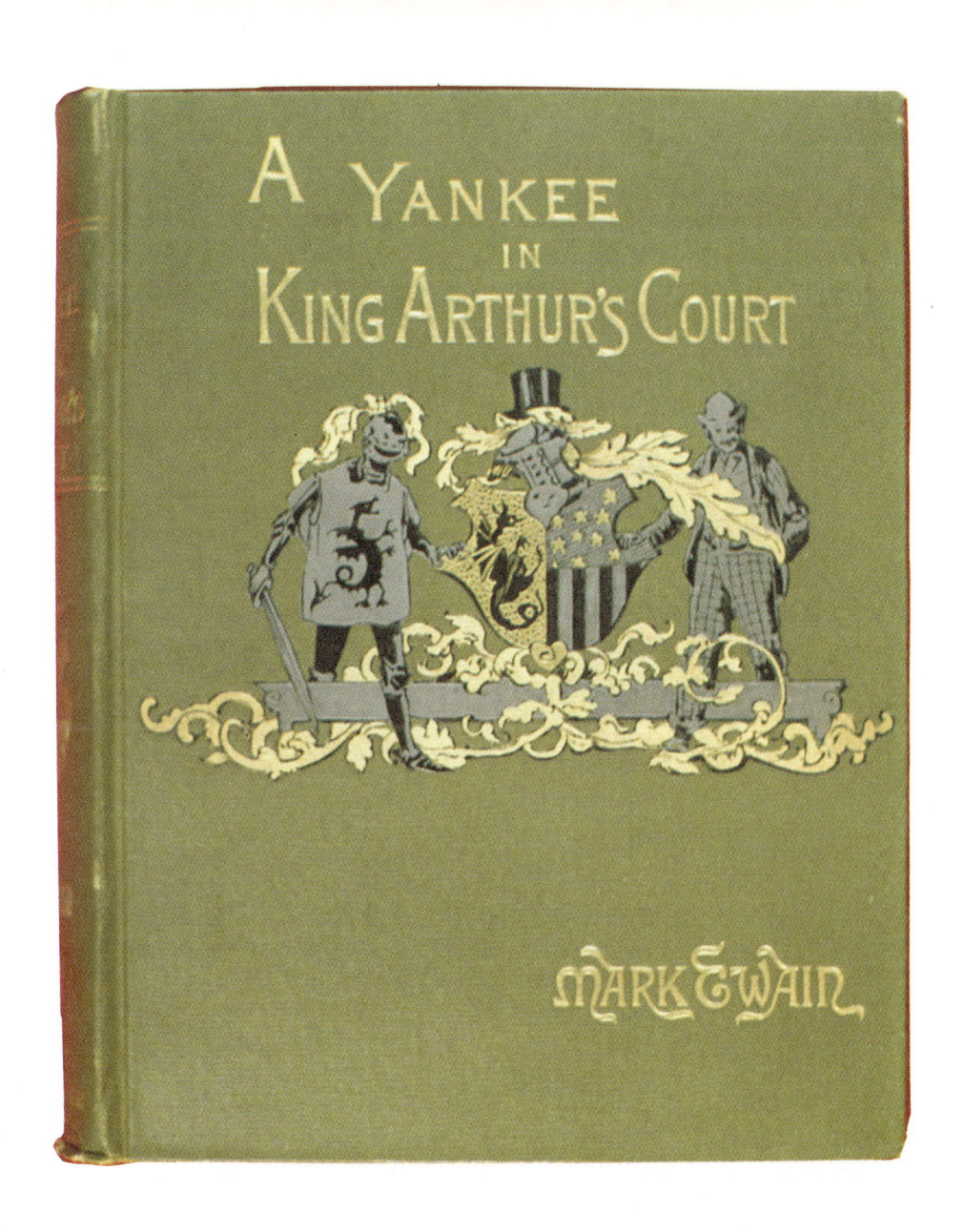

Plate 7. A Connecticut Yankee in King Arthur's Court.

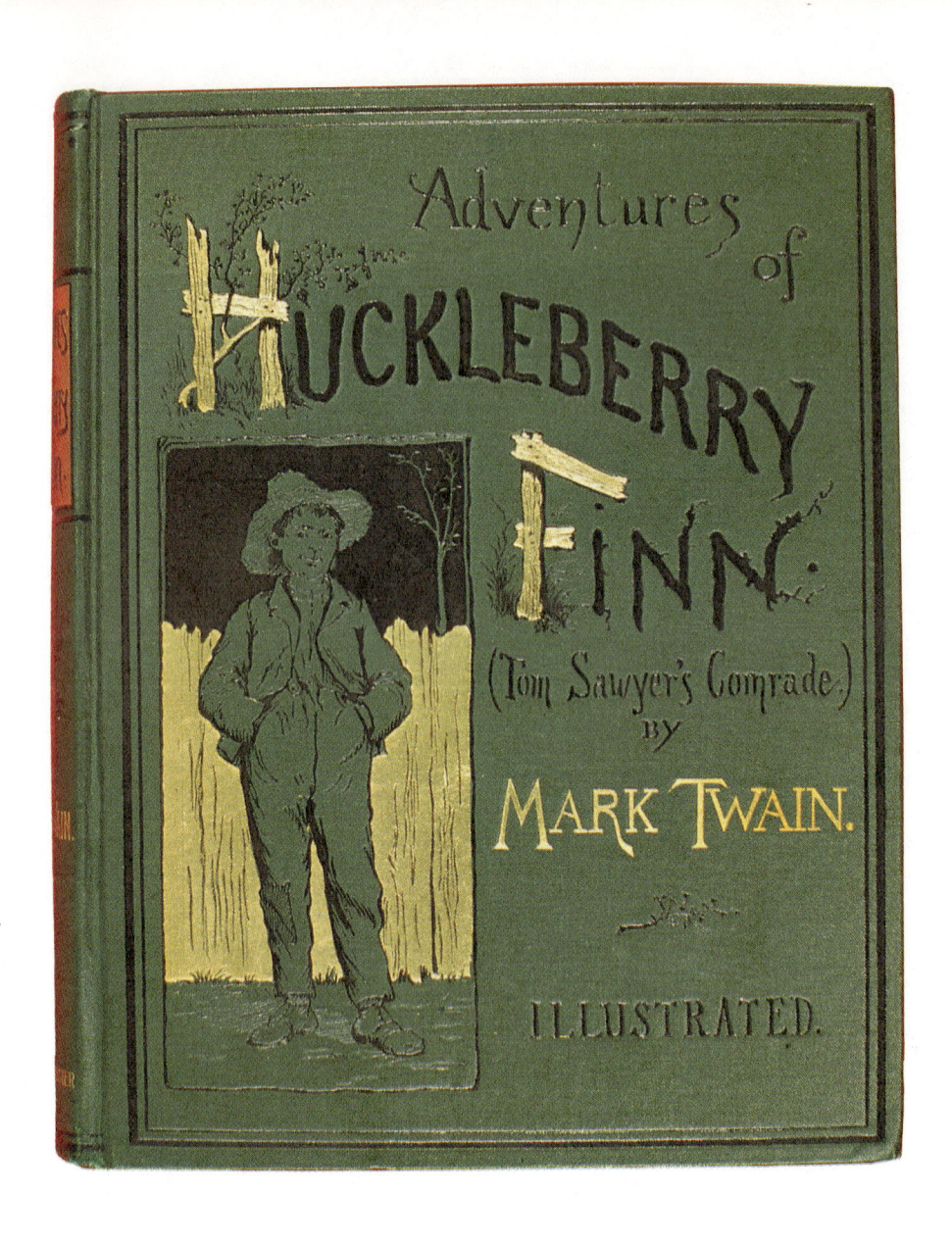

Plate 8. Adventures of Huckleberry Finn. *green cloth.*

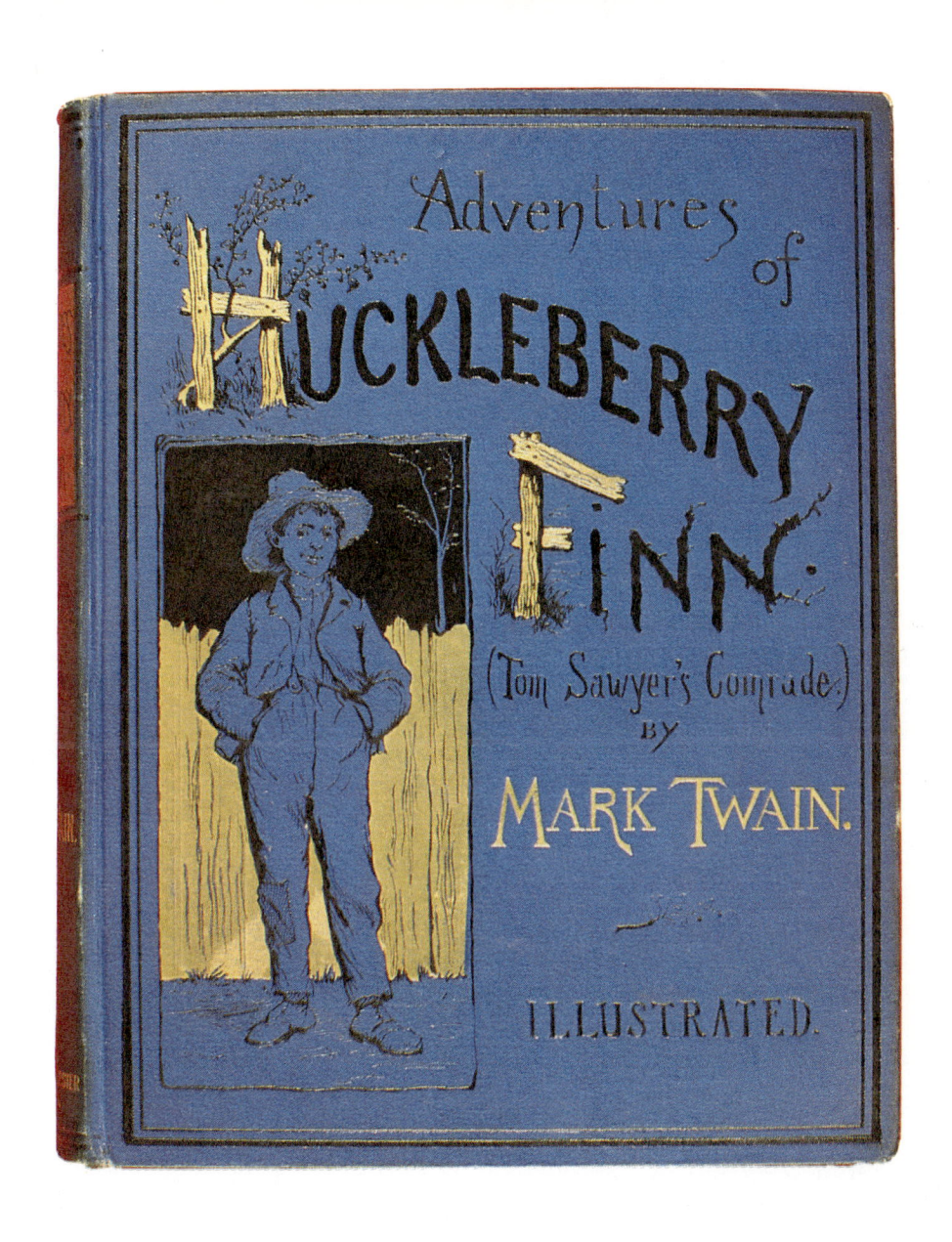

Plate 9. Adventures of Huckleberry Finn. *blue cloth.*

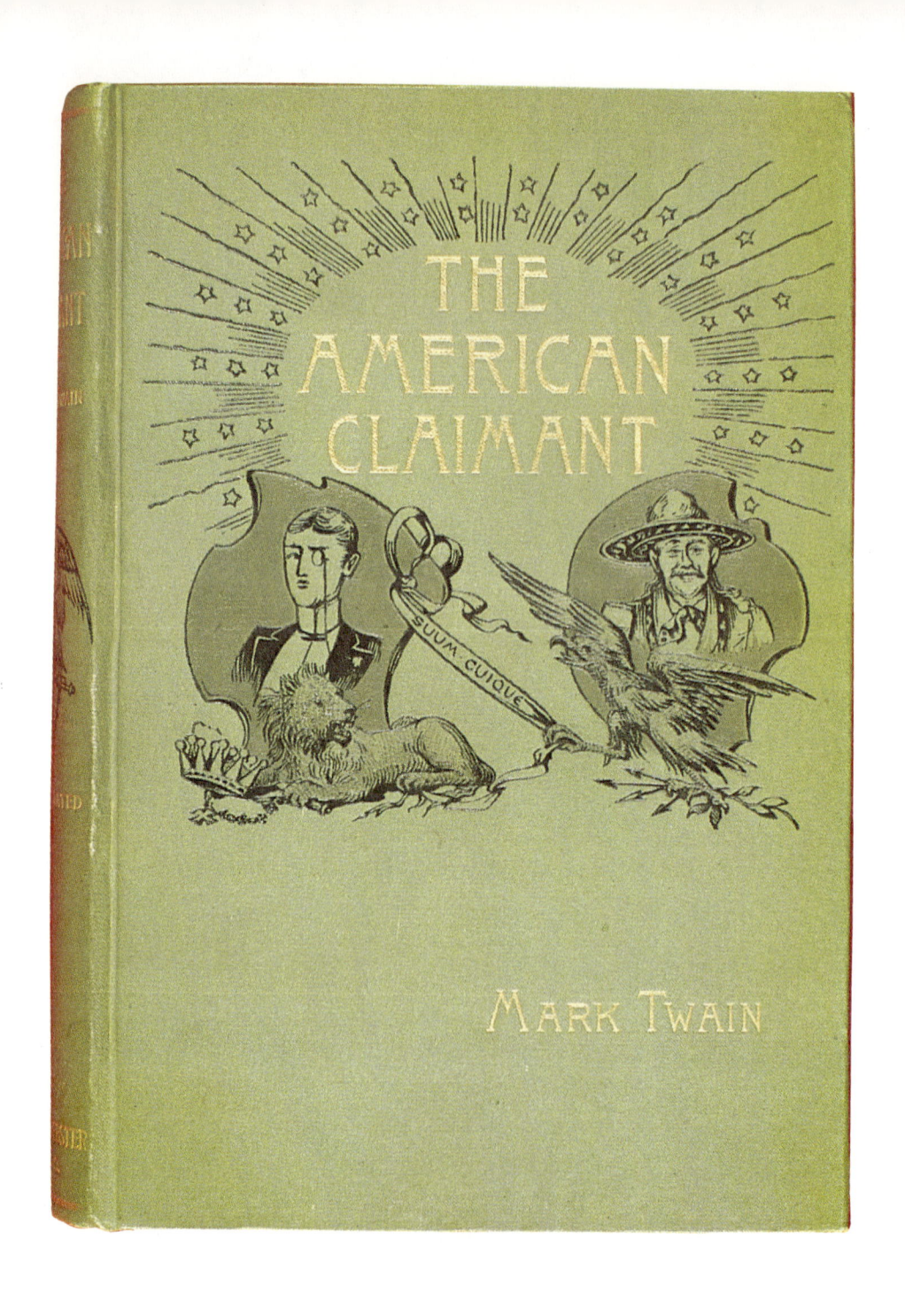

Plate 10. The American Claimant.

Plate 11. The £ 1,000,000 Bank Note.

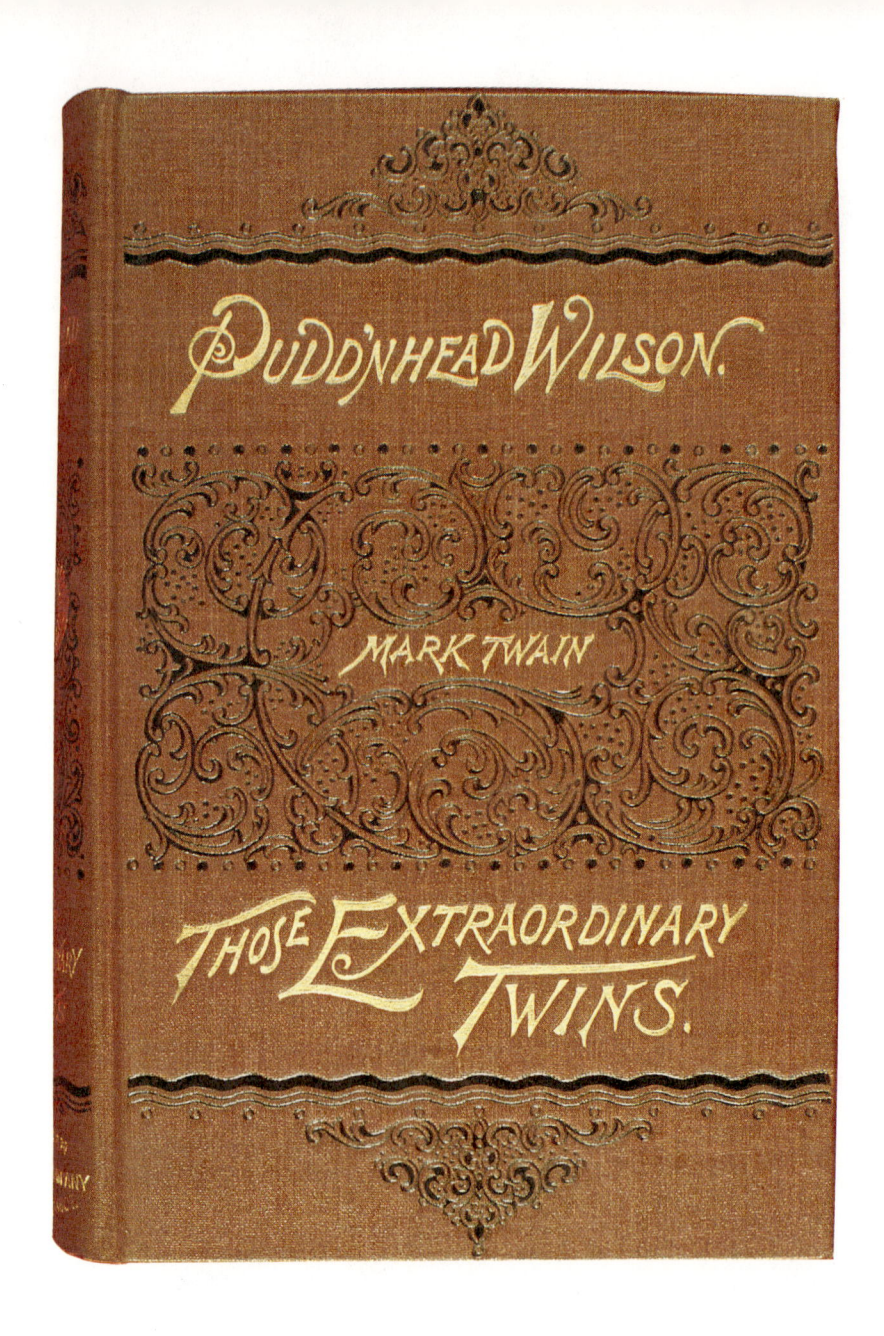

Plate 12. The Tragedy of Pudd'nhead Wilson. *etc.*

Plate 13. The Man That Corrupted Hadleyburg. *First English edition.*

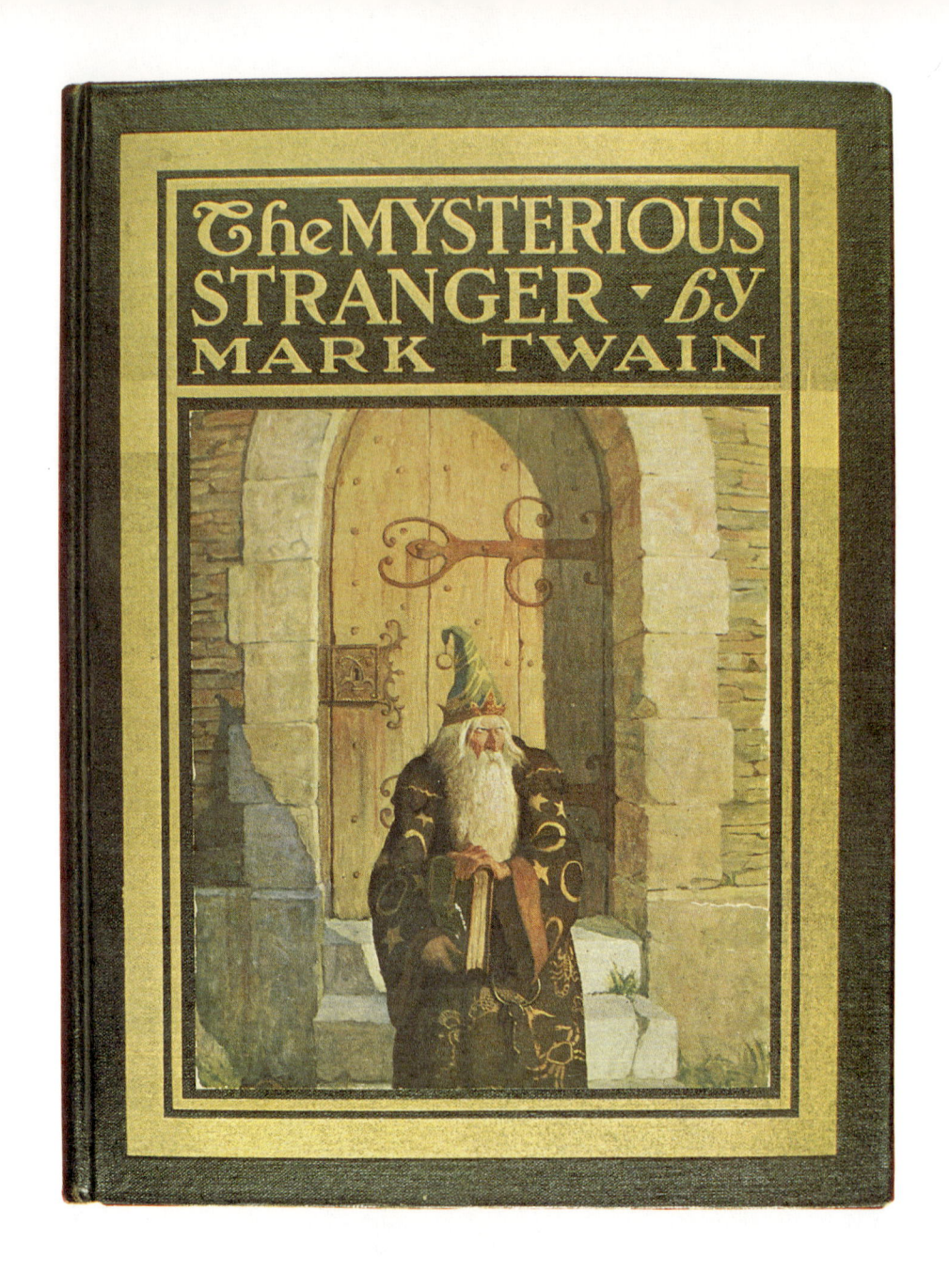

Plate 14. The Mysterious Stranger.

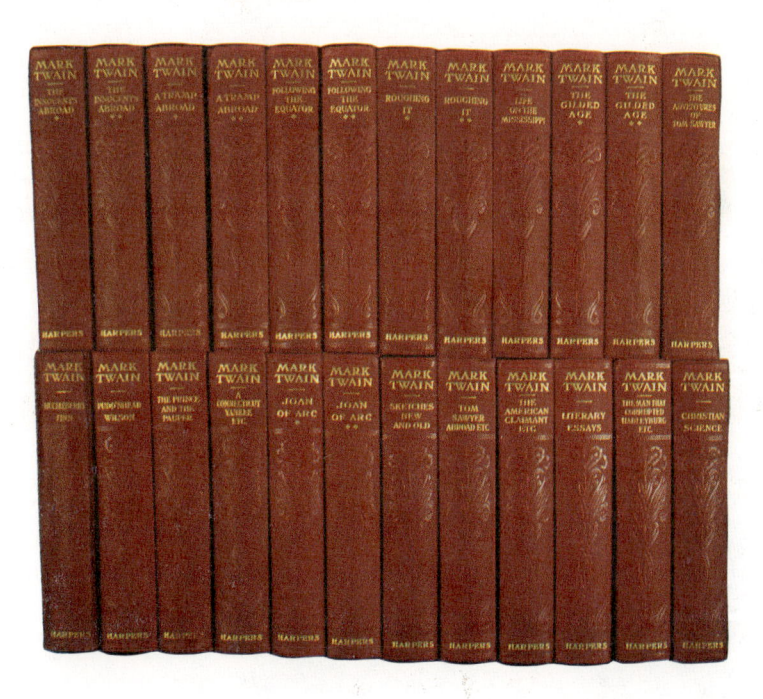

Plate 15. The Works of Mark Twain.

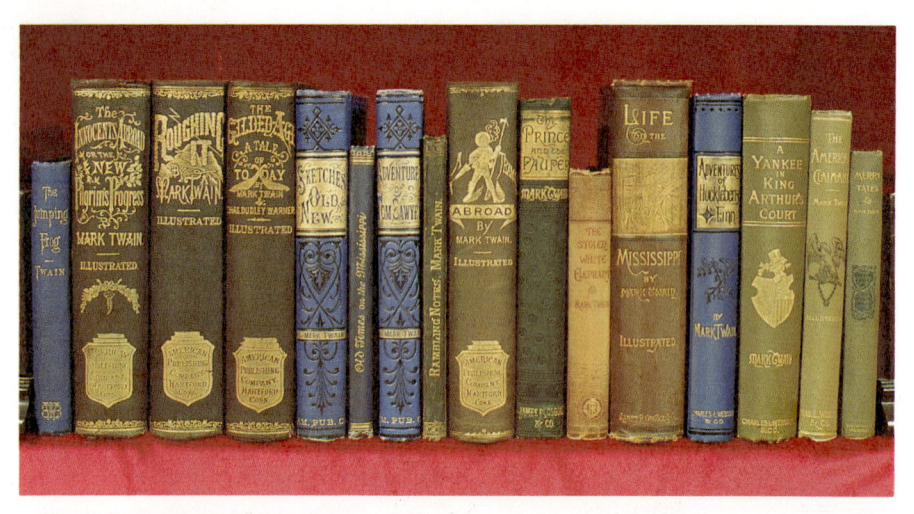

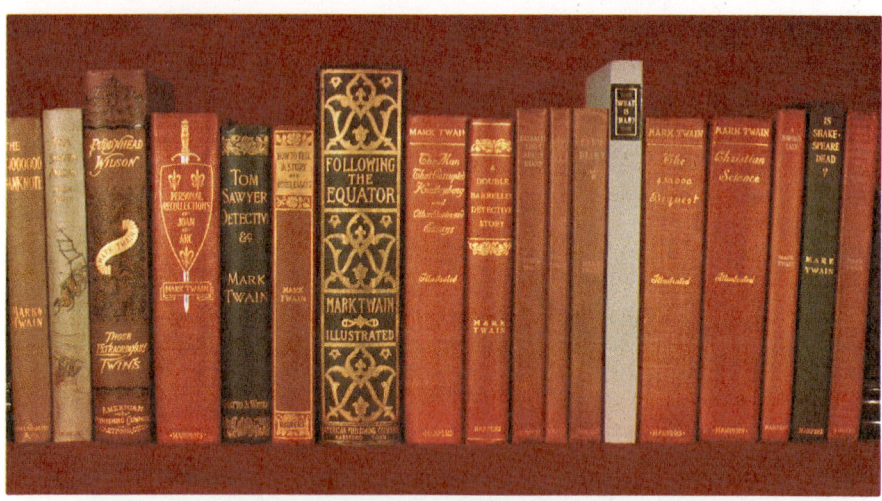

Plate 16. First Editions of Mark Twain 1867-1910.

First Editions 1867-1892.
(left to right)

1. The Celebrated Jumping Frog of Calaveras County.
2. The Innocents Abroad, or The New Pilgrim's Progress.
3. Roughing It.
4. The Gilded Age, a Tale of To-Day.
5. Mark Twain's Sketches, New and Old.
6. Old Times on the Mississippi. (Toronto).
7. The Adventures of Tom Sawyer.
8. An Idle Excursion. (Toronto).
9. A Tramp Abroad.
10. The Prince and The Pauper.
11. The Stolen White Elephant.
12. Life on the Mississippi.
13. Adventures of Huckleberry Finn.
14. A Connecticut Yankee in King Arthur's Court.
15. The American Claimant.
16. Merry Tales.

First Editions 1893-1909.
(left to right)

1. The £1,000,000 Bank Note.
2. Tom Sawyer Abroad.
3. The Tragedy of Pudd'nhead Wilson
4. Personal Recollections of Joan of Arc.
5. Tom Sawyer, Detective. (London).
6. How to Tell a Story.
7. Following the Equator.
8. The Man That Corrupted Hadleyburg.
9. A Double-Barrelled Detective Story.
10. Extracts From Adam's Diary.
11. A Dog's Tale.
12. Eve's Diary.
13. What is Man?
14. The $30,000 Bequest.
15. Christian Science. etc.
16. A Horse's Tale.
17. Is Shakespeare Dead?
18. Extract from Captain Stormfield's Visit to Heaven.

First Editions (various).
(left to right)

1. Mark Twain's Speeches.
2. The Mysterious Stranger.
3. The Innocents at Home. (London).
4. Roughing It. (London).
5. The Adventures of Tom Sawyer. (London).
6. The Adventures of Tom Sawyer. (Toronto).
7. A Tramp Abroad. (London).
8. A Tramp Abroad. (Toronto).
9. The Prince and The Pauper. (London).
10. The Stolen White Elephant. (London).
11. Adventures of Huckleberry Finn. (Montreal).
12. The Adventures of Huckleberry Finn. (London).
13. A Yankee in the Court of King Arthur's Court. (London).
14. The American Claimant. (London)
15. The £1,000,000 Bank Note. (London).
16. The Man That Corrupted Hadleyburg. (London).
17. What is Man? (London).

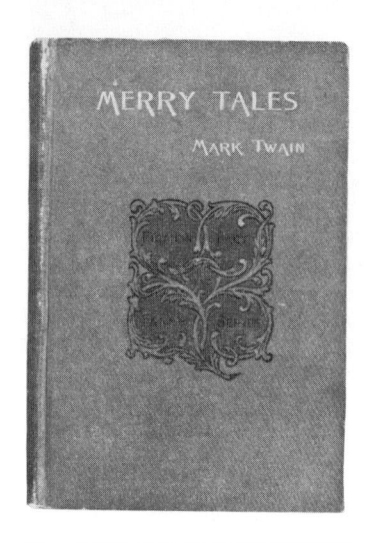

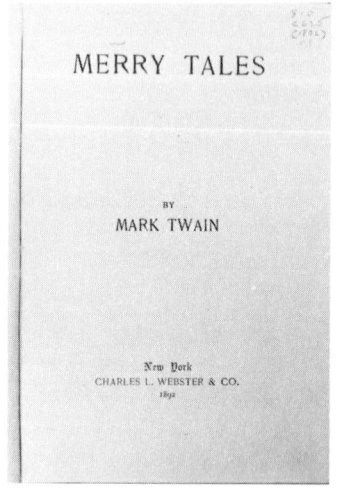

Merry Tales.

New York, 1892: Charles L. Webster & Co. Grey-green cloth. First issue with decorated endpapers and no portrait frontispiece.

BAL 3435

Susy and Mark Twain as Hero and Leander, at the Onteora Club, Tannersville, New York, 1890.

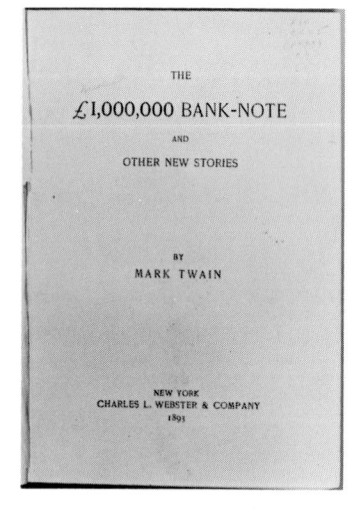

The £1,000,000 Bank-note and Other New Stories.
New York, 1893: Charles L. Webster & Company. Tan cloth:
BAL 3436   three copies.

The £1,000,000 Bank-note and Other New Stories.
London, 1893: Chatto & Windus, Piccadilly.
        First English edition.
        Red cloth stamped in black and gold.

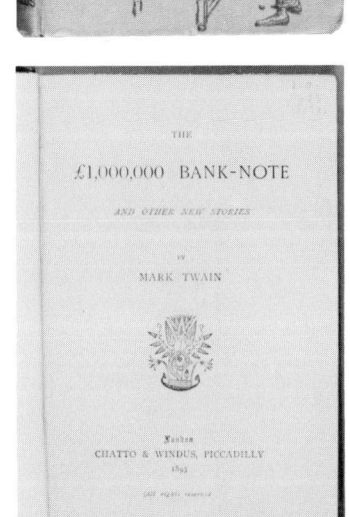

The £1,000,000 Bank-note and Other Pieces of American Humor.
Harstellung, Druck, (1963): Ferdinand Schoningh,
        Paderborn and J.D. Broelemann.
        Edited by Wilhelm Mensing.
        Also includes pieces by O. Henry,
        Robert Benchley, Christopher
        Morley and Ring Lardner.
        Pictorial paper wrappers.

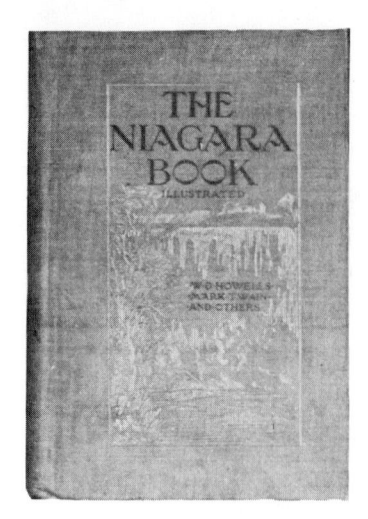

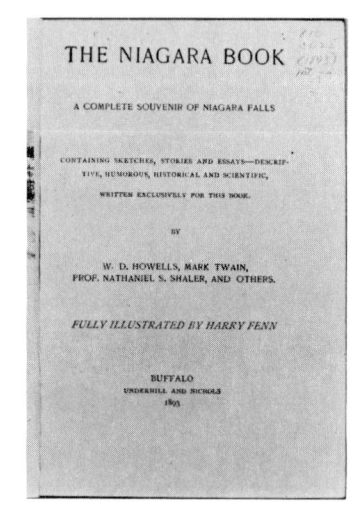

The Niagara Book.
Buffalo, 1893: Underhill & Nichols.
By Clemens and W.D. Howells, Prof. Nathaniel S. Shaler and others. First issue with copyright notice in three lines and page (226) blank.
Illustrated by Harry Fenn.

BAL 3437   Green cloth: two copies.

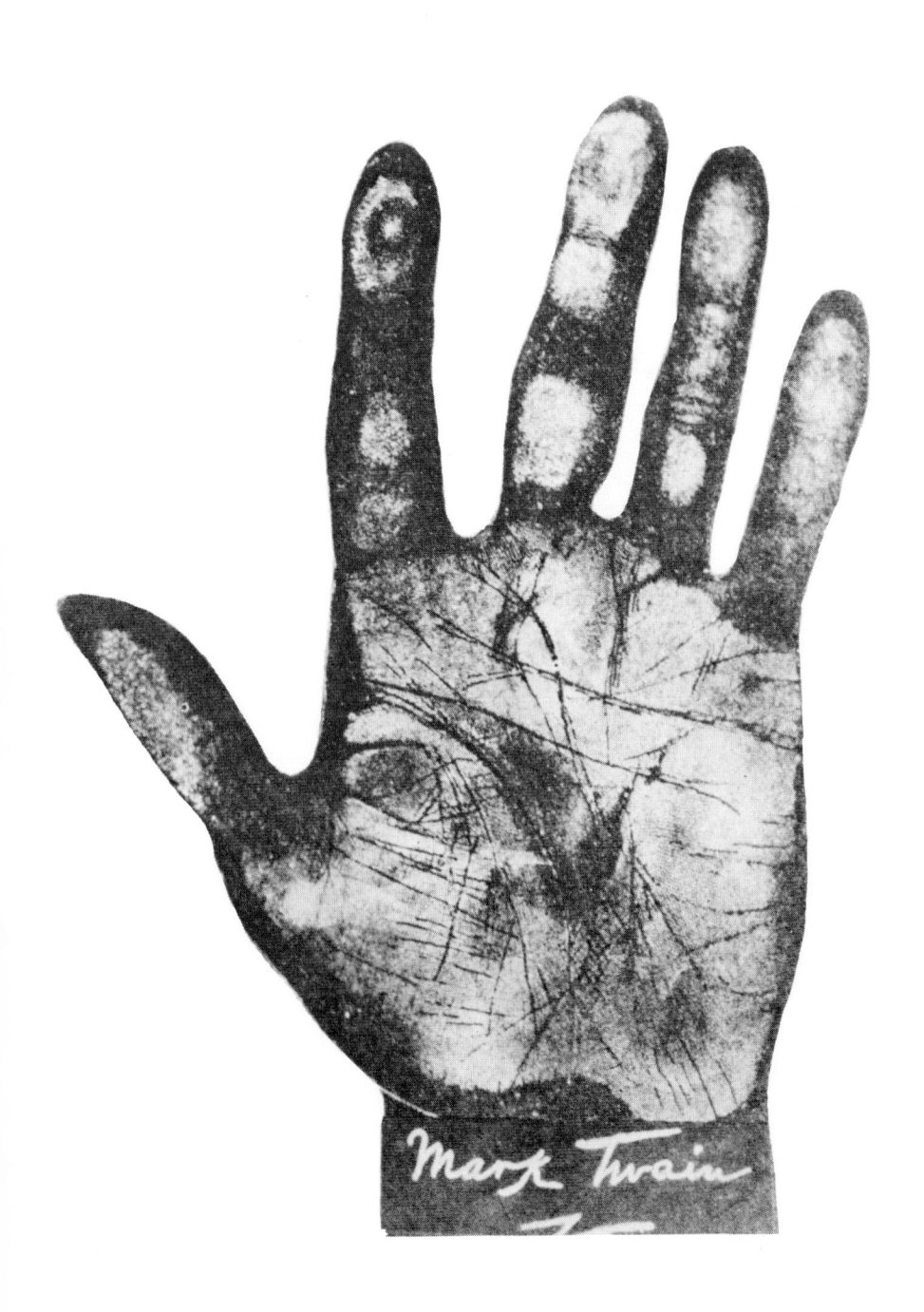

Mark Twain's right hand, about 1895.

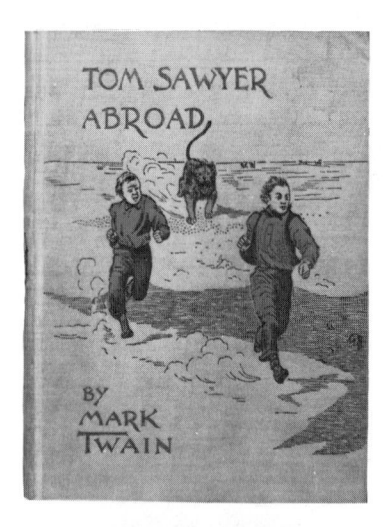

Tom Sawyer Abroad by Huck Finn Edited by Mark Twain.
New York, 1894: Charles L. Webster & Company.
        Tan pictorial cloth.
        First issue binding with 5 3/8" between *WEBSTER* and *TWAIN* on spine.
        Illustrated by Dan Beard.
        Bookplate of William Hartmann Woodin.
        F.e.p. inscribed:
BAL 3440   *First Edition/Merle Johnson.*

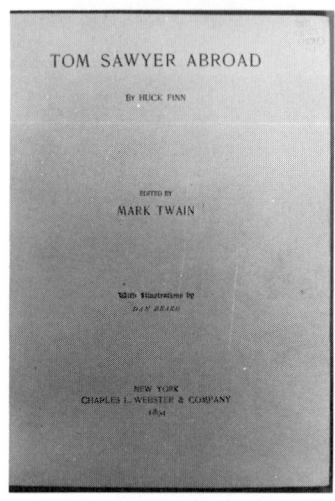

Tom Sawyer Abroad by Huck Finn. etc.
New York, 1894: Charles L. Webster & Company.
        Second issue binding with 5 5/8" between names on spine.
        Tan pictorial cloth.

Tom Sawyer Abroad.
London, 1894: Chatto & Windus, Piccadilly.
        First English edition.
        Illustrated by Dan Beard.
        Red cloth stamped in black and gold.

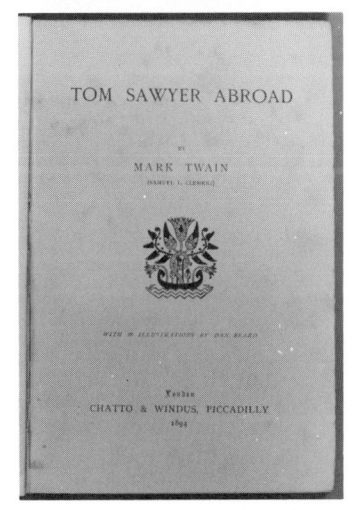

Tom Sawyer Abroad, Tom Sawyer Detective, and Other Stories, Etc., Etc.
Hartford, 1899: The American Publishing Company.
Volume XX of
The Writings of Mark Twain.
Autograph Edition of the Edition de Luxe.
Bound in:
ALS by Arthur Burdett Frost to Mr. Bliss, 1¼ pp., 1899 September 11.
Three-quarter morocco.

Tom Sawyer Abroad, Tom Sawyer Detective, and Other Stories, Etc., Etc.
Hartford, 1899: American Publishing Company.
Volume XX of
The Writings of Mark Twain.
Edition de Luxe.
Set #54 of 1000.
Uses the same plates as the Autograph Edition.
Green cloth.

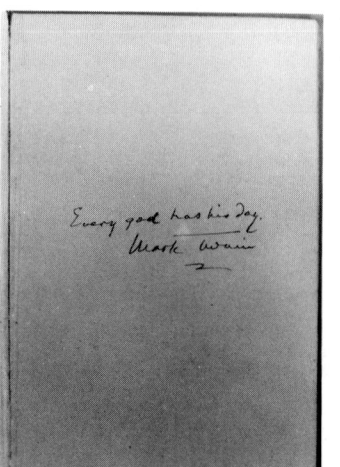

Tom Sawyer Abroad, Tom Sawyer Detective.
New York, 1904: Harper & Brothers Publishers.
Volume XX of
The Writings of Mark Twain.
Hillcrest Edition.
Three-quarter morocco.
Inscribed copy:
Every god has his day./Mark Twain.

Tom Sawyer Abroad, Tom Sawyer, Detective.
New York and London, (1915): Harper & Brothers
Publishers.
Volume XX of
The Writings of Mark Twain.
Author's National Edition.
Red cloth.

Tom Sawyer Abroad, Tom Sawyer, Detective and Other Stories.
New York and London, (1917): Harper & Brothers
Publishers.
Limp leather edition.
Red leather with dustjacket.

Tom Sawyer Abroad, Tom Sawyer, Detective and Other Stories.
New York and London, (1918): Harper & Brothers
Publishers.
Volume XX of
The Writings of Mark Twain.
Author's National Edition.
Green cloth.

Tom Sawyer Abroad, Tom Sawyer, Detective and Other Stories.
New York, (1921): P.F. Collier & Son Company.
"Harper & Brothers Edition."
Blue cloth.

Tom Sawyer Abroad, Tom Sawyer, Detective and Other Stories.
New York and London, (1927): Harper & Brothers
Publishers.
Blue cloth: two copies.

Tom Sawyer Abroad.
New York and London, 1928: Harper & Brothers.
First edition thus.
Introduction by Commander
Richard E. Byrd.
Blue cloth.

Tom Sawyer Abroad, Tom Sawyer Detective and other stories.
New York, 1929: Harper & Brothers.
Volume 19 of
The Stormfield Edition of
The Writings of Mark Twain.
Set #212 of 1024.
Blue cloth stamped in gold.

Tom Sawyer Abroad & Tom Sawyer, Detective.
Garden City, N.Y., n.d. (c. 1960): Dolphin Books, Doubleday & Company, Inc.
Dolphin Book #C256; price 95¢.
Cover illustrated by Lawrence Beall Smith.
Pictorial paper wrappers.

Tom Sawyer Abroad and Tom Sawyer Detective.
New York, 1965: Dell Publishing Company.
Laurel Leaf Library edition.
Dell #8943; price 45¢.
"First printing — February, 1965"
Cover illustrated by Blake Hampton.
Pictorial paper wrappers.

Tom Sawyer Abroad and Tom Sawyer Detective.
New York, (1966): Airmont Publishing Company, Inc.
Airmont Classics Series edition #CL126; price 50¢.
Introduction by Beryl Rowland.
Pictorial paper wrappers.

Tom Sawyer Abroad and Tom Sawyer Detective.
New York, (1968): Lancer Books, Inc.
Magnum Easy Eye Book #65, catalog number 13-441, price $1.25.
Pictorial paper wrappers.

Mark Twain in 1897.

Pudd'nhead Wilson's Calendar for 1894.
New York, 1893: The Century Company.
"Set up and printed for Mr. Wilson by Henry Butts, Dawson's Landing, Mo."
First issue with 5: *count four*; 15: *$4.00 a year*, and inner back wrapper: *Do not fail to read* . . .

BAL 3439   Paper wrappers.

Third issue of Pudd'nhead Wilson's Calendar *for 1894, page I.*

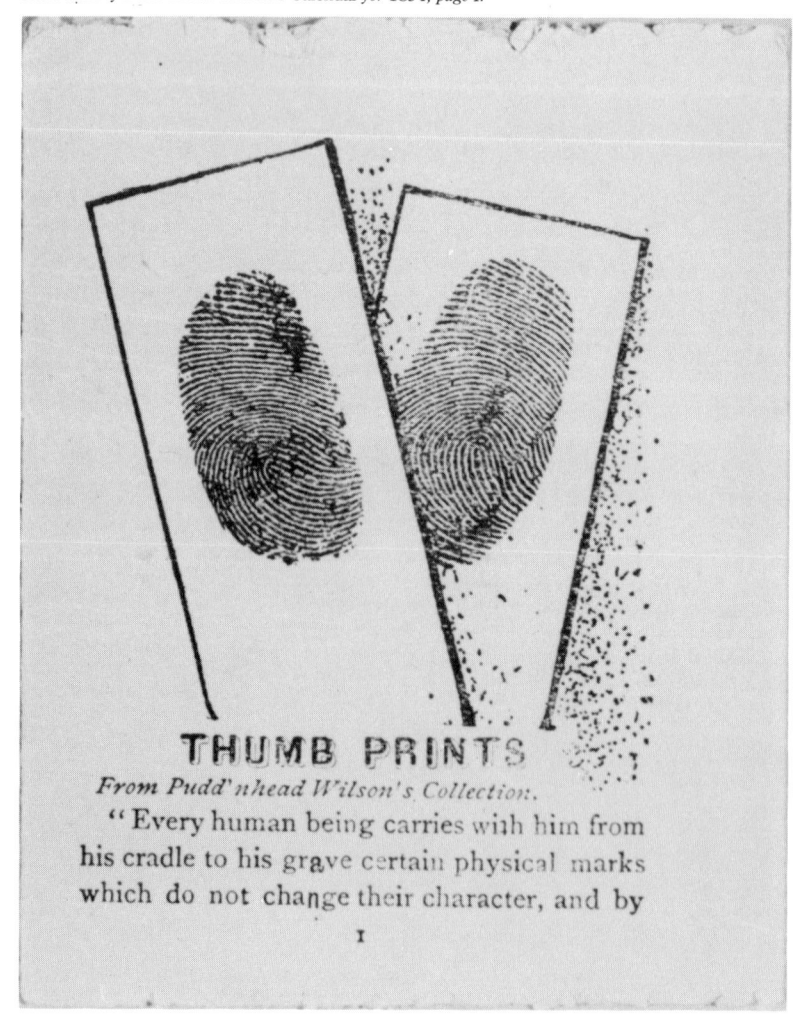

THUMB PRINTS
From Pudd'nhead Wilson's Collection.
"Every human being carries with him from his cradle to his grave certain physical marks which do not change their character, and by

I

Pudd'nhead Wilson's Calendar for 1894.
New York, 1893: The Century Company.
Third issue with 1: illustration of thumbprints; 5: *count a hundred*; 15: *news-stands*, and inner back wrapper: *Portrait of Mark Twain.*
Paper wrappers.
Laid in:
card 4 13/16" x 5 3/4" printed: *From/"Puddin' Head Wilson"/Few things are harder/to bear than the annoy-/ance of a good example./By Mark Twain/*

BAL 3439 (signature of:) *Mark Twain.*

From

"PUDDIN' HEAD WILSON"

FEW things are harder to bear than the annoy-ance of a good example.

By MARK TWAIN

Mark Twain

The Tragedy of Pudd'nhead Wilson and the Comedy of Those Extraordinary Twins.

Hartford, 1894: American Publishing Company. First issue with title leaf integral and length of facsimile signature on frontispiece 1 7/16" wide and sheets bulk about 1 1/8".

BAL 3442

Brown cloth: five copies.
Three-quarter morocco: two copies.

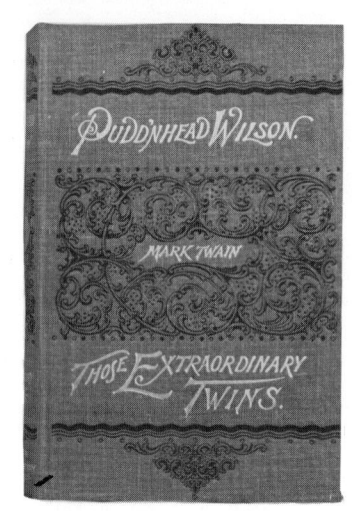

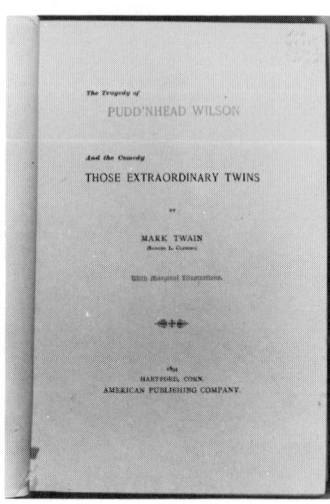

Pudd'nhead Wilson.
Leipzig, 1895: Bernhard Tauchnitz.
Paper wrappers.
See note on Tauchnitz editions under *The Innocents Abroad* (page 9).
Last title listed opposite title page is *More Tramps Abroad* (1897).

Pudd'nhead Wilson and Those Extraordinary Twins.
Hartford, 1899: The American Publishing Company.
Volume XIV of
The Writings of Mark Twain.
Autograph Edition of
the Edition de Luxe.
Three-quarter morocco.

Pudd'nhead Wilson and Those Extraordinary Twins.
Hartford, 1899: The American Publishing Company.
Volume XIV of
The Writings of Mark Twain.
Edition de Luxe.
Set #54 of 1000.
Uses the same plates as the
Autograph Edition.
Green cloth.

Pudd'nhead Wilson and Those Extraordinary Twins.
New York and London, (1899, actually no earlier than 1909 and no later than January, 1912): Harper & Brothers Publishers.
Red cloth.

Pudd'nhead Wilson and Those Extraordinary Twins.
New York and London, 1904: Harper & Brothers.
Harper's Library Edition.
Purple cloth.

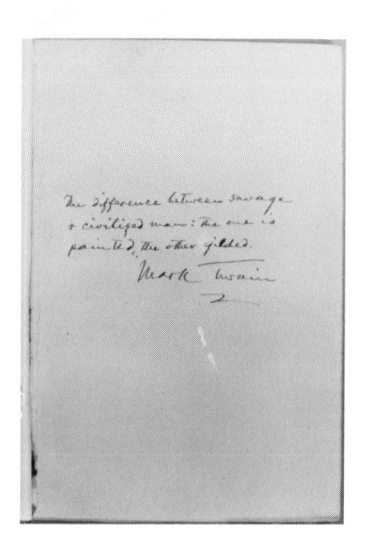

Pudd'nhead Wilson.
New York, 1904: Harper & Brothers Publishers.
    Volume XIV of
    The Writings of Mark Twain.
    Hillcrest Edition.
    Three-quarter morocco.
    Inscribed copy:
    The difference between savage/&
    civilized man: The one is/painted, the
    other gilded./Mark Twain.
    (*Notebook*, p. 392, a major variant)

Pudd'nhead Wilson and Those Extraordinary Twins.
New York and London, (1915): Harper & Brothers
    Publishers.
    Volume XIV of
    The Writings of Mark Twain.
    Author's National Edition.
    Red cloth.

Pudd'nhead Wilson and Those Extraordinary Twins.
New York and London, (1919): Harper & Brothers
    Publishers.
    Limp leather edition.
    Red leather with dustjacket.

Pudd'nhead Wilson and Those Extraordinary Twins.
New York and London, (1919): Harper and Brothers
    Publishers.
    Volume XIV of
    The Writings of Mark Twain.
    Author's National Edition.
    Green cloth.

Pudd'nhead Wilson and Those Extraordinary Twins.
New York and London, (1927): Harper & Brothers
    Blue cloth.

Pudd'nhead Wilson and Those Extraordinary Twins.
New York, 1929: Harper & Brothers.
>Volume 16 of
>The Stormfield Edition of
>The Writings of Mark Twain.
>Set #212 of 1024.
>Appreciation by E.V. Lucas.
>Introduction by Albert
>Bigelow Paine.
>Blue cloth stamped in gold.

Pudd'nhead Wilson.
New York, (1955): Grove Press, Inc.
>Introduction by F. R. Leavis.
>"Eleventh printing" (first was in 1955).
>Pictorial paper wrappers.

Pudd'nhead Wilson.
New York, 1964: Bantam Books.
>Introduction by Langston Hughes.
>#FC252; price 50¢.
>"5th printing June 1964" (first was November 1959).
>Pictorial paper wrappers.

Pudd'nhead Wilson.
New York, (1966): Airmont Publishing Company, Inc.
>Introduction by Francis R. Gemme.
>Classics Series #CL124, price 50¢.
>Pictorial paper wrappers.

Pudd'nhead Wilson and Those Extraordinary Twins.
San Francisco, (1968): Chandler Publishing Company.
>A Facsimile of the first edition.
>With an introduction, note on the text and bibliography by Frederick Anderson.
>Paper wrappers.

Pudd'nhead Wilson and Pudd'nhead Wilson's Calendar.
Avon, Conn. (1974): The Heritage Press.
>Introduction by Edward Wagenknecht.
>Illustrated by John Groth.
>Pictorial paper over boards with leather spine and slipcase.

"This series of 7 photographs registers with scientific precision, stage by stage, the progress of a moral purpose through the mind of the human race's Oldest Friend. SLC Aug. 29/06." Dublin, New Hampshire.

"No. 1 *Shall* I learn to be good? . . . I will sit here and think it over."

"No. 2 There do seem to be so many diffi..."

"No. 3 And yet if I should *really* try..."

"No. 4 . . . . and I just put my whole heart in it . . ."

"No. 5 . . . . But then I couldn't break the Sab . . ."

"No. 6 . . . . and there's *so* many
other privileges
that . . . perhaps . . ."

"No. 7 Oh, never mind, I reckon
I'm good enough just as I am."

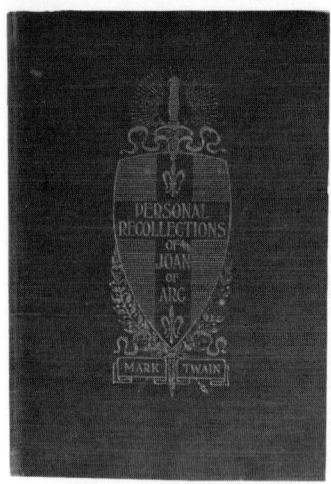

Personal Recollections of Joan of Arc.
New York, 1896: Harper & Brothers Publishers.
First issue with (463): *The Abbey Shakespeare*; and *Memoirs of Barras* described as in four volumes, I-II at *$3.75 each* and III-IV *just ready*.
Illustrated by F.Y. DuMond.

BAL 3446   Red cloth: three copies.

Personal Recollections of Joan of Arc.
New York, 1896: Harper & Brothers Publishers.
Red cloth.
First issue.
Inscribed by Ida Langdon:
Ida Langdon/Fisher's Island./July the twenty-second./1896.

Personal Recollections of Joan of Arc.
London, 1896: Chatto & Windus, Piccadilly.
>First English edition.
>Blue pictorial cloth.
>Inscribed copy:
>*Colonel Swinton Jacob./Now if I could only foregather/with you again! There is no/such good fortune for me;/but neither I nor the rest/will forget that we have had/that privilege once./Sincerely yours/Mark Twain/London, January, 1897.*

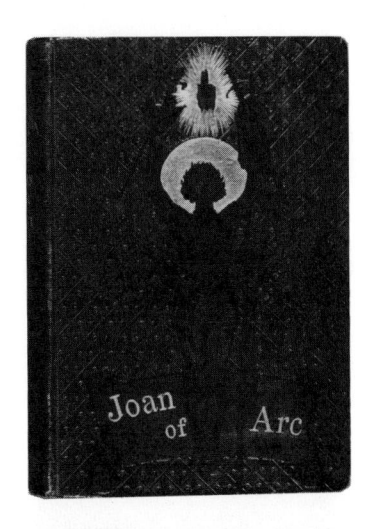

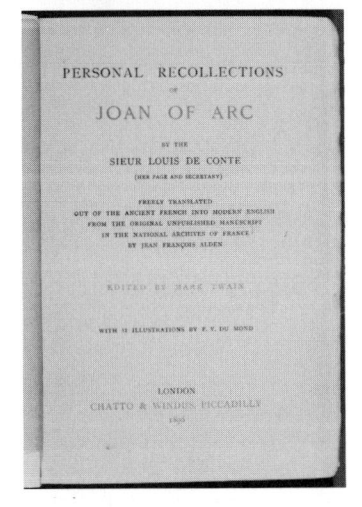

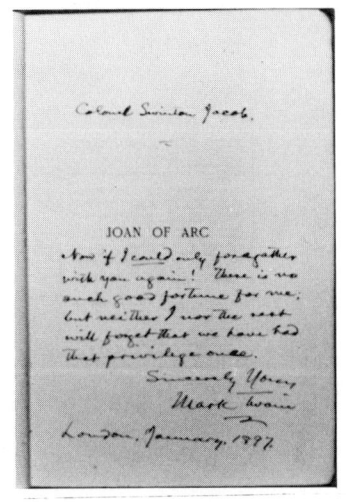

Personal Recollections of Joan of Arc.
New York and London, (1896, actually no eariler than 1909 and no later than January 1912): Harper & Brothers Publishers.
From the "Uniform Edition."
Last listed title on copyright page: *Is Shakespeare Dead?* (1909).
Red cloth.

Personal Recollections of Joan of Arc.
Hartford, 1899: The American Publishing Company.
Volumes XVII & XVIII of The Writings of Mark Twain.
Autograph Edition of the Edition de Luxe.
Three-quarter morocco.

Personal Recollections of Joan of Arc.
Hartford, 1899: American Publishing Company.
Volume XVII & XVIII of The Writings of Joan of Arc.
Edition de Luxe.
Set #54 of 1000.
Uses the same plates as the Autograph edition.
Green cloth.

Personal Recollections of Joan of Arc.
New York and London, 1905: Harper & Brothers Publishers.
Volume (I missing) & II.
Harper's Library Edition.
Purple cloth.

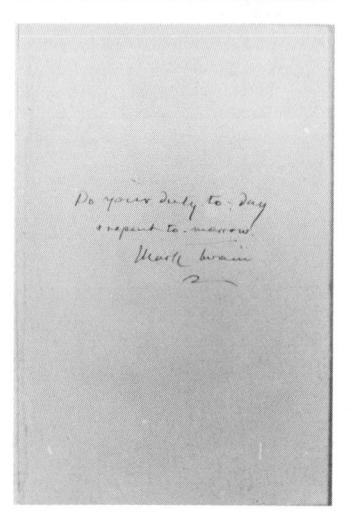

Personal Recollections of Joan of Arc.
New York, 1904: Harper & Brothers Publishers.
Volumes XVII & XVIII of The Writings of Mark Twain.
Hillcrest Edition.
Three-quarter morocco.
Volume XVII inscribed:
The trouble ain't that there is/too many fools, but that/the lightning ain't distributed/right./Mark Twain.
(*More Maxims of Mark*, p. 13)
Volume XVIII inscribed:
Do your duty to-day/& repent to-morrow./Mark Twain.
(*More Maxims of Mark*, p. 6)

Personal Recollections of Joan of Arc.
New York and London, 1906: Harper & Brothers
Publishers.
Volumes XVII & XVIII of
The Writings of Mark Twain.
Hillcrest Edition.
Green cloth.

Personal Recollections of Joan of Arc.
New York and London, (1915): Harper & Brothers
Publishers.
Volumes XVII & XVIII of
The Writings of Mark Twain.
Author's National Edition.
Red cloth.

Personal Recollections of Joan of Arc.
New York and London, (1917): Harper & Brothers
Publishers.
Red cloth.

Personal Recollections of Joan of Arc.
New York and London, (1917, 1919): Harper &
Brothers Publishers.
Volumes XVII and XVIII of
The Writings of Mark Twain.
Author's National Edition.
Green cloth.
A mismatched pair; the 1919
edition is slightly smaller.

Personal Recollections of Joan of Arc.
New York and London, (1918): Harper & Brothers
Publishers.
Volumes XVII & XVIII of
The Writings of Mark Twain.
Author's National Edition.
Green cloth: two sets.

Personal Recollections of Joan of Arc.
New York and London, (1926): Harper & Brothers
Publishers.
Two volumes in one.
Blue cloth.

Personal Recollections of Joan of Arc.
New York and London, (1925, 1927): Harper &
Brothers Publishers.
Two volumes.
Limp leather edition.
Red leather with dustjackets.
A mismatched pair with differing
Harper's date codes on the copyright
page.

Personal Recollections of Joan of Arc.
New York and London, (1926): Harper & Brothers Publishers.
Two volumes in one.
Blue cloth with dustjacket.

Personal Recollections of Joan of Arc.
New York and London, 1926: Harper & Brothers.
Illustrated by G.B. Cutts.
First illustrated edition thus.
Black cloth with color plate on front cover.
Date code on copyright page I-A or September 1926.

Personal Recollections of Joan of Arc.
New York and London, (1927): Harper & Brothers Publishers.
Two volumes in one.
Blue cloth: two copies.

Personal Recollections of Joan of Arc.
New York, 1929: Harper & Brothers.
Volumes 17 & 18 of The Stormfield Edition of The Writings of Mark Twain.
Set #212 of 1024.
Appreciation by E.V. Lucas.
Introduction by Albert Bigelow Paine.
Blue cloth stamped in gold.

Personal Recollections of Joan of Arc.
Hartford, 1980: The Stowe-Day Foundation.
Introduction by John Seelye.
Paper wrappers.

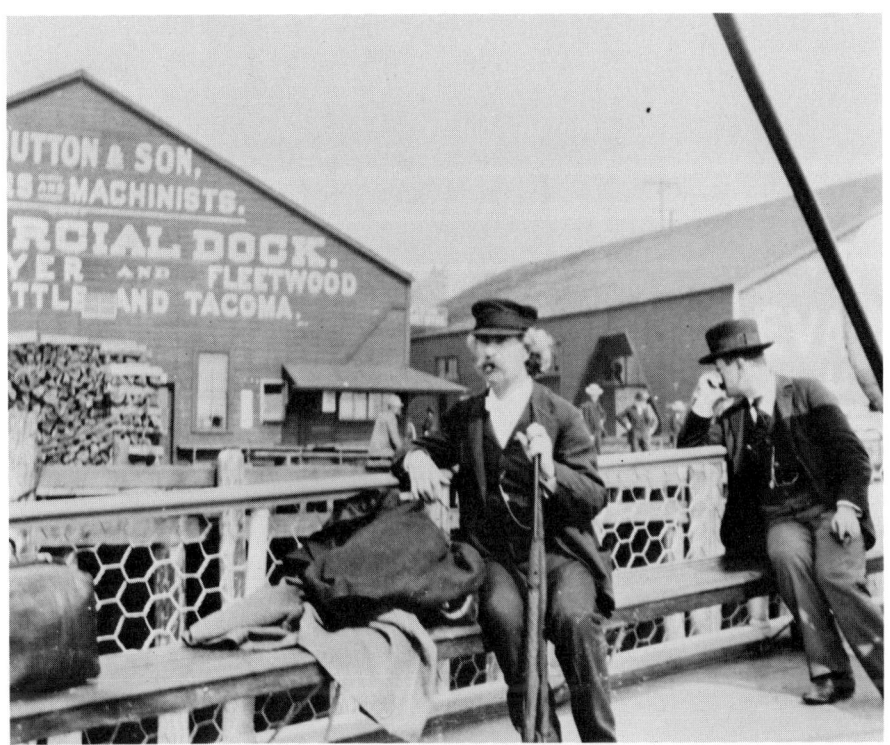

Mark Twain waiting to board the steamer Warrimoo *at Victoria, British Columbia, August 23, 1895.*

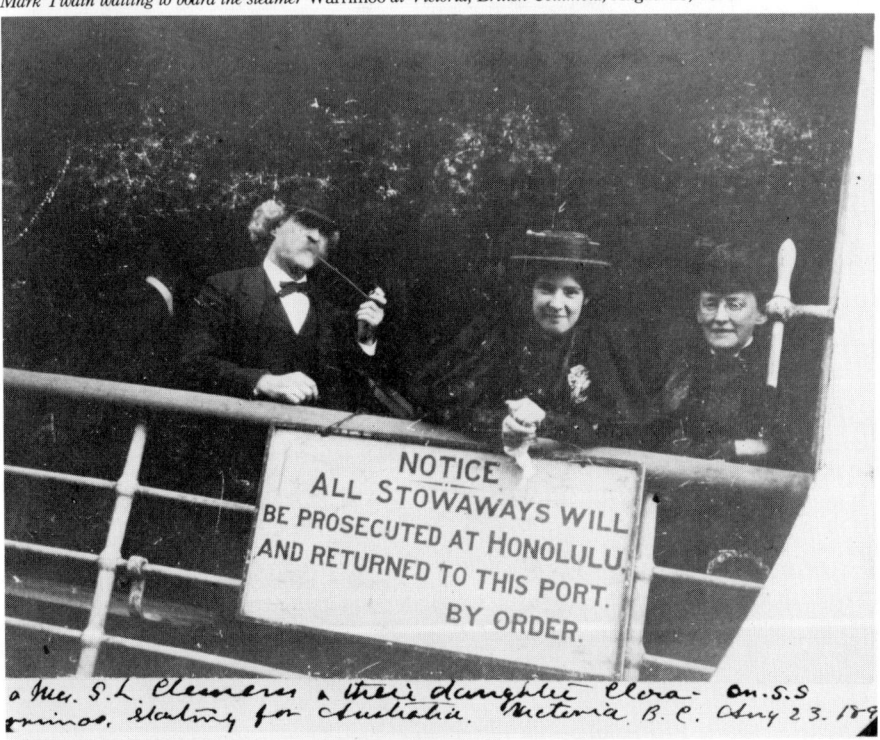

Mark Twain, Clara and Livy aboard the Warrimoo, *August 23, 1895.*

183

Mark Twain and his daughter, Clara, about 1890.

Mark Twain in 1900.

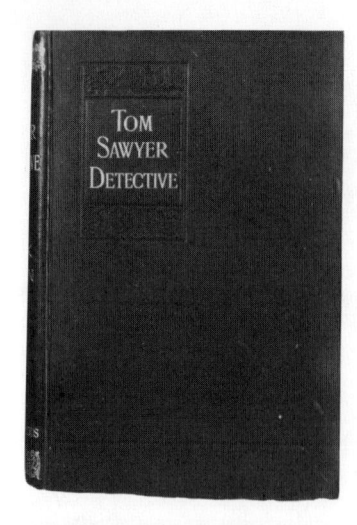

Tom Sawyer, Detective, as told by Huck Finn and Other Tales.
London, 1897: Chatto & Windus.
                First English edition.
BAL 3448   Blue cloth.

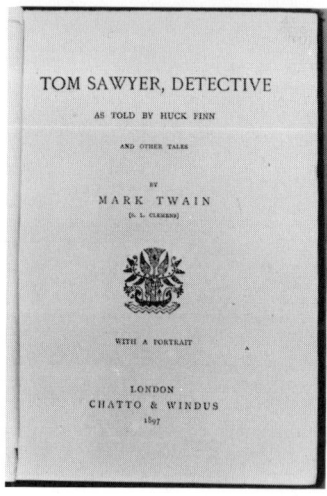

Tom Sawyer, Detective, as told by Huck Finn, and Other Tales.
London, 1901: Chatto & Windus.
        "A new edition with a portrait"
        Blue cloth.

NOTE: See other entries containing this title under *Tom Sawyer Abroad*.

Mark Twain in 1901.

Une Aventure de Tom Sawyer Detective.
(Paris, 1979): Editions Gallimard.
> In French.
> Translated by Francois de Gail.
> Illustrated by Bernard Heron.
> Cover illustrated by Paul Hogarth.
> Pictorial paper wrappers.

Tom Sawyer, Detective.
Barcelona, n.d.: Editorial Mateu.
> In Spanish.
> Adapted by Simon Santaines.
> Illustrated by Farinas.
> Pictorial paper over boards.

Tom Sawyer, En El Extranjero.
Buenos Aires, 1951: Espasa-Calpe Argentina.
> In Spanish.
> Translated by Maria Alfaro.
> #1049 Coleccion Austral.
> Paper wrappers.

Mark Twain at Dollis Hill, London, in 1900.

How to Tell a Story and Other Essays.
New York, 1897: Harper & Brothers Publishers.
BAL 3449   Red cloth.

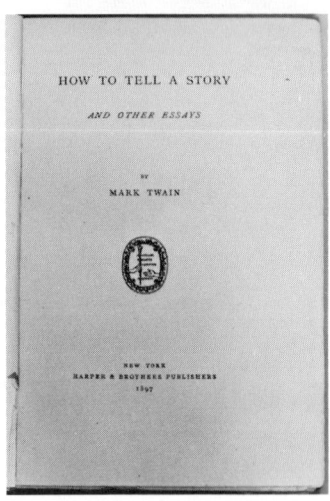

How to Tell a Story and Other Essays.
New York, (1897, actually no early than 1909
            and no later than January 1912):
            Harper & Brothers Publishers.
            Red cloth.

How to Tell a Story and Other Essays.
Hartford, 1900: The American Publishing Company.
                 Volume XXII of
                 The Writings of Mark Twain.
                 Autograph Edition of the Edition
                 de Luxe.
BAL 3458   Three-quarter morocco.

How to Tell a Story and Other Essays.
Hartford, 1900:   American Publishing Company.
      Volume XXII of
      The Writings of Mark Twain.
      Edition de Luxe.
      Set #54 of 1000.
      Uses the same plates as the
      Autograph Edition.
      Green cloth.

How to Tell a Story & Other Essays.
New York, 1904: Harper & Brothers Publishers.
      Volume XXII of
      The Writings of Mark Twain.
      Hillcrest Edition.
      Three-quarter morocco.
      Inscribed copy (possibly by Clara):
      In literature,/imitations do not imitate./Mark Twain.
      (More Maxims of Mark, p. 8)

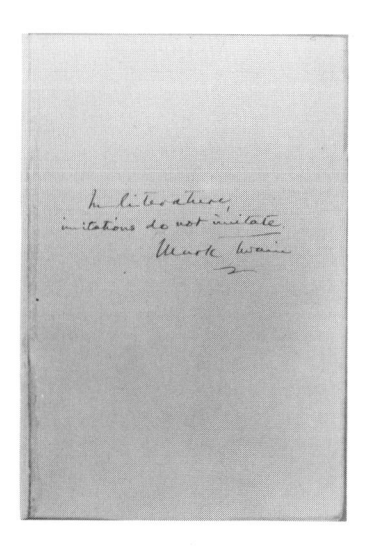

How to Tell a Story and Other Essays.
New York and London, (1917): Harper & Brothers
      Publishers.
      Red cloth.

Following the Equator. etc.
Hartford, 1897: The American Publishing Company. Publisher's prospectus.
Includes three broadsides:
1: Following the Equator. A Journey Around the World./The Surviving Innocent Abroad.
2: Mark Twain's New Book of Travel.
3: Canvass for *"Following the Equator."*
Samples of red leather and library leather binding on inside front cover.
Blue cloth: two copies.

FOLLOWING THE EQUATOR
A JOURNEY AROUND THE WORLD BY MARK TWAIN
THE SURVIVING INNOCENT ABROAD

Be good + you will be lonesome.
Mark Twain

Broadside included in the prospectus for Following the Equator.

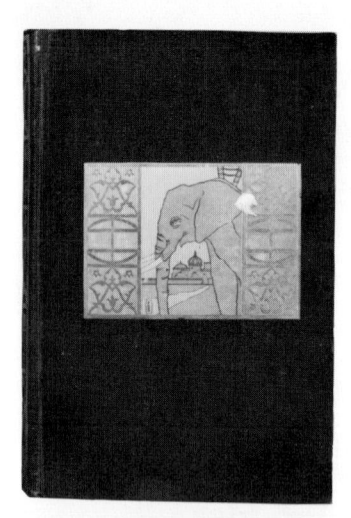

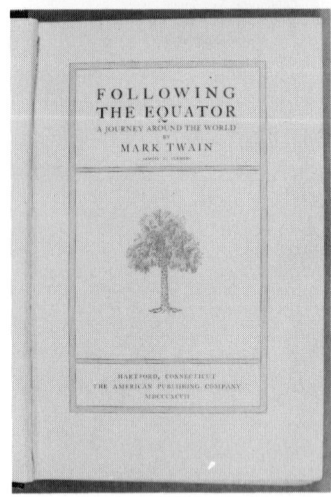

Following the Equator. A Journey Around the World.

Hartford, 1897: The American Publishing Company. Presumed first issue with Hartford only on title-page imprint.
Blue cloth: fifteen copies.

BAL 3451 Three-quarter morocco: one copy.

Following the Equator. etc.
Hartford and New York, 1897: The American Publishing Company. Doubleday & McClure.
Presumed second issue with Hartford and New York on title-page imprint.
Three-quarter blue morocco (a color not offered in the prospectus): one copy.
Blue cloth: one copy.

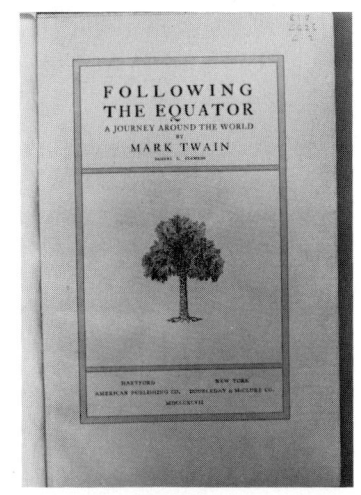

Following the Equator. etc.
Hartford, 1897: The American Publishing Company.
First issue.
With the bookplate of Rudolph Howard Krause.
Blue cloth.
Inscribed copy:
To/Mr. + Mrs. R. Howard Krause/with the kindest regards of/The Author./Vienna, Feb. 11, 1898.

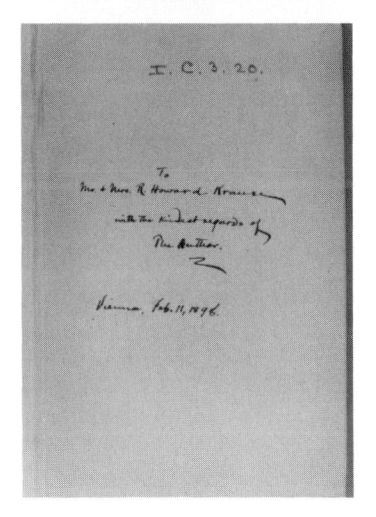

Following the Equator. etc.
Hartford, 1897: The American Publishing Company.
First issue.
Three-quarter morocco.
Inscribed copy:
Truly yours/S.L. Clemens/ Mark Twain

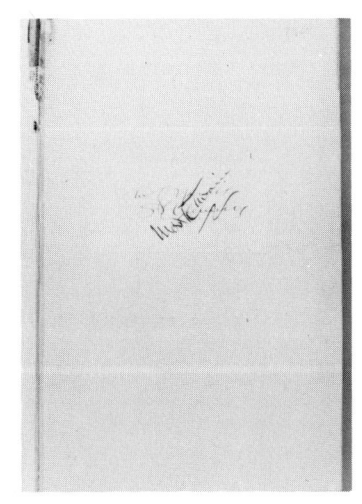

195

Following the Equator. etc.
Hartford, 1898: The American Publishing Company.
First limited signed edition.
#50 of 250.
Green cloth.
Inscribed copy:
S.L. Clemens/Mark Twain. Bound in:
Facsimile ALS by Clemens to
(T.F. Frisbie) 1897 October 25
concerning a carriage Clemens used
BAL 3451   during the trip.

Following the Equator. etc.
Hartford, 1898: The American Publishing Company.
Blue cloth: two copies.

Following the Equator. etc.
Hartford, 1899: The American Publishing Company.
Volumes V & VI of
The Writings of Mark Twain.
Autograph Edition of the Edition
de Luxe.
Bound into Volume V:
ALS from B. West Clinedinst to
Frank E. Bliss, 1¼ pp., 1899
January 19.
Bound into Volume VI:
ALS from Daniel Beard to Frank E.
Bliss, 1½ pp., 1897 November 22.
Three-quarter morocco.

Following the Equator. etc.
Hartford, 1899: American Publishing Company.
Volumes V & VI of
The Writings of Mark Twain.
Edition de Luxe.
Set #54 of 1000.
Uses the same plates as the
Autograph Edition.
Green cloth.

Following the Equator. etc.
New York and London, 1903: Harper & Brothers
Publishers.
Two volumes in one.
Red cloth.

Following the Equator.
New York, 1904: Harper & Brothers Publishers.
    Volumes V & VI of
    The Writings of Mark Twain.
    Hillcrest Edition.
    Three-quarter morocco.
    Volume V inscribed:
    The burnt child shuns the/fire until next day./Mark Twain.
    (*More Maxims of Mark Twain*, p. 6)
    Volume VI inscribed:
    Our morals are not imported/from heaven. We know it/because Government/lets them in free./Mark Twain.
    (Not located)

Following the Equator. etc.
New York and London, 1906: Harper & Brothers Publishers.
    Volumes V & VI of
    The Writings of Mark Twain.
    Hillcrest Edition. Green cloth.

Following the Equator. etc.
New York and London, (1915): Harper & Brothers Publishers.
    Volumes V & VI of
    The Writings of Mark Twain.
    Author's National Edition.
    Red cloth.

Following the Equator. etc.
New York and London, (1918): Harper & Brothers Publishers.
    Volumes V & VI of
    The Writings of Mark Twain.
    Author's National Edition.
    Green cloth.

Following the Equator. etc.
New York and London, (1923): Harper & Brothers Publishers.
    Two volumes in one.
    Blue cloth: two copies.

Following the Equator. etc.
New York and London, (1925): Harper & Brothers. Publishers.
    Two volumes in one. Blue cloth.

Following the Equator. etc.
New York, 1929: Harper & Brothers.
    Volumes 20 & 21 of
    The Stormfield Edition of
    The Writings of Mark Twain.
    Set #212 of 1024. Blue cloth stamped in gold.
    Appreciation by William McFee.
    Introduction by Albert Bigelow Paine.

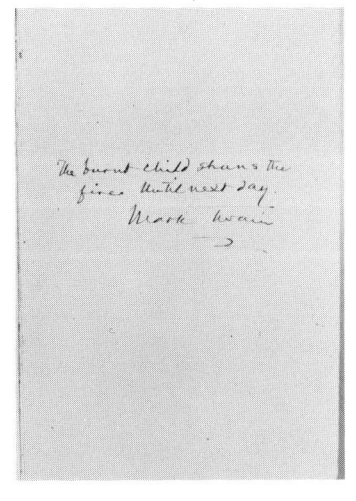

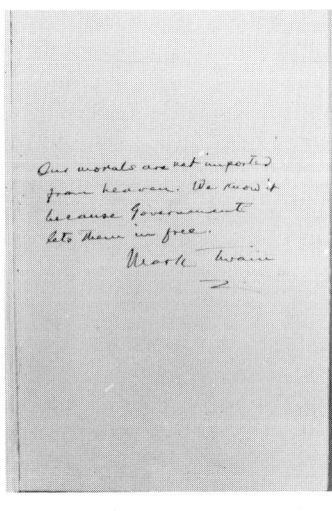

Mark Twain, near Dollis Hill, London, 1900.

Mark Twain with a friend, a dog, Clara and Livy Clemens at Dollis Hill, London, in 1900.

More Tramps Abroad.
London, 1897: Chatto & Windus.
> First English edition of *Following the Equator*.
> Maroon cloth.
> Halftitle signed:

BAL 3453 *J.S. Sherwood/Dec 97.*

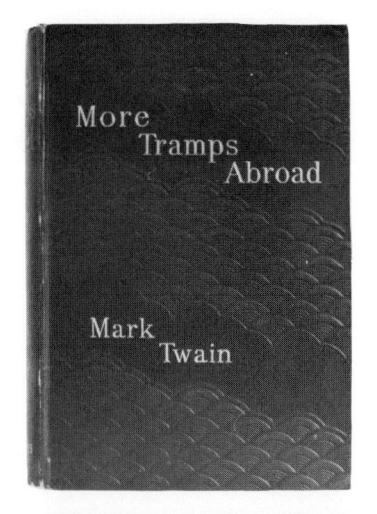

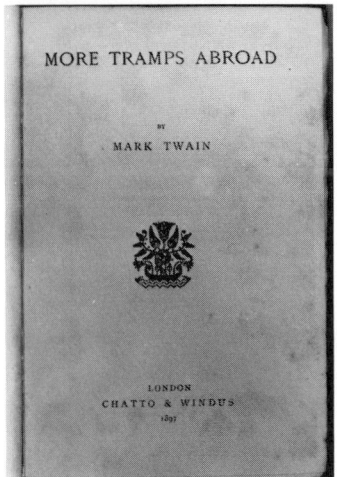

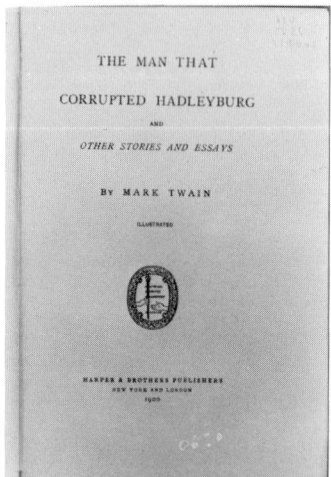

The Man That Corrupted Hadleyburg and Other Stories and Essays.
New York and London, 1900: Harper & Brothers Publishers.

BAL 3459

Third issue with sheets bulk about 1 1/4" and *Page 2* absent from plate opposite page 2.
Red cloth.

Mark Twain at Tyringham, Massachusetts, 1904, photographed by Joseph Gaylord Gessford, New York society photographer.

The Man That Corrupted Hadleyburg and Other Stories and Sketches.
London, 1900: Chatto & Windus.
          First English edition.
          Frontispiece by Lucius Hitchock.
BAL 3460   Orange pictorial cloth.

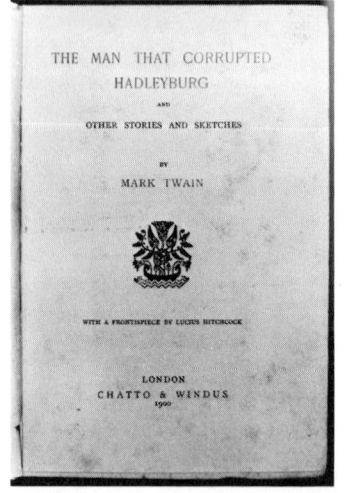

The Man That Corrupted Hadleyburg. etc.
London, 1900: Chatto & Windus.
          First English edition.
          Orange pictorial cloth.
          Inscribed copy:
To/Mr. Spalding/with the kindest regards of/The Author/London, Sept. 2, 1900.
          Bookplate of Frederick R. Kirkland.
            Included:
          1: TL from Kirkland, 1958 December 2, to *"the gentleman that is taking Wector's place in the Mark Twain division."*
          2: TLS from Frederick Anderson to Kirkland, 1958 December 12, concerning the identity of *"Mr. Spalding"* (an *"Englishman"*)
          3: TL from Kirkland to Walter Bliss on the same subject.

Mark Twain at Dollis Hill, London, 1900.

The Man That Corrupted Hadleyburg. etc.
New York and London, 1902: Harper & Brothers
 Publishers.
 Red cloth: two copies.

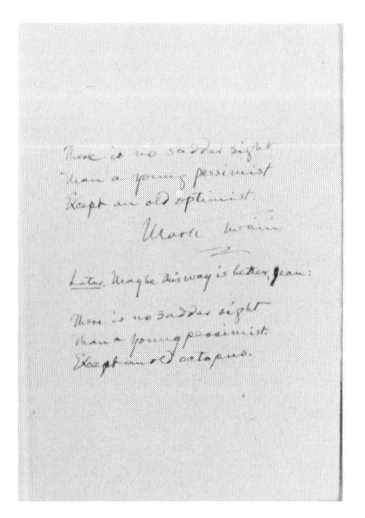

The Man That Corrupted Hadleyburg. etc.
New York, 1904: Harper & Brothers Publishers.
 Volume XXIII of
 The Writings of Mark Twain.
 Hillcrest Edition.
 Three-quarter morocco.
 Inscribed copy:
 *There is no sadder sight/than a young pessimist./Except an old optimist. */ Mark Twain/Later. Maybe this way is better, Jean:/There is no sadder sight/ Than a young pessimist./Except an old octopus.*
 (* — Mark Twain's Notebook, p. 385)

The Man That Corrupted Hadleyburg. etc.
New York and London, 1906: Harper & Brothers
 Publishers.
 Harper's Library Edition.
 Purple cloth.

The Man That Corrupted Hadleyburg. etc.
New York and London, (1915): Harper & Brothers
 Publishers.
 Volume XXIII of
 The Writings of Mark Twain.
 Author's National Edition.
 Red cloth.

The Man That Corrupted Hadleyburg. etc.
New York and London, (1918): Harper & Brothers
        Publishers.
        Volume XXIII of
        The Writings of Mark Twain.
        Author's National Edition.
        Green cloth.

The Man That Corrupted Hadleyburg. etc.
New York and London, (1926): Harper & Brothers
        Publishers.
        Blue cloth: two copies.

Mark Twain's The Man That Corrupted Hadleyburg.
Franklin, Ohio, 1976: Eldredge Publishing Co.
        "A Dramatization in Two Acts"
        Written by Richard W. Harris and
        Edgar L. Kloten.
        Yellow paper.

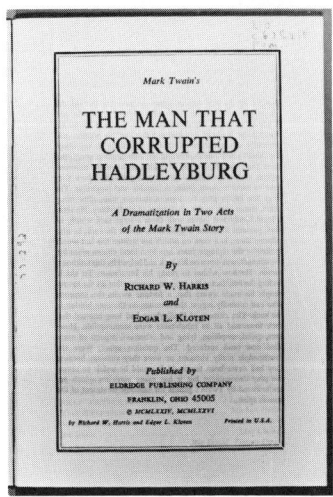

El Hombre Que Corrompio A Una Ciudad.
Buenos-Aires, (1947): Espasa-Calpe Argentina, S.A.
>>In Spanish.
>>Translated by Leon Mirlas.
>>First edition thus.
>>Coleccion Austral.
>>Paper wrappers: two copies.

El Hombre Que Corrompio A Una Ciudad.
Madrid, 1967: Espasa-Calpe, S.A.
>>In Spanish.
>>Translated by Leon Mirlas.
>>Third edition.
>>Paper wrappers.

Mark Twain in 1900.

English As She Is Taught.
London, 1887: T. Fisher Unwin.
                Commentary by Clemens.
BAL 3420   Cloth.

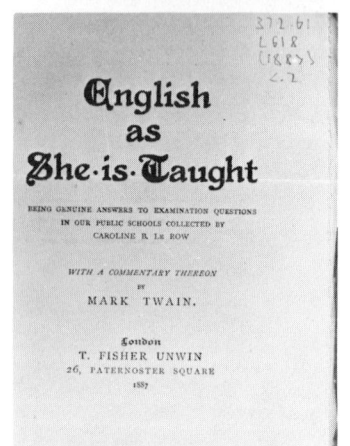

English As She Is Taught.
Boston, (1900):   Mutual Book Company.
                    With a biographical sketch of the
                    author by Matthew Irving Lans.
BAL 3465   Printed paper wrappers.

English As She Is Taught.
Boston, (1887, actually c. 1917): The A.M. Davis Co.,
                Publishers.
BAL 3645   Pictorial paper wrappers.

To the Person Sitting in Darkness.
(New York, 1901: Anti-Imperialist League of
        New York.)
             "Reprinted by permission from
                the North American Review,
                February, 1901."
BAL 3470   Paper self-wrappers: two copies.

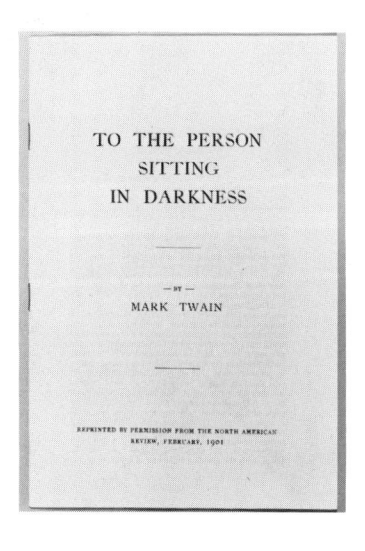

To the Person Sitting in Darkness and
Concerning the Rev. Mr. Ament.
Privately printed, 1926.
              #184 of 250 copies.
              One page anonymous introduction.
BAL 3698   Brown wrappers.

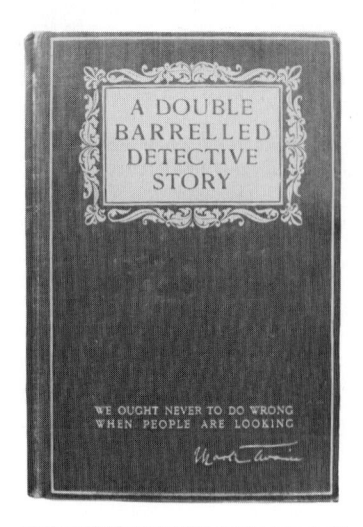

A Double Barrelled Detective Story.
New York and London, 1902: Harper & Brothers Publishers.
Illustrated by Lucius Hitchcock.
BAL 3471   Red cloth: four copies.

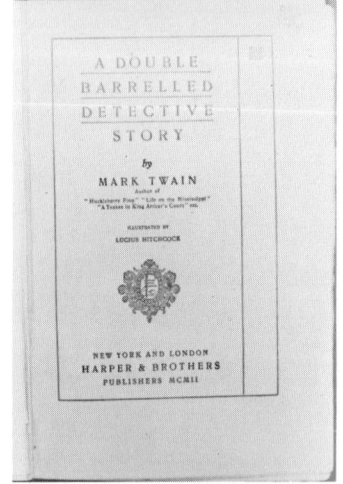

A Double Barrelled Detective Story.
Evanston, Ill., 1954: Row, Peterson & Co.
"A Mystery Comedy in three acts adapted for the stage and with a note by Robert St. Clair. Manuscript editing and general revisions by Verne E. Powers."
Red cloth with dustjacket.

My Debut as a Literary Person with Other Essays and Stories.
Hartford, 1903: The American Publishing Company.
Volume XXIII of
The Writings of Mark Twain.
Autograph Edition of the
Edition de Luxe.
Bound in:
ALS from Francis Luis Mora to
Bliss, 1 p., 1902 July 31
BAL 3476 Three-quarter morocco.

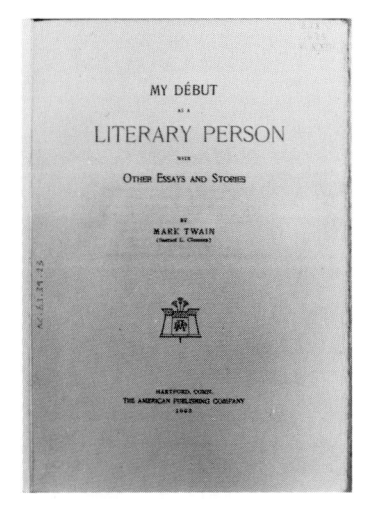

My Debut as a Literary Person. etc.
Hartford, 1903: The American Publishing Company.
Volume XXIII of
The Writings of Mark Twain.
Edition de Luxe.
Set #54 of 1000.
Uses the same plates as the
Autograph Edition.
Green cloth.

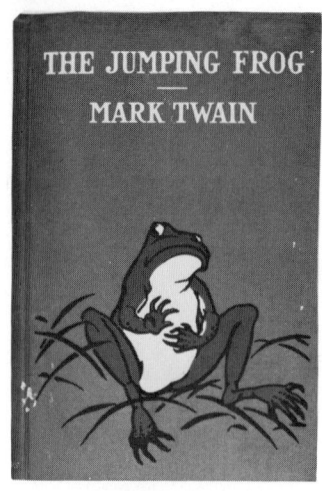

The Jumping Frog in English, Then in French, Then Clawed Back into a Civilized Language Once More by Patient Unremunerated Toil.
New York and London, 1903: Harper & Brothers Publishers.
Illustrated by F. Strothman.
BAL 3477   Red pictorial cloth: two copies.

The Jumping Frog. etc.
New York and London, 1903: Harper & Brothers Publishers.
Illustrated by F. Strothman.
Full leather with diamond-shaped panels (on front and back covers) which looks suspiciously like leopard frog skin.
Includes:
On notepaper of the Express Printing Company, Buffalo, an inscription:
With pleasure/Yrs truly/Saml. L. Clemens/"Mark Twain"/Jno. H. Gourlie, Esq.

The Notorious Jumping Frog of Calaveras County.
New York, 1932: Philip C. Duschnes.
Paper over boards.

Mark Twain at the Quarry Farm study, 1903.

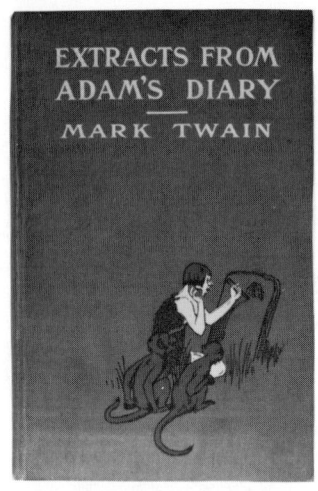

Extracts from Adam's Diary Translated from the Original MS.
New York and London, 1904: Harper & Brothers Publishers.
Illustrated by F. Strothman.
BAL 3480   Red pictorial cloth: two copies.

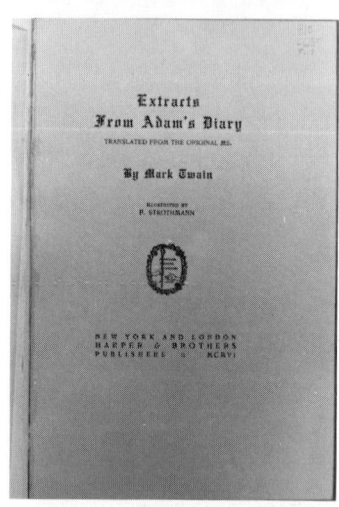

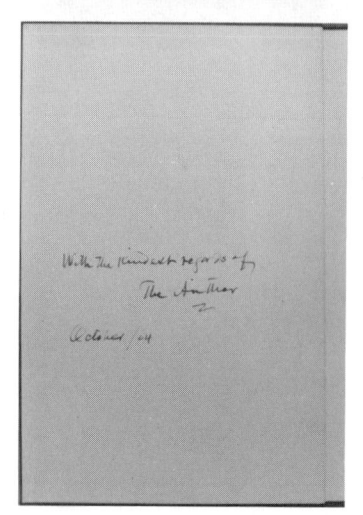

Extracts from Adam's Diary. etc.
New York and London, 1904: Harper & Brothers Publishers.
Illustrated by F. Strothman.
Red pictorial cloth with dustjacket.
Inscribed copy:
With the kindest regards of/The Author/October/04.

Extracts from Adam's Diary. etc.
New York and London, 1906: Harper & Brothers.
                Red pictorial cloth: four copies.

Extracts from Adam's Diary. etc.
New York and London, (1914): Harper & Brothers
                Publishers.
                Red pictorial cloth.

Fragmentos del Diario de Adan y Diario de Eva.
Buenos Aires, (1947): Espasa-Calpe Argentina, S.A.
                In Spanish.
                Translated by Leon Mirlas.
                First edition thus.
                Coleccion Austral.
                Paper wrappers.

Fragmentos del Diario de Adan y Diario de Eva.
Madrid, 1961: Espasa-Calpe, S.A.
                In Spanish.
                Translated by Leon Mirlas.
                Third edition.
                Paper wrappers.

A Dog's Tale.
New York and London, 1904: Harper & Brothers Publishers.
Illustrated by W.T. Smedley.
BAL 3483   Red pictorial cloth.

A Dog's Tale.
New York and London, 1904: Harper & Brothers Publishers.
Illustrated by W.T. Smedley.
Red pictorial cloth.
Inscribed copy:
To Ida Langdon/with the love of her uncle/The Author./Sept. 22/04.

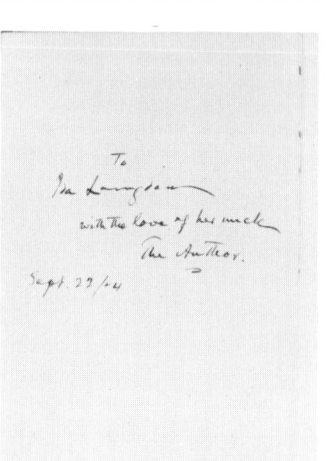

A Dog's Tale.
(London, 1903, actually 1904):
"Reprinted by permission from Harper's Magazine Christmas Number, 1903 by Mark Twain"
BAL 3479   Paper wrappers.

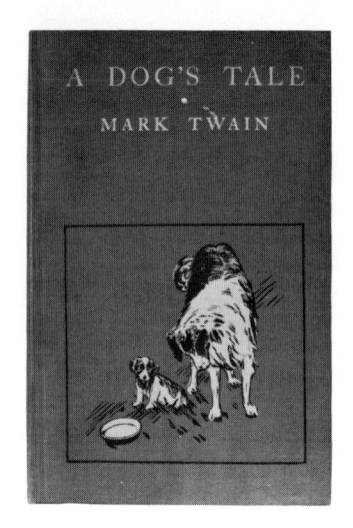

A Dog's Tale.
New York and London, 1905: Harper & Brothers Publishers.
Illustrated by W.T. Smedley.
Red pictorial cloth.

A Dog's Tale.
New York and London, (1920): Harper & Brothers Publishers.
Red pictorial cloth.

An Unexpected Acquaintance.
New York and London, (1904): Harper & Brothers.
Publishers.
Reprinted from *A Tramp Abroad.*
First separate edition.
BAL 3664   Paper self-wrappers: two copies.

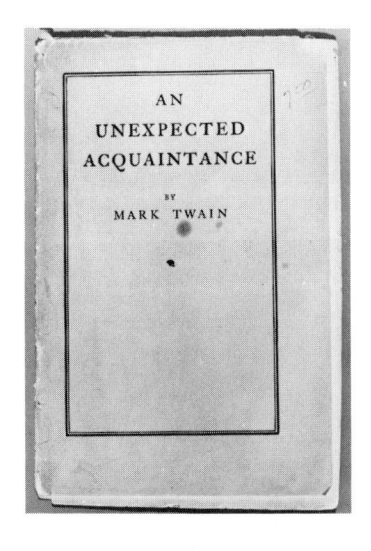

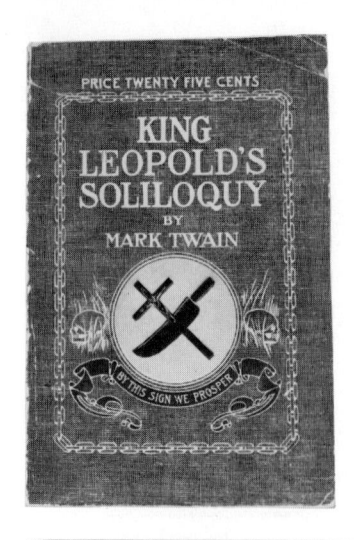

King Leopold's Soliloquy. A defense of his Congo rule.
Boston, 1905: The P.R. Warren Co.
                Second edition, with those words on the title page.
BAL 3485   Pictorial paper wrappers.

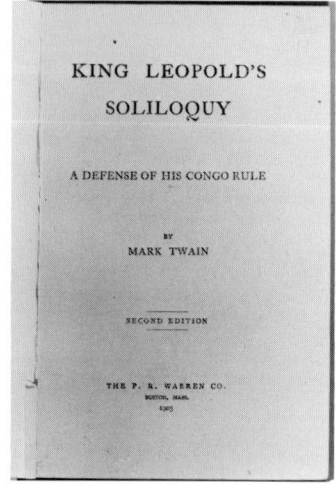

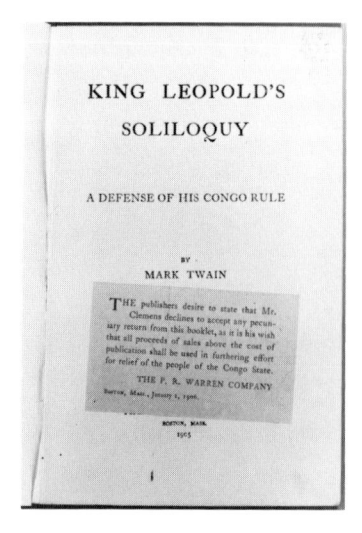

Editorial Wild Oats.
New York and London, 1905: Harper and Brothers
   Publishers.
   Illustrated by F. Strothman.
   Frontispiece by F. Opper.
BAL 3665   Red pictorial cloth.

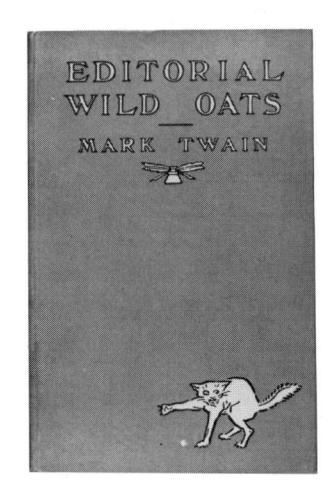

Editorial Wild Oats.
New York and London, 1905: Harper & Brothers
   Publishers.
   Red pictorial cloth with dustjacket.
   Inscribed in an unknown hand:
   First Edition/Autographed and Dated by/Mark Twain/on His Seventieth Birthday.
   Inscribed by Clemens on a bookplate of the Bryn Mawr Book Fair:
   Truly yours/Mark Twain/Nov. 30, 1905/b. "30, 1835.

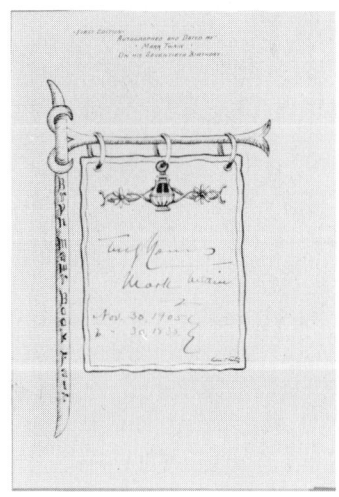

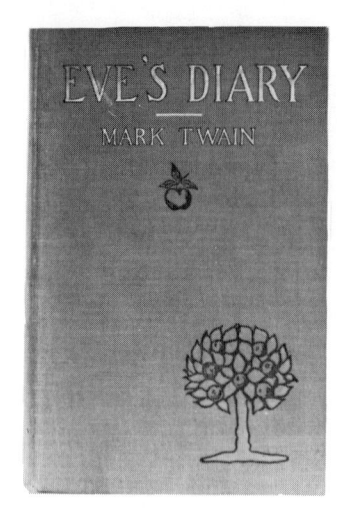

Eve's Diary Translated from the Original MS.
London and New York, 1906: Harper & Brothers
          Publishers.
          Illustrated by Lester Ralph.
BAL 3489   Red pictorial cloth: five copies.

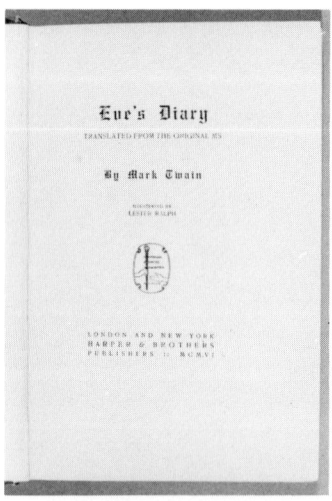

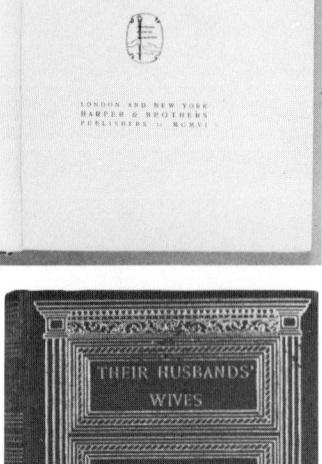

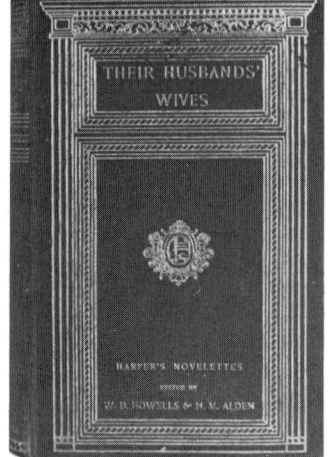

"Eve's Diary"
New York and London, 1906: Harper & Brothers
          Publishers.
          "In Their Husband's Wives.
          Harper's Novelettes."
          Edited by William Dean Howells and
          Henry Mills Alden.
          Pages (1)-27.
BAL 3488   Olive green cloth.

Eve's Diary Translated from the Original MS.
London and New York, 1906: Harper & Brothers Publishers.
Red pictorial cloth.
Inscribed copy:
Dear Mrs. Whitmore—/This-/With the compliments of/The Authoress/ + the love of/The Translator./Dublin, N.H., June 25/06.

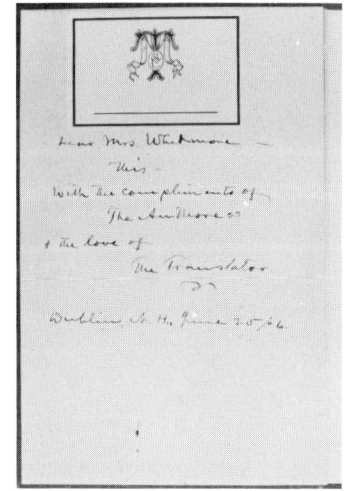

Eve's Diary Translated from the Original MS.
London and New York, 1906: Harper & Brothers Publishers.
Red pictorial cloth.
Inscribed copy:
Mrs. Harry Rogers, jr/with the compliments of/The Authoress/ + the kind regards of/The Translator./July 4/06.

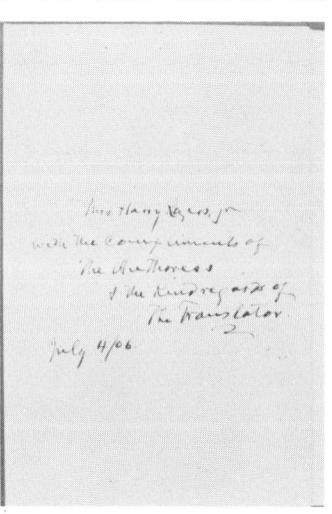

Eve's Diary Translated from the Original MS.
London and New York, 1906: Harper & Brothers Publishers.
Red pictorial cloth.
Front flyleaf is inscribed with the emblem and names of the Saturday Morning Club of Hartford (1906).

Eve's Diary Translated from the Original MS.
New York and London, (1920): Harper & Brothers Publishers.
Red cloth.

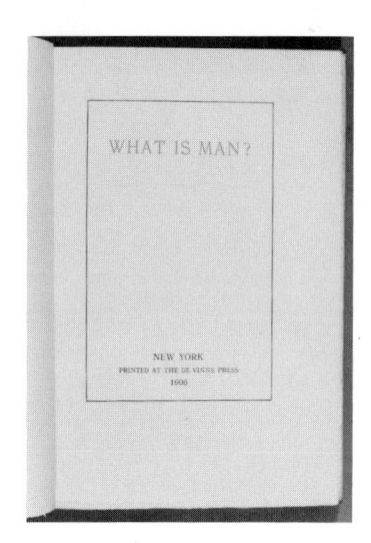

What is Man?
New York, 1906: DeVinne Press.
    Written anonymously.
    Grey-blue cartridge boards: two copies, one with slipcase and tissue wrapper.
    First issue with 131 ending:
BAL 3490   *thinks about/it.*

An expanded version of this title was published by Harper & Brothers in 1917 and is BAL 3524.

What is Man?
London, 1910: Watts & Co.
    First English edition.
    First disclosure of authorship.
    Blue cloth.

Mark Twain, at billiards, on the third floor of 351 Farmington Avenue, Hartford, in 1905.

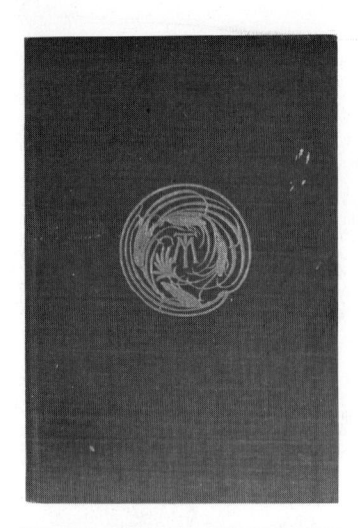

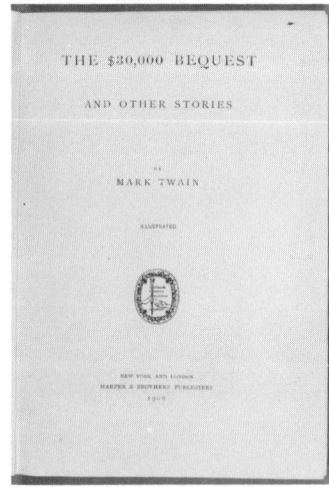

The $30,000 Bequest and Other Stories.
New York and London, 1906: Harper & Brothers Publishers.
Second issue with boxed ad on copyright page (first lacks it).
BAL 3492   Red cloth.

Mark Twain at Tuxedo, New York, 1907.

The $30,000 Bequest and Other Stories.
New York and London, (1906): Harper & Brothers
        Publishers.
        Red cloth.

The $30,000 Bequest and Other Stories.
New York and London, 1906: Harper & Brothers
        Publishers.
        Volume XXIV of
        The Writings of Mark Twain.
        Hillcrest Edition.
        Green cloth.

The $30,000 Bequest and Other Stories.
Hartford, 1907:   The American Publishing Company.
        Volume XXIV of
        The Writings of Mark Twain.
        Autograph Edition of
        the Edition de Luxe.
        "This edition is printed by Harper & Brothers, the exclusive publishers of Mark Twain's works, as an accommodation to purchasers of their earlier volumes with a view to making their sets uniform."
        Three-quarter leather.

The $30,000 Bequest and Other Stories.
Hartford, 1907: American Publishing Company.
Volume XXIV of
The Writings of Mark Twain.
Edition de Luxe.
Set #54 of 1000.
Uses the same plates as the
Autograph Edition.
Green cloth.

The $30,000 Bequest and Other Stories.
New York and London, (1915): Harper & Brothers
Publishers.
Volume XXIV of
The Writings of Mark Twain.
Author's National Edition.
Red cloth.

The $30,000 Bequest and Other Stories.
New York and London, (1918): Harper & Brothers
Publishers.
Volume XXIV of
The Writings of Mark Twain.
Author's National Edition.
Green cloth.

The $30,000 Bequest and Other Stories.
New York and London, (1927): Harper & Brothers
Publishers.
Blue cloth with dustjacket.

The $30,000 Bequest.
New York, (1929): Harper & Brothers.
Authorized Edition of
The Complete Works of Mark
Twain.
Green cloth.

The $30,000 Bequest and Other Stories.
New York, 1929: Harper & Brothers.
Volume 24 of
The Stormfield Edition of
The Writings of Mark Twain.
Set #212 of 1024.
Appreciation by E.V. Lucas.
Introduction by Albert
Bigelow Paine.
Blue cloth stamped in gold.

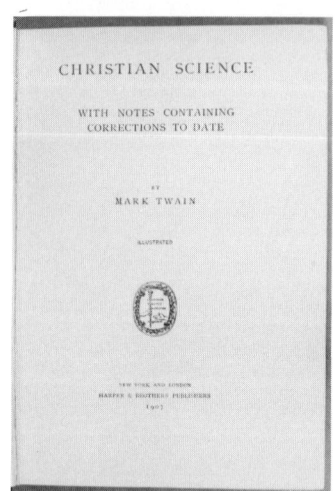

Christian Science with Notes Containing Corrections to Date.
New York and London, 1907: Harper & Brothers Publishers.
    Red cloth: three copies.
    BAL point: 1 2 3 4 5
    Copy 1:   A B* A A B
    Copy 2:   A A A B A
    Copy 3:   B B A A B
    Point 1: A: Copyright-page boxed ad lists 17 titles
               B: Ad lists 18 titles
    Point 2: A: p.(iii): type, including heading is eight lines long.
               B: Type is six lines long.
    Point 3: A: frontispiece dated (1906)
               B: frontispiece dated (1907)
    Point 4: A: 3:9: *farmhouse*
               B: 3:9: *fa mhouse*
    Point 5: A: 5:14: *W* in *Why* standard
               B: 5:14: *W* in *Why* heavy

BAL 3497

*BAL does not list this combination of 17 titles and a six-line list of illustrations.

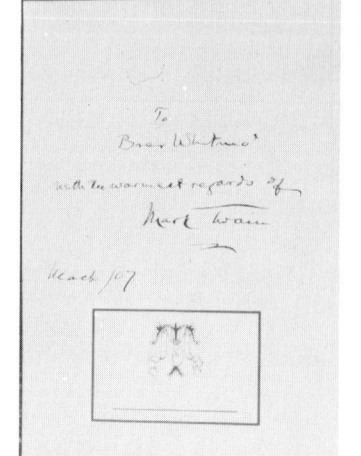

Christian Science. etc.
New York and London, 1907: Harper & Brothers Publishers.
    Red cloth.
    Same as Copy 2 (above).
    Inscribed copy:
    To/Brer Whitmo'/with the warmest regards of/Mark Twain/March/07.

A A

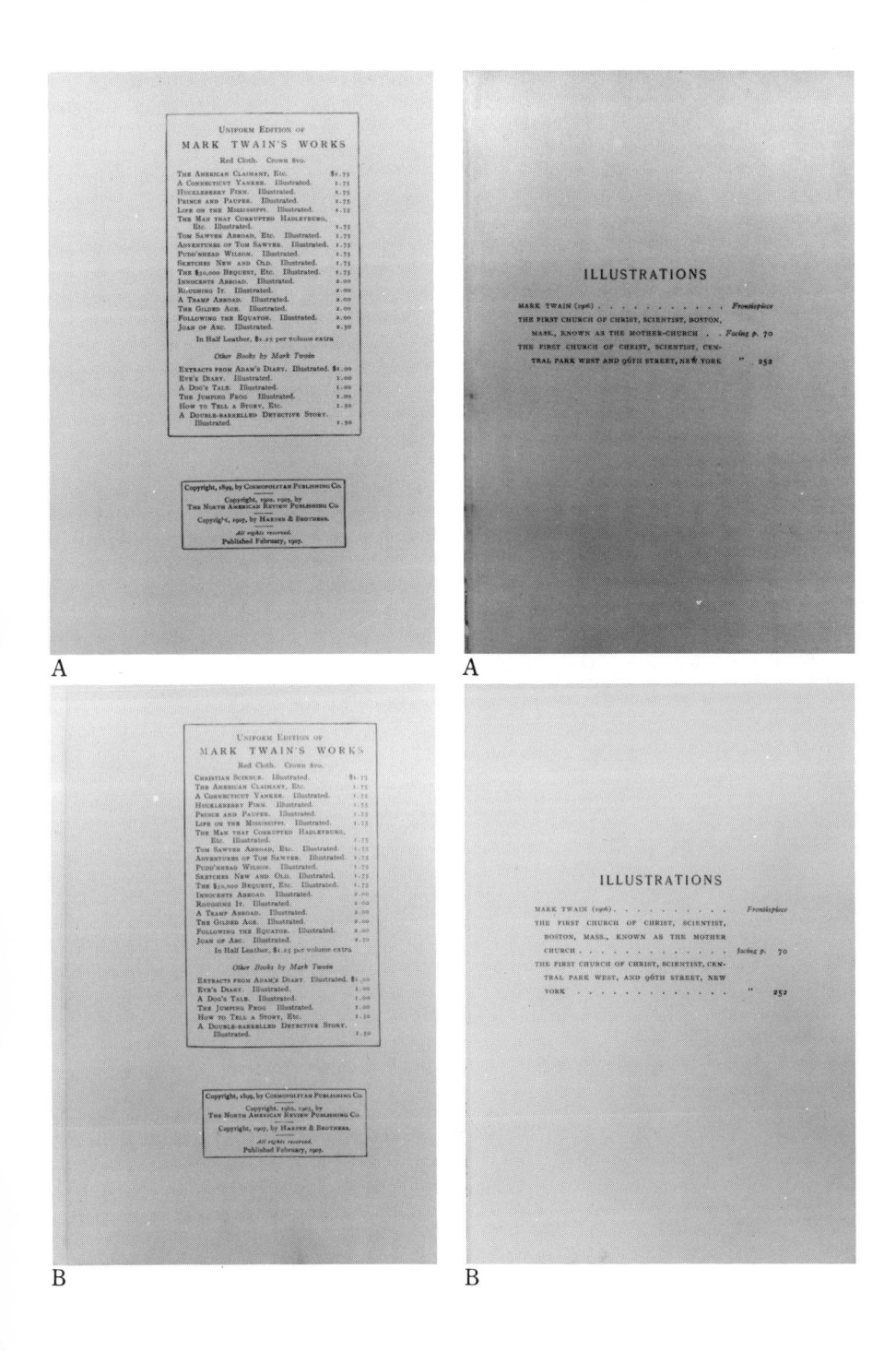

B B

BAL states that the first issue should have copyright page A and illustration list A, the second issue copyright page B and list B. Copy 1 of our collection has copyright page A and list B.

Christian Science. etc.
Hartford, 1907: The American Publishing Company.
Volume XXV of
The Writings of Mark Twain.
Autograph Edition of the Edition
de Luxe.
Actually printed by Harper &
Brothers (see note under *The
$30,000 Bequest.*).
Three-quarter morocco.

Christian Science. etc.
Hartford, 1907: The American Publishing Company.
Volume XXV of
The Writings of Mark Twain.
Edition de Luxe.
Set #54 of 1000.
Uses the same plates as the
Autograph Edition.
Green cloth.

Christian Science. etc.
New York and London, (1915): Harper & Brothers
           Publishers.
           Limp leather Edition.
           Red leather.

Christian Science. etc.
New York and London, (1917): Harper & Brothers
           Publishers.
           Volume XXV of
           The Writings of Mark Twain.
           Author's National Edition.
           Green cloth.

Christian Science. etc.
New York and London, (1918): Harper & Brothers
           Publishers.
           Volume XXV of
           The Writings of Mark Twain.
           Author's National Edition.
           Green cloth.

Christian Science. etc.
New York and London, (1924): Harper & Brothers
           Publishers.
           Blue cloth with dustjacket.

Christian Science. etc.
New York, 1929: Harper & Brothers.
           Volume 25 of
           The Stormfield Edition of
           The Writings of Mark Twain.
           Set #212 of 1024.
           Introduction by Albert
           Bigelow Paine.
           Blue cloth stamped in gold.

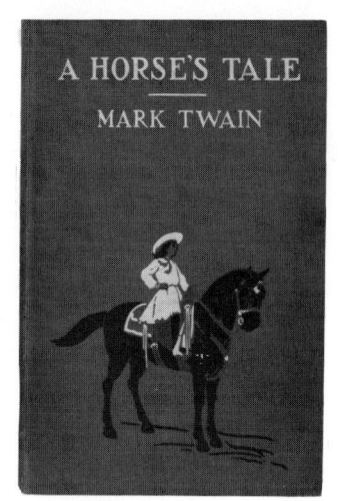

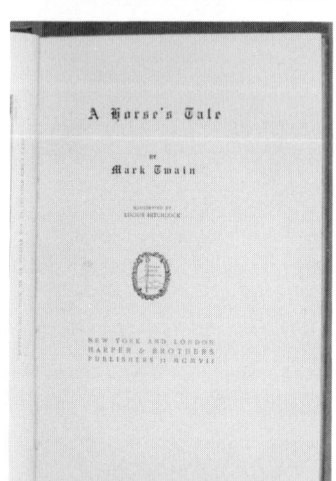

A Horse's Tale.
New York and London, 1907: Harper & Brothers Publishers.
Illustrated by Lucius Hitchcock.
Red pictorial cloth:
BAL 3500   three copies, one with dustjacket.

Is Shakespeare Dead? From My Autobiography.
New York and London, 1909: Harper & Brothers Publishers.
First issue with no inserted leaves mentioning Greenwood's *Shakespeare Problem.*
Green cloth: two copies, one with a plain brown paper unprinted dustjacket with an oval cutout at the spine title.

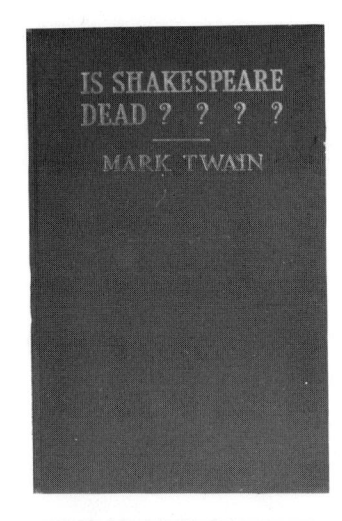

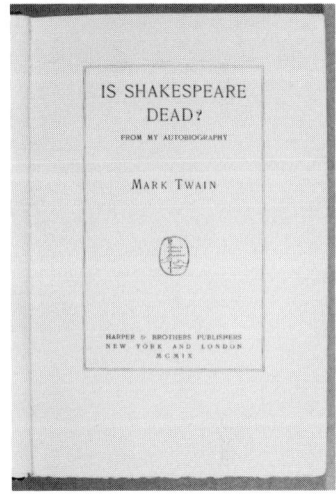

BAL 3509

Is Shakespeare Dead? From My Autobiography.
New York and London, 1909: Harper & Brothers Publishers.
Third issue with leaf mentioning Greenwood at (151).
Two copies, both rubberstamped *Printed in U.S. of America* on copyright page, thus export copies.
Green cloth.

Extract from Captain Stormfield's Visit to Heaven.
New York and London, 1909: Harper & Brothers
>Frontispiece illustrated by Albert Levering.

BAL 3511   Red pictorial cloth.

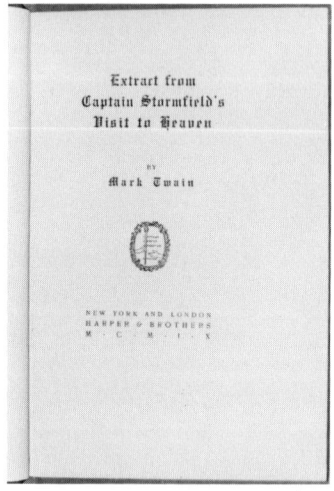

Extract from Captain Stormfield's Visit to Heaven.
New York and London, (1909): Harper & Brothers
>Publishers.
>Red pictorial cloth.

Mark Twain's Speeches.
New York and London, 1910: Harper & Brothers Publishers.
Introduction by William Dean Howells.
Compiled by F.A. Nast.

BAL 3513   Red cloth: four copies.

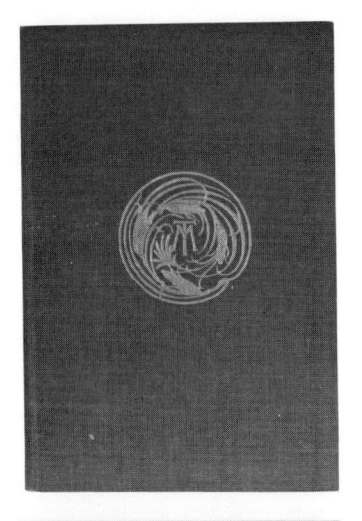

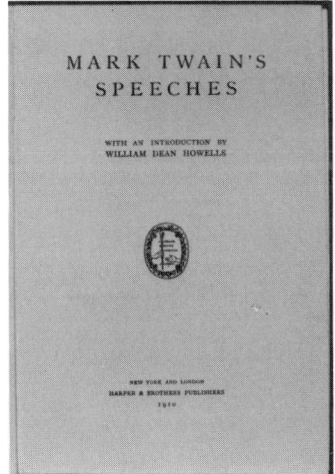

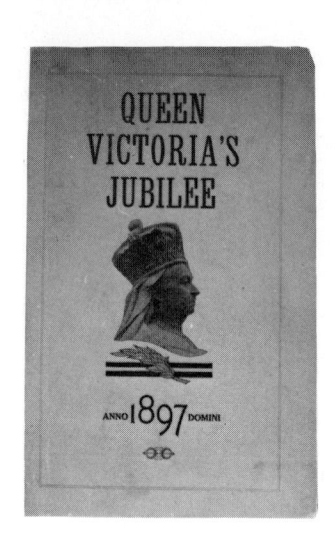

Queen Victoria's Jubilee.
Privately printed for private distribution only, (1910).
"The Great Procession of June 22, 1897, in the Queen's Honor, Reported both in the Light of History, and as a Spectacle."
Copies 62 and 181 of 195 made.
Printed white boards with cloth shelfback.

BAL 3514

Travels at Home.
New York and London, 1910 : Harper & Brothers Publishers. Selected and introduced by Percival Chubb.

BAL 3673   Green cloth.

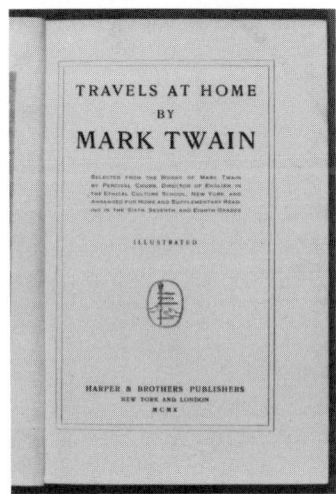

Mark Twain's Letter to the California Pioneers.
Oakland, Cal., 1911: DeWitt & Snelling.

	One page anonymous Publisher's Note.
	#298 of 750, signed *DeWitt & Snelling.*
BAL 3516	Tan paper wrappers.

Death-Disk.
New York, 1913: Edgar S. Werner.
BAL 3676   Printed wrappers: three copies.

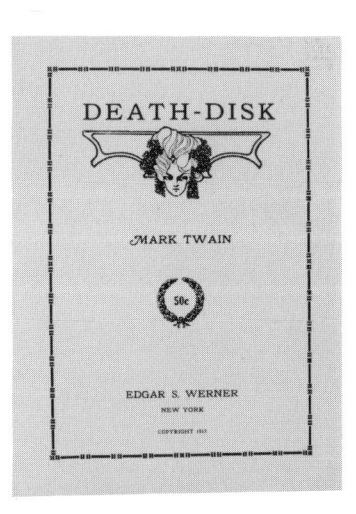

The Suppressed Chapter of "Life on the Mississippi."

n.p., n.d. (actually New York, c. 1913): no publisher.
BAL 3519   Paper wrappers.

Literary Essays.
New York and London, (1915): Harper & Brothers
           Publishers.
           Volume XXII of
           The Writings of Mark Twain.
           Author's National Edition.
           Biographical sketch by Samuel E.
           Moffett.
           Red cloth.

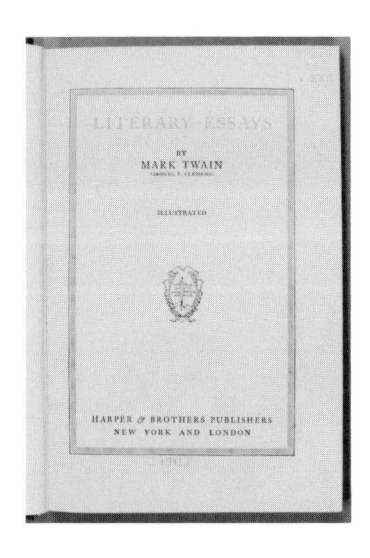

Literary Essays.
New York and London, (1918): Harper & Brothers
           Publishers.
           Volume XXII of
           The Writings of Mark Twain.
           Author's National Edition.
           Green cloth.

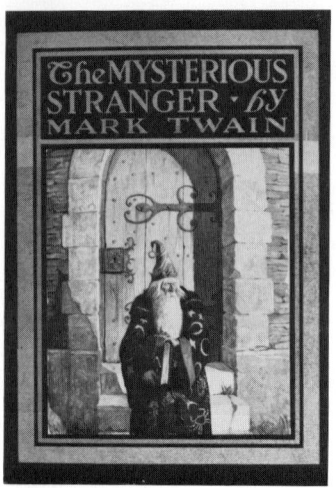

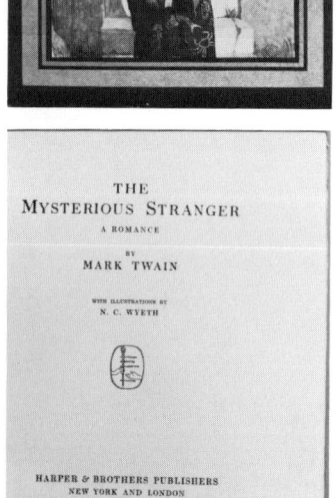

The Mysterious Stranger. A Romance.
New York and London, (1916): Harper & Brothers
Publishers.
Illustrated by N.C. Wyeth.
BAL 3520
Black cloth stamped in gold and with a color plate on the front cover.

The Mysterious Stranger. A Romance.
New York and London, (1916): Harper & Brothers
Publishers.
Illustrated by N.C. Wyeth.
A set of unbound sheets, rubber-stamped on first leaf
MYSTERIOUS STRANGER.

Who Was Sarah Findlay?
London, 1917: Privately printed by Clement Shorter.
"With a Suggested Solution of the Mystery by J.M. Barrie."
#17 of 25, signed by Shorter.
Two page prefactory by Shorter.

BAL 3523   Grey paper wrappers.

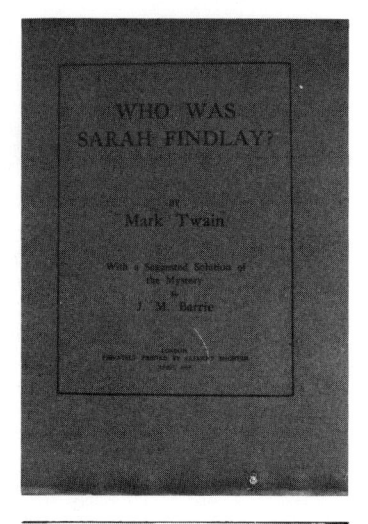

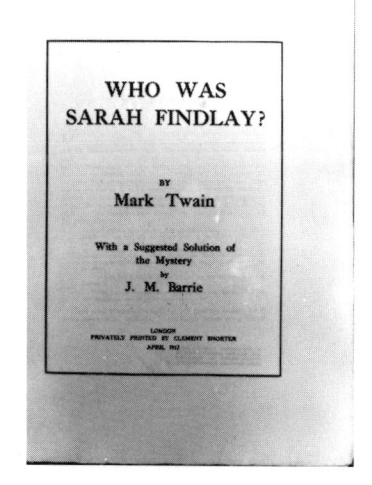

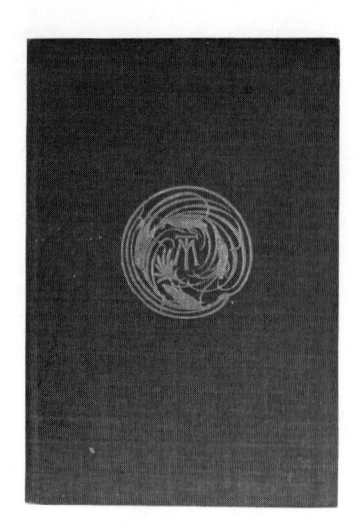

Mark Twain's Letters.
New York and London, (1917): Harper & Brothers
        Publishers.
        Two volumes.
           "Arranged with Comment by
           Albert Bigelow Paine."
BAL 3525   Red cloth: four sets.

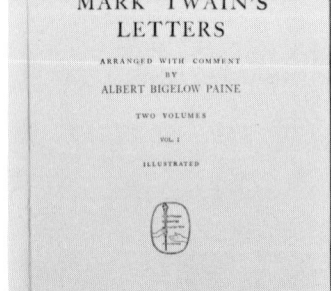

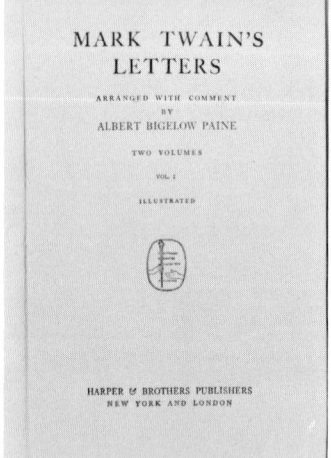

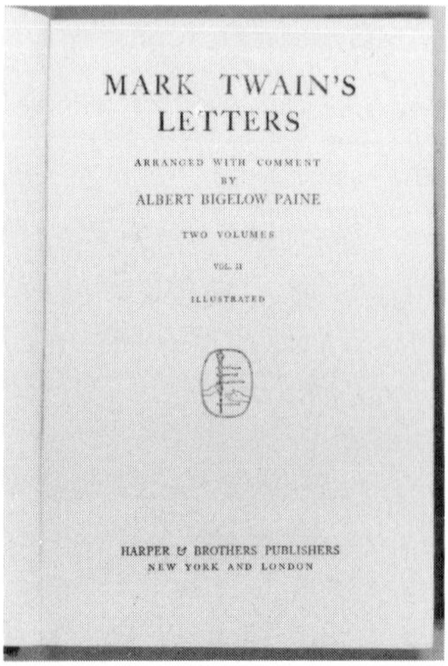

Mark Twain's Letters.
New York and London, (1917): Harper & Brothers
        Publishers.
        Two volumes.
           "Arranged with Comment by
           Albert Bigelow Paine."
        Limited edition.
        One of 350 sets "bound with uncut
        edges and paper labels."
        Tan boards with cloth shelfback.

Mark Twain's Letters.
New York and London, (1917): Harper & Brothers
Publishers.
Two volumes.
Front e.p. of Volume I is inscribed by Paine:
Dear Mr. Briggs: I am satisfied that/ Yours is the best part of this/book; certainly the hardest/to do. I grow daily more/grateful for your index./Faithfully and sincerely/Albert Bigelow Paine/Dec 4:17
Flyleaf is inscribed, likely by Isabel Lyon:
I think Paine has sacrificed/the value of these volumes to glorify. his Biography: Scraps of letters these, which/should be in full here.
Red cloth.

Mark Twain's Letters.
New York, 1929: Harper & Brothers.
Volumes 34 & 35 of
The Stormfield Edition of
The Writings of Mark Twain.
Set #212 of 1024.
Appreciation by E.V. Lucas.
Introduction by Albert Bigelow Paine.
Blue cloth stamped in gold.

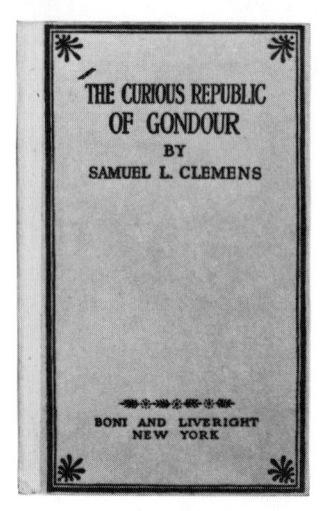

The Curious Republic of Gondour and Other Whimsical Sketches.
New York, 1919: Boni & Liveright.

BAL 3527

Rough yellow paper boards with white cloth shelfback: four copies.

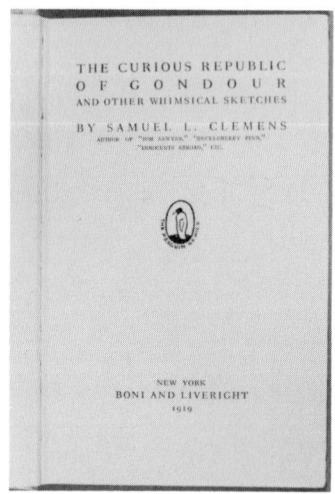

Saint Joan of Arc.
New York and London, 1919: Harper & Brothers Publishers.
Illustrated by Howard Pyle.
Main text reprinted from *The $30,000 Bequest*; the "Translator's Preface" and "Conclusion" from *Personal Recollections of Joan of Arc*.
First issue with the marginal illustration on page 18 right side up and the endpapers printed.

BAL 3683   Black cloth with color plate on cover.

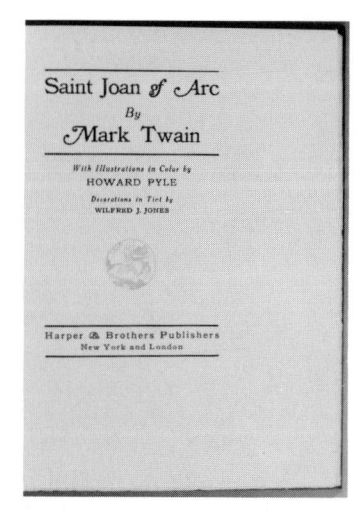

Saint Joan of Arc.
New York and London, 1919: Harper & Brothers.
Illustrated by Howard Pyle.
Second issue with marginal illustration on page 18 upside down and the endpapers plain.
Black cloth with color plate on cover.

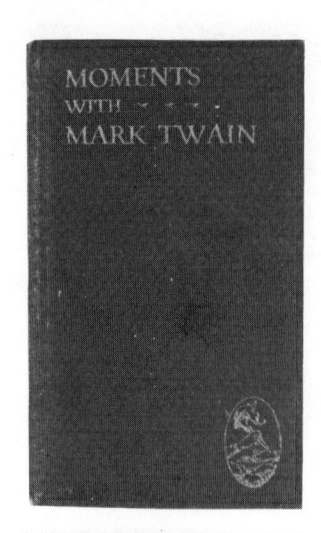

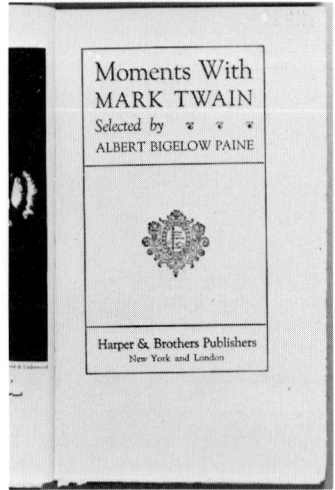

Moments with Mark Twain.
New York and London, 1920: Harper & Brothers Publishers.
Selected by Albert Bigelow Paine.
Excerpts from earlier works.

BAL 3686   Green cloth.

Mark Twain Able Yachtsman Interviews Himself on Why Lipton Failed to Lift the Cup.
(n.p., actually New York; 1920).
White boards with cloth shelfback.
#51 of 109 copies.
Inscribed by Merle Johnson:
First edition/One of twelve/copies bound in boards — with the extra picture on cover — /Merle Johnson

BAL 3529

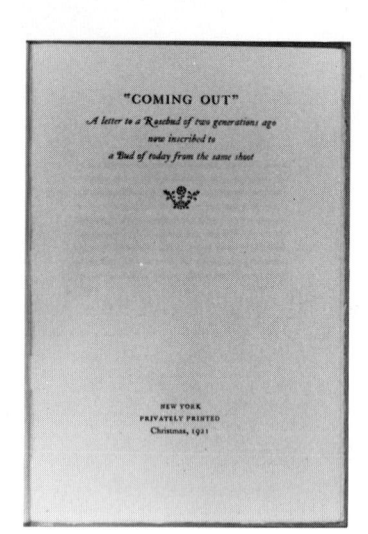

"Coming Out" A letter to a Rosebud of two generations ago now inscribed to a Bud of today from the same shoot.
New York, 1921: Privately Printed, Christmas.
                Printed by The Marchbanks Press for Thomas Nast Fairbanks.
BAL 3533   Rose paper boards.

The Mysterious Stranger and Other Stories.
New York and London, (1922): Harper & Brothers Publishers.
BAL 3534   Red cloth.

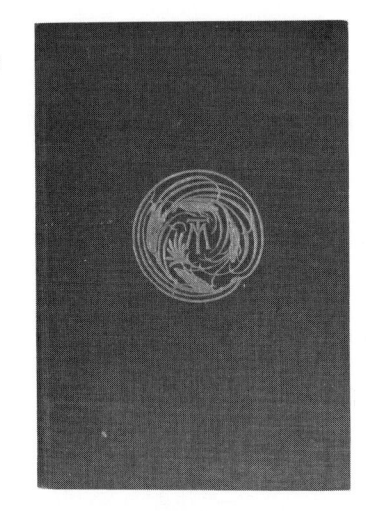

The Mysterious Stranger and Other Stories.
New York, (1929): Harper & Brothers.
Blue cloth.

The Mysterious Stranger and Other Stories.
New York, (1929): Harper and Brothers.
    Authorized Edition of
    The Complete Works of Mark Twain.
    Green cloth.

The Mysterious Stranger and Other Stories.
New York, 1929: Harper & Brothers.
    Volume 27 of
    The Stormfield Edition of
    The Writings of Mark Twain.
    Set #212 of 1024.
    Appreciation by E.V. Lucas.
    Introduction by Albert Bigelow Paine.
    Blue cloth stamped in gold.

The Mysterious Stranger.
Berkeley and Los Angeles, 1970: University of California.
    Edited with an Introduction by William M. Gibson.
    Tan cloth with dustjacket.

The Mysterious Stranger and Other Stories.
(New York, 1962): New American Library.
    Signet Classic edition #CD68, 50¢.
    Foreword by Edmund Reiss.
    "First printing, February, 1962"
    Pictorial paper wrappers.

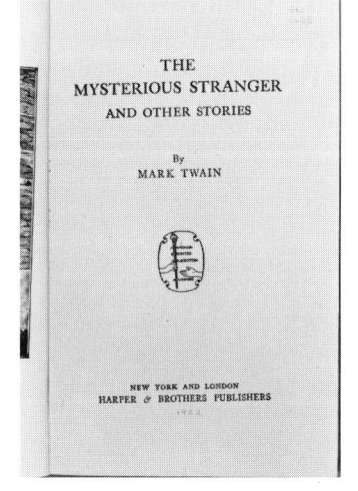

Mark Twain's Speeches.
New York and London, (1923): Harper & Brothers
        Publishers.
        Introduction by Albert Bigelow
        Paine.
        Appreciation by William Dean
        Howells.
        Date code D-X on copyright
        page.
BAL 3535   Red cloth.

Mark Twain's Speeches.
New York and London, (1925): Harper & Brothers
        Publishers.
        Edited by Albert Bigelow Paine.
        Appreciation by William
        Dean Howells.
        Blue cloth.

Mark Twain's Speeches.
New York, (1929): Harper and Brothers.
        Authorized Edition of
        The Complete Works of
        Mark Twain.
        Green cloth.

Mark Twain's Speeches.
New York, 1929: Harper & Brothers.
        Volume 29 of
        The Stormfield Edition of
        The Writings of Mark Twain.
        Set #212 of 1024.
        Appreciation by E.V. Lucas.
        Introduction by Albert
        Bigelow Paine.
        Blue cloth stamped in gold.

Europe and Elsewhere.
New York and London, (1923): Harper & Brothers Publishers.
Appreciation by Brander Matthews.
Introduction by Albert Bigelow Paine.
Red cloth: three copies, one with part of a dustjacket, one with a full dustjacket.

BAL 3536

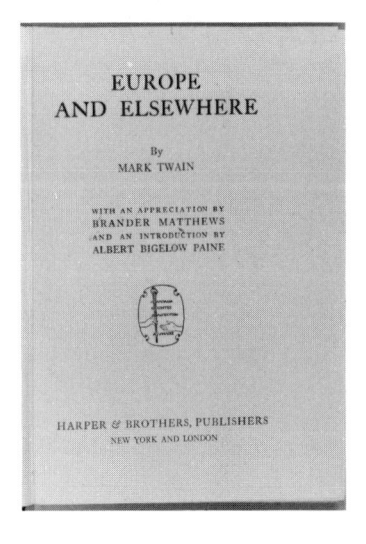

Europe and Elsewhere.
New York and London, (1923): Harper & Brothers Publishers.
Second printing with L-X date code on copyright page.
Red cloth.

Europe and Elsewhere.
New York, 1929: Harper & Brothers.
Volume 29 of
The Stormfield Edition of
The Writings of Mark Twain.
Set #212 of 1024.
Appreciation by Brander Matthews.
Introduction by Albert Bigelow Paine.
Blue cloth stamped in gold.

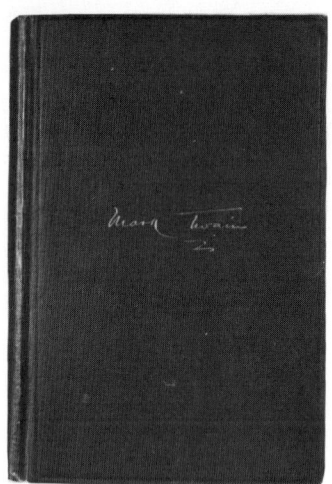

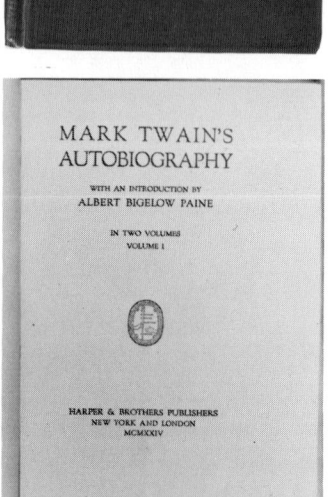

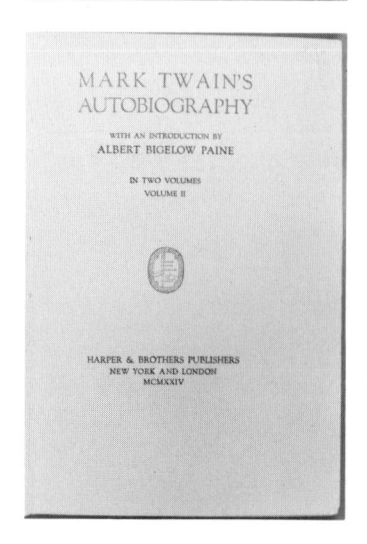

Mark Twain's Autobiography.
New York and London, 1924: Harper & Brothers Publishers.
Introduction by Albert Bigelow Paine.
Two volumes.
Blue cloth: five sets.
Four sets of first editions (one with dustjackets).
One set of second printings with L-Y date code on copyright page.

BAL 3537

Mark Twain's Autobiography.
New York and London, 1924: Harper & Brothers
Publishers.
Blue cloth: two volumes.
Introduction by Albert
Bigelow Paine.
Inscribed by Merle Johnson:
*Isabel Lyon/from/Merle Johnson/
January 1935*
Inscribed by Lyon:
*Selections from/Autobiography
(-"buried"-)/in N.A. Review
1906-09./also in Sunday Magazine of
St. Louis Republic/Oct. 29-1907 To
Sept. — 1908/This in arrangement
with Col. Harvey/for Mr. Clemens
wished to reach his submerged readers
— Those who could not afford to buy
his books —/There was no money in it
for/SLC he didn't want that —/but the
Harpers got/some for the advertising/of
the books, MT's idea/This would not be
an Autobiography:/it is a collection/of
notes dictated in 1906 — to be used
autobiographically,/sparingly, &
severely edited.*

Mark Twain's Autobiography.
New York, 1929: Harper & Brothers.
Volumes 36 & 37 of
The Stormfield Edition of
The Writings of Mark Twain.
Set #212 of 1024.
Appreciation by E.V. Lucas.
Introduction by Albert
Bigelow Paine.
Blue cloth stamped in gold.

The Autobiography of Mark Twain.
New York, 1959: Harper & Brothers, Publishers.
"Including chapters now published
for the first time."
Arranged, edited, with an introduction and notes by Charles Neider.
Blue and yellow cloth with
dustjacket:
four copies. (A-I date code on
copyright page of all.)

The Autobiography of Mark Twain.
New York, (1961): Washington Square Press, Inc.
Introduction, notes and a special
essay by Charles Neider.
Pictorial paper wrappers.

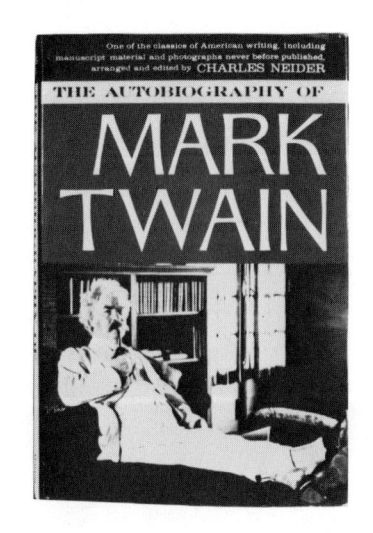

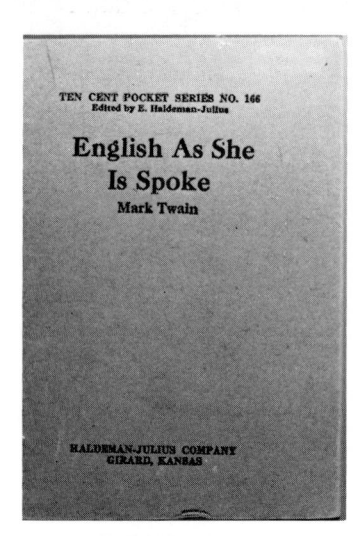

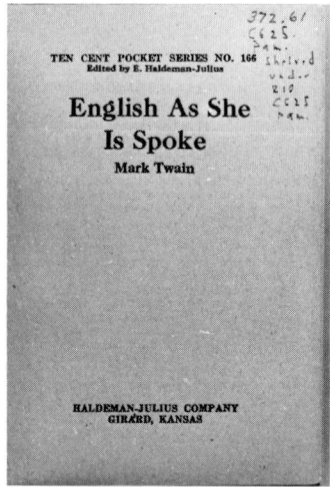

English As She Is Spoke.
Girard, Kansas, n.d. (actually c. 1921): Haldeman-Julius Company.
Biographical sketch by Matthew Irving Lans.
Two copies:
Copy 1: Blue paper wrappers with *Ten Cent Pocket Series No. 166* on front cover and title page.
Copy 2: Orange paper wrappers with the above on title page only.

BAL 3688

Humorous Sketches.
Girard, Kansas, n.d. (actually c. 1924): Haldeman-Julius Company.
Ten Cent Pocket Series #231.
Pictorial paper wrappers.

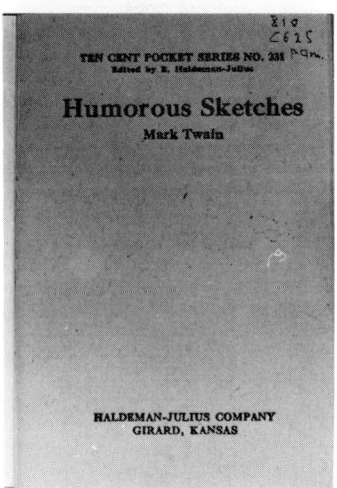

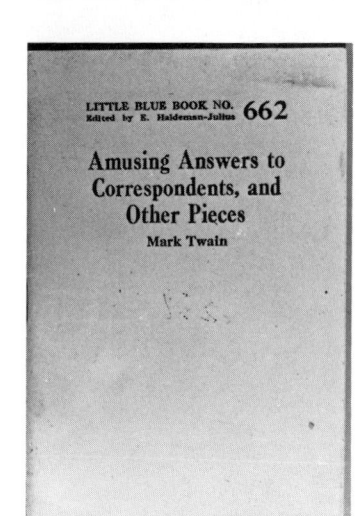

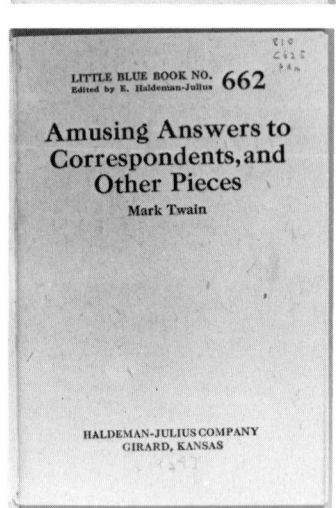

Amusing Answers to Correspondents, and Other Pieces.
Girard, Kansas, n.d.(actually 1924): Haldeman-Julius Company.
Little Blue Book No. 662.
Edited by E. Haldeman-Julius.
BAL 3693   Manila wrappers.

Humorous Fables.
Girard, Kansas, n.d. (actually c. 1924): Haldeman-Julius Company.
Little Blue Book No. 668.
BAL 3694 Brown paper wrappers.

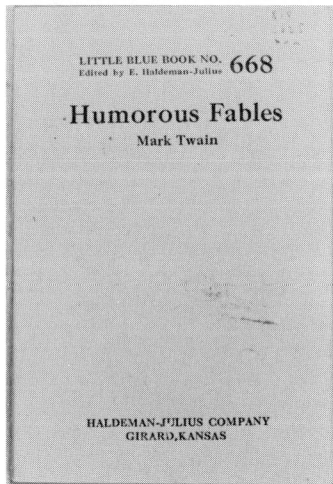

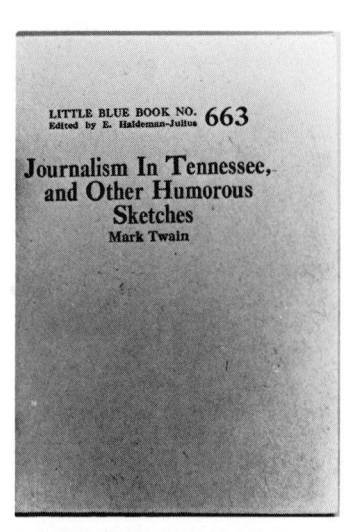

Journalism in Tennessee, and Other Humorous Sketches.
Girard, Kansas, n.d.(actually c. 1924): Haldeman-Julius Company.
Little Blue Book No. 663.
BAL 3695   Blue paper wrappers.

A Curious Experience And Other Amusing Pieces.
Girard, Kansas, n.d. (actually 1925): Haldeman-Julius
                Company.
                First separate edition of this
                collection.
                Little Blue Book No. 932.
BAL 3697   White paper wrappers.

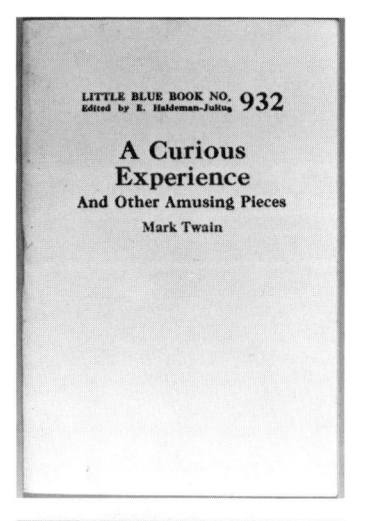

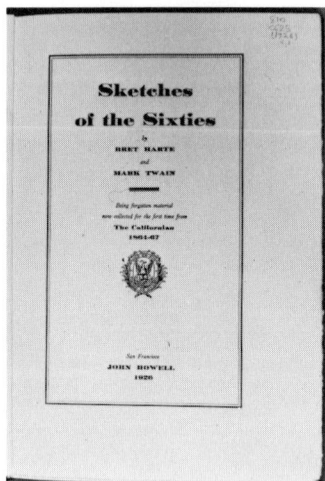

Sketches of the Sixties.
San Francisco, 1926: John Howell.
    Items by Clemens and Bret Harte.
    "being forgotten material now collected for the first time from *The Californian* 1864-67."
    One of 2000.
    Title page by Edwin Grabhorn.
    Paper over boards with cloth shelfback and pictorial dustjacket: two copies.

BAL 3539

Sketches of the Sixties.
San Francisco, 1927: John Howell.
    "Second edition, with new material and illustrations."
    Inscribed by Howell:
    To Christopher Morley/Our American "Kit Marlowe"/with a dash of Harte/& Twain, but most/of all his agreeable/ own Self/from a fellow/Roxburger the/ publisher John Howell/April 2, 1933/ San Francisco
    Tan laid paper boards.

More Maxims of Mark.
(New York), 1927: no publisher.
Checkered batik boards with cloth shelfback: two copies.
Copy 1: one of 50, this copy unnumbered.
Copy 2: "Printer's Copy"
Laid in:
TNS by Philip C. Duschnes, reading in part:
*(This copy purchased by me on October, 1959, from the own-/er of Harvard Press, New York, who printed this book and se-/veral other ephemeral pieces of Mark Twain, Sinclair Lewis,/Stephen Crane. These appear in my catalogue No. 141, except/*More Maxims of Mark, *because there was only one copy to be/had, i.e. the last copy — owned by the printer)./Philip C. Duschnes/Nov. 5, 1959.*

BAL 3542

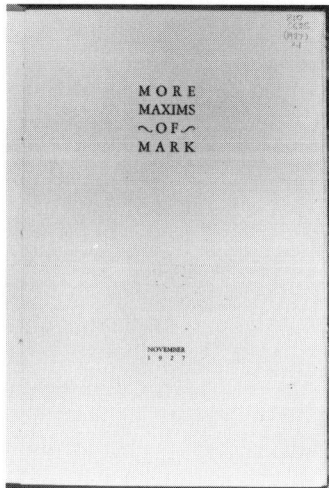

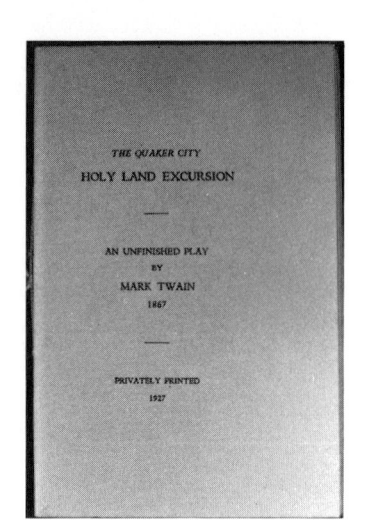

The Quaker City Holy Land Excursion.
(New York), 1927: Privately Printed.
An unfinished play by Mark Twain 1867.
Wrappers: two copies.
Each is one of 200, printed on Normandy Vellum.
Introduction by Albert Bigelow Paine reprinted from *Mark Twain: A Biography.*

BAL 3543

The Adventures of Thomas Jefferson Snodgrass.
Chicago, 1928: Pascal Covici, Publisher, Inc.
　　　　　　Edited by Charles Honce.
　　　　　　Foreword by Vincent Starrett.
　　　　　　Note on "A Celebrated Village Idiot"
　　　　　　by James O'Donnell Bennett.
　　　　　　Brown laid paper boards with cloth shelfback:
　　　　　　two copies, one with dustjacket.
　　　　　　Copy 1: #199 of 375.
BAL 3544　　Copy 2: #312 of 375.

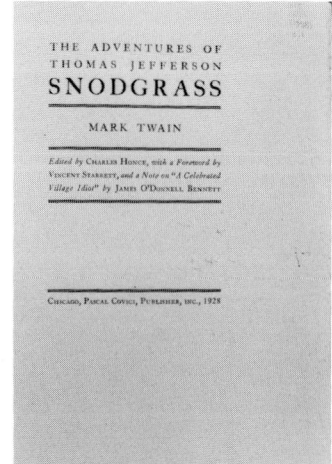

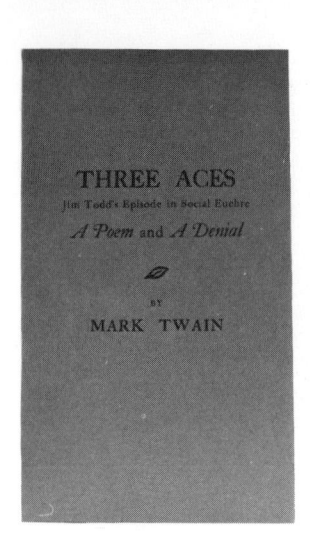

Three Aces. Jim Todd's Episode in Social Euchre.
A Poem and a Denial by Mark Twain.
(Westport, Conn., 1929): (privately printed).
Stiff orange paper wrappers.
One of 50 copies *"for friends of Robin and Marian MacVicars, — in their studio at Westport-in-Connecticut.*
BAL 3549 *Christmas Season 1929."*

A Champagne Cocktail and a Catastrophe.
Two Acting Charades by Mark Twain.
(New York, Xmas 1930): (privately printed).
                Self-wrappers.
                "Printed from the original manuscript in the possession of Robin and
BAL 3551   *Marian MacVicars . . ."*

Mark Twain's Early Writings in Hannibal Missouri Papers.
Santa Monica, California, January 1931: Willard S.
                Morse.
                Complied by Willard Morse.
                Consists of photostats of the originals from the newspapers; clippings of articles (on early writings of Clemens) by Minnie M. Brashear and C.J. Armstrong are stated to be present but are absent from a pocket in the back of the binder.

Be Good, Be Good. A Poem by Mark Twain.
New York, 1931: Privately printed.
BAL 3553   Laid paper wrappers.

Mark Twain in 1901, photographed by T.C. Marceau.

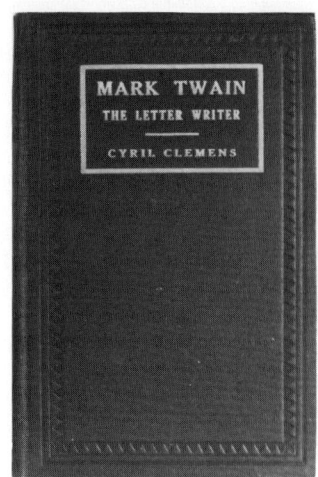

Mark Twain The Letter Writer.
Boston, 1932: Meador Publishing Company. Prepared by Cyril Clemens. Purple-red cloth with pictorial dustjacket.

BAL 3554

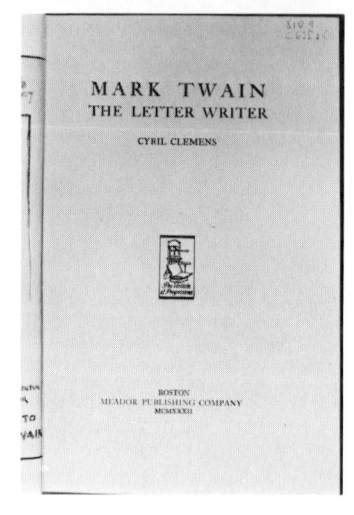

Mark Twain in 1907.

Mark Twain. Wit and Wisdom.
New York, 1935: Frederick A. Stokes Company.
Edited by Cyril Clemens.
Preface by Stephen Leacock.
Grey cloth: two copies.

The Family Mark Twain.
New York and London, (1935 or later): Harper & Brothers.
Biographical summary by Albert Bigelow Paine.
In Homage to Mark Twain by Owen Wister.
BAL 3704   Terra cotta cloth.

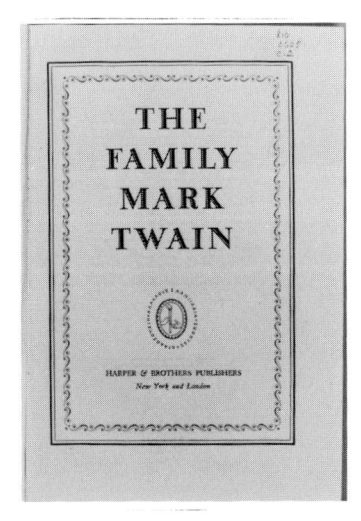

The Favorite Works of Mark Twain.
New York (1939): Garden City Publishing Co., Inc.
Revised edition.
Edited from The Family Mark Twain.
Pictorial buckram with dust-jacket.

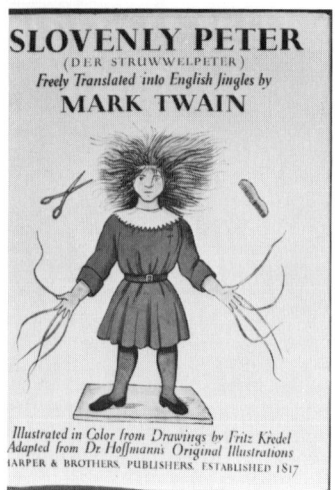

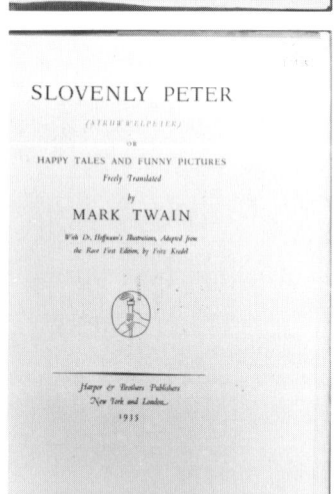

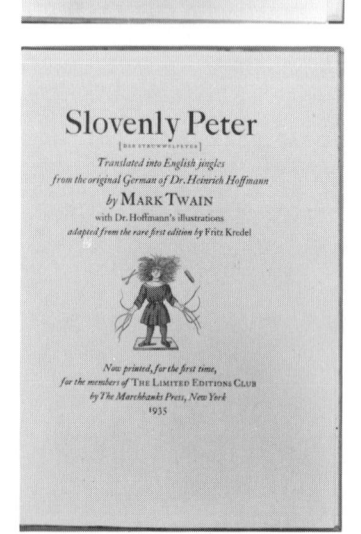

Slovenly Peter (Der Struwwelpeter).
New York and London, 1935: Harper & Brothers.
"Freely Translated into English Jingles by Mark Twain"
Pictorial paper over boards with matching dustjacket.
Illustrated in color by Fritz Kredel adapted from Dr. Hoffman's Original Illustrations.

Slovenly Peter.
New York, 1935: The Limited Editions Club.
Printed by the Marchbanks Press.
Illustrated by Fritz Kredel.
"The Translation by Mark Twain was made in Berlin in 1891."
#1377 of 1500 copies.

BAL 3555

Pictorial cloth with tissue dustjacket, folding box and slipcase.

Mark Twain in 1908.

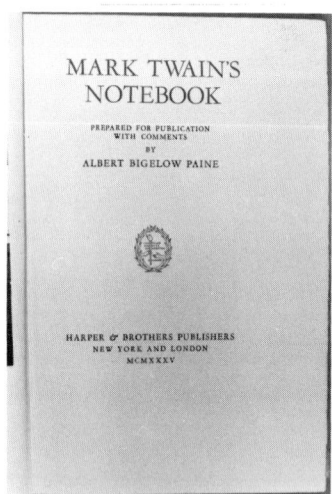

Mark Twain's Notebook.
New York and London, 1935: Harper and Brothers
            Publishers.
            Prepared by Albert Bigelow Paine.
BAL 3556   Blue cloth with dustjacket.

Mark Twain's Notebook.
New York and London, 1935: Harper and Brothers
            Publishers.
            Prepared by Albert Bigelow Paine.
            Second edition.
            Blue cloth.

Mark Twain's Notebook.
New York, (1936): Harper & Brothers.
            Authorized Edition of
            The Complete Works of Mark
            Twain.
            Green cloth.

Letters from the Sandwich Islands Written for the Sacramento Union by Mark Twain.
San Francisco, 1937: The Grabhorn Press.
Introduction and conclusion by G. Ezra Dane.
Illustrated by Dorothy Grover.
Paper over boards with cloth shelfback:
two copies, one with plain green dustjacket.

BAL 3558 Each is one of 550 copies.

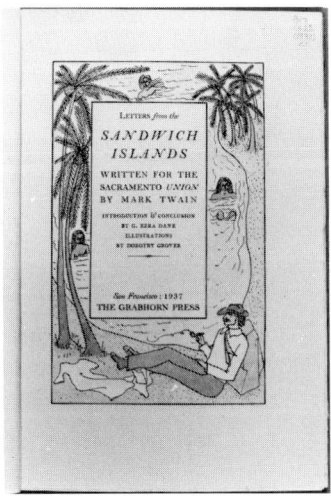

The Washoe Giant in San Francisco.
San Francisco, 1938: George Fields.

BAL 3559

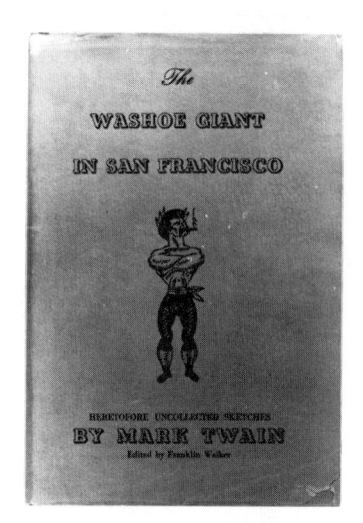

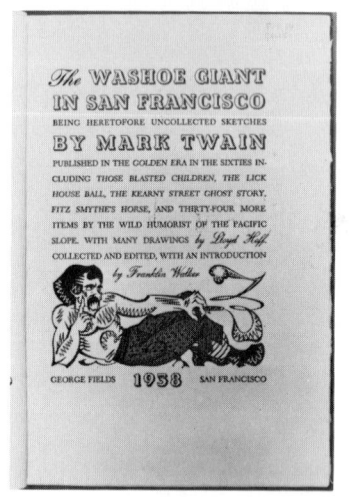

"Being heretofore uncollected sketches published in *The Golden Era* in the Sixties . . ." Drawings by Lloyd Hoff. Collected and edited with an introduction by Franklin Walker. Paper over boards with cloth shelfback and dustjacket.

Mark Twain's Letter to William Bowen.
San Francisco, 1938: The Book Club of California.
Letter written Februrary 6, 1870 at Buffalo, New York.
Prefatory Note by Clara Clemens Gabrilowitsch.
Foreword by Albert W. Gunnison.
Printed blue paper boards with cloth shelfback.
One of 400 copies printed by The Grabhorn Press.

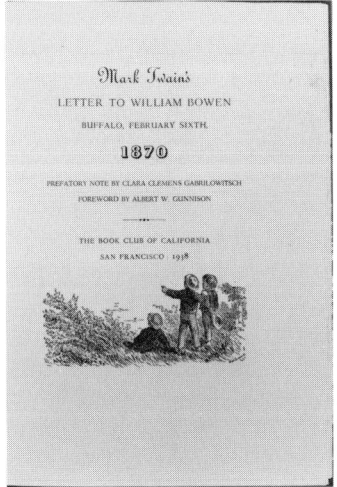

BAL 3560

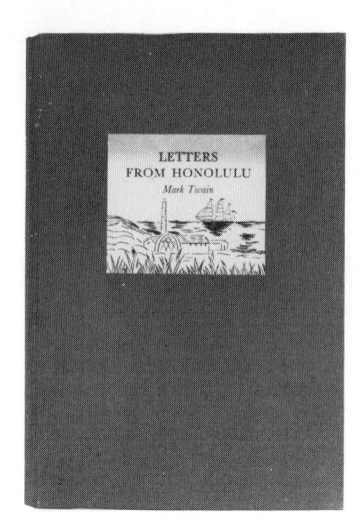

Letters from Honolulu Written for the Sacramento Union.
Honolulu, 1939: Thomas Nickerson.
Introduction by John W. Vandercook.
Blue green cloth: two copies.
BAL 3561 Each is from the edition of 1000.

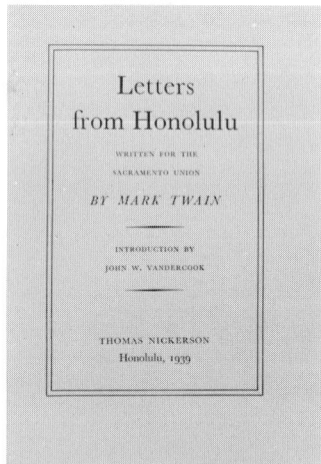

Mark Twain in 1904. The dog is believed to be Osman, Stephen Crane's dog.

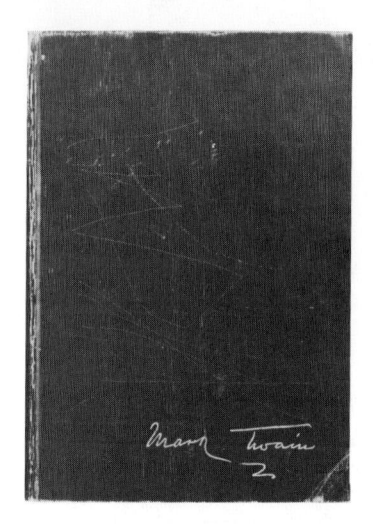

The Complete Short Stories and Famous Essays.
New York, (1928, actually about 1940): P.F. Collier & Son Corporation.
    One Volume Edition.
    Flexible brown cloth.

Mark Twain's Travels with Mr. Brown.
New York, 1940: Alfred A. Knopf.
"being heretofore uncollected sketches . . . for the San Francisco *Alta California* in 1866 & 1867, describing the adventures of the author & his irrepressible companion in Nicaragua, Hannibal, New York, & other spots on their way to Europe."
Collected and edited with an introduction by Franklin Walker and G. Ezra Dane.
#827 of 1795 copies.
Typography and design by W.A. Dwiggins.

BAL 3563   Green cloth with dustjacket.

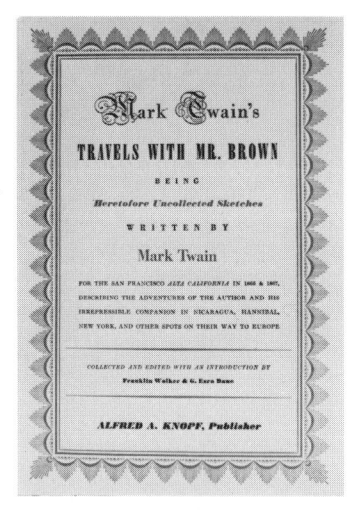

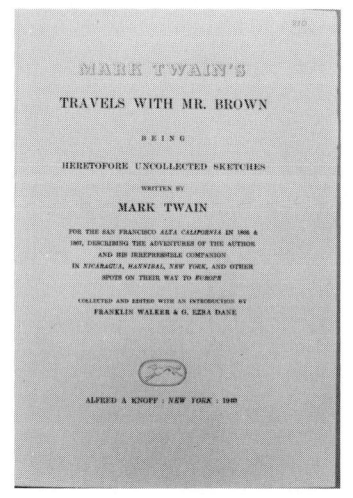

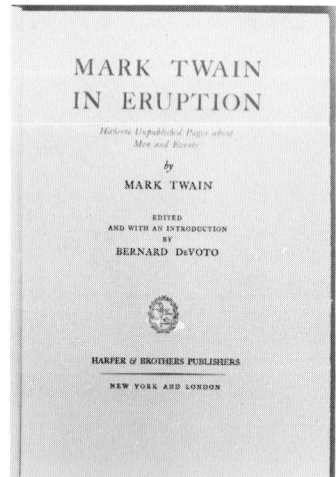

Mark Twain in Eruption.
New York and London, (1940): Harper & Brothers Publishers.
Edited with an introduction by Bernard DeVoto.
BAL 3564 Terra-cotta cloth.

Mark Twain in Eruption.
New York and London, (1940): Harper & Brothers Publishers.
Second edition.
From the library of Isabel Van Kleeck Lyon.
Terra-cotta cloth.

Mark Twain in Eurption.
New York and London, (1940): Harper & Brothers Publishers.
Third edition.
Terra-cotta cloth.

Mark Twain's Letters in the Muscatine Journal.
Chicago, 1942: The Mark Twain Association of America.
Edited with an introduction by Edgar M. Branch.
BAL 3569   Blue paper wrappers.

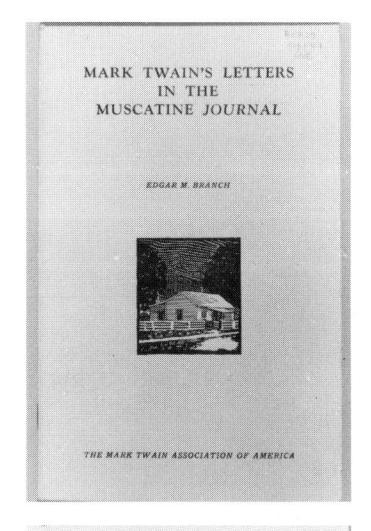

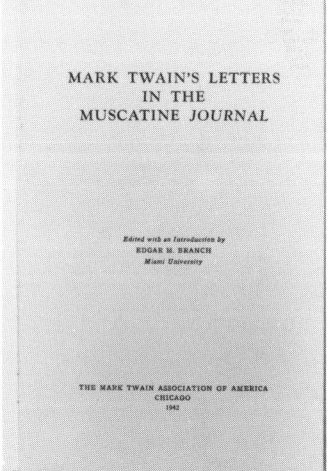

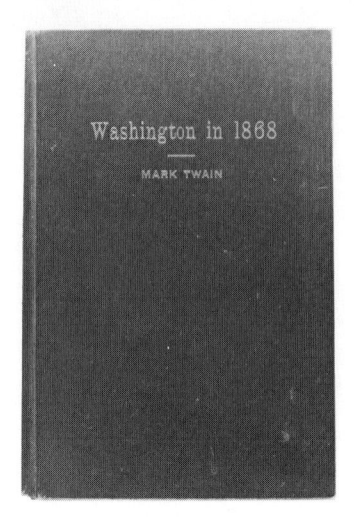

Washington in 1868.
Webster Groves, Missouri, 1943: International Mark Twain Society and London: T. Werner Laurie, Limited. Edited with an introduction and notes by Cyril Clemens. Foreword by W.W. Jacobs.
BAL 3570   Purple cloth.

A Murder, A Mystery, and a Marriage.
(New York), 1945. (Manuscript House.)
"as Written . . . in April 1876 and Now for the First Time Privately Printed."
BAL 3572   Printed grey paper wrappers.

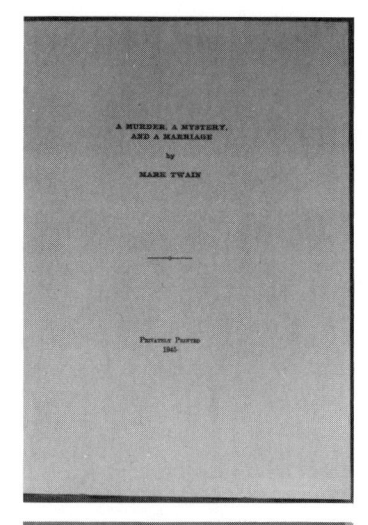

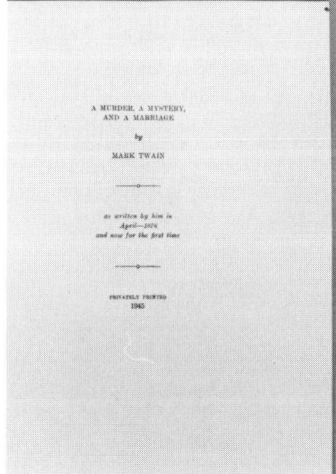

Mark Twain, Businessman.
Boston, 1946: Little, Brown and Company.
                Edited by Samuel Charles Webster.
                Signed by the editor.
BAL 3573   Blue cloth with dustjacket.

Mark Twain, Businessman.
Boston, 1946: Little Brown and Company.
        Third printing.
        Blue cloth.

The Portable Mark Twain.
New York, 1946: The Viking Press. Edited with an introduction by Bernard DeVoto.
BAL 3574   Yellow-orange cloth.

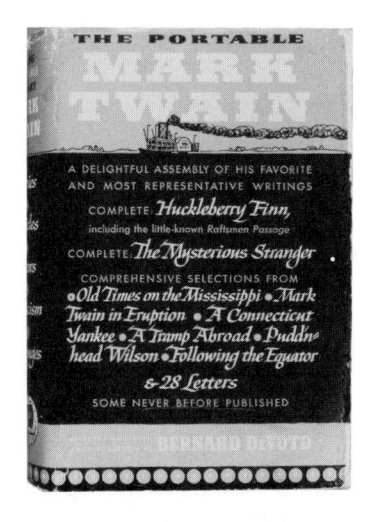

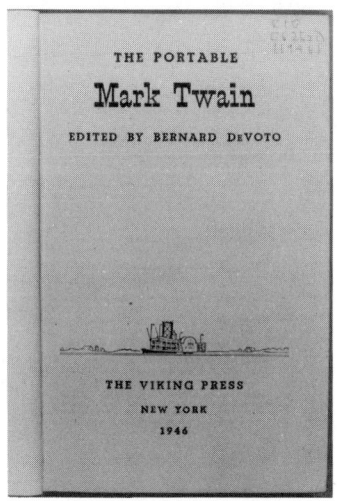

The Portable Mark Twain.
New York, (1956): The Viking Press. "Fifth printing May 1956" Pictorial paper wrappers.

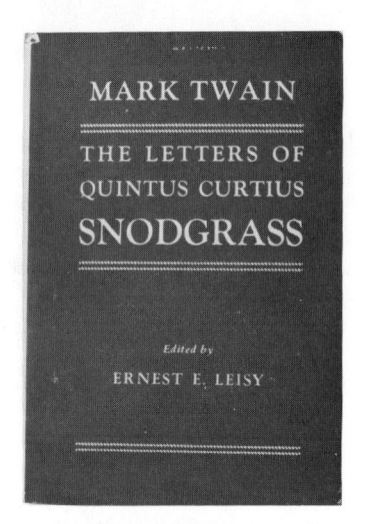

The Letters of Quintus Curtius Snodgrass.
Dallas, 1946: University Press, Southern Methodist University.
Edited by Ernest E. Leisy.
BAL 3575   Light brown cloth.

Mark Twain with John T. Lewis, at the Quarry Farm, July 17, 1903.

Mark Twain. In Three Moods.
San Marino, 1948: Friends of the Huntington Library.
"Three new items of Twainiana."
Edited by Dixon Wecter.
One of 1200 copies; this copy unnumbered.
Printed by the Ward Ritchie Press.
Brief note at the end by Charles Erskine Scott Wood.

BAL 3577   Paper over boards.

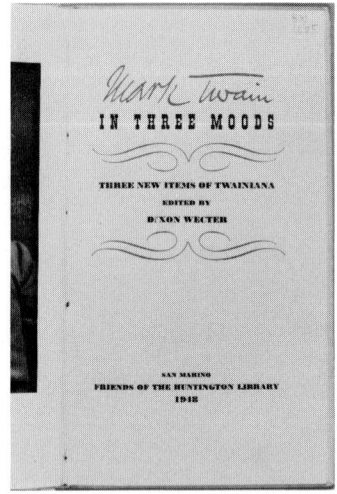

Mark Twain at Your Fingertips.
New York,(1948):Beechhurst Press, Inc.
　　　　　　Edited by Caroline Thomas
　　　　　　Harnsberger.
　　　　　　Signed by the editor.
BAL p.254　　Cloth.

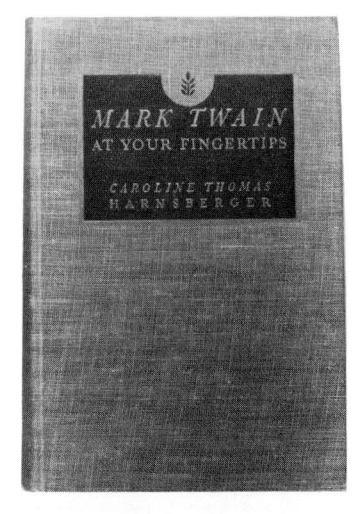

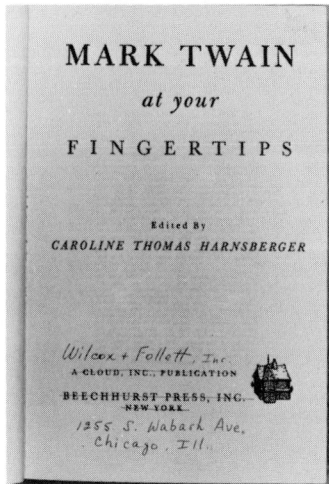

Mark Twain.
New York, 1948: The Bigger Press, Inc.
    Privately printed for C. Charles Burlingame, M.D.
    Illustrated by Kathryn Howard.
    Introduction by C. Charles Burlingame.
    White pictorial paper over boards with tissue dustjacket: five copies, two with dustjacket.

Mark Twain to Mrs. Fairbanks.
San Marino, California, 1949: Huntington Library.
Edited by Dixon Wecter.
BAL 3578　　Medium blue cloth: two copies.

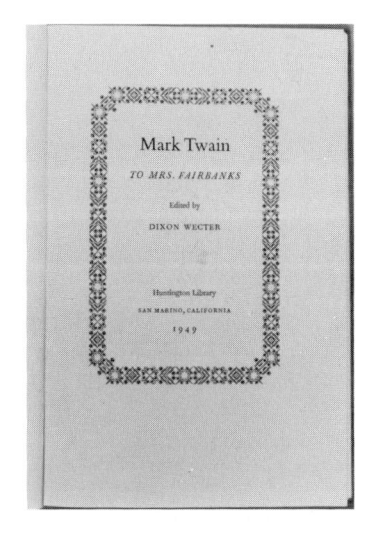

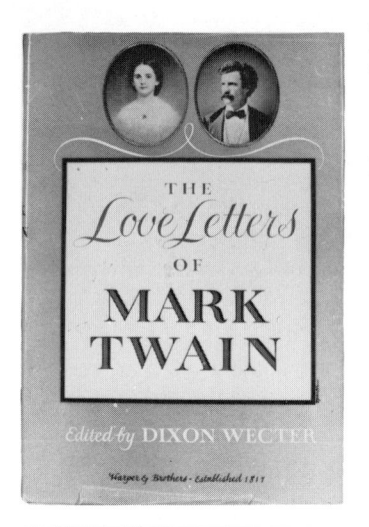

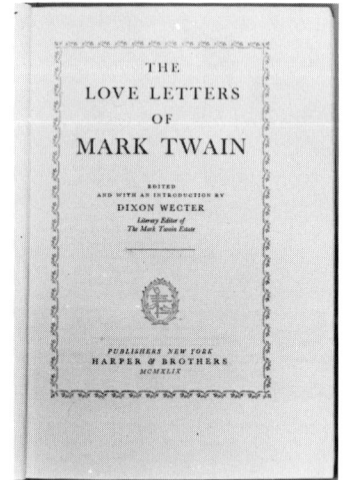

The Love Letters of Mark Twain.
New York, 1949: Harper & Brothers.
Edited with an introduction by Dixon Wecter.
Blue cloth: two copies, one with dustjacket.

BAL 3579

Clara, Mrs. Clemens and Mark Twain at Dollis Hill, London, in 1900. The glass plate negative has cracked.

Mark Twain at Quarry Farm, 1903.

Some Thoughts on the Science of Onanism.
n.p., January 1952: no publisher.
"Being an Address Delivered Before the Members of the Stomach Club Paris 1879."
Limited to 100 copies.
BAL 3580   Self-wrappers.

```
January          SOME THOUGHTS
 1952               ON THE
                   SCIENCE
                      OF
                   ONANISM
                      BY
                  MARK TWAIN
Limited     * * Being an Address Delivered . . .
to 100      Before the Members of the . . . .
Copies      . . . Stomach Club . . . Paris . . . 1879
   z

ONE HUNDRED COPIES of this brochure have been printed
for a microscopically few members of the great Fraternity to
which Mark Twain belonged and in behalf of whose rites he
speaks with so much feeling and depth of insight into his
subject. . . .
```

Some Thoughts on the Science of Onanism or Mark Twain in Erection with Apologies to Bernard DeVoto.
n.p., 1964: Privately printed for the Trade.
One of 1000.
Paper self-wrappers: two copies.

Report from Paradise.
New York, 1952: Harper & Brothers Publishers. Introduction by Dixon Wecter. Drawings by Charles Locke. Printed by the Golden Hind Press. This copy not a first edition (date code E-E means May 1955). Aqua paper over boards with cloth shelfback and dustjacket.

BAL 3581

Mark Twain's First Story.
(Iowa City, Iowa, 1952): A Prairie Press Publication.
                Introduction by Franklin J. Meine.
                Illustrated by Dale Ballantyne.
                Printed beige laid paper wrappers:
BAL 3582   three copies.

Mark Twain's First Story.
(Iowa City, Iowa, 1952): A Prairie Press Publication.
                Second printing, "completely reset".
                Inscribed by Franklin J. Meine.
                Terra-cotta wrappers.

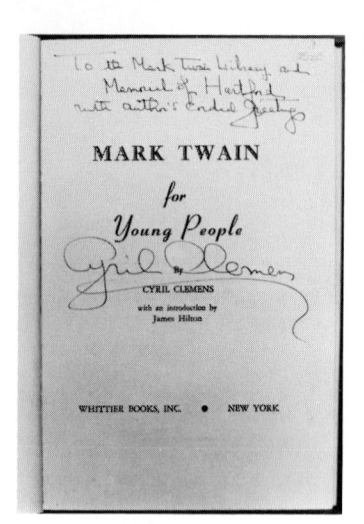

Mark Twain for Young People.
New York, (1953): Whittier Books, Inc. Complied by Cyril Clemens. Introduction by James Hilton. Inscribed by the compiler. Red cloth.

Mark Twain's Letters from Hawaii.
New York, 1956: Appleton-Century.
Edited with an introduction by A. Grove Day.
Signed by the editor.
Patterned paper over boards with cloth shelfback and dustjacket.

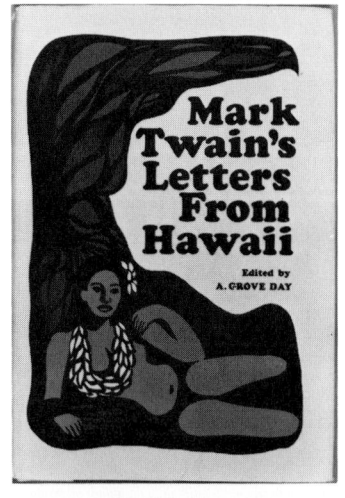

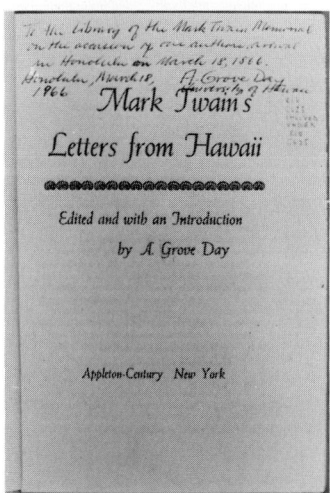

Mark Twain of the Enterprise.
Berkeley and Los Angeles, 1957: University of California Press.
"Newspaper articles & other documents, 1862-64."
Edited by Henry Nash Smith with the assistance of Frederick Anderson.
Designed by Adrian Wilson.
Pictorial cloth over boards: two copies.

Mark Twain: San Francisco Virginia City Territorial Enterprise Correspondent.
San Francisco, 1957: The Book Club of California.
"Selections From His Letters To The Territorial Enterprise: 1865-66."
Edited by Henry Nash Smith and Frederick Anderson.
One of 400 copies.
Paper over boards with cloth shelfback.

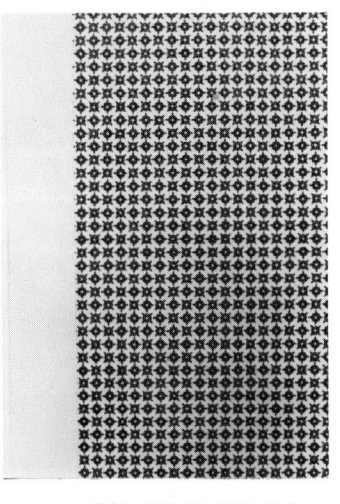

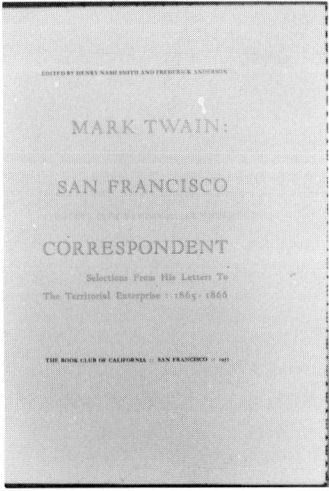

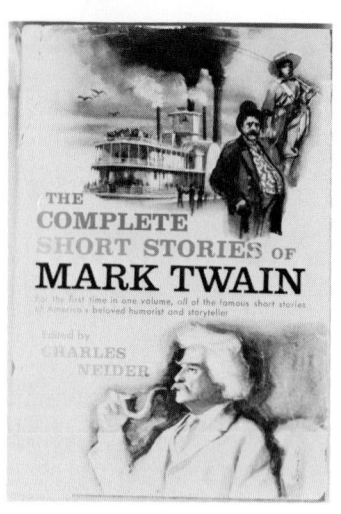

The Complete Short Stories of Mark Twain.
Garden City, 1957: Hanover House.
    Edited with an introduction by
    Charles Neider.
    Yellow and orange cloth with dust-jacket.

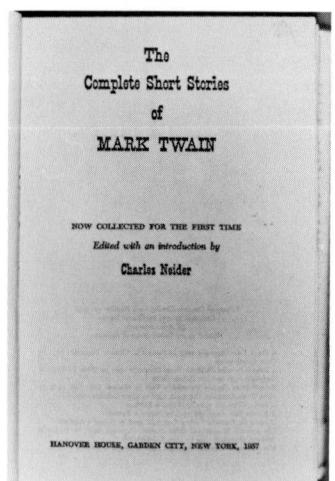

The Complete Short Stories of Mark Twain.
Garden City, 1958: Hanover House.
    Second printing.
    See above for binding.

The Complete Short Stories of Mark Twain.
New York, 1958: Bantam Books.
    Edited with an introduction by
    Charles Neider.
    Pictorial paper wrappers.

The Complete Short Stories of Mark Twain.
New York, (1964): Bantam Books.
    Edited with an introduction by
    Charles Neider.
    "5th printing, August 1964"
    Bantam Classic #NC259, price 95¢.
    Pictorial paper wrappers.

Mark Twain's Jest Book.
Kirkwood, Mo., 1957: Mark Twain Journal.
    Edited by Cyril Clemens.
    Foreword by Carl Sandburg.
    Inscribed by the editor.
    Pictorial paper wrappers.

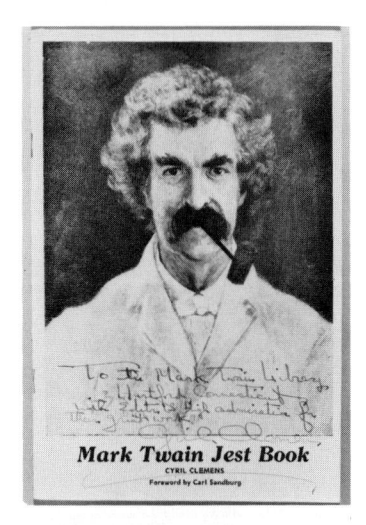

Mark Twain's Jest Book.
Kirkwood, Mo., 1963: Mark Twain Journal.
    Edited by Cyril Clemens.
    "Second edition with new material"
    Inscribed by the editor.
    Pictorial paper wrappers.

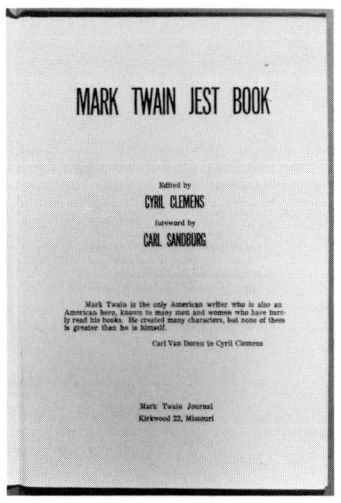

Mark Twain's Jest Book.
Kirkwood, Mo., 1965: Mark Twain Journal.
    Edited by Cyril Clemens.
    "Third edition with new material"
    Inscribed by the editor.
    Pictorial paper wrappers.

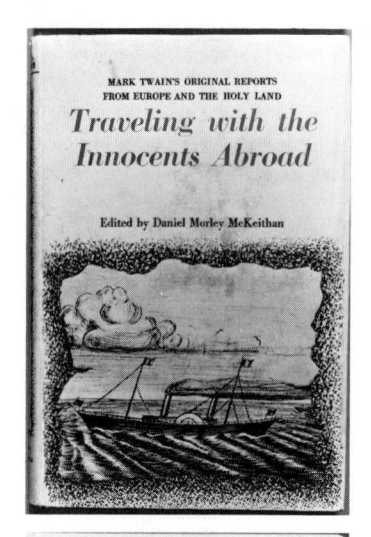

Travelling with the Innocents Abroad.
Norman, (1958): University of Oklahoma Press.
"Mark Twain's Original Reports from Europe and the Holy Land." Edited by Daniel Morley McKeithan.
Terra-cotta cloth with dustjacket.

The Art, Humor and Humanity of Mark Twain.
Norman, 1959: University of Oklahoma Press.
Edited by Minnie M. Brashear and Robert M. Rodney.
Introduction by Edward Wagenknecht.
Green cloth with dustjacket.

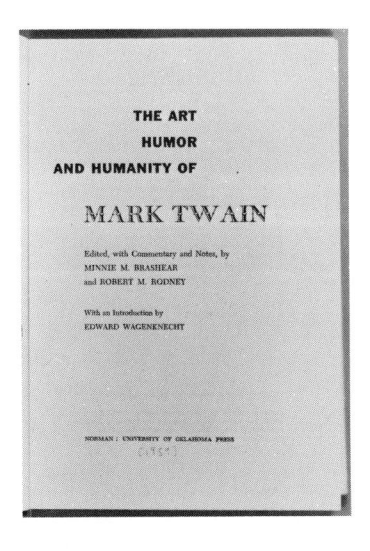

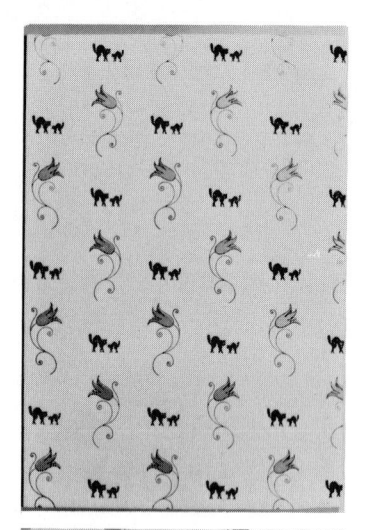

Concerning Cats. Two Tales.
San Francisco, 1959: The Book Club of California.
Introduction by Frederick Anderson.
Printed at the Grabhorn Press for
The Colt Press.
One of 450 copies.
Pictorial paper over boards with
cloth shelfback.

Mark Twain. A Laurel Reader.
(New York, 1960): Dell Publishing Co., Inc.
        Edited by Edmund Fuller.
        #LC 111, price 50¢.
        Second printing, November 1960
        (First was October, 1958).
        Pictorial paper wrappers.

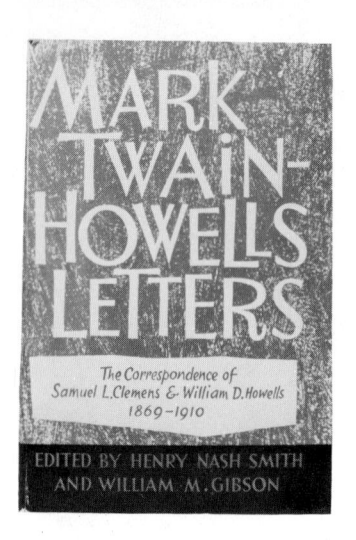

Mark Twain-Howells Letters.
Cambridge, Mass., 1960: The Belknap Press
of Harvard University Press.
"The Correspondence of Samuel L. Clemens and William Dean Howells 1872-1910."
Edited by Henry Nash Smith, William M. Gibson and Frederick Anderson.
Two volumes.
Blue cloth with dustjacket: two sets.
Set 1: as above.
Set 2: with publisher's promotional band around the pair.

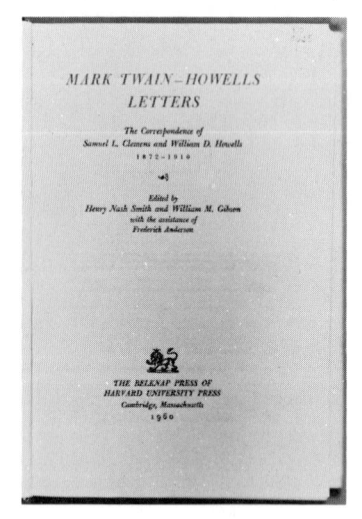

Selected Mark Twain-Howells Letters 1872-1910.
Cambridge, 1967: The Belknap Press of Harvard University Press.
Edited by Henry Nash Smith, William M. Gibson and Frederick Anderson.
Blue cloth with dustjacket.

Mark Twain. Wit and Wisecracks.
Mount Vernon and New York, (1961): The Peter Pauper Press.
Selected by Doris Benardete.
Illustrated by Henry R. Martin.
Yellow pictorial paper over boards with matching dustjacket.

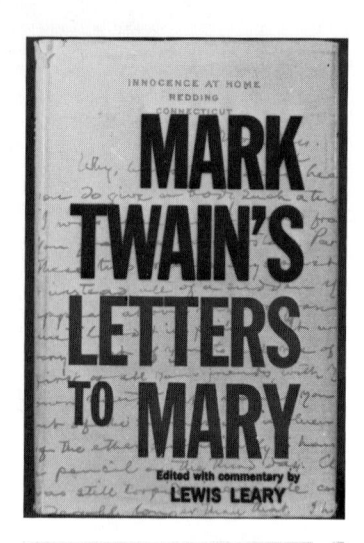

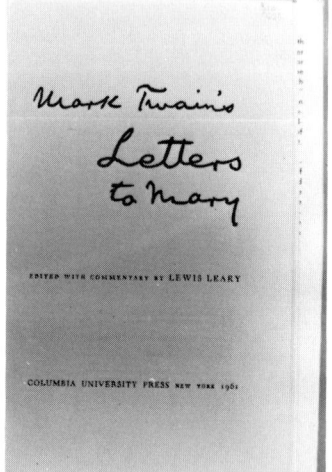

Mark Twain's Letters to Mary.
New York, 1961: Columbia University Press.
> Edited with commentary by Lewis Leary.
> White cloth with dustjacket: two copies, one autographed by the editor.

Mark Twain: Life as I Find It.
Garden City, 1961: Hanover House.
Edited with an introduction by Charles Neider.
Cloth with dustjacket.

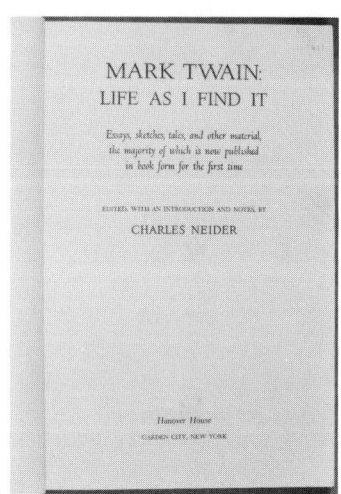

"Ah Sin" A Dramatic Work.
San Francisco, 1961: The Book Club of California.
Written with Bret Harte.
Edited by Frederick Anderson.
Designed, decorated with woodcuts and printed by Vivien and Mallette Dean. One of 450 copies.
Pictorial paper over boards with cloth shelfback and plain paper dustjacket: two copies.

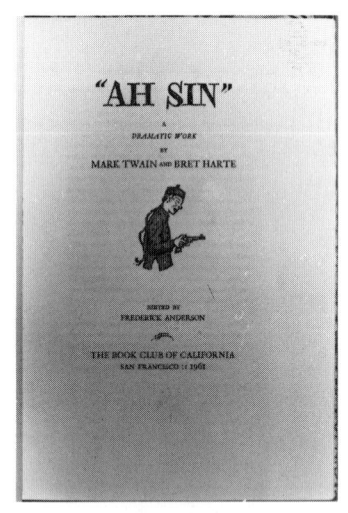

The Complete Humorous Sketches and Tales of Mark Twain.
Garden City, (1961): Hanover House.
        Edited with an introduction by Charles Neider.
        Drawings by Mark Twain.
        Cloth with pictorial dustjacket.

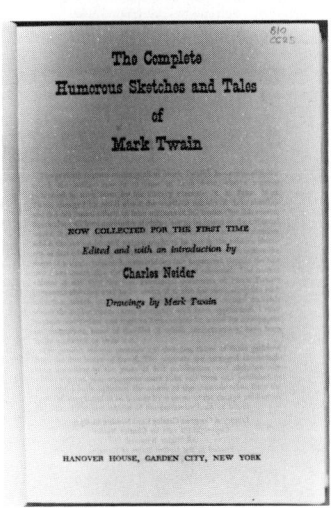

Mark Twain on the Damned Human Race.
New York, (1962): American Century Series, Hill and Wang.
Edited with an introduction by Janet Smith.
Preface by Maxwell Geismar.
First edition thus, September 1962.
Paper wrappers.

Mark Twain's Best: Eight Short Stories by America's Master Humorist.
New York, (1962): Scholastic Book Services.
          Introduction by Morris Goldberger.
          Eleventh printing.
          Paper wrappers.

Letters from the Earth.
New York and Evanston, (1962): Harper & Row.
        Edited by Bernard DeVoto.
        Preface by Henry Nash Smith.
        Black cloth with pictorial dustjacket.

Letters from the Earth.
Greenwich, Conn., (1963): Fawcett Publications, Inc.
        The Crest reprint edition, first printing.
        Pictorial paper wrappers.

Selected Shorter Writings of Mark Twain.
Boston, (1962): Houghton Mifflin Company.
                Edited with an introduction by
                Walter Blair.
                Riverside Edition A58.
                Paper wrappers.

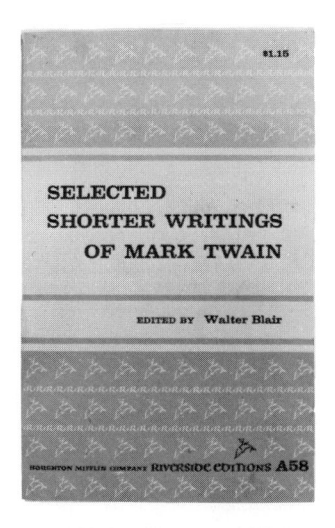

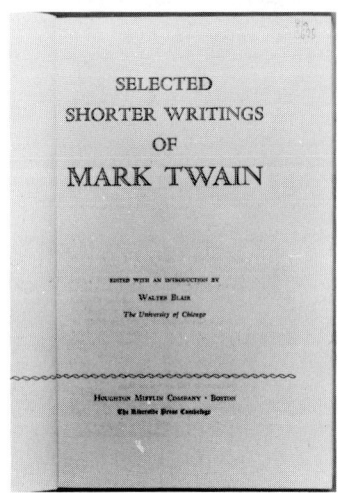

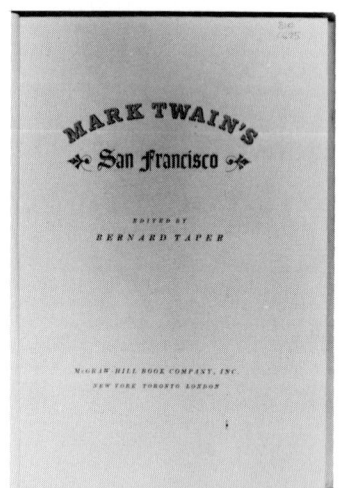

Mark Twain's San Francisco.
New York, Toronto, London, (1963): McGraw-Hill Book Co.
Edited with an introduction by Bernard Taper.
Paper over boards with cloth shelfback and dustjacket.

Simon Wheeler, Detective.
New York, 1963: The New York Public Library.
Edited with an introduction by Franklin R. Rogers.
Green cloth with tissue wrapper: two copies from the edition of 1500.

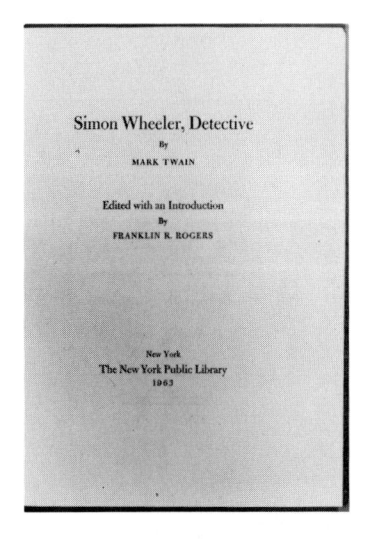

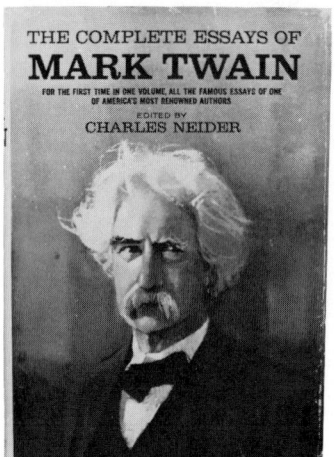

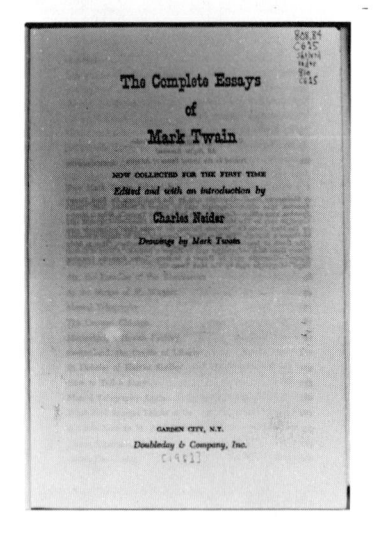

The Complete Essays of Mark Twain.
Garden City, 1963: Doubleday & Company, Inc.
  "Now Collected for the First Time."
  Edited with an introduction by
  Charles Neider.
  Drawings by Mark Twain.
  Black cloth with pictorial dustjacket.

The Forgotten Writings of Mark Twain.
New York, (1963): The Citadel Press.
        Edited by Henry Duskis.
          "First paperbound edition,
          June 1963."
          Paper wrappers: two copies.

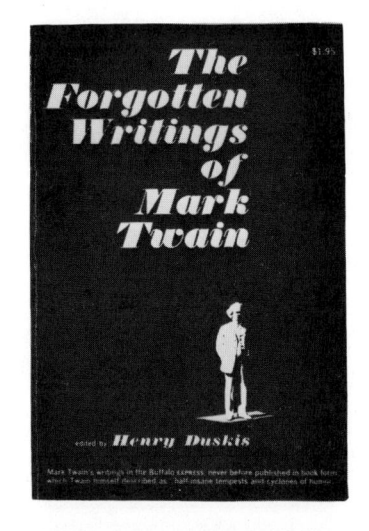

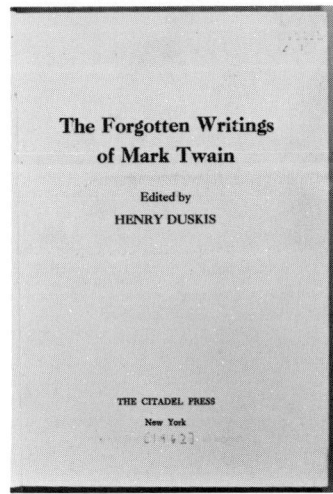

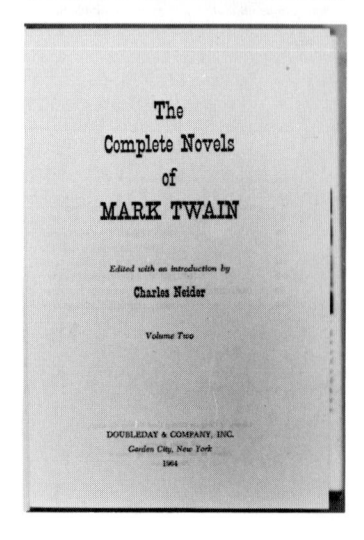

The Complete Novels of Mark Twain.
Garden City, 1964: Doubleday and Co., Inc.
Edited by Charles Neider.
Two volumes.
Green cloth with pictorial dustjackets and slipcase.

Mark Twain: A Cure for the Blues.
Rutland, Vt., (1964): Charles Tuttle Co. Includes "The Enemy Conquered; or Love Triumphant" by Ragsdale McClintock.
Paper over boards with dustjacket.

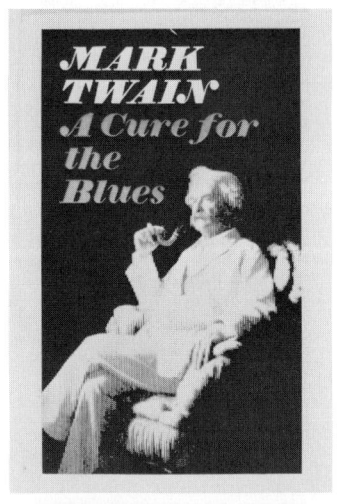

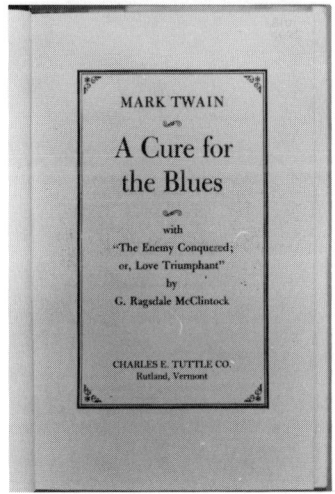

Susy and Mark Twain: Family Dialogues.
New York, (1965): Harper & Row, Publishers. Arranged and edited by Edith Colgate Salsbury.
Red cloth with pictorial dustjacket.

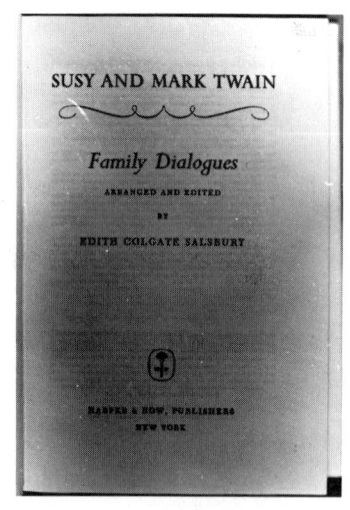

Short Stories of Mark Twain.
New York, (1967?): Funk & Wagnalls.
        Cover illustration by Bill Hoffman.
        Funk and Wagnalls Paperback F18,
        price $1.50.
        Pictorial paper wrappers.

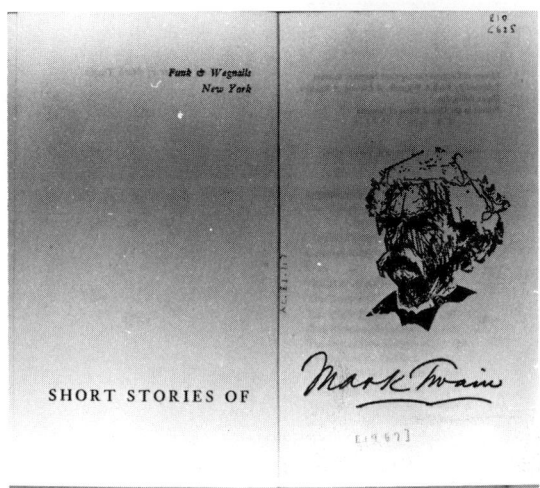

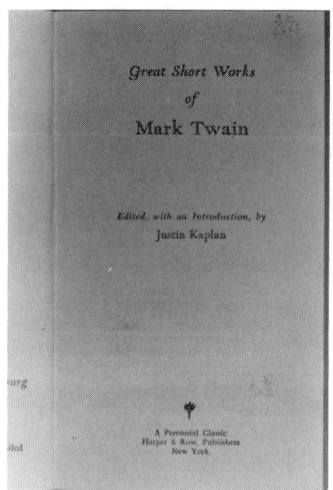

Great Short Works of Mark Twain.
New York, (1967): Harper & Row.
>Perennial Classic #P3075, price 95¢.
>Cover illustration by
>Leonard Baskin.
>Edited with an introduction by
>Justin Kaplan.
>Pictorial paper wrappers.

A Treasury of Mark Twain.
(Kansas City, Mo., 1967): Hallmark Editions.
"The Wit and Wisdom of a Great Writer."
Edited by Edward Lewis and Robert Myers.
Illustrated by James Parkinson.
Paper over boards with dustjacket.

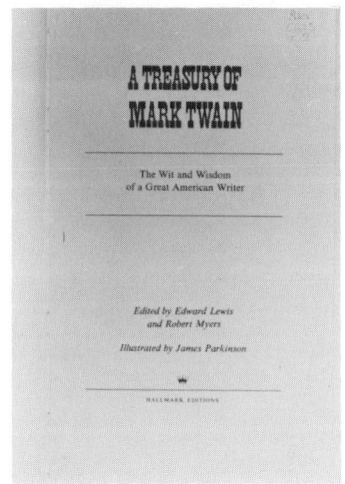

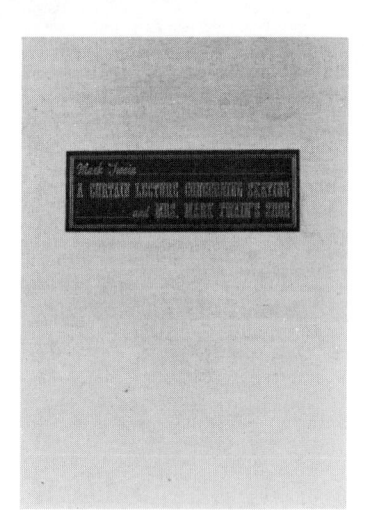

A Curtain Lecture concerning Skating; and, Mrs. Mark Twain's Shoe.
Denver, 1967: Ralph Baldwin, Printer.
>Edited by Donald M. Kunde.
>#229 of 265 copies.
>Signed by the editor.
>Cloth with leather label stamped in gold.

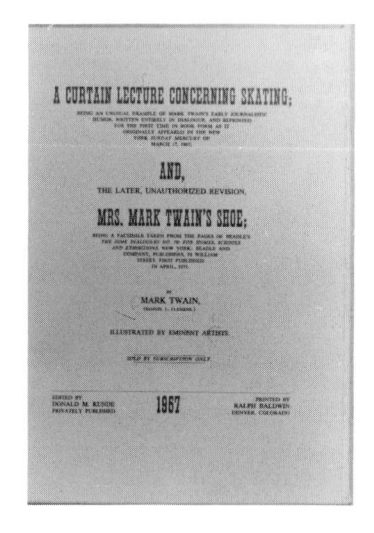

Mark Twain's Satires and Burlesques.
Berkeley and Los Angeles, 1967: University of California Press.
Edited with an introduction by Franklin R. Rogers.
Grey cloth with dustjacket.

Mark Twain's Satires and Burlesques.
Berkeley and Los Angeles, 1968: University of California Press.
Second printing.
Grey cloth with dustjacket.

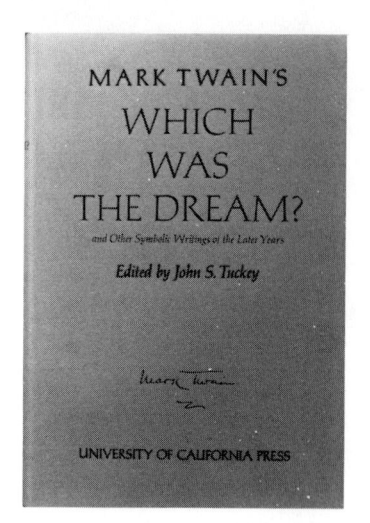

Which Was the Dream? And Other Symbolic Writings of the Later Years.
Berkeley and Los Angeles, 1967: University of
    California Press.
    Edited with an introduction by
    John S. Tuckey.
    Grey cloth with dustjacket.

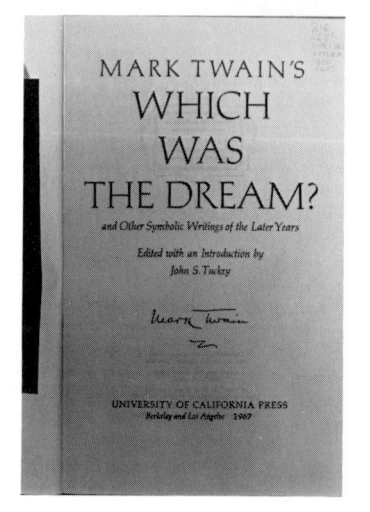

Which Was the Dream? etc.
Berkeley and Los Angeles, 1968: University of
    California Press.
    Second printing.
    Grey cloth with dustjacket.

Mark Twain's Letters to His Publishers 1867-1894,
Berkeley and Los Angeles, 1967: University of California Press.
Edited with an introduction by Hamlin Hill.
Grey cloth with dustjacket.

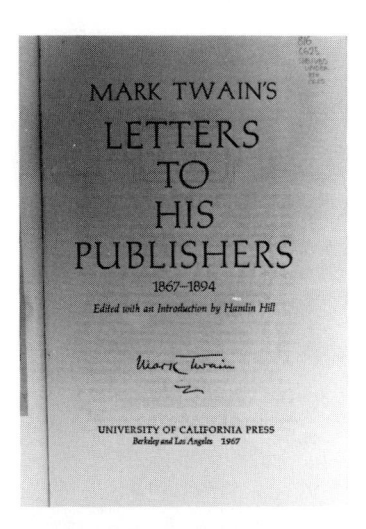

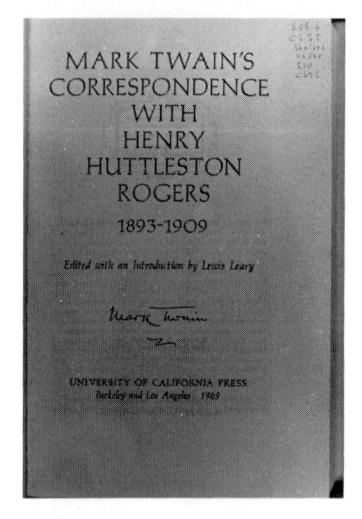

Mark Twain's Correspondence with Henry Huddleston Rogers 1893-1909.
Berkeley and Los Angeles, 1969: University of California Press.
Edited with an introduction by Lewis Leary.
Grey cloth with dustjacket.

Mark Twain's Mysterious Stranger Manuscripts.
Berkeley and Los Angeles, 1969: University of California Press.
Edited with an introduction by William M. Gibson.
Grey cloth with dustjacket.

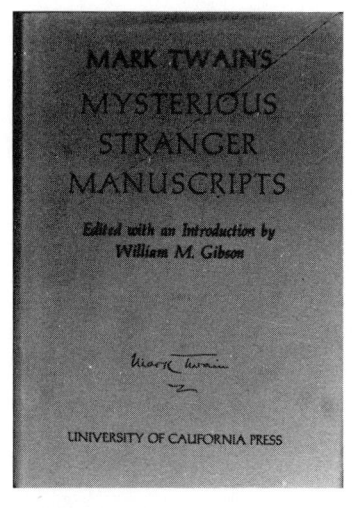

Mark Twain's Hannibal, Huck & Tom.
Berkeley and Los Angeles, 1969: University of California Press.
Edited with an introduction by Walter Blair.
Grey cloth with dustjacket.

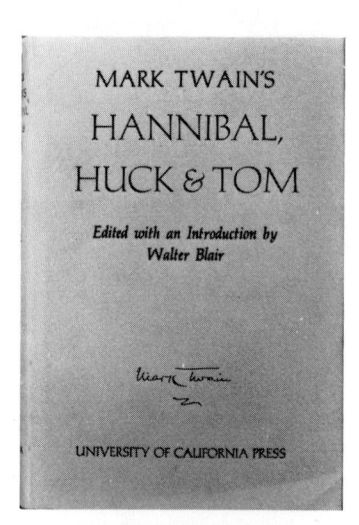

Man is the only animal that blushes or needs to.
(New York, 1970): Stanyan Books, Random House.
"The wisdom of Mark Twain"
Selected by Michael Joseph.
Sixth printing.
Pictorial paper over boards with dustjacket.

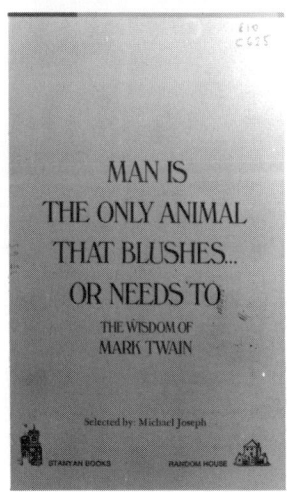

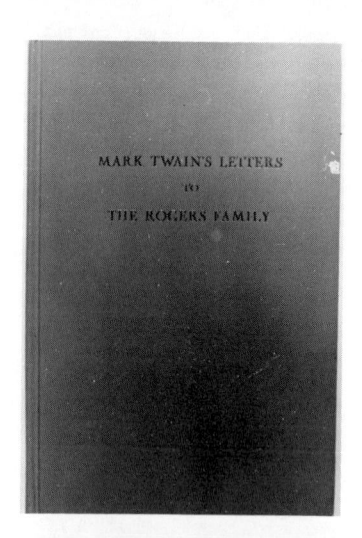

Mark Twain's Letters to the Rogers Family.
(New Bedford, Mass., 1970: Reynolds-DeWalt Printing Inc.)
The Millicent Library Collection.
Edited with notes and an introduction by Earl J. Dias.
Red cloth with tissue dustjacket: two copies, one signed by the editor.

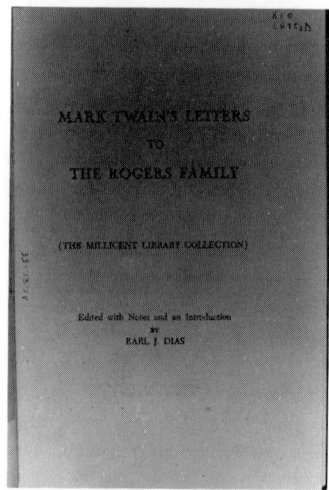

The War Prayer.
(New York, 1970): A St. Crispin Press Book.
           Published in association with
           Harper & Row.
           Drawings by John Groth.
           First Harper Colophon edition.
           Printed paper wrappers.

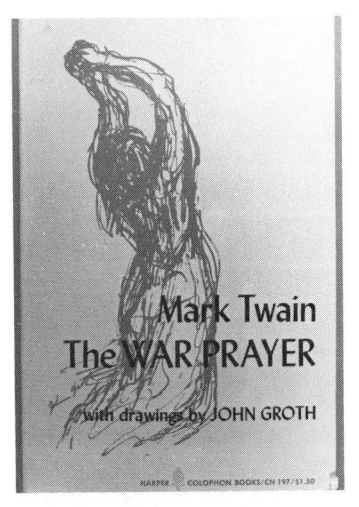

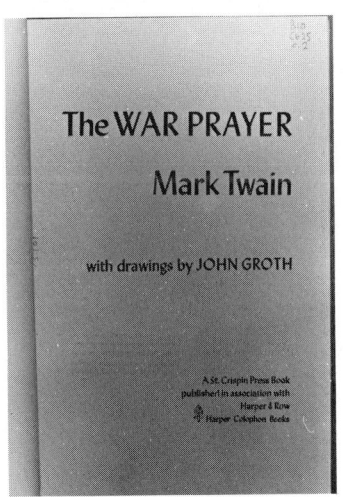

The War Prayer.
(New York, 1971): A Crispin Press Book.
           Published in association with
           Harper & Row.
           First Perennial Library edition.
           Printed paper wrappers.

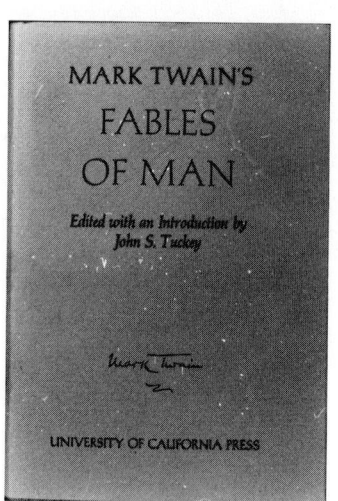

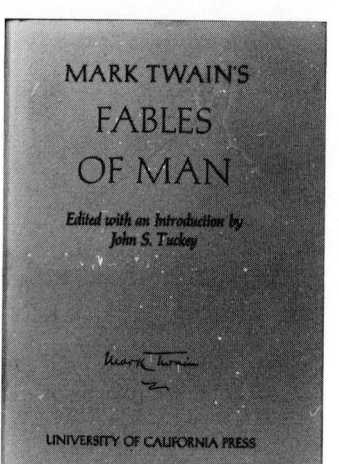

Mark Twain's Fables of Man.
Berkeley, Los Angeles, London, 1972: University of California Press.
Edited with an introduction by John S. Tuckey.
Text established by Kenneth Sanderson and Bernard L. Stein.
Grey cloth with dustjacket.

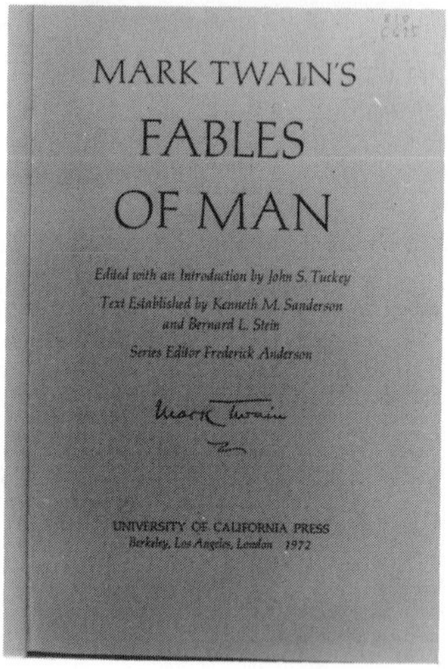

Mark Twain on Man and Beast.
New York and Westport, Conn., 1972: Lawrence Hill & Co.
Compiled by Janet Smith.
Pictorial paper wrappers.

A Mark Twain Turnover: Advice for Good Little Girls. (with) Mark Twain and the Devil.
New Britain, Conn., 1972: Robert E. Massmann.
   Miniature book.
   Pictorial cloth over boards.

Everyone's Mark Twain.
South Brunswick, N.J. and New York, (1972):
>A.S. Barnes and Company. London:
Thomas Yoseloff Ltd.
Complied by Caroline Thomas
Harnsberger.
Signed by the compiler.
Black cloth.

A Pen Warmed-up in Hell.
New York, Evanston, San Francisco, London, (1972):
    Harper & Row, Publishers.
    Edited by Frederick Anderson.
    Cloth with pictorial dustjacket.

A Pen Warmed-up in Hell.
New York, Evanston, San Francisco, London, (1973):
    Harper & Row, Publishers.
    First Perennial Library edition.
    #P279, price $1.50.
    Paper wrappers.

Mark Twain and the Three R's. (Race, Religion, Revolution and Related Matters).
Indianapolis, New York, (1973): The Bobbs-Merrill Company, Inc.
Edited with an introduction by Maxwell Geismar.
Mustard cloth with dustjacket.

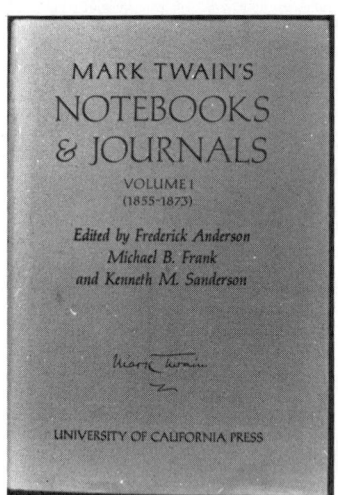

Mark Twain's Notebooks and Journals: Volume I (1855-1873).
Berkeley, Los Angeles, London, 1975: University of California Press.
Edited by Frederick Anderson, Michael B. Frank and Kenneth M. Sanderson.
Grey cloth with dustjacket.

Mark Twain's Notebooks and Journals: Volume II (1877-1883).
Berkeley, Los Angeles, London, 1975: University of California Press.
Edited by Frederick Anderson, Lin Salamo and Bernard L. Stein.
Grey cloth with dustjacket.

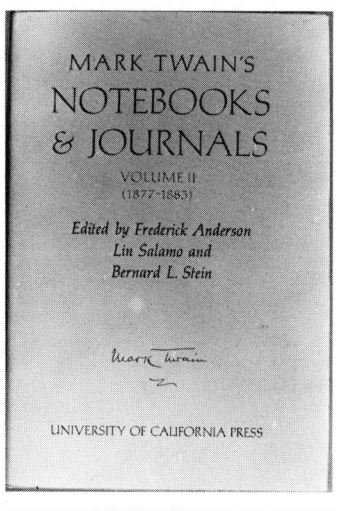

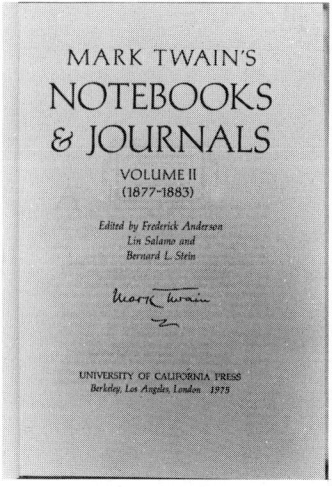

Mark Twain's Notebooks and Journals: Volume III (1883-1891).
Berkeley, Los Angeles, London, 1979: University of California Press.
Edited by Robert Pack Browning, Michael B. Frank and Lin Salamo.
Grey cloth with dustjacket.

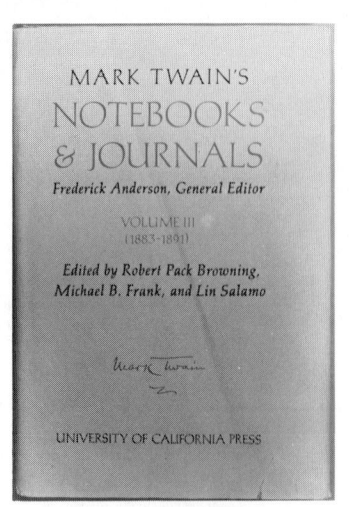

The Higher Animals: A Mark Twain Bestiary.
New York, (1976): Thomas Y. Crowell Company.
>> Edited by Maxwell Geismar.
>> Drawings by Jean-Claude Suares.
>> Terra-cotta cloth with dustjacket.

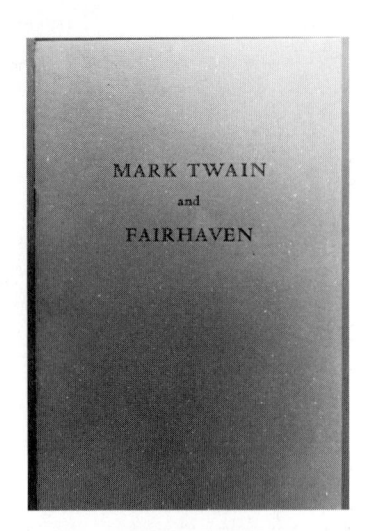

Mark Twain and Fairhaven.
Fairhaven, Mass., (1976): The Millicent Library.
Introduction by Earl J. Dias.
Revised edition.
(First edition was 1913, second was 1926).
Yellow-gold paper wrappers.

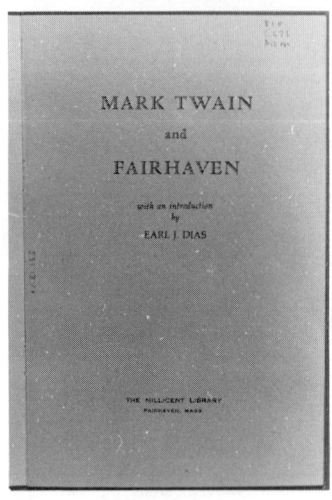

The Unabridged Mark Twain.
Philadelphia, (1976): Running Press.
> Opening remarks by Kurt Vonnegut, Jr.
> Edited by Lawrence Teacher.
> Fifth printing.
> This copy inscribed by Vonnegut: *Eternal life/to the Mark/Twain Memorial — Kurt Vonnegut/*/ Hartford/May 30, 1979*
> Brown cloth with pictorial dustjacket.

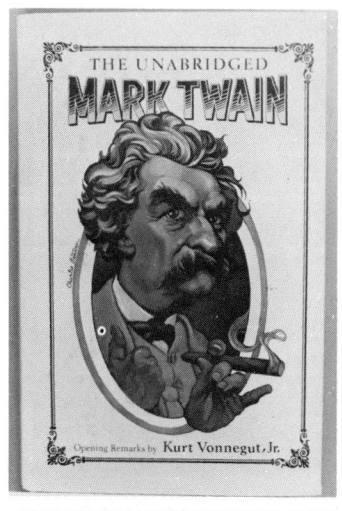

The Unabridged Mark Twain. Volume II.
Philadelphia, (1979): Running Press.
> Edited by Lawrence Teacher.
> Brown cloth with pictorial dustjacket.

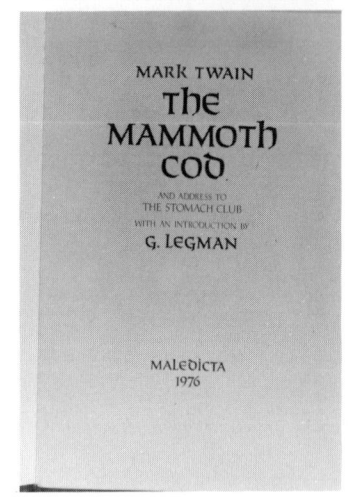

The Mammoth Cod and Address to the Stomach Club.
(Milwaukee), 1976: Maledicta, Inc.
>Introduction by G. Legman.
>No. 1019 of an unspecified number.
>Green cloth with pictorial dustjacket.

The Comic Mark Twain Reader.
Garden City, 1977: Doubleday & Company, Inc.
        Edited with an introduction by
        Charles Neider.
        Paper over boards with cloth
        shelfback and pictorial dustjacket.

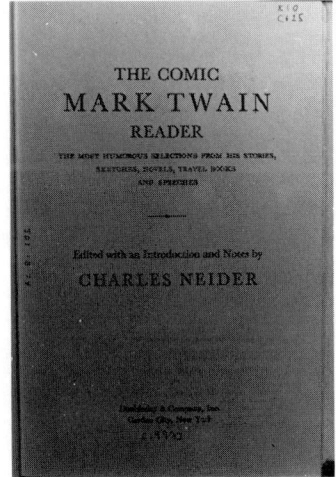

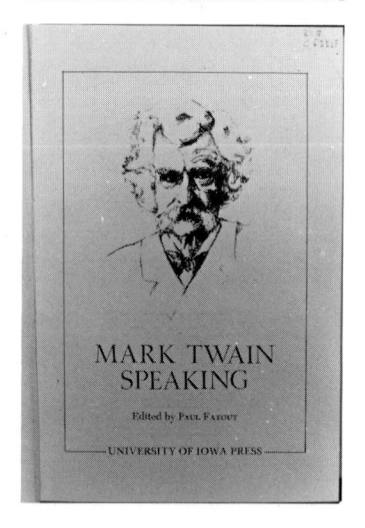

Mark Twain Speaking.
(Iowa City, Iowa, 1976): University of Iowa Press.
    Edited by Paul Fatout.
    Second printing.
    Purple cloth with dustjacket.

Mark Twain Speaks for Himself.
West Lafayette, In., 1978: Purdue University Press.
　　　　　Edited by Paul Fatout.
　　　　　Cloth with dustjacket.

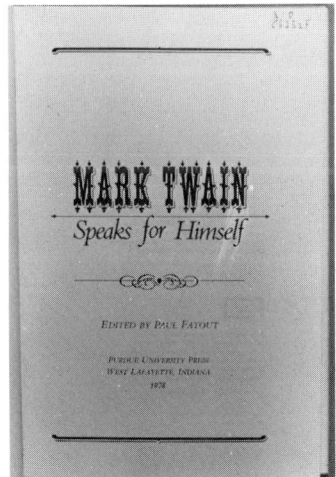

Early Tales & Sketches: Volume I (1851-1864).
Berkeley, Los Angeles, London, 1979: University of California Press for the Iowa Center for Textual Studies.
Edited by Edgar Marquess Branch and Robert H. Hirst with the assistance of Harriet Elinor Smith. Orange cloth with dustjacket.

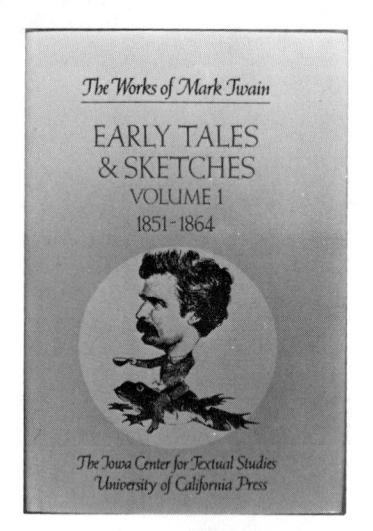

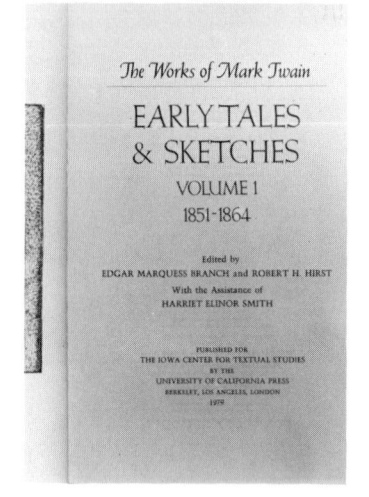

Early Tales & Sketches: Volume II (1864-1865).
Berkeley, Los Angeles, London, 1981: University of California Press for the Iowa Center for Textual Studies.
Edited by Edgar Marquess Branch and Robert H. Hirst with the assistance of Harriet Elinor Smith.
Orange cloth with dustjacket.

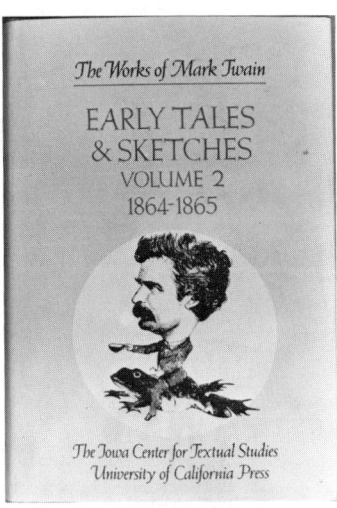

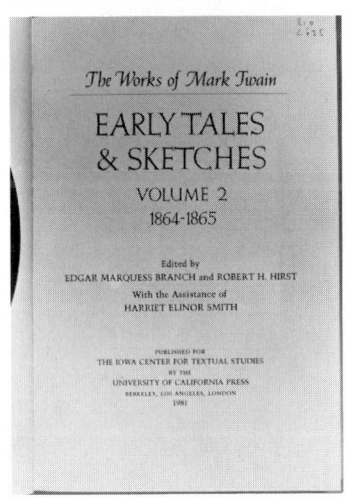

Jim Wolf and the Cats.
Buffalo, 1979: The Hillside Press.
>Miniature book.
>Introduction by Kevin J. Bochynski.
>#32 of 225 copies.
>Pictorial grey cloth with decorated slipcase.

Mark Twain: Social Critic for the 80s.
San Francisco, 1980: AT Press.
           Edited by William L. McLinn and
           Stuart W. White.
           Social Issues Program Edition.
           Cloth with dustjacket.

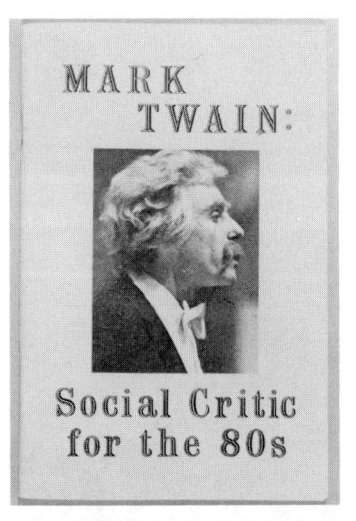

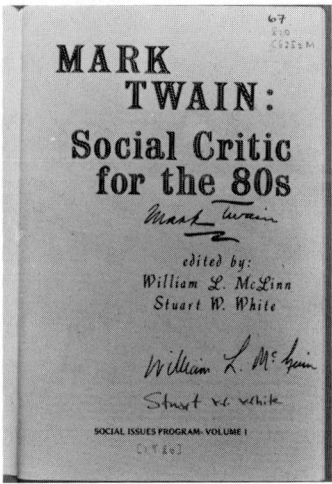

Mark Twain in 1903.

Letters by Mark Twain.

This section describes letters and other communications of Clemens. They are listed chronologically, when date is known, and the few items which could not be dated are listed at the end of this section. The summaries of content were prepared by Diana Royce, Chief Librarian of the Stowe-Day Foundation Library. Occasionally, a summary quotes a sentence or more from a letter where Clemens turned a particularly good phrase.

Abbreviations

ACI : Autograph card, initialed
AL : Autograph letter
ALI : Autograph letter, initialed
ALS : Autograph letter, signed
AN : Autograph note
ANI : Autograph note, initialed
CY : Copy
D   : Document
DS : Document, signed
LS : Letter, written and signed for the author, not in his hand
TL : Typed letter
TLS : Typed letter, signed

WESTMINSTER HOTEL,
cor of Irving Place and 16th St New York.

Roberts & Palmer Prop'rs

New York, June 1, 1867.

Gov. Frank Fuller—

Dear Sir: Please take charge of my affairs while I am gone to Europe, (as per previous understanding,) & in the absence of a better, let this note be full & sufficient authority. Call at the ten cents a copy due me on all sales of my book ("The Jumping Frog & Other Sketches — by Mark Twain,")

ALS to Governor Frank Fuller.
1867 June 1/New York, New York/2 pp.
> Arrangements for Fuller to maintain Clemens' affairs (especially royalties from *The Jumping Frog*) while he is away. Receipts to go to his mother. Sails on Quaker City, June 8.

TLcy to Elisha Bliss, Jr.
1867 December 1/Washington, D.C./1½pp.
> Regards publication of and terms for a book based on his Quaker City letters.

ALS to Jervis Langdon.
(1868) December 2/New York, New York/8 pp.
> Apologizes for not being particularly sociable during his recent visit. Regards Mrs. Crane's departure from the Langdon house. Lecture at Newark (Dec 9) sold out. Invited to return to Pittsburgh. Business matters: purchase of *Tribune* shares; possible editorship of a new Frank Leslie paper. Generally a witty but cautious letter.

Mark Twain, about 1867.

TL to (Elisha, Jr.) Bliss.
1869 April "Something"/Elmira, New York/½ p.
> "*All the names were correct I think, except/Messerano. Jam the Queen of Greece in anywhere. She is the/ daughter of the Emperor of Russia/ and can stand it. No —/put her in Grecian chapter that will be better.*"

TL to (Elisha, Jr.) Bliss.
1869 April 12/Elmira, New York/1 p.
> Regards engravings and title for *The Innocents Abroad*.

Autograph.
1869 September 7/Buffalo, New York/1 p.
> "With pleasure/Yrs truly/ Saml. L. Clemens/"Mark Twain"/Jno. H. Gourlie, Esq.".

472, 22d, 6 P.M.
1870.

Brother Theodore —

I enclose you an official letter, acknowledging rec't of Check.

All right — I will come down & break one of the horses while you break the other. But are you sure your plan is good? It looks feasible, but at the same time I cannot feel certain that it is the safest way. My custom heretofore, when I wanted to break a

AL to (Orion Clemens).
(1870) 11th/Buffalo, New York/4pp. possibly
    incomplete.
    Has no desire to publish in quantity
    nor even see his name in print.

ALS to "Friend" Bliss.
1870 January 22/Elmira, New York/3½ pp.
    Will not copyright *"Round the World"* letters as advertising is too good as the matter stands. Regards *"Noah's Ark book"*; great pains he will take with it; the wish that Mrs. Fairbanks would *"keep still about (it)."* Webb may grant him copyright on *The Jumping Frog.* Business news and his concern as he is to be married February 2.

Mark Twain, about 1870.

ALS to Jervis Langdon.
1870 March 2-3/(Buffalo, New York)/5 pp.
    Thank-you for the replacement of the "Peace". Business: arrangements for Kennett 'indebtedness". A rumor that they intend to leave for Hartford. Impression arose out of his last visit there.

ALS to Hattie Booth.
1870 March 18/Buffalo, New York/½ p.
    Probably answering a fan's letter.

ALS to Theodore Crane.
1870 (April) 22/(Buffalo, New York)/2½ pp.
    Receipt for check. Chatty letter.

TL to ("Frank") Anonymous.
1870 April 26/Buffalo, New York/1½ pp.
    Cannot contract insurance with Frank. Regards publishing and "John Quill".

ALS to Jervis Langdon.
(1870) May 22/(Buffalo, New York)/6 pp.
    Mr. Langdon's recovery. $150. from Theodore (Crane) to Charles (Langdon) for the purchase of a microscope for Clemens. $15,000. offered for Tennessee land. Orion would take it reserving 1000 acres; he would sell all at $30,000. Family news.

ALS to "Friend" Bliss.
1870 June 9/Elmira, New York/2 pp.
>Requests that Bliss paste enclosure in copy of his book (*Innocents Abroad?*) and send to Edward H. House of the *Tribune*.

ALS to Daniel (Slote?).
(1870?) June 27/(Elmira, New York)/1¼ pp.
>Charley (Langdon) returning home from London. Father very ill. Dan to convey whatever news there is to Charles.

ALS to Francis E. Bliss.
1870 September 15/Buffalo, New York/1½ pp.
>Cannot attend Bliss marriage; young lady in household ill with typhoid. Obliged and necessary to remain. Nor can they attend Chas. Langdon's wedding in mid-Oct.

ALS to Olivia (Lewis) Langdon, Mrs. Jervis.
1870 November 7/Buffalo, New York/Telegram.
>"*Langdon Clemens was/born at eleven this morning Mother/& child doing well. Mr. Fairbanks is coming/Samuel L. Clemens/Theodore/Please preserve this/O.L.*"

ALS to Charles Jervis Langdon.
(1870 after November 7)/Buffalo, New York/4 pp.
>Thank-you for baby shoes for Langdon. There follows "conversation" between Father and son. Delightful.

ALS to (Eunice Langdon Ford, Mrs.)
(1870) November 11/Buffalo, New York/16 pp.
>Text written for son Langdon. Trials and tribulations of being 4 days old without any human rights or dignity. Wonderful letter.

ALS to Haney.
(1870) November 14/Buffalo, New York/1½ pp.
>Refuses to "*meddle with Almanac business*". Discusses a caricature of himself & son.

ALS to (Olivia (Lewis) Langdon, Mrs. Jervis).
(1870) November 19/Buffalo, New York/4 pp.
>Thank-you for apples. Request for suspenders. Encourages her visit at Thanksgiving as Livy is lonely. Family correspondence.

ALS to (Eunice Langdon Ford, Mrs.)
1870 December 25/(Buffalo, New York)/2 pp.
>Written for and to accompany present from Langdon. Holiday wishes.

ALS Olivia (Langdon) Clemens, Mrs. Samuel L. to Alice (Hooker) Day, Mrs. John C.
1871 January 25/Buffalo, New York/8 pp.
>She writes a great deal of her father's death and of her new baby boy. She and Mr. Clemens have read Mr. Warner's book and enjoyed it. Clemens adds a note begging Mrs. Hooker's pardon for sending such a curt telegram last time he was in Hartford.

ACS to Jane (Lampton) Clemens, Mrs. John Marshall.
(?1871 August) n.p.
>His love and good wishes.

ALS to Charles E. Perkins.
1872 May 8/Elmira, New York/1 p.
>Regards Bliss's check for *Roughing It.* Asks him to acknowledge check and accompany it with necessary protest.

ALS to (Olivia Susan Clemens).
(1872) May 9/(Cleveland, Ohio)/3½ pp.
>Father's loving letter to daughter not yet 2 months old. *"My child, be virtuous and you will be happy."*

ALS to Olivia (Lewis) Langdon, Mrs. Jervis.
(1872) December 3/(Buffalo, New York)/7½ pp.
>Misses Mrs. Langdon after her stay. Regards Beecher-Tilton Scandal. Nasby just gone after hurried hour's visit.

ALS to Anonymous — Lee.
(1873) n.d./(London, England)/ 6 pp.
>Gene's plans for seeing things in London he wants his wife to see.

ALS to Olivia (Lewis) Langdon, Mrs. Jervis.
(1873 May)/On board ship/1½ pp.
>Departure for England. Farewell.

ALS to (Olivia (Lewis) Langdon, Mrs. Jervis).
(1873 October 12)/1 p.
>Will go to new hotel if better than St. Nicholas. Resting before lecturing.

Farmington Avenue,
Hartford.

Dec. 22.

Dear Brother:

I have been confined to the house & in the doctor's clutches for about 3 weeks — otherwise I could not & would not have delayed so long to tell you how thoroughly delighted I am with the Cyclopedia & how much the book

ALS to (Charles E.) Perkins.
(1874) May 8/Elmira, (New York)/10 pp. + enc., 2 pp.
> Regards the use of Livy's horse and carriage. Also a note to the city authorities in Clemens' hand regards the renewing and widening of the sidewalk on Farmington Avenue.

ALS to (Edward Tuckerman Potter).
(1874) May 8/Elmira, New York/2 pp.
> Regards design and arrangement of butler's pantry and nursery of the Hartford house. Per order of Mrs. Clemens.

Check + enc.
to F. Bubser.
1875 April 21/Hartford.
> Cancelled check to the amount of $23.

Mark Twain, about 1875.

ALS to Olivia (Lewis) Langdon, Mrs. Jervis.
(1875) December 22/Hartford/2 pp.
> Confined to the house and would have written his delight with the cyclopedia sooner.

AL to (John Calvin) Day.
(1876) September 27/(Hartford) 1 p.
> RSVP. *"Mr. & Mrs. Clemens will be happy to see Mr. & Mrs. Day on Friday evening from 7 till 11 . . . ."*

ALS to (Charles E.) Perkins.
(1876) October 5/2 pp.
> Regards pirating from Clemens various books. What should he do? Regards a tax list from the assessors. Regards a check.

ALI to (Charles E. Perkins).
(1876) October 16/1 p.
> Regards a list and a clause beginning *"By the law of 1872."*

ACS to Charles E. Perkins.
(1876) October 16/Hartford.
> Regards the Philadelphia checks.

ALS, cy. to John T. Raymond.
1876 October 27/Hartford/1½ pp.
> (Copied by Charles E. Perkins with notation regards what was written.) Clemens has made arrangements to go to Europe in April. He will make one more effort to come to an understanding. Regards piracy of his writings.

371

ACS to Charles E. Perkins.
(1876 December)/Hartford.
 Raymond waits for contract. Please draw it. He has another contract to be drawn and a deed to be examined.

ACI to Charles E. Perkins.
(1876) December 20/Hartford.
 Regards going to New York and the Parsloe contracts.

ALS to Charles E. Perkins.
(1877?) n.d./(Hartford)/1 p.
 Regards his approval (of an engraving) to be sent to Davies & Company.

ACI to Charles E. Perkins.
(1877) January 22/Hartford.
 Do not send document to R(aymond). There is a very important alteration to be made.

ACS to (Charles E. Perkins).
(1877) April 26/Baltimore, Maryland
 Tell Bergen that you are awaiting instructions.

Memorandum to (Charles E.) Perkins.
(1877 May bet. 4-16)/2 pp.
 Regards investments during the past sixteen months. Please straighten up the interest account and report your findings to me.

DS to G(eorge) P. Bissell & Company.
1877 May 15/Hartford/1 p.
 Authorizing Perkins to endorse checks payable to Clemens for deposit.

ACS to (Charles E. Perkins).
(1877) May 15/2 pp.
 Regards Harte and his indebtedness to Clemens. Keep a memorandum of all deposits.

ALS to (Charles E. Perkins).
(1877) July 4/Elmira, (New York)/2 pp.
 Regards fire insurance and one's ability to claim full value in case of a loss. He requests that insurance on the furniture and barn be reduced.

ACI to (Charles E. Perkins).
(1877) July 7/Elmira, (New York)/2 pp.
 Regards the Hartford property. It should be in "her" name. Regards taxes.

Telegraph to Charles E. Perkins.
1877 July 7/Hartford.
> *"Telegraph me Bergens address."*

ALS to Charles E. Perkins.
(1877 August 3)/Elmira, (New York)/2 pp.
> Regards insurance, interest deposits and *"hot Scotch whisky."*

ACS to (Charles E. Perkins).
(1877) August 3/Elmira, (New York)/2 pp.
> Regards his and Harte's shares from the play *Ah Sin*.

ACI to Charles E. Perkins.
(1877) August 11/Elmira, New York.
> Apply to Parsole. *"I don't know that joint-agent's name myself."* (Card is torn.)

ALS to (Charles E.) Perkins.
(1877) September 20/1 p.
> Tell Bergen to add $2 to his wages after October 2.

ACS to (Charles E. Perkins).
(1877) September 21.
> Regards Bergen and dramatics.

ALS to (Charles E. Perkins).
(1877 September 21 or after)/1 p.
> Regards the engraving *"*Christ Leaving the Praetorium.*" "Shall I pay, or refuse"* is the closing by Clemens.

ACS to Charles E. Perkins.
(1877) September 24/Hartford.
> Regards Edward's sending some money. A note on reverse side states: Rec'd and ans. 25./77

ACS to Charles E. Perkins.
(1877 October 4)/Hartford.
> Regards the "Dramatic" year which he will not concede yet.

ALS to (Routledge & Company).
1877 October 14/Hartford/2 pp.
> Regards a tramp in London. Regards *"that box and contents."*

ACI to (Charles E. Perkins).
(1877) October 18. n.p.
> *"Send this or tear it up."* If you send it, tell them to hold the picture a few days.

ACI to Charles E. Perkins.
(1877) December 28/Hartford.
> Regards Bergen. Hopes he is out of luck.

D to George P. Bissell & Company.
(1878) February 9/Munich, (Germany)/1 p.
> Asks them to pay Orion Clemens $25.

ALS to (Frank Woodbridge Cheney).
(1878) c. February 23/(Hartford)/7 pp.
> Regards Welsey Hart, evidently an inmate at Wethersfield State Prison.

LS to John T. Raymond.
1878 March 16/Hartford/1 p.
> Regards the appointment of Charles E. Perkins as his agent.

ALS Olivia (Langdon) Clemens, Mrs. Samuel L. to (Saturday Morning Club, Hartford).
1878 March 25/Hartford/4 pp.
> (Written in Clemens' hand on blue-embossed initialed stationery.) Thank-you for flowers. *"I am too proud of my patriarchal position in the Club to be willing to either resign it or allow another to occupy it in the interregnum. I long, instead, the privilege of appointing a vacant chair, of ordinary pattern, to represent me & my wisdom on occasions when I ought to be present in my official capacity — & mark you, there are malignants who will tell you that a vacant chair is able to represent me & my wisdom very well...."*

ALS to Olivia (Lewis) Langdon, Mrs. Jervis.
1878 April 20/At Sea/2¼ pp.
> Written on their evening's menu. Appetite and enjoyable voyage.

ALS to George P. Bissell & Company.
1878 May 23/Heidelberg, (Germany)/1 p.
> Asks them to pay Rev. Mr. Twichell $300 and charge to his account.

ALS to Olivia (Lewis) Langdon, Mrs. Jervis.
1878 September 13/Geneva, Switzerland/7½ pp.
> Family out shopping. Travels with the Rev. Twichell. Susie's philosophical nature. Wonderful letter.

ALS to Olivia (Lewis) Langdon, Mrs. Jervis.
1878 December 2/Munich, Germany/6 pp. + env.
    Receipt of birthday present (*"covered Krug of beaten brass & gilded in addition"*). Humorous account of the difficulties with their lodgings.

ALS Olivia (Langdon) Clemens, Mrs. Samuel L. to Olivia (Lewis) Langdon, Mrs. Jervis.
1878 December 7/Munich, Germany/15 pp. + env.
    Livy's news of the children, particularly Clara. Regards Christmas presents from and to members of the Langdon family. Susy's concern that Santa Claus will not come as he will be German. Susy's letter dictated to her father.

ALI to Olivia (Lewis) Langdon, Mrs. Jervis.
(1878 or 1879)/4 pp.
    Thank-you for *"Faust"*, his Christmas present. Family news.

ALS to Olivia (Lewis) Langdon, Mrs. Jervis.
(1879) February 23/Munich, Germany/5½ pp. + env.
    Snow storm. *"I've got the airs for my musical box selected at last . . . ."* Sam Moffett has joined them. Charles Langdon maintaining Livy's affairs. Leaving for Paris.

AL to Olivia (Lewis) Langdon, Mrs. Jervis.
1879 March 30/Paris, France/4½ pp. + env.
    Aches and family pains. Includes message dictated by Susy; child's activities.

ALS to Charles Jervis (Langdon).
(1879) June 17/Paris, France/2 pp.
    Encourages Charley to join them. Plans to go from Paris to London in early July.

ALS to George P. Bissell & Company.
1879 September 8/Elmira, New York/1 p.
    Asks them to pay $25 to E.S. Cleveland and charge to his account. Rowe and Swift on reverse side.

ALS to George P. Bissell & Company.
1879 October 13/Elmira, New York/1 p.
    Asks them to pay Federick Schweppe $250. and charge to his account.

Elmira, Sept. 3/81.

Well, my dear old Whitmore —

I owe you money on that hotel bill, but we will let her rest for the present, as I am in bed, exhausted by six days' work done in three.

I mustn't be writing letters; but this only a note. I wanted to say, I'm away out here in the woods, far from all sources of information, & I want to ask you what I had better do about the Omaha pf & Omaha common? Sell at the price I paid, or leave them alone a while longer? Of course I would prefer to sell each at an advance of about 4 points. This would average my Denver very neatly, & make my 200 stand me in about 85. Love to you both

Ys
SLC.

ALS to (Olivia (Lewis) Langdon, Mrs. Jervis).
(1879?) December 5/2 pp.
>Thank-you for shaving stand. Visit by Mr. Slee. Missed her telephone exhibition.

DS to George H. Warner.
1880 May 24/Hartford/1 p.
>A promise to pay Warner $900. A notation that principal plus interest were paid on July 6.

AL to Olivia (Lewis) Langdon, Mrs. Jervis.
1880 August 19/Quarry Farm, (Elmira, New York)/1 p.
>Letter written for 3-week old Jean. She has a scarcity of hair.

Telegram to George Griffin.
1880 September 11/Elmira, New York.
>*"Show this telegram to Mr. Perkins & get twenty dollars."*

ALI to (Charles E.) Perkins.
1880 September (13) or after/(Hartford)/1½ pp.
>Regards his cash balance, it is too large. (This is added to Bissell & Company's letter.)

ALS to (Mary Caroline (Robinson), Mrs. Nathaniel) Shipman.
(1880-1881) "Sunday"/(Hartford)/3 pp.
>Their enjoyment of gift of flowers and jelly.

Telegram & env. to H(erbert) M. Lawrence.
1881 May 9/(Elmira, New York?).
>*"What is earlist date you can begin decorating our/house. Answer to New York paid Mark Twain."*

ALI to (Charles E.) Perkins.
1881 July 2/Branford/1 p. + env.
>Regards a swindle.

ALS to Franklin G. Whitmore.
1881 August 8/Elmira, New York/4 pp. + env.
>Attack of lumbago. Children as travellers.

ALI to (Franklin G.) Whitmore.
1881 September 3/Elmira, New York/1 p. + env.
>Business: regards debt to Whitmore and Omaha stock.

ALS to (Charles E.) Perkins.
(1881) December 12/Hartford/1 p. + card.
>Regards his claim against Ives.

Mark Twain, about 1880.

ALS to (Charles E.) Perkins.
1882 September 2/Elmira, (New York)/2 pp.
> Regards taxes. Regards Orion's and his mother's checks.

ALS to (Charles E.) Perkins.
1882 September 6/1 p.
> Asks him to extract a certificate from his safety deposit box and mail it to Mr. Webster.

ANS to Charles Jervis Langdon.
1883 January 15/Hartford/½ p.
> Authorizes Langdon to pay his assessment on Susquehanna and South Western Railroad Company stock.

TL to (Matthew A.) Hewins.
1883 April 10/Hartford/½ p.
> New cushions not needed. Hewins was state billiard champion.

ALI Olivia (Langdon) Clemens, Mrs. Samuel L. to Charles Jervis Langdon.
1883 April 24/(Hartford)/4 pp.
> Rejects Charley's invitation to Elmira because of Livy's health which has begun to improve but there is need of caution.

ALS to Ellen Teresa (Clark) Taft, Mrs. Cincinnatus A.
1883 August 14/Elmira, New York/4 pp.
> Written by Mr. Clemens for the family. Their concern for the health of Dr. Taft; his admirable calling and character. Praise of the good physician.

ALS to Olivia (Lewis) Langdon, Mrs. Jervis.
1883 August 19/Quarry Farm, (Elmira, New York) /3 pp.
> Mrs. Langdon has presented gifts to the Clemenses on her birthday. "Thank-you" for the "rauchgeschirr" from Livy, too.

ALS to Jervis (Langdon).
1883 December 19/Hartford/2½ pp.
> (In pencil) Hopes Jervis will like the Robin Hood book. Clemens has reread text and it still holds his fancy. *"I have always regretted that I did not belong to Robin Hoods' gang."* Samuel and Olivia Clemens gave the book as a Christmas present to Jervis.

ALS to (Cincinnatus A. Taft).
(Before 1884)/½ p. (incomplete).
>Apparently a description of his schedule and busy routine.

ALS to (Cincinnatus A. Taft).
(Before 1884) "Saturday Evening"/(Hartford)/3 pp.
>Offers Hartford house at his disposal while family is in Elmira. Would provide the peace and quiet to cure his fatigue.

ALS to Ellen Teresa (Clark) Taft, Mrs. Cincinnatus A.
(1884?)/(Elmira, New York?/1 p. (incomplete).
>After Dr. Taft's death, Mrs. Taft and daughter, Laura will be missed.

ANS to Francis E. (Bliss).
1884 (after May 11)/(Hartford)/¼ p.
>Written at top of letter to Bliss, May 11, 1884, 1 p. by George P. Walliham. Send to Walliham such books as he has published by Clemens charged to Clemens.

ALS to Isabella (Beecher) Hooker, Mrs. John.
1884 May 27/Hartford/1 p.
>*"Mrs. Clemens & I have conferred together, & decided that if you can get the subscriptions you may hold us responsible for fifty dollars a year toward your proposed salary (in Woman Suffragist movement). Would like to give more but must go according to our ability."*

ALS to Charles H. Clark.
1884 June 24/Elmira, New York/1½ pp. + env.
>Regards news of Dr. (Cincinnatus A.) Taft of whom they have heard nothing. Clark is at *Courant* office.

ALS to Ellen Teresa (Clark) Taft, Mrs. Cincinnatus A.
(1884) July 10/Elmira, New York/3½ pp.
>Praise and admiration for the late Dr. Taft. Delayed writing as have dental problems.

ALI to Editor of the *Courant*.
(1884) July 18/Elmira, New York/11½ pp.
>Clemens' own copy of eulogy to Dr. (Cincinnatus A.) Taft.

Elmira, July 17/86.

My Dear Warner:

Thank you ever so much for your effort in the matter of the land. It is tempting; still, the figure is too high by $1500 — that is, for this year. By & by, if business prospects continue as they now look, I could more easily & would more cheerfully pay ten thousand than half that sum now. If that prospect should prove a delusion, we

ALS to T. W. Russell.
1884 October 14-16/Hartford/2 pp. + env.
    Regrets but must decline. Sympathies are with the independent movement.

ALScy to My dear Kinney.
1885 December 15/Hartford/1 p.
    Thank you for invitation for January 6th, but I am not able to accept as I shall be absent from town.

ALS to Franklin G. Whitmore.
1886 June 15/New York, New York/1 p. + env.
    Has forgotten field-glass. Please send to Elmira. *"I suppose it is in the billiard room . . . ."*

ALS to Franklin G. Whitmore.
1886 July 12/Elmira, New York/3 pp. + env.
    Enjoyable trip. Cigars arrived. Sell the American Exchange. He is sending $3000. for Bissell. Business affairs.

Mark Twain, about 1885.

ALS to (George H.) Warner.
1886 July 17/Elmira, New York/2¼ pp.
    Business regards purchase of land. Rug received (for Clara Spauldings wedding present).

ALS to (Franklin G.) Whitmore.
1886 July 17/Elmira, New York/4 pp. + env.
    "My idea is to have the type-setter going constantly in New York, every day & all day long . . . ." Business and arrangements regards the typesetter.

ALI to Franklin G. Whitmore.
1886 July 28/Elmira, New York/1 p. + env.
    "I am not crying because the Thorne machine failed . . . ." Business.

ALS to (James W.)Paige.
1886 August 16/Elmira, New York/4 pp.
    Instructions for Mr. Paige to arrange a test of the typesetter's ability. A competition with prizes will settle the issue.

ALS to Franklin G. Whitmore.
1886 August 17/Elmira, New York/2 pp.
    Clemens' prospectus for the typesetter. Proposes incentive rewards for "Will", $300. paid as his speed in typesetting increases.

ALS to Elizabeth (Foote) Jenkins, Mrs. Edward H.
18(86) October 2/Hartford/1 p. + env.
  Regards tile for the side of a bedroom fireplace.

ALS to Olivia (Lewis) Langdon, Mrs. Jervis.
1886 October 19/Hartford/2 pp. + env.
  Invitation to visit. New boiler satisfies all want for hot water.

ALS to Elizabeth (Foote) Jenkins, Mrs. Edward H.
1886 October 20/(Hartford)/1 p.
  Regards money owed to her by Mrs. Clemens.

ALS to Olivia (Lewis) Langdon, Mrs. Jervis.
(1886?) October 21/Hartford/1¾ pp. + env.
  In "Sunday" best awaiting 30 guests for whist. Anxious for her arrival.

ALS to Dora ((Wheeler) (Keith), Mrs. Boudinot.
1887 February 15/Hartford/2 pp.
  Embarrassed invitation. Miss Keith was to paint Clemens' portrait, being commissioned by Harper and Brothers.

Envelope to Linus T(ryon) Fenn.
1887 July 5/Elmira, New York.

ALI to Franklin G. Whitmore.
1887 July 11/New York, New York/1 p. + env.
  Sending Grant's *Memoirs* to Mr. Quinn. Give as present or sell at cost to him.

ALI to Franklin G. Whitmore.
1887 July 15/Hartford/1 p.
  Regards article on "electro-motors" already out as they plan for the type-setter. Royalties from American Publishing Co. for 3 mos. + $163.26.

Telegram to Franklin G. Whitmore.
1887 July 23/Elmira, New York/2 pp. + env.
  Will talk business Wed. at home.

ALI to Franklin G. Whitmore.
1887 August 14/Elmira, New York/2 pp. + env. (?).
  Instructs Whitmore to look over (typesetter) motor himself; to withold money until it is completed. Delay in its completion troublesome. They have a monopoly on the market.

ALI to Franklin G. Whitmore.
1887 August 22/Elmira, New York/1 p.
> Exchanging billiard tables. Hewins should take and recover Whitmore's. Can see financing of typesetter through without hitting "New York Firm."

ALI to Franklin G. Whitmore.
1887 August 27/Elmira, New York/½ p. + env.
> *"All right, then, we will not sell or spout those bonds 'till we are obliged to. Your judgement is correct."*

ALS to Olivia (Lewis) Langdon, Mrs. Jervis.
1888 April 19/Hartford/2 pp.
> Livy's health steadily improving. Dr. Kellogg, the family physician, since Dr. Taft's death. He leaves for Montreal regards Canadian copyright.

ALS to Susan (Langdon) Crane, Mrs. Theodore.
1888 April 28/Hartford/1 p.
> Receipt and enjoyment of trout. Livy improves. "We're getting along; slowly, but getting along."

ALS to Ellen (Bunce) Welch, Mrs. Archibald A.
1888 June 9/Hartford/2 pp.
> Regards artistic praise.

ALS to Anonymous ("To whom it may concern").
1888 July 12/Hartford/1 p.
> Letter of introduction for Lilly G. Foote.

ALS to John J(ames) McCook.
1888 July 15/Elmira, New York/½ p. + env.
> *"That paper is delicious. I do not/often find literature that will bear reading/ twice, but this does. I am glad you/gave me a chance to see it."*

ALI to Franklin G. Whitmore.
1888 July 16/Elmira, New York/¾ pp. + env.
> Business.

ALI to Franklin G. Whitmore.
1888 August 10/Elmira, New York/1 p. + env.
> Instructions to borrow for *"3 or 4 months"*. No money from Webster until Sheridan book comes out. Business.

ACS to Olivia (Lewis) Langdon, Mrs. Jervis.
1888 August 19/(Elmira, New York?).
    "With love to Mother/from/Livy and Samuel/Aug. 19, 1888." Verso: *"Mr. and Mrs. S. L. Clemens"* (inked out).

ALS to Franklin G. Whitmore.
1888 September 10/Elmira, New York/½ p. + env.
    "Please bank the enclosed $8,300." Typesetter: *"Tell me when the machine is done."*

ALI to Franklin G. Whitmore.
1888 September 17/Elmira, New York/1 p. + env.
    If machine works, desires $150,000 insurance. Protection ("watch") necessary.

ALS to Franklin G. Whitmore.
1888 September 26/(New York, New York)/½ p. + env.
    Deposit $4004. in "U.S. Bank with the other type-setter ammunition."

ALS to (J. C.) Kinney.
1888 October 16/Hartford/4 pp.
    Apologies for not attending Foot Guard dinner. Description of Nook Farm-Forest St. vs. Farmington Ave. Essay on street lights, cf. MS of same date by Clemens.

ALI to Olivia (Langdon) Clemens, Mrs. Samuel L.
1888 November 27/Hartford/1 p.
    Love.

ALS to Olivia (Lewis) Langdon, Mrs. Jervis.
1888 December 6/Hartford/1 p.
    Thank-you for supplementary volumes and index of the Britannica as her choice for their Christmas present. Britannica, the best cyclopedia.

ALS Olivia (Langdon) Clemens, Mrs. Samuel L. to Olivia (Lewis) Langdon, Mrs. Jervis.
1888 December 14 & 19/Hartford/3½ pp.
    Wishes Mrs. Langdon was in Hartford for the holidays. Theodore (Crane) feeling poorly, and, consequently, Susan. Clemens writes that Livy is shopping for economical but thoughtful Christmas presents — "the expression of love & a low financial condition."

ALS to Olivia (Lewis) Langdon, Mrs. Jervis.
1889 April 17/Hartford/1½ pp.
>Awaiting her arrival. Livy would
>write but Dr. Bacon forbids the use of her
>eyes. Spring has come. All going to
>ball — Mrs. Colt's for Union for
>Home Work, May 7th.

ALI to Franklin G. W(hitmore).
1889 June 15/Hartford/¾ pp. + env.
>Financial arrangements made. If
>Bissell account needs payment, will
>do so.

ALI to Franklin G. Whitmore.
1889 August 20/Quarry Farm, Elmira, New York/2 pp.
> + env.
>Regards typesetter: speed rather
>than clean proof; to prove setting
>6,000/hr.

**ALS to Ellen (Bunce) Welch,
Mrs. Archibald A.**
1889 September 7/Elmira, New York/2 pp. + env.
>Possibly a "cosmic" digression and
>congratulations regards the institu-
>tion of marriage.

ALScy to Dear Kinney.
1889 September 28/(Hartford)/1 p.
>Thank you for thinking of me.

ALS to Olivia (Lewis) Langdon, Mrs. Jervis.
1889 October 7/Hartford/2 pp. + env.
>Livy still prevented from writing
>because of her eyes. Household set-
>tled; Mrs. Moffett returns West after
>week's visit. Regards Annie Price
>and family.

ALS to Olivia (Lewis) Langdon, Mrs. Jervis.
1889 November 9/Hartford/1½ pp.
>Visit from David Robinson and
>"Miss Nelly". Family upstairs
>rehearsing Thanksgiving production
>Mrs. Langdon's room painted
>together with the furniture.

ALS to Olivia (Lewis) Langdon, Mrs. Jervis.
1889 December 18/Hartford/2 pp. + env.
>A delightful visit with Mrs. Langdon
>and Susan (Crane). Livy occupied
>with Christmas presents. He has a
>cold and postponed West Point
>engagement for 3 weeks.

July 6/90.

Dear Bro:

I want Ned Bunce to see the machine. Pilot him thither.

And be sure you either take Batterson to see it, or have Bunce do it. Early — right away.

SLC

I am waiting for news from Goodman.

SL Clemens
Tannersville, Greene Co. N.Y.
Care Mrs. Candace Wheeler.

TL cy to (C. P. Everitt).
(1889) December 20.
> Regards source of illustrations for text of *A Connecticut Yankee in King Arthur's Court*. Identifies Dan Beard as illustrator.

ALS to Olivia (Lewis) Langdon, Mrs. Jervis.
1889 December 22/Hartford/1 p.
> Receipt of money from Mrs. Langdon for Livy. Spent in New York for *"mighty nice & satisfactory things...."*

ALS to Olivia (Lewis) Langdon, Mrs. Jervis.
1889 December 27/Hartford/½ p. + env.
> Warm thanks for receipt of (Brittanica) volumes.

Envelope to Olivia (Lewis) Langdon, Mrs. Jervis.
(before 1890) February 21/Buffalo, New York.

ACS to (Olivia (Lewis) Langdon, Mrs. Jervis).
(before 1890) Christmas.
> *"Merry Christmas to Mother,/together with a word of love/from Livy & Samuel."*

ALS to John J(ames) McCook.
(1890) April 8/Hartford/2 pp. + env.
> Will forward questions to his firm at once. Regards attempt on his income by "Mr. House." *"I'm never going to law again with a man who is willing to tell lies & swear to them."* Type-setter is all right. On loan from The Antiquarian & Landmarks Society of Connecticut, Inc.

ALS to Franklin G. Whitmore.
1890 July 6/Tannersville, New York/1 p. + env.
> Instructs Whitmore to have Ned Bunce "see the machine" (Paige Typesetter). (James G.) Batterson must also see it. Awaiting news from Goodman.

ALI to Franklin G. Whitmore.
1890 August 5/Tannersville, New York/2 pp. + env.
> Let machine (typesetter) be given all-day, all-night trial in Hartford. May work despite Davis and Paige's doubts. Then will test machine in N.Y. Wants shoes and socks.

Mark Twain, about 1885.

ALI to Franklin G. Whitmore.
1890 August 13/New York, New York/2 pp. + env.
    Apology. Paige joins him tomorrow and together they go to Jones about typesetter. If (typesetter) crew would remain with half wages "we might be able to stand it awhile . . . ."

ALS to Mary Monteith (Smith) Keller, Mrs. George.
1890 September 12/Onteora Club, Tannersville, New York/1 p. + env.
    Thanks her for sending (*Plain Tales From the Hills*). Reminds him that *"whereas Kipling's stories are plenty good enough on a first reading they very greatly improve on a second".*

ALS to Charles Jervis (Langdon).
(1891) September 22/"Afloat on the Rhone"/2 pp.
    Boat trip down the Rhone. Family at Ouchy. Clemens will return to Ouchy then on to Berlin. Rheumatic arm of aggravation to him.

ALI to Franklin G. Whitmore.
(1891) November 9/Berlin, Germany/1 p. + env.
    Receiving 2 copies of *Harper's*. Unnecessary. Will Whitmore tend to it?

ALI to (Franklin G. Whitmore).
1891 November 23 & 28/Berlin, Germany/2¼ pp. + env. + enc.
    Pay repair bill for sofa. Please forward mail coming to Hartford. By the 28th arm recovered so as to write himself. Send Clemens' photograph to H. J. McGivern, W. VA.

ALS Olivia (Langdon) Clemens, Mrs. Samuel L. to George H. Warner.
1891 December 1/Berlin, Germany/3 pp. + env.
    Aggravation with his arm limits writing. Considerations for *"cheap paper-cover form"* of his book. Livy describes their German experience and impressions. (Clemens' signature taped to first sheet).

ALS to (Thomas W.) Williams.
1892 January 25/Berlin, Germany/1 p.
    Glad that Williams will manage L.A.L. Clemens lost a bet on his acceptance of the position.

ALS to Franklin G. Whitmore.
1892 May 22/Venice, Italy/2 pp. + env.
    Make necessary green-house repairs. John to estimate amt' of coal for winter. Will return home in June while Livy goes to German bath.

ALS to Charles Jervis (Langdon).
(1892) August 7/(Frankfort, Germany)/3 pp.
    Regrets not seeing him in Brussels because of Livy's health. Parting with Sue was too much for Livy.

ALI to Franklin G. Whitmore.
(1892) October 16/Berlin, Germany/1 p. + env.
    Pay Clemens' taxes. Word of typesetter. Thinking of friends.

ALS to (Franklin G. Whitmore).
1892 November 2/Florence, Italy/3 pp.
    Change mailing address to Florence. Wants to cancel Amer. Pub. Co. contract, because Webster & Co. making no profit as middlemen. Wants "Perique" tobacco.

ALI to Franklin G. Whitmore.
1893 March 2/Florence, Italy/1¼ pp. + env.
    Some unknown Smith-Hamersley elected neatly. *"Let the house be painted."* He will leave for home for a few days, sailing from Genoa on the 22nd.

ALI to Franklin G. Whitmore.
1893 March 16/Florence, Italy/1½ pp. + env.
    He and/or Whitmore failed to pay Player's Club dues; therefore, he is dismissed; *"the only Club I took any interest in or cared to belong to."*

ALS to Susan (Langdon) (Crane), Mrs. Theodore.
1893 March 19 & 20/Florence Italy/4 pp.
    Susy is 21 today. Perhaps melancholy resume of his own life. New of friends. Won't Susy give machine royalties to girls for security.

ALS to Franklin G. Whitmore.
1893 May 1/New York, New York/2 pp. + env.
    Health is better. He is at Dr. Rice's. Leave for Elmira tomorrow; hopes to go to Hartford to see Ned Bunce. Take care of Dr. Porter's bill.

QUARRY FARM
ELMIRA N.Y.

June 26/95.

Dear Mr. Rogers:

How exasperating it is! The Devil & Colby would necessarily choose this time for junketing when I am tied by the hind leg & can't go & 'tend to my matters myself. Why good Lord, I *must* make a book-contract with somebody before I leave this country; can't have the books standing still any longer. Dang it, I'm getting desperate. This carbuncle is not going to allow me to stand on my feet for two or three weeks yet. It is slower than chilled molasses. I'll go to Cleveland on a stretcher, sure.

ALI to Ida (Clark) (Langdon), Mrs. Charles J.
1893 May 11/New York, New York/2½ pp.
> Cannot make it to Hartford, but *"the Murray Hill* (hotel in N.Y.C.) *is but a suburb of Hartford"* and has many people. Sails on Sat.

AL to Franklin G. Whitmore.
1893 September 13/New York, New York/1½ pp. + env.
> In Hartford unexpectedly. Clara in Elmira, then to visit Twichells, Mazie Robinson. Clemens at Dr. Rice's.

ALI to Franklin G. Whitmore.
1893 November 4/New York, New York/2 pp. + env.
> At Player's Club. Wants *"perpetual free-ticket to Irving's theatres".* Its description with illustration follows.

Mark Twain, about 1894.

Telegram to (Henry Huddleston) Rogers.
1894 June 29/Paris France/
> *"Unavoidably detained".*

ALS to G(eorge) W(illard)? Knowlton.
1894 August 11/Hartford/1 p. + env.
> Young lady in question will be of no concern under Mrs. Mary B. Willard's care. Mrs. Willard is in Berlin, Germany.

Telegram to (Alice (Hooker) Day, Mrs. John C.).
1894 October 16/Southampton/
> *"S.S. Spree (N.G.L.) Southampton/ wish you all bon voyage."*

ALS to (Franklin G. Whitmore).
1894 November 16/Paris, France/1½ pp.
> Misplaced rugs. If Whitmore needs money go to Stern & Rushmore as Amer. Pub. Co. does. Attack of gout. Must be "carted" to new address on letter — a small house furnished by an American.

Telegram to (Henry Huddleston) Rogers.
1894 December 21/Paris, France,
> *"Can you delay final action/one month."*

ALS to Franklin G. Whitmore.
1895 January 8/Paris, France/3 pp. + env.
> Must pay creditors of C.L. Webster & Co. *"a heavy sum"* this year. Therefore, house repairs cut to $15/mo. (Orion) still to have $50/mo. Will Whitmore or associate continue at half rate — $20/mo. for former services and a monthly itemized account. *"We've got to rent that house."*

ALS to Elizabeth Hart (Jarvis) Colt, Mrs. Samuel.
1895 February 15/Paris, France/3 pp.
> Condolences on the death of her son.

ALS to George H. Warner.
1895 March 9/New York, New York/2 pp. + env.
> Will Warner not let him know when he is coming to N.Y.C. Clemens sails for France on the 27th but will come to Hartford before departing.

AL to Franklin G. Whitmore.
1895 March 24/New York, New York/1½ pp. + env.
> When Whitmore has the money pay *Courant* bill and cancel subscription. Ineptness as a business man.

AL to Franklin G. Whitmore.
1895 March 27/New York, New York/1½ pp. + env.
> In haste. Regards business. *". . . but next it occurred to me that I am warned every day to venture no orders concerning Mrs. Clemens' properties & affairs."*

AL to Franklin G. Whitmore.
1895 April 7/Paris, France/1½ pp. + env.
> Mrs. Clemens says gentleman was to sell piano. If possible. No arrangement for himself to buy it and money go for new one. Will Whitmore present a bill for piano?

AL to Franklin G. Whitmore.
1895 May 30/Quarry Farm, Elmira, New York/2½ pp. + env.
> Mr. (John C.) Day knows Whitmore is agent for Clemens. Forget "lecture-applications," work enough without them. Send them to Maj. Pond. Gout attack. *"If they double-track* (Farmington) *Avenue we shall want to start in early & hunt up a purchaser for our house."*

ALS to (Henry Huddleston) Rogers.
1895 June 26/Quarry Farm, Elmira, New York/2 pp.
>Will he not meet with J. Henry Harper to amend and sign contract. Clemens confined by carbuncle. Arrange so that both parties can quit contract after 10 yrs.

Telegram to H(enry) H(uddleston) Rogers.
1895 August 7/Spokane, Washington.
>*"Certainly no objection. Would like a/typewritten copy of it mailed/to Melbourne all well and send/love to you all".*

Telegram to Henry Huddleston Rogers.
(1895?) August 15/Fair Haven, Minnesota.
>"Steamer does not sail/until the twentieth."

ALI to (Henry Huddleston) Rogers.
1896 April 24/Curepipe, Mauritius/3½ pp.
>Regards voyage and need of holiday. Description of Mauritis.

ALI to (Henry Huddleston) Rogers.
1896 May 26/Pretoria, S.A.R./2 pp.
>Politics hot in South Africa. Has spoken to (political) prisoners. Regrets lecture circuit is ending. Family well.

ALI to (Henry Huddleston) Rogers.
1896 June 6/Queenstown, Cape Colony, Africa/2 pp.
>Will *Joan* not be published in book form? Itinerary. African politics.

ALS to (Clara (Clemens) Gabrilowitsch Samossoud, Mrs. Jacques)
1896 June 8/Kingstown/1 p.
>Her birthday which he had forgotten.

AL to (Henry Huddleston) Rogers.
1896 June 19/Port Elizabeth/4 pp.
>Quotes Livy's quote from Harper's letter to Rogers regards *Joan of Arc*. He wants it *"dramatized & produced."* Agrees that Bliss can exchange rights to Clemens' book with Harper's for Webster publications. Business.

ALI to (Henry Huddleston) Rogers.
1896 July (22)/S.S. "Norma", On the Equator/3½ pp.
> Regards business and Rogers' help. Might not Harper's sell single vols.; Bliss, the sets by subscription. Slavery of lecturing at the end.

ANI to (Henry Huddleston) Rogers.
1896 July 31/Southampton, England/1 p.
> Just arrived. Will telegraph London for letters.

ALI to (Henry Huddleston) Rogers.
1896 August 12/Guilford, England/4 pp.
> Arrangements bet. Bliss and Harper's: Bliss to pay 8% on retail price of Clemens' books for use of plates. 12% to Clemens. That can be reduced to 10%. Business.

ALI to Charles Jervis (Langdon).
1896 September 13/London, England/2 pp.
> Susy's memory. His appreciation for Charley's and wife, Ida's, care and support of Livy.

ALI to Franklin G. Whitmore.
1896 September 14/London, England/2 pp. + env.
> Arrangements for the Hartford house.

ALI to (Franklin G. Whitmore).
1896 September 14/(Chelsea, England?)/3¼ pp.
> (Shortly after Susy's death). Press John Day or his agent for money. Inventory (of house) not to include books. Barney's to pay $100/mo. for use of "horse-part of barn." John O'Neil into Patrick's quarters. Furnace repaired but watch cost. Wait about ceilings. Withdrawn from Authors Club. The John Day's damage in the house.

AN + env. to Franklin G. Whitmore.
1896 September 23/London, England.
> P.S.: Maintain insurance on (Hartford) house.

ALS to Edward Bunce.
1896 October 16/London, England/2 pp.
> At time of Susy Clemens' death. Details sorrow and loss at Susy's passing.

ALS to (Henry Huddleston) Rogers.
1897 April 14/London, England/½ p. + env.
    Introducing Mr. F.N. Doubleday who wants to discuss publishing business with Rogers. Enclosure describes Doubleday's association with Scribner's and S.S. McClure Co.

Calling card.
1897 July 16.
    Calling card. Printed card with black border; pencilled directions to send mail for listed family members to Villa Buhlegg, Weggis. Verso: *"For Postmaster/By S.L. Clemens".*

ALS to Mr. Hurst, The Consul General, U.S. of America.
(1897) October 8/Hotel Metropole, Vienna, Austria/ 1 p. + env.
    Refuses accommodation at Wohring for his daughter. Includes calling card:" John Fletcher Hurst/Hawley/ Pennsylvania".

ALS to Anonymous ("Dear Sir").
1897 October 25/Vienna, (Austria)/1½ pp.
    Thank-you for pictures.

TL to (Francis E.) Bliss.
1897 November 4/Vienna, Austria/1½ pp.
    His debts, his health, his writing.

ALI to Franklin G. Whitmore.
1898 July 9/Vienna, Austria/2 pp. + partial env.
    Aggravated with 6-month-old mail forward by Whitmore. P. & W. bill withdrawn. A.C. Dunham and Dr. Parker joined family last week.

ANI to Franklin G. Whitmore.
1898 July 20/(Vienna, Austria?)/ + env.
    Post-script possibly to letter of July 9. Send $1500. of the $2500. to Mr. (Henry) Rogers. Also Bliss *"July ½-year money"* to Rogers.

ACS
1898 August 2/Kaltenlentgeben.
    "Truly yours/Mark Twain". Includes ref. to grease spot and lithographed drawing of Clemens.

[1900]

Elmira, Aug. 18.

My Dear Whitmore —

I clear forgot that ten dollars which Mrs. Whitmore lent Mrs. C. However, it has since been jammed into the Gilsey bill, & now she won't ever see it any more. The bill came, in due time, ($67. 70/—) of which sum, $20.10 was charged to you. As your room was only $4, I could not see why it was so large. They seemed to have got too much dinner charged to you. So I wrote & asked them to send

ALS to Mrs. Edward Bunce.
1898 December 2/Vienna, Austria/2 pp. + env.
    Writes of their mutual bereavement, the death of Susy Clemens and Edward Bunce.

ANI to Franklin G. Whitmore.
(1899) January 21/(Vienna, Austria)/ + env.
    Press Bliss for January statement. Check to go to London bank in Mrs. Clemens' account.

ALS to (Frank E.) Bliss.
1899 March 31 & April 2/Hotel Krantz, (Vienna, Austria)/4 pp.
    Orders deluxe edition *(The Writings of Mark Twain)* for Mr. (Henry) Rogers; uniform edition for "Miss Harrision". Mrs. Clemens wants biographical sketch of Clemens added to anthology, written by Mark Twain and edited by nephew, Samuel E. Moffett, editor of *New York Journal.* Signing autograph sheets. Wrote to Twichell for information about *"the Christian Science articles."* Suggests title for book.

AL to Franklin G. Whitmore.
1899 October 26/London, England/2 pp. + env.
    Business: Mr. Rogers and Mr. Bliss. Eager to sell (Hartford) house — *"a profitless drain & dead expense".*

ALI to (Franklin G. Whitmore).
(1890's) August 6/½ p.
    Requests pipe.

ALS to Franklin G. Whitmore.
(1900) August 18/Elmira, New York/3 pp. + env.
    The $10. Mrs. Clemens borrowed from Mrs. Whitmore settled in Clemens' payment of Gilsey bill for hotel and dinner accommodations. Enclosing Watrous letter to be shown around regards conductor.

ALS to (Frank E.) Bliss.
1900 September 18/(London, England)/2 pp.
    Regards business and writing. Author's Club claim to the copyright on *"The Californian's Tale",* *"a swindle".*

1900

ALI to (Henry Huddleston) Rogers.
(1900) November 21/New York, New York/1 p.
>Has lunch and a tea on for Sat. by and by will join Rogers and Rice for billiards that night.

TL to Robert N. Stanley.
1901 January 21/1 p. + handwritten env.
>Believes *"things which I have been saying tally with the feelings . . . in the hearts of all intelligent men in the nation, but I shall not except many of them to come out and confess it."*

ALS to William Carey.
1901 February 20/(New York) City/½ p. + env.
>*"Carey says he knows I would rather write than be President. This has all the ear-marks of one of Carey's ordinary every-day lies."*

ALS to Franklin G. Whitmore.
1901 September 29/New York, New York/1 p. + env.
>Closing out at "that" bank. New address.

AN to Franklin G. Whitmore.
1901 October 26/(New York, New York)/
>Written note at bottom of Whitmore's TLS of October 25, 1901. Whitmore has enclosed self-explanatory letter and sent book for autograph. Clemens answers that, in the future, paste in prepared autographs. Autograph business tires him.

ANS to Ida (Langdon).
1901 December 24 "Xmas Eve"/Riverdale, (New York)/1 p.
>(Presumably an enclosure with a gift.) Regards his gift. *"Remember the Great Oath of Our Order: 'Silence should be seen, not heard."*

ANS to A. Schonstadt.
1902 January 30/New York, New York/with envelope.
>In answer to a request for a photograph.

ALI to (Henry Huddleston Rogers)
(1902) May 16/Riverdale, New York/1½ pp.
> Leave for New York Harbor in late June. Mrs. Clemens did not approve of invitation to Mr. Rogers — the form not the intention. Mrs. Clemens' heart condition. Will go to Osteopath as cheaper than housecall and Hartford house is not sold.

ALI to (Franklin G Whitmore).
1902 May 19/(Tarrytown, New York?)/2½ pp.
> Regards sale of Hartford house. Only one Hartford bid. What about Mrs. George Perkins or James Goodwin's son? What about levelling house and stable so as to have land to sell? House be torn down before it goes to "base uses".
> Packing, shipping mantel.

Telegram to Henry Huddleston Rogers.
1902 June 27/York Depot, Maine.
> *"Housed and at home by noon had a perfectly lovely/voyage."*

ANI to Franklin G. Whitmore.
1902 July 3/York, Maine/ + env.
> Written at bottom of partial TLS on F.G. Whitmore's letter; requests more autographs. Clemens replies that he has no cards, etc.

ACS to Franklin G. Whitmore.
1902 July 30/York Harbor, (Maine)
> Business.

ALI to (Franklin G. Whitmore).
(1902) August 21/York Harbor, (Maine)/1½ pp.
> Livy dangerously ill. That they could sell the house. Inform friends but let them not write.

ALS to Ida (Clark) Langdon, Mrs. Charles J.
1902 August 28/York Harbor, Maine/1½ pp. + env.
> Refuses invitation. Regards Livy's health. Perhaps this letter purposely makes light of Livy's condition (cf. preceding letters).

Telegram to Henry Huddleston Rogers.
1902 August 28/York Harbor, Maine.
> *"Thank you without limit will/write you my later scheme".*

AL to (Franklin G. Whitmore).
1902 October 6/York, Maine/1¼ pp.
    If Mr. Roberts will pay *"what the land cost ($32,000.)"* "can have house, stable & green house for nothing". Regards Western buyer.

AL to (Franklin G. Whitmore).
1902 November 24/(York, Maine?)/1 p.
    ". . . get obstruction removed that the scoundrel Chamberlin put upon the green house lot, I mean to put the house up at auction." "Expenses are $10,000. a year heavier than . . . a year ago."

ALS to (Josephine Sarah (Lippincott) Goodwin, Mrs. James J. ?).
(1902?) December 6/New York/3 pp.
    (Dictated to Isabel V. Lyon.) Gladly be "your guest." No music while he reads. Length of reading determined by audience reaction and her wishes. Mrs. Clemens improved.

ALS to Charles Jervis Langdon.
1902 December 26/(New York, New York)/2¼ pp. + env.
    Receipt of Christmas greetings and a check. Livy ill; Jean has pneumonia. His fear. Emotional letter.

ANI to (Henry Huddleston) Rogers.
(1902 December or 1903 January)/(Riverdale, New York).
    Note written on Harvey's letter. Wishes for a Happy New Year and directs Rogers' attention to Harvey's reply.

ALI to Franklin G. Whitmore.
(1903 April 5)/New York, New York/1½ pp. + env.
    Monthly expenses at $4000. *". . . sell or rent that God damned house."* P.S.: error in mathematics. Expenses-$2000./mo.

AL to (Franklin G. Whitmore.
1903 April 28/(Riverdale, New York?)/1 p.
    Take Witherbee offer. Tarrytown property rented to Gould family lawyer with option to buy at $7000. profit.

AL to (Franklin G. Whitmore).
1903 May 7/(Riverdale, New York)/2 pp.
>Moving difficulties because of their collective infirmities. Moving must be organized and based on Mrs. Clemens' memory of 12 yrs. ago. Regards Bissell's letter to Whitmore.

AL to (Franklin G. Whitmore).
1903 May 9/(Riverdale, New York)/1 p. (incomplete?).
>3 or 4 sets of billiard balls worth $50./set. Paid $200. for safe. Painted windows in Hartford not part of house. Made in England after house was finished.

AL & ALS (Olivia (Langdon) Clemens, Mrs. Samuel L. to Franklin G. Whitmore.
1903 May 11/Riverdale, New York/5 pp. + env.
>Because Mrs. Day has moved furnishings about, makes packing, selling, and saving by memory difficult. Lists items, and their location which should be saved. Clemens adds 3 items to go to Susan Crane, Elmira.

AL to Franklin G. Whitmore.
1903 May 20/Riverdale, New York/3 pp.
>Bust to (Isabella) Hooker. Mrs. Clemens wants Mrs. Whitmore to present the "Mercury" to one of the libraries. Jean wants birdseye maple table from pink room. Mirror and stained glass windows to be sold. Nursery and pink room carpets to Mary McAlear. Letter dictated to Isabel Lyon.

ALS to Harriet (Goulder) Whitmore, Mrs. Franklin G.
1903 June 16/Riverdale, New York/1½ pp.
>Mrs. Clemens' gift of the "Mercury". Pleasure from their hospitality. Livy progressing.

L to Roycrofters.
(1903 before July 4)/Riverdale on the Hudson/1 p.
>(Written by Isabel Lyon.) Regrets unable to accept invitation of July 4, 1903.

ALS to Harriet (Goulder) Whitmore, Mrs. Franklin G.
1903 July 25/Quarry Farm, Elmira, New York/2 pp.
>Arrangements: *Courant* letter, Gifford picture, Mrs. Clemens' lace in the bank.

ALS to William Gillette.
1903 October 22/New York, N.Y./1 p. + env.
> About some verses ("ungodly rhymes") Gillette sent to Clemens. Includes envelope with notation by Will Gillette.

ALS to E. B. Caulfield.
1903 November 18 & (22)/Florence, Italy/1 p. + 2 enc. + env.
> Should the Clemens call on Caulfield, also in Florence next Sunday? Encs., Clemens' calling cards written on the Sun. of his visit to Caulfield: *"I waited till 10:30/-was then obliged/to go; very good-we will/call it (sic) 10 next Sunday./This time I had to run/away and hunt for a doctor."*

ALS to Charles Jervis Langdon.
1904 February 14/Florence, Italy/3¼ pp. + env.
> Dividend from Charley for Livy. Deposit $1000. in bank. His work for *Harper's* will meet extra costs. Livy endures her illness.

ALS to Charles Jervis Langdon.
1904 May 27/Florence, Italy/2 pp. + env.
> Business, health and weather.

Telegram to Langdon family.
(1904 June 6)/Florence, Italy.
> *"She passed peacefully away last night".*

ALS to Charles Jervis Langdon.
1904 June 8/Florence, Italy/2 pp. + env.
> Clara's 30th birthday. She *"lies motionless & wordless"* (nervous breakdown after Livy's death). Livy's passing.

Telegram to Langdon family.
1904 June 8/(Florence, Italy).
> *"The ruined household undivided sail in Prince Oscar June 28 homeward/bound."* Note to Susan (Crane) regards 37th anniversary of Quaker City departure.

AL to Charles Jervis Langdon.
(1904) June 13/(Florence, Italy)/2¼ pp. + env.
> Livy's last gift to children, pair of grey mares, sent by boat with Italian butler, Ugo. Arrangements for their arrival. (Isabel) Lyon, Ugo, and Italian maid, Teresa will tend to lodgings, rented from Gilder of the *Century*.

ALS to Charles Jervis Langdon.
1904 June 19/(Florence, Italy)/4 pp. + env.
> Life without Livy. Items on which they may have to pay duties. Financial trials.

ALS to Charles Jervis (Langdon).
1904 June 26/Rome, Italy/2½ pp.
> Remained in Florence while "mourning gowns" were finished. Both Clara and Jean unwell. Concern for children.

ALS to Mary (Bushnell) Cheney, Mrs. Frank Woodbridge.
1904 July 21/Lee, Massachusetts/3 pp. + env.
> In answer to her condolences when learning of Livy's death. Regards Mrs. Cheney's written praise one time of Susy which Livy treasured.

ALS to Charles Jervis Langdon.
1904 July 25/Lee, Massachusetts/2 pp. + env.
> Witty commentary on an unwanted shaving brush. Charley has picture of Livy unknown to Clemens.

ALS to Clara (Clemens) Gabrilowitsch Samossoud, Mrs. Jacques.
1904 July 26/(Lee, Massachusetts)/2 pp.
> Father's letter to daughter; concerned for her health. Quote from Helen Keller.

ANI to (Franklin G. Whitmore).
1904 September 10/New York, New York.
> Where is the mantel piece from Hartford?

AL to Franklin G. Whitmore.
1904 October 28/New York, New York/2 pp. + env.
> Can mahogany-room set be bought back? Clara at rest-cure on 69th St.

Clara's Birthday
Wednesday afternoon
June 8/04.

Dear Charley:

Thirty years ago, to-day, Clara lay in the hollow of her happy mother's arm — just the top of her head showing — & Susy was admitted, to see the new wonder: & said admiringly, "L at bay got boofu' hair." And now Susy is gone, the happy mother is gone, & Clara lies motionless & wordless — & has so lain ever since Sunday night brought our irremediable disaster. We were wholly unprepared, we were not dreaming of danger.; Livy had been brightly chatting a moment before — & in an

ALI to Franklin G. Whitmore.
1904 November 11/New York, New York/1 p. + env.
    Thank-you for trying regards
    mahogany-room set.

Calling card (black edged).
to (Clara (Clemens) Gabrilowitsch
Samossoud, Mrs. Jacques).
(c. 1904-1909).
    "Be happy, dear & don't/forget us./We think your little/chimney pests are fledged/& gone./Father."

ALS to Susan (Langdon) Crane,
Mrs. Theodore.
(1905 March 13)/New York, New York/½ p.
    (incomplete) + env.
    She should pray to St. Peter for him.

AL to (Henry Huddleston) Rogers.
1905 September 7/(Tuexdo, New York?)/1½ pp.
    Will bring Twichells' letter when he
    finds it. Lameness lingers.

ACS to Annie Eliot (Trumbull).
1905 December 6 & 9/New York, New York.
    Thank-you for his 70th birthday
    wishes. Signed *"Mark Twain"*.
    Verso: Appreciation of poem. Signed
    "S.L. Clemens".

ALS to William R. Coe.
1905 (December 26)/New York, New York/1 p.
    Thank-you for Christmas present.
    Clemens has been delayed by
    publisher.

ALS to Anonymous ("Dear Sir").
1906 February 15/New York, New York/1½ pp.
    Regards identity of original Huck
    Finn, *"a magistrate in a far Western*
    State . . . ."

ALS to John J. McCook.
(1906 February 16) "Friday"/Hartford/1 p. + env.
    Urges him to look at *"machine set*
    type " at Pratt & Whitney (Tool and
    Die). *"It performs well."*

ALS to Charles Jervis Langdon.
1906 April 4/New York, New York/1 p. + env.
    Was there a Mrs. Lee on the
    "Quaker City"?

Mark Twain in 1903.

Telegram to Henry Huddleston Rogers.
1906 June 6/Dublin, New Hampshire.
"Yes, still am investor to/amount formally mentioned Come up/here both of you and/I will return with you if properly invested".

AL to (Henry Huddleston) Rogers.
1906 June 13/Dublin, New Hampshire/1 p.
(Dictated to Isabel Lyon; signed by Clemens). Get Christian Science book from Harper's and put in safe until Clemens comes.

Telegram cy to Henry Huddleston Rogers.
1906 September 3/Dublin, New Hampshire.
Not in Clemens' hand. *"God be thanked have found/some of the things send another trunk this one leaked."*

ALS to Clara (Clemens) Gabrilowitsch Samossoud, Mrs. Jacques.
1907 July 27/Tuxedo Park, New York/3½ pp.
In bed with bronchitis but shall sail for Bermuda next wk. with Col. Harvey. Has Wedgewood locket for her. What genius is.

ALI to Henry Huddleston (Rogers).
(1907 July 29)/Tuxedo Park, New York/2½ pp.
Out of temper with bronchitis. News of friends and notables. Regards Mr. Rogers' health.

ALS to Clara (Clemens) Gabrilowitsch Samossoud, Mrs. Jacques.
1907 September (4?)/Tuxedo Park, New York/2½ pp. + env.
Expected her but she did not arrive. Quotes Paine on the changability of hers and Clemens' mind.

ALS to (Mai (Rogers) Coe, Mrs. William R.)
(1908) "2 p.m. Monday"/Bermuda/2 pp.
Mr. Rogers is better in Bermuda climate. He is awaiting picture of baby.

AC to Franklin G. Whitmore.
1908 (January 1).
"Happy New Year/to my dear Whitmore/from "The Great White Brer." (Post card depicts Clemens in bed writing and cigar-smoking; card is autographed *"Mark Twain"* and labelled *"Mark Twain's Muse").*

ALS to (Jane Lampton) Clemens.
(1908)* January 27/Bermuda/2 pp. + env.
>*Envelope dated "1908" (cf. Paine. *Mark Twain. A Biography.* v.iii., p. 1435). Has arrived and seen to hotel. Many tourists and friends there. Among them, Woodrow Wilson.

ALS to Charles Jervis Langdon.
1908 February 11/New York, New York/1½ pp. + env. (incomplete).
>(First page has been cropped, from salutation to end paragraph.)Jean has taken a house in Greenwich; Clara is well; he is satisfactory. Bermuda trip cured his bronchitis. Charley is in Pasadena. Regards Jervis, Mr. Carnegie, and visit to the new organ.

ALI to (Mai (Rogers) Coe, Mrs. William R.).
1908 July 27/(Stormfield, Redding?)/2 pp.
>Thank-you for photograph. Invitation.

AL to Clara (Clemens) Gabrilowitsch Samossoud, Mrs. Jacques.
1908 October 6/Redding/2 pp.
>Pleased that she has located an apartment. The trouble with securing servants.

ALS to Charles Jervis (Langdon).
1908 December 12/Redding/2¼ pp.
>Receipt of $25. (Atlantic Gas coupon). Miss (Isabel) Lyon will attend to business. Visiting.

ACS to Harriet (Whitmore) Enders, Mrs. John Ostrom.
1908 December 25/Redding/ + env.
>Thank-you for muffler and portraits.

ACI to Harriet (Goulder) Whitmore, Mrs. Franklin G.
1908 December 25/Redding/ + env.
>Thank-you for book.

ALI to Coe family.
1909 January 18/Stormfield, Redding/1 p.
>Refuses invitation as he goes to N.Y.C. to deliver speech and "guestship" at young Robert Collier's house.

REDDING
CONNECTICUT

Dec. 28/09.

She is out of it all, dear Mrs. Whitmore — the first kindness that has come to her from the Source of All Kindness in sixteen years. She & I had a long & loving chat the night before the blow fell, & she gave me a commission for you. I said I would write you my side of that matter, & I proceeded to map it out, but she stopped me & asked me not to write in that heated vein — & not to try to write at all, because I would not be able to

ALI to Coe family.
1909 February 3/Stormfield, Redding/2 pp.
> *"It has arrived"* and delighted Miss Lyon who is ill. Thank-you.

Telegram to Henry Huddleston Rogers.
1909 April 26/Redding.
> "I will spend tomorrow night with you."

ALS to William R. Coe.
1909 June 16/Stormfield, Redding/4 pp.
> In from difficult Baltimore trip. Will finish Mr. Rogers' eulogy when the text suits him. Real eulogy are the references to Mr. Rogers in his *Autobiography. "Mr. Ashcroft & Miss Lyon are still being investigated, but the finish is near."* Mr. Rogers initiated investigation. Regards document which would hand over all Clemens' possessions to Ashcroft and Miss Lyon.

Mark Twain in 1907.

ALI to Franklin G. Whitmore.
1909 June 21/Redding/3 pp. + env.
> Wants Hartford checkbooks for household expenses. Jean at Redding. Also Clara. P.S.: regards Fred Quarles his cousin to whom he wishes to send a stipend of $5./mo.

ALI to (William R.) Coe.
1909 June 27/Redding/2 pp.
> Farewell. Ashcroft-Lyon business over and they have departed. Must stay put because of his health.

ALS to (William Henry) Bishop.
1909 October 11/Redding/3½ pp. + env.
> Describes physical complaints and his treatment.

ALI to (Mai (Rogers) Coe, Mrs. William R.).
1909 December 27/Redding/4 pp.
> Really not melancholy after Jean's death. His ability to regain happiness. Jean's last months.

ALS to Harriet (Goulder) Whitmore, Mrs. Franklin G.
1909 December 28/Redding/2½ pp.
> (Includes env. with note by Mrs. Whitmore stating that this is Mr. Clemens' last letter to her). Jean is gone. Regards some unpleasant matter or opinions in Hartford. In fact, no condolences from Hartford.

ALS to Mr. Stone.
n.y.(February 2) "Monday"/Hartford/2 pp. + env.
"Young" Wheeler's visits are welcomed but would Mr. Stone mention the subject of his not staying to dinner. (Wheeler was resident at Deaf & Dumb Asylum).

ALI to (Charles E.) Perkins.
n.y. February 3/1¼ pp.
Regards "new clauses" and to see if all his suggestions have been adopted.

ALS to (Charles E.) Perkins.
n.y. February 25/1 p.
Regards Mills' agreement for Colorado.

ACI to Charles H(opkins) Clark.
n.y. (March 6)/Hartford/2 pp. + env.
Humorous defense of his supposed treatment of Indians.

ALS to Franklin G. Whitmore.
n.y. May 18/Hartford/2 pp. + env.
Thank-you for *"those delightful little creatures" "served up broiled"*. Regards Mrs. Clemens and two new suits.

TL to (Elisha Bliss, Jr.).
n.y. July 22/Elmira, New York/2½ pp.
The business of publishing his next book. Written in an indignant if not somewhat ironic vein in which Clemens "contends" that he is not complaining.

ALS to (Charles E.) Perkins.
n.y. September 9/1 p.
"Keep the keys til we come."

ACS to Charles E. Perkins.
n.y. September 29/Hartford.
Regards interest on loans.

ACS to (Charles E.) Perkins.
n.y. October 25.
Regards enlarging Orion's check as of November.

ALS to Editor, "Atlantic Monthly".
n.y. November 22/Hartford/10 pp.
> Considers it unnecessary and a complete waste of time and money for a letter writer to have to write anything but the first line and the name the city on an envelope — *"no need of decrees to compel a man to make a letter, address full".*

ALS to George Keller.
n.y. November 25/New York, New York/1 p.
> Is *"hopelessly busy,"* but if he runs across *"Chauncey"* will put the matter before him.

AC to Monday Afternoon Club.
n.y. December 31/Hartford.
> Acceptance of invitation to Monday Afternoon Club.

ALS to (William) Hamersley.
n.d. "Thursday"/1 p.
> Awaiting Peyton to return from West Indies. *". . . he is the financial lever".* (Regards Paige typesetter).

ACI to (Charles E.) Perkins.
n.d. "Thursday".
> Regards items to be transferred to his checking account. We leave for New York on Monday.

AL (cy) to (Henry Robinson).
n.d. "Friday"/New York, New York/2 pp.
> Thank you for money; put in Whitmore's name for Mrs. Clemens' trust. Will be applied to Stern & Rushmore debt. Creditors have been understanding. Original at Robinson, Robinson & Cole Law Offices, 799 Main St., Hartford.

TL to Anonymous.
n.d./1p. (incomplete).
> p. 2: Regards MS and prospectus for forthcoming book, (possibly *The Gilded Age*). His stock rising, requests increasing for lectures, and offer arrived for 12 articles (at $6000.).

ACI to (Richard E.) Burton.
n.d./2 pp.
> Wishes him a good time.

ANI to (Mai (Rogers) Coe, Mrs. William R.).
n.d.
>Written note at end of typewritten *"Endless Chain Prayer"* which Clemens has received in the mail. Evidently forwarded to Mrs. Coe for her salvation, too.

ALS to Austin Cornelius Dunham.
n.d./(Hartford)/2 p. + env.
>Invitation to dinner.

ACS to (Elizabeth) Hall.
n.d.
>*"For Miss Hall/S.L. Clemens./Hotel Krautz/Neuer Market/Vienna/Austria."* Possibly in Clemens' handwriting.

ALS to (Langdon).
n.d./½ p. (fragment).
>Will "pay" Charley to visit and increase payment relative to the amount of family he brings with him.

Scrap of paper to (Charles E. Perkins).
n.d.
>Regards Raymond's contracts and the originals.

ANI to (Henry Huddleston Rogers).
n.d./+ enc.
>*"I used to pray to God, too, but now/when I want a thing/pulled off sudden/I know where I can do better."* Regards communication of sentence described by enclosed newspaper clipping.

AL to (Franklin G. Whitmore).
n.d./Quarry Farm, Elmira, New York/1 p.
>Will he please show "little book" to postmaster and forward it on to "the Grosvenor", N.Y.C.

This section lists appearances of Mark Twain's writings in collections and anthologies and is limited to those published during his lifetime.

Contributions by Mark Twain to Collections & Anthologies.

William Dean Howells, Mark Twain, George Harvey (president of Harper's), Henry Mills Alden (editor of Harper's Magazine), *David Munro (editor of the* North American Review), *and M. W. Hazeltine (former literary editor of the New York* Sun), *at Lakewood, New Jersey, in 1908.*

"The Dandy Frightening the Squatter." IN: The Carpet-Bag. Boston, May 1, 1852; Volume II, No. 5.

BAL 3550*

Clemens' first published story. This copy part of a bound set of the publication.

*: collection in *Tall Tales of the Southwest*, New York, 1930.

"Mark Twain on Fritz Smythe's Horse" IN:
Beadle's Dime No. 3. Book of Fun.
New York, (1866): Beadle and Company, Publishers, 118 William Street.
"Comprising Good Things from the Best Wits, and a Rare Collection of Laughable Stories and Jokes."
BAL 3309   Pictorial paper wrappers.

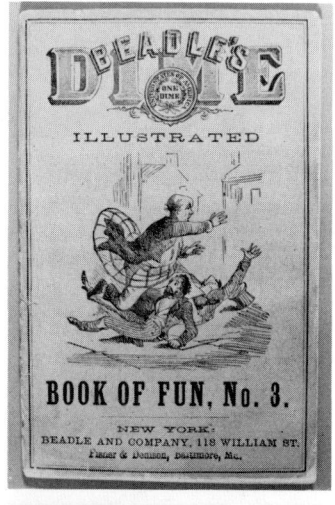

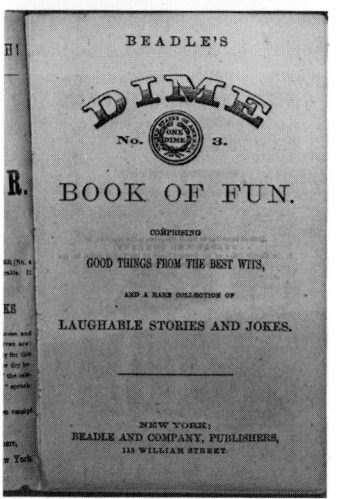

"Getting Under Way" IN:
Good Selections in Prose and Poetry.
New York, 1872: J.W. Schermerhorn & Co.
"for use in Schools and Academies, Home and Church Sociables, Lyceums and Literary Societies, etc., by W.M. Jelliffe"
Green cloth stamped in black and gold.
Inscribed copy:
BAL 3330   A.S. Stevens from Schermerhorn & Co.

"How I Edited an Agricultural Paper Once" IN:
Good Selections in Prose and Poetry.
New York, 1872: J.W. Schermerhorn & Co.
BAL 3330   *See above for binding.*

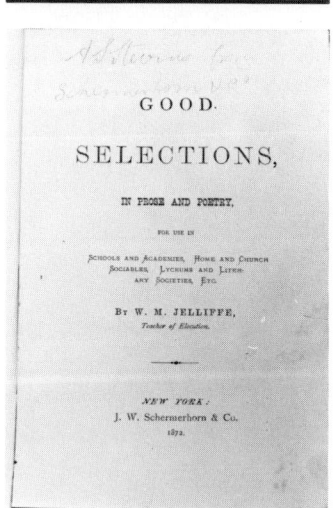

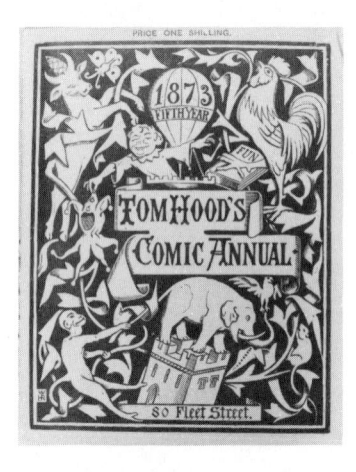

"How I Escaped Being Killed in a Duel" IN:
Tom Hood's Comic Annual for 1873.
London, (n.d., actually 1872): Fun Office, 80 Fleet Street, E.C.
BAL 3347   Paper wrappers.

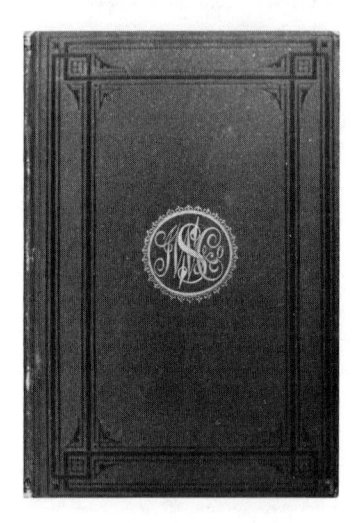

"Mark Twain on Juvenile Pugilists" IN:
Choice Selections in Poetry and Prose, no. 6.
Philadelphia, 1874: P. Garrett & Co.
            Compiled and arranged by Phineas
BAL 3350   Garrett.

"Introductory" IN:
(Wright, William) Dan De Quille. History of the Big Bonanza.
Hartford, 1876: American Publishing Company.
            San Francisco, Cal.: A.L. Bancroft &
BAL 3370   Co. Blue cloth.

"Introduction" IN:
Carolino, Pedro.
The New Guide of the Conversation in Portuguese and English in two parts.
Boston, 1883: James R. Osgood and Company.
            Brown cloth.
            Additional copies in printed wrappers and yellow cloth.
            Inscribed copy by Clemens:
            Miss Laura Taft/With the kindest/ regards of/The Author/Hartford/June
BAL 3412   *'83.*

The New Guide of the Conversation in Portuguese and English.
New York, 1966: Halcyon-Commonwealth Foundation.
            Introduction to the "Introduction by Mark Twain" by Brendan Gill.

"Mark Twain Tells About a Pipe" IN:
Cope's Tobacco Leaves for the Smoking Room.
Liverpool, May, 1885: Office of "Cope's Tobacco Plant"
            Part I. Pictorial paper wrappers.

Camden's Compliment to Walt Whitman May 31, 1889.
Philadelphia, 1889: David McKay, Publisher.
"Notes, Addresses, Letters, Telegrams edited by Horace L. Traubel."
Green cloth.
Inscribed by Traubel:
Altoona/June 28th iv/Gable asked me to write/my name in this book./I do so willingly because/I always think with a glad heart of the incident/it celebrates & like to/humor anybody who/reminds me of it/Horace Traubel.

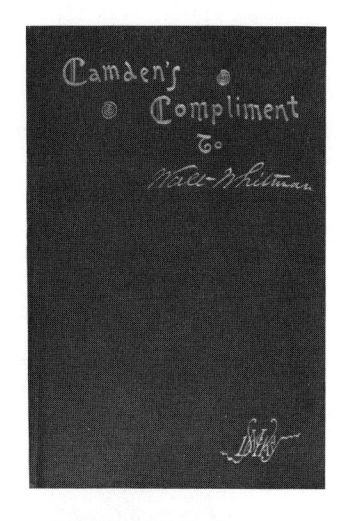

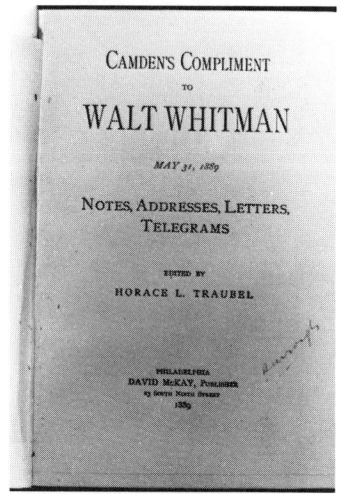

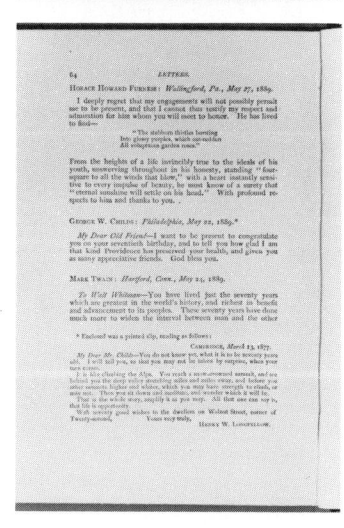

"The Californian's Tale" IN:
The First Book of the Authors Club Liber Scriptorum.
New York, 1893: Published by the Authors Club.
BAL 3438　　　Brown leather.

"The Panama Railroad" IN:
Sixty and Six Chips from Literary Workshops.
New York, (1897): New Amsterdam Book Company,
　　　　　　　156 Fifth Avenue.
BAL 3452　　　Item No. 52.

"The Author's Soldiering" IN:
Masterpieces of American Eloquence (Christian Herald Selection).
New York, 1900: The Christian Herald, Louis
　　　　　　　Klopsch,
　　　　　　　Proprietor.
　　　　　　　Introduction by Julia Ward Howe.
BAL 3462　　　Red cloth.

"The Discounts of an Author" IN:
Masterpieces of American Eloquence (Christian Herald Selection).
New York, 1900: The Christian Herald, Louis
　　　　　　　Klopsch,
　　　　　　　Proprietor.
　　　　　　　Introduction by Julia Ward Howe.
BAL 3462　　　Red cloth.

"Speech" IN:
Modern Eloquence.
Philadelphia, (1901): John D. Morris and Company.
　　　　　　　Edited by Thomas B. Reed.
　　　　　　　"A Library of Famous After-Dinner Speeches, Classic and Popular Lectures, The Best Occasional Addresses, Anecdotes and Short Stories."
　　　　　　　Ten Volumes.
　　　　　　　Clemens item is in Volume I, After-
BAL 3467　　　Dinner Speeches.

"Testimonial" IN:
Special Performance of Hansel and Gretel by the Lonreid Metropolitan Opera Company.
n.p., March 15th, 1906: (published by the company).
　　　　　　　"for the benefit of the Legal Aid Society at the Metropolitan Opera House. . . ."
　　　　　　　"Testimonial" by Clemens is dated Dec. 12 at New York.

Ephemeral Material by or about Mark Twain.

In England he was asked why he always carried a cheap cotton umbrella. He answered: "Because that's the only kind of umbrella that an Englishman won't steal"

Mark Twain's Patent Scrapbook.

Patent No. 140,245, issued June 24, 1873.

These illustrations show various descriptive leaflets and, below, the cover of one of the scrapbooks.

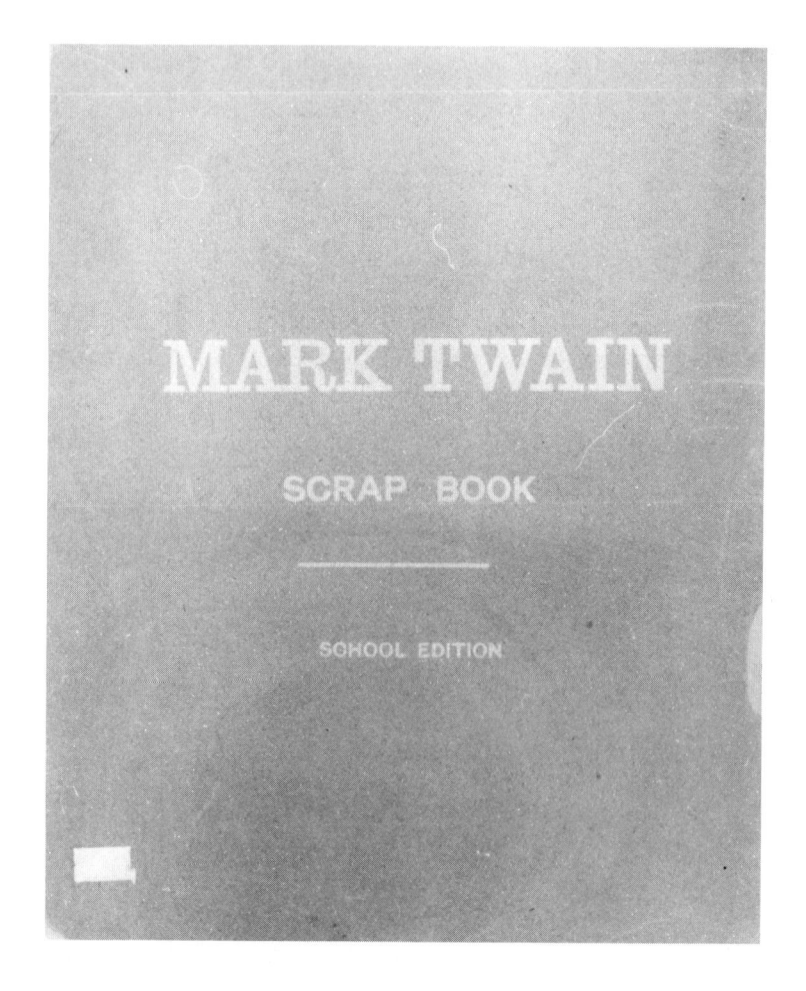

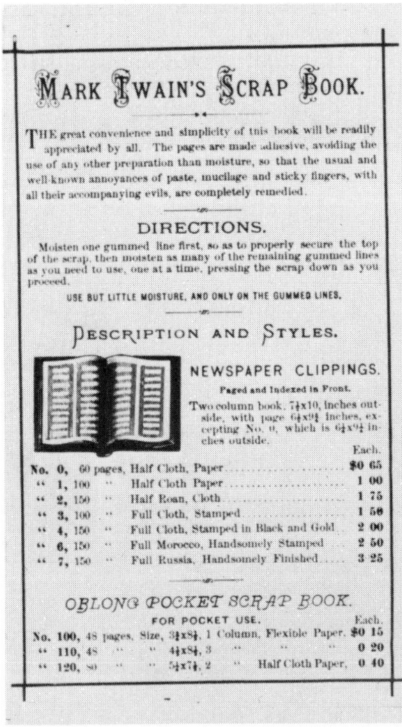

MARK TWAIN'S SCRAP BOOK.

THE great convenience and simplicity of this book will be readily appreciated by all. The pages are made adhesive, avoiding the use of any other preparation than moisture, so that the usual and well-known annoyances of paste, mucilage and sticky fingers, with all their accompanying evils, are completely remedied.

DIRECTIONS.

Moisten one gummed line first, so as to properly secure the top of the scrap, then moisten as many of the remaining gummed lines as you need to use, one at a time, pressing the scrap down as you proceed.

USE BUT LITTLE MOISTURE, AND ONLY ON THE GUMMED LINES.

DESCRIPTION AND STYLES.

NEWSPAPER CLIPPINGS.

Paged and Indexed in Front.

Two column book, 7¼x10, inches outside, with page 6¼x9¼ inches, excepting No. 0, which is 6¼x9½ inches outside.

			Each.
No. 0,	60 pages,	Half Cloth, Paper	$0 65
" 1,	100 "	Half Cloth Paper	1 00
" 2,	150 "	Half Roan, Cloth	1 75
" 3,	100 "	Full Cloth, Stamped	1 50
" 4,	150 "	Full Cloth, Stamped in Black and Gold	2 00
" 6,	150 "	Full Morocco, Handsomely Stamped	2 50
" 7,	150 "	Full Russia, Handsomely Finished	3 25

OBLONG POCKET SCRAP BOOK.

FOR POCKET USE.

			Each.
No. 100,	48 pages, Size, 3¼x8¼, 1 Column,	Flexible Paper,	$0 15
" 110,	48 " " 4¼x8¼, 3 "	" "	0 20
" 120,	80 " " 5¼x7¼, 2 "	Half Cloth Paper,	0 40

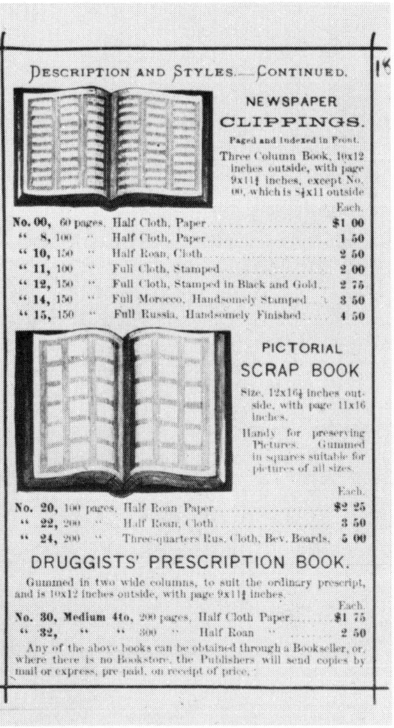

DESCRIPTION AND STYLES.—CONTINUED.

NEWSPAPER CLIPPINGS.

Paged and Indexed in Front.

Three Column Book, 10x12 inches outside, with page 9x11¼ inches, except No. 00, which is 8¼x11 outside

			Each.
No. 00,	60 pages,	Half Cloth, Paper	$1 00
" 8,	100 "	Half Cloth, Paper	1 50
" 10,	150 "	Half Roan, Cloth	2 50
" 11,	100 "	Full Cloth, Stamped	2 00
" 12,	150 "	Full Cloth, Stamped in Black and Gold	2 75
" 14,	150 "	Full Morocco, Handsomely Stamped	3 50
" 15,	150 "	Full Russia, Handsomely Finished	4 50

PICTORIAL SCRAP BOOK

Size, 12x16¼ inches outside, with page 11x16 inches.

Handy for preserving Pictures. Gummed in squares suitable for pictures of all sizes.

			Each.
No. 20,	100 pages,	Half Roan Paper	$2 25
" 22,	200 "	Half Roan, Cloth	3 50
" 24,	200 "	Three-quarters Rus. Cloth, Bev. Boards,	5 00

DRUGGISTS' PRESCRIPTION BOOK.

Gummed in two wide columns, to suit the ordinary prescript, and is 10x12 inches outside, with page 9x11¼ inches.

			Each.
No. 30,	Medium 4to, 200 pages,	Half Cloth Paper	$1 75
" 32,	" " 300 "	Half Roan "	2 50

Any of the above books can be obtained through a Bookseller, or, where there is no Bookstore, the Publishers will send copies by mail or express, pre paid, on receipt of price.

PROFANITY

MARK TWAIN'S DESCRIPTION OF HIS INVENTION:

HARTFORD, Monday Evening

MY DEAR SLOTE:—I have invented and patented a new Scrap Book, not to make money out of it, but to economise the profanity of this country. You know that when the average man wants to put something in his scrap book he can't find his paste—then he swears; or if he finds it, it is dried so hard that it is only fit to eat—then he swears; if he uses mucilage it mingles with the ink, and next year he can't read his scrap—the result is barrels and barrels of profanity. This can all be saved and devoted to other irritating things, where it will do more real and lasting good, simply by substituting my self-pasting Scrap Book for the old-fashioned one.

If Messrs. Slote, Woodman & Co. wish to publish this Scrap Book of mine, I shall be willing. You see by the above paragraph that it is a sound moral work, and this will commend it to editors and clergymen, and in fact to all right feeling people. If you want testimonials I can get them, and of the best sort, and from the best people. One of the most refined and cultivated young ladies in Hartford (daughter of a clergyman) told me herself, with grateful tears standing in her eyes, that since she began using my Scrap Book she has not sworn a single oath.

Truly yours, MARK TWAIN.

ADVANTAGES OF THE NEW STYLE SCRAP BOOK.

MARK TWAIN'S
PATENT
SCRAP BOOK
Mark Twain
FOR SALE BY
J. B. LIPPINCOTT & CO.,
PUBLISHERS, BOOKSELLERS AND STATIONERS,
715 & 717 Market Street, Philadelphia.

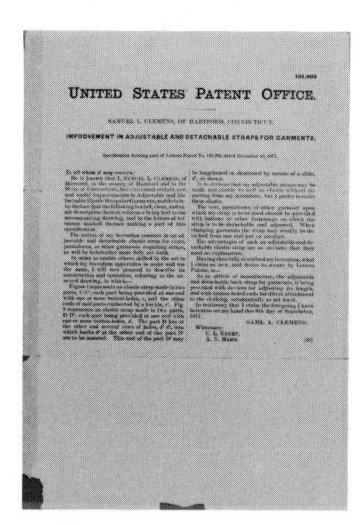

Improvement in Adjustable and Detachable Straps for Garments.
(Washington, D.C., 1871): United States Patent Office. Patent No. 121,992, issued December 19, 1871. Single sheet.

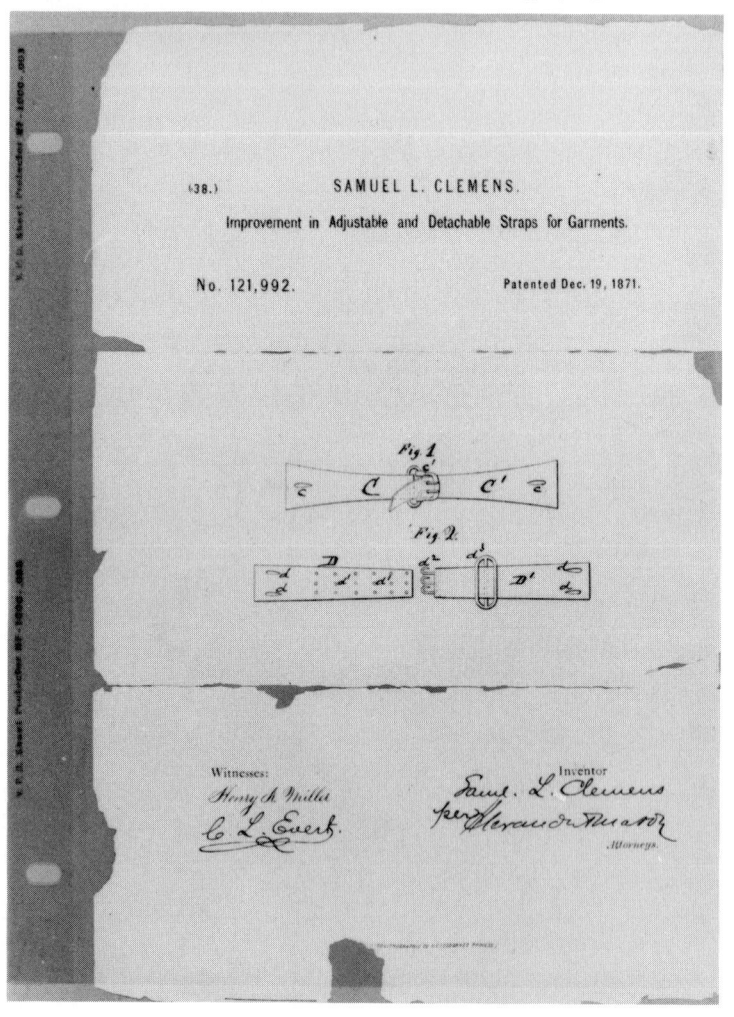

Fortifications of Paris.
Buffalo, Sept. 17th, 1870: Buffalo Express.
BAL 3320   Newspaper supplement.

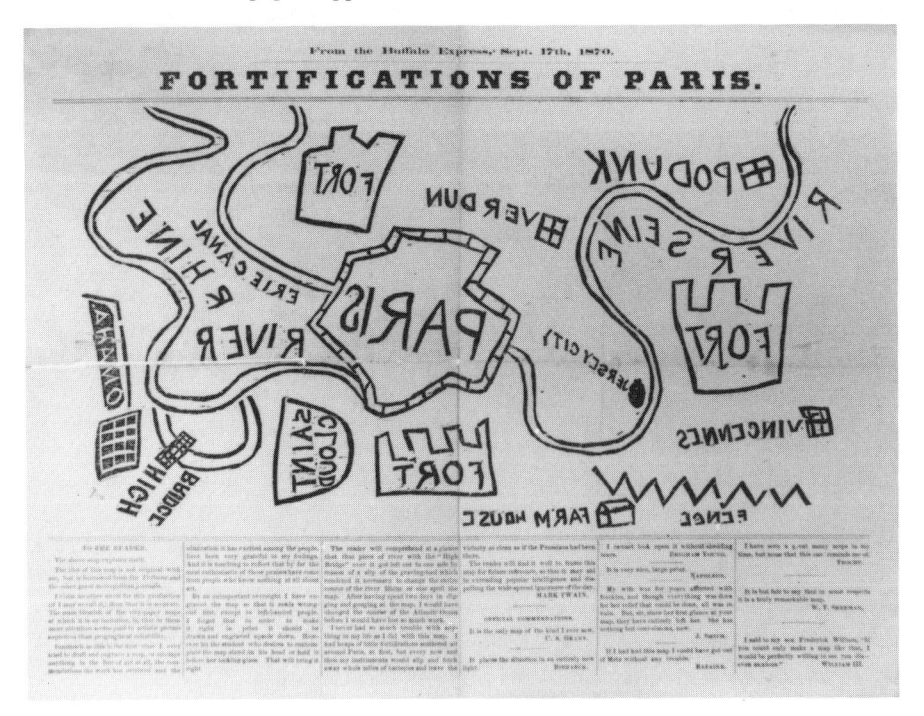

**Address. To His Imperial Majesty: —
Alexander II. Emperor of Russia.**
Yalta, August 26th, 1867.
BAL 3311   Broadside.

ADDRESS.

To His Imperial Majesty:--
     ALEXANDER II. Emperor of Russia.

We, a handful of citizens of the United States, travelling for recreation—and unostentatiously, as becomes our unofficial state,—have no excuse for presenting ourselves before your Majesty, save a desire to offer our grateful acknowledgments to the Lord of a Realm which, through good and through evil report, has been the steadfast friend of our Native Land.

We could not presume thus to present ourselves did we not know that the words we speak and the sentiments we utter, reflect the thoughts and feelings of all our countrymen; from the green hills of New England to the snowy peaks of the far Pacific. Though few in number, we utter the voice of a Nation.

One of the brightest pages that has graced the world's history, since written history had its birth, was recorded by your Majesty's hand when it loosed the bonds of twenty millions of men, and Americans can but esteem it a privilege to do honour to a ruler who has wrought so great a deed. The lesson then taught us we have profited by, and our Country is as free in fact today, as before it was in name.

America owes much to Russia: is indebted to her in many ways; and chiefly for her unwavering friendship in the season of her greatest need. That the same friendship may be hers in time to come, we confidently pray; that she is, and will be gratefull to Russia, and to her Sovereign for it, we know full well; that she will ever forfeit it by any premeditated, unjust act, or unfair course, it would be treason to believe.

Samuel Clemens, Wm Gibson, T D Crocker, S N Sanford, P Kinney, Committee

Respectfully tendered on behalf of the excursionists of the American Steam Yacht Quaker City.

Yalta August 26th 1867.

In Memoriam. Olivia Susan Clemens.
Died August 18, 1896; Aged 24.
(Lake Lucerne, Switzerland, August 18, 1897)
BAL 3450   Single sheet, folded.

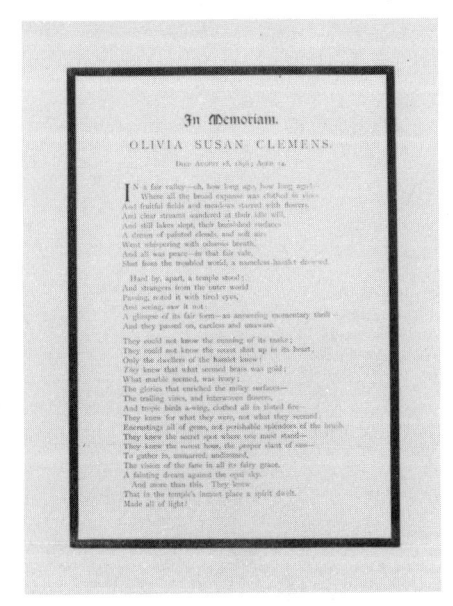

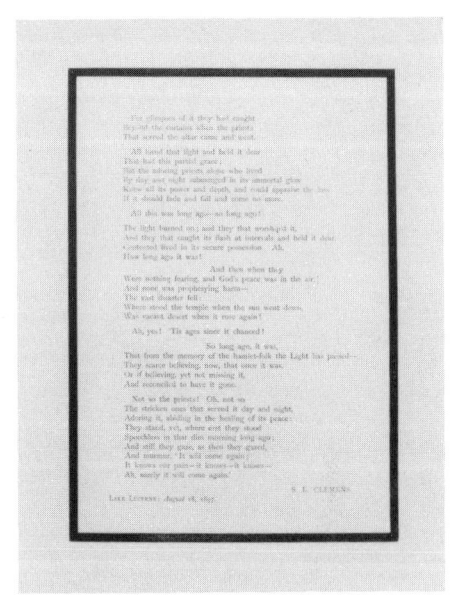

Horse-Car Poetry.
New York, 1876: G.W. Carleton & Co., Publishers.
BAL 3366A   Paper wrappers.

HORSE-CAR POETRY.

EARLY in April, 1875, the city line of the New York and Harlem Railroad Company, having adopted the punch system, posted in the panels of their cars a card of information and instruction to conductors and passengers, both of whom were indirectly requested to watch each other. It read as follows:

The CONDUCTOR, when he receives a Fare, must immediately PUNCH in the presence of the passenger,
A BLUE Trip Slip for an 8 Cents Fare,
A BUFF Trip Slip for a 6 Cents Fare,
A PINK Trip Slip for a 3 Cents Fare.
FOR COUPON AND TRANSFER TICKETS, PUNCH THE TICKETS.

The poesy of the thing was discovered almost as "immediately" as the conductor "immediately" punched, and all sorts of jingles were accommodated to the measure.

The regular patrons of the Fourth Avenue Line heard something new almost every day. But it was not until the 27th of September, 1875, that the first poem appeared in print. Two gentlemen connected with the New York Press, Mr. Bromley, of the *Tribune*, and Mr. Brooks, of the *Times*, in the summer of 1875, "were riding down town in car No. 101, having the whole car to themselves," wrote "Winkelried Wolfgang Brown," in Scribner's *Bric-a-Brac*. "Brooks was dozing. Bromley's attention was riveted to the notice, which always had a strange fascination for him. At length he started up with:

" 'It's poetry, by George! Brooks, it's poetry!'

This section lists, alphabetically by author, biographical and critical works about Mark Twain and his writings. Items listed in Tenney's *Mark Twain: A Reference Guide* (G.K. Hall, 1977) and the two supplements, have his item number listed. (Note: TSI means *Tenney Supplement I* and TSII means *Tenney Supplement II.*)

Biographical & Critical Books about Mark Twain.

Mark Twain at Oxford, England, in 1907.

Ade, George.
Revived Remarks on Mark Twain.
Chicago, 1936: Privately printed.
    "Also the Address of John T. McCutcheon Commemorating the Centenary of Mark Twain's Birth." Compiled by George Hiram Brownell.
    Orange printed wrappers: three copies, each one of 500 unnumbered, unsigned copies. (500 additional copies were each signed by Ade.) Laid onto one copy is the printed poem *The Microbe's Serenade*, signed by Ade.

T1936.A1

Allen, Jerry.
The Adventures of Mark Twain.
Boston, 1954: Little, Brown and Co.
    Black cloth with dustjacket: three copies, one with dustjacket.
T1954.A1   All are reprints.

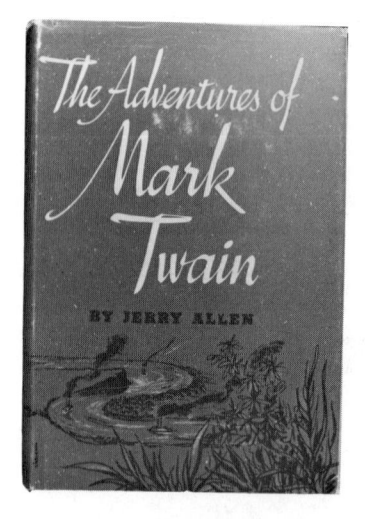

Babcock, C. Merton.
Mark Twain and the Dictionary.
Springfield, Mass., 1966: G. & C. Merriam Company.
    Volume 42, Number 1, (October 1966) of *Word Study*, a periodical.
T1966.B13   Paper wrappers.

Baldanza, Frank.
Mark Twain: An Introduction and Interpretation.
New York, 1961: Barnes and Noble, Inc.
    American Authors and Critics Series #AC3, price $1.25.
    "Second printing, 1963."
    Signed by the author.
T1961.A1   Paper wrappers.

Beck, Warren.
Huck Finn at Phelps Farm.
(Paris), 1968: Archives des Lettres Modernes.
"An essay in defense of the form of
Mark Twain's novel."
No. 13-15 of the periodical.
Paper wrappers.

Bell, Raymond Martin.
**The Ancestry of Samuel Clemens,
Grandfather of Mark Twain.**
Washington, Pennsylvania, 1980:
Introduction by Ralph Gregory.
Unpublished photocopy.

Bellamy, Gladys Carmen.
Mark Twain as Literary Artist.
Norman, 1950: University of Oklahoma Press.
T1950.A3 Green cloth.

Bingham, Robert W.
Buffalo's Mark Twain.
Buffalo, 1935: Buffalo Historical Society.
Volume 2, Nos. 4-6 of *Museum Notes.*
"Mark Twain Centennial Number."
T1935.B17 Brown printed wrappers: two copies.

Black, Robert H.
Mark Twain and Education.
n.p., 1952: McKinley Publishing Co.
"Reprint from May 1952 issue
of *The Social Study*."
Paper wrappers.

Blair, Walter.
Mark Twain & Huck Finn.
Berkeley and Los Angeles, 1960: University of
California Press.
T1960.A1 Black cloth with dustjacket.

Blair, Walter.
Mark Twain & Huck Finn.
Berkeley and Los Angeles, 1962: University of
California Press.
"Second printing 1962 (First
paper-bound Edition)."
Pictorial paper wrappers.

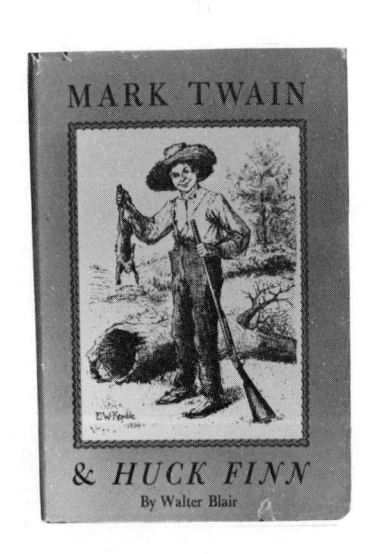

Bliss, Walter.
Twainiana Notes from the Annotations of Walter Bliss.
Hartford, (1930): The Hobby Shop.
Edited by Frances M. Edwards.
Blue cloth: three copies (numbers 64, 303 and 323 of the edition of 1000):
T1930.A1   one copy signed by the editor.

Bluefarb, Sam.
The Escape Motif in the American Novel: Mark Twain to Richard Wright.
(Columbus, 1972): Ohio State University Press.
Orange cloth with blue cloth shelfback.

Blues, Thomas.
Mark Twain and the Community.
Lexington, (1970): The University Press of Kentucky.
Paper over boards with matching
T1970.A2   dustjacket: two copies.

Branch, Edgar M., ed.
Clemens of the Call: Mark Twain in San Francisco.
Berkeley and Los Angeles, 1969: University of California Press.
Pictorial cloth over boards with
T1969.A1   dustjacket: two copies.

430

Brashear, Minnie.
Mark Twain Son of Missouri.
Chapel Hill, 1934: The University of North Carolina Press.
T1934.A1   Blue cloth with dustjacket.

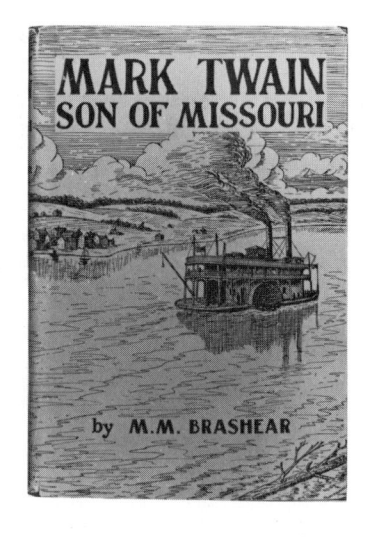

Brooks, Van Wyck.
The Ordeal of Mark Twain.
New York, (1920): E.P. Dutton & Co.
T1920.A1   Black cloth: two copies, probably first editions.

Budd, Louis J.
The Southward Currents Under Huck Finn's Raft.
Cedar Rapids, Iowa, 1959: The Mississippi Valley Historical Review.
Reprinted from Volume 46, Number 2, September 1959.
T1959.B10   Grey wrappers.

Budd, Louis J.
Twain, Howells, and Boston Nihilists.
n.p., 1959: The New England Quarterly.
Reprinted from Volume 32, Number 3, September 1959.
T1959.B11   Paper wrappers.

Butrym, Alexander J.
Mark Twain's The Adventures of Huckleberry Finn and other works.
New York, (1964): Thor Publications, Inc.
Monarch Notes #00649, price $1.00.
Pictorial wrappers: two copies.
One copy is earlier, but no printing number is indicated on either.

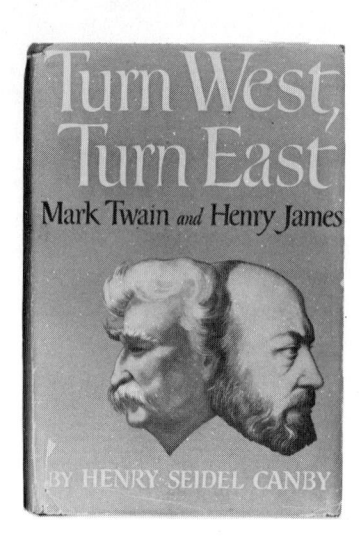

Canby, Henry Seidel.
Turn West, Turn East. Mark Twain and Henry James.
Boston, 1951: Houghton Mifflin and Co.
                Bluegreen cloth with dustjacket:
T1951.A3   two copies.

Cardwell, Guy A.
Twins of Genius.
(Lansing), 1953: The Michigan State College Press.
                About Clemens and George W.
BAL 3707   Cable.
T1953.A1   Green cloth.

Carter, Paul J., Jr.
The Influence of the Nevada Frontier on Mark Twain.
n.p., 1959: The Western Humanities Review.
                Reprinted from Volume 13,
                Number 1, Winter 1959.
T1959.B13   Grey paper wrappers: two copies.

Carter, Paul J., Jr.
The Influence of William Dean Howells Upon Mark Twain's Social Satire.
n.p., 1953: University of Colorado Studies.
                Reprinted from "Series in Language
                and Literature No. 4, July 1953."
T1953.B8   Printed wrappers.

Carter, Paul J., Jr.
Mark Twain and the American Labor Movement.
n.p., 1957: The New England Quarterly.
                Reprinted from Volume 30,
                Number 3, September 1957.
T1957.B17   Green wrappers.

Carter, Paul J., Jr.
Mark Twain Describes a San Francisco Earthquake.
New York, 1957: Modern Language Association of
                America.
                Reprinted from Volume 72,
                Number 5, December 1957.
T1957.B18   Blue wrappers: two copies.

Carter, Paul J., Jr.
Mark Twain Material in the *New York Weekly Review.*
n.p., 1958: The Bibliographical Society of America.
Reprinted from *Papers* of the Society, Volume 52, First Quarter 1958.
T1958.B9 Tan wrappers.

Carter, Paul J., Jr.
Mark Twain: "Moralist in Disguise."
n.p., 1957: University of Colorado Studies.
Reprinted from "Series in Language and Literature, Number 6, January 1957."
T1957.B19 Wrappers: two copies.

Carter, Paul J., Jr.
Olivia Clemens Edits *Following the Equator.*
n.p., 1958: American Literature.
Reprinted from Volume 30, Number 2, May 1958.
T1958.B10 Printed wrappers: two copies.

Chambliss, Amy.
The Friendship of Helen Keller and Mark Twain.
n.p., 1970: The Georgia Review.
Excerpted pages from Volume 24, Number 3, Fall 1970.
T1970.B12

Clemens, Clara.
My Father Mark Twain.
New York and London, 1931: Harper & Brothers Publishers.
Contains "hitherto unpublished letters of Mark Twain."
Blue cloth with dustjacket.
Three copies, all autographed by the author, one with dustjacket. Two second printings, one third printing.
T1931.A3

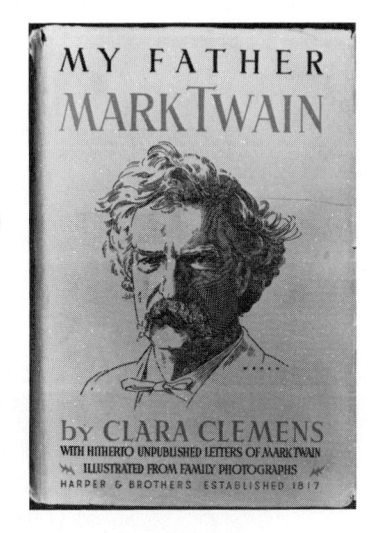

433

Clemens, Cyril.
Mark Twain and Harry S Truman.
Webster Grove, Missouri, 1950: International Mark Twain Society.
London, 1950: T. Werner Laurie Limited.
Foreword by Louis Johnson.
Inscribed by the author.

T1950.A5   Grey wrappers.

Clemens, Cyril.
Mark Twain and John F. Kennedy.
Kirkwood, Missouri, 1962: Mark Twain Journal.
Preface by Sir Geoffrey Shakespeare, Bart.
Dedication by John Masefield.
Inscribed by Clemens.

T1962.A4   Printed paper wrappers.

Clemens, Cyril.
Mark Twain and Mussolini.
Webster Groves, Missouri, 1934: International Mark Twain Society.
Foreword by Patrick Braybrooke.
Two copies:
Copy 1: Blue cloth with dustjacket.

T1934.A2   Copy 2: Red printed wrappers.

Clemens, Cyril.
Mark Twain and Richard M. Nixon.
Kirkwood, Missouri, 1970: Mark Twain Journal.
Foreword by Herbert Hoover.
Dedication by William H. Taft.

TSI, p.366   Light green wrappers.

Clemens, Cyril.
My Cousin Mark Twain.
Emmaus, Penn., 1939: Rodale Press.
"Second edition (revised, with additional material)."
Orange cloth.

T1939.A3   Autographed by the author.

Clemens, Cyril, ed.
Mark Twain Anecdotes.
n.p., 1929: Mark Twain Society.
"Tributes to S.L. Clemens by G.K. Chesterton and John Galsworthy, Members of the Society."
Yellow-gold wrappers: two copies,
T1929.A2   one signed by the editor.

Clemens, Will M.
**Mark Twain: His Life and Work:
A Biographical Sketch.**
San Francisco, 1892: The Clemens Publishing
Company.
"Pacific Library No. 1, July, 1892"
T1892.A1   Pictorial wrappers.

Coard, Robert L.
The Dictionary and Mark Twain.
Springfield, Mass., 1968: G. & C. Merriam Company.
Volume 43, Number 3, February,
1968 issue of *Word Study*.
T1968.B22   Paper wrappers.

Cox, James M.
Mark Twain: The Fate of Humor.
Princeton, N.J., 1966: Princeton University
Press.
Grey cloth with dustjacket:
T1966.A2   two copies.

Darbee, Henry, ed.
Mark Twain in Hartford.
Hartford, 1958: The Mark Twain Library &
Memorial Commission.
T1958.A2   Pictorial paper wrappers: two copies.

Darbee, Henry, ed.
Mark Twain in Hartford.
Hartford, 1966: The Mark Twain Library and
Memorial Commission.
Second edition.
Pictorial paper wrappers.

Darbee, Henry, ed.
Mark Twain in Hartford.
Hartford, 1974: Mark Twain Memorial.
Third edition.
Pictorial paper wrappers.

Darbee, Henry, ed.
Mark Twain's House.
Hartford, 1977: Mark Twain Memorial.
Fourth edition.
Pictorial paper wrappers.

Day, Katharine Seymour.
Mark Twain's First Years in Hartford and Personal Memories of the Clemens Family.
(Hartford, 1936): not published.
    "A Thesis submitted in partial fulfillment of the requirements for the degree of Master of Arts, in History at Trinity College, Hartford, Connecticut, May 13, 1936."
    Early draft and final typescripts.

DeCasseres, Benjamin.
When Huck Finn Went Highbrow.
New York, 1934: Thomas F. Madigan, Inc.
    "with a facsimile reproduction."
    Paper over boards with imitation vellum shelfback and tissue dustjacket.
T1934.A3   #1 of 125 copies.

DeVoto, Bernard.
Mark Twain at Work.
Cambridge, Mass., 1942: Harvard University Press.
T1942.A4   Green cloth: two copies.

DeVoto, Bernard.
Mark Twain's America and Mark Twain at Work.
Boston, 1967: Houghton Mifflin Company.
    "Sentry Edition 1967."
    #SE50. price $2.45.
    Illustrated by M.J. Gallagher.
    Pictorial wrappers.

Duckett, Margaret.
Mark Twain and Bret Harte.
Norman, (1964): University of Oklahoma Press.
T1964.A2   Grey cloth with dustjacket.

Eaton, Jeanette.
America's Own Mark Twain.
New York, 1958: William Morrow & Company.
                Illustrated by Leonard
                Everett Fisher.
T1958.A3   Blue cloth with dustjacket.

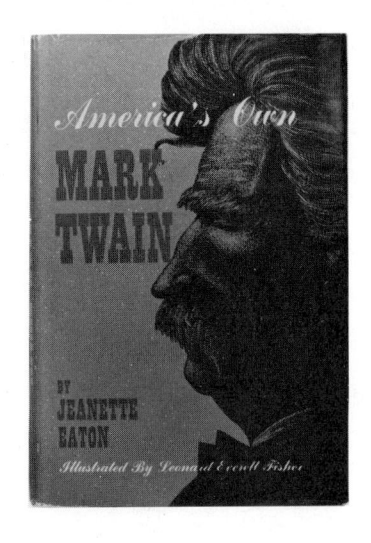

Egan, Michael.
Mark Twain's Huckleberry Finn: Race Class and Society.
(London), 1977: Sussex University Press.
TSII, p.208

Ensor, Allison.
Mark Twain and The Bible.
(Lexington, 1969): University of Kentucky Press.
T1969.A5   Terra-cotta cloth.

Fatout, Paul.
Mark Twain in Virginia City.
Bloomington, 1964: Indiana University Press.
                "Second printing, July 1964"
T1964.A3   Grey cloth with dustjacket.

Fatout, Paul.
Mark Twain on the Lecture Circuit.
Bloomington, 1960: Indiana University Press.
T1960.A3   Green cloth with dustjacket.

Faude, Wilson H.
The Renaissance of Mark Twain's House. Handbook for Restoration.
Larchmont, N.Y., (1978): Queens House.
     Introduction by Oliver Jensen.
TSII, p.216   Brown cloth with dustjacket.

Ferguson, DeLancey.
Mark Twain: Man and Legend.
Indianapolis and New York, (1943): The Bobbs-Merrill Co.
     Red cloth with dustjacket: four
T1943.A3   copies, two signed by the author.

Finger, Charles J.
Mark Twain: The Philosopher Who Laughed at the World.
Girard, Kansas, (1924): Haldeman-Julius Company.
    Little Blue Book No. 517.
    Edited by E. Haldeman-Julius.
T1924.A3   Blue paper wrappers: two copies.

Fisher, Henry W.
Abroad with Mark Twain and Eugene Field.
New York, 1922: Nicholas L. Brown.
    "Tales They Told a Fellow Correspondent."
T1922.A2   Blue cloth.

Foner, Philip S.
Mark Twain Social Critic.
New York, 1958: International Publishers.
T1958.A4   Blue cloth.

Frederick, John T.
Mark Twain, American Author.
(Chicago), 1943: Northwestern University on the air.
    Transcript of "a radio conversation over the Columbia Broadcasting System."
    Volume 2, No. 47: August 28, 1943.
    Paper wrappers: two copies, one signed by the author.

French, Bryant Morey.
Mark Twain and *The Gilded Age.*
Dallas, (1965): Southern Methodist University Press.
T1965.A2   Orange cloth with dustjacket.

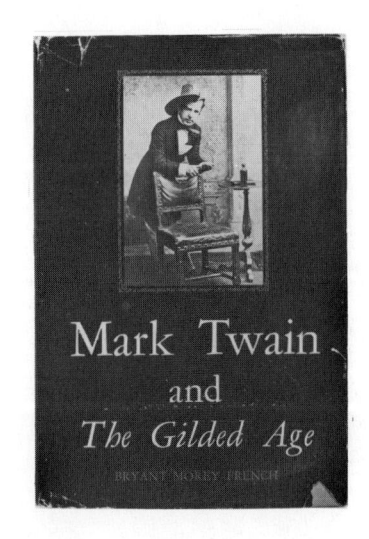

Frevert, Patricia Dendtler.
Mark Twain: An American Voice.
Mankato, Minn., (1981): Creative Education, Inc. Pictorial cloth.

Ganzel, Dewey.
Mark Twain Abroad: The Cruise of the "Quaker City."
Chicago and London, (1968): The University of Chicago Press.
T1968.A1   Blue green cloth with dustjacket.

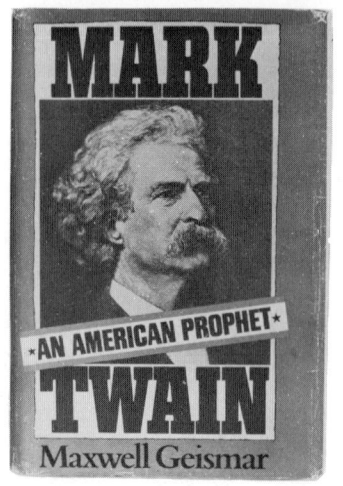

Geismar, Maxwell.
Mark Twain An American Prophet.
Boston, 1970: Houghton Mifflin Company.
T1970.A5   Brown cloth with dustjacket.

Gillis, William R.
Gold Rush Days with Mark Twain.
New York, 1930: Albert & Charles Boni.
    Introduction by Cyril Clemens.
    Illustrated with woodcuts by
    H. Glintenkamp.
T1930.A2   Blue green cloth.

Gillis, William R.
Memories of Mark Twain and Steve Gillis.
Sonora, Calif., March 1924: The Banner.
T1924.A2   Green wrappers: two copies.

Goad, Mary Ellen.
The Image and the Woman in the Life and Writings of Mark Twain.
Emporia, Kansas, (1971): The Emporia State
    Research Studies.
    Reprint from Volume 19, Number 3,
    March 1971.
T1971.B28   Paper wrappers.

Grant, Douglas.
Twain.
Edinburgh and London, 1962: Oliver and Boyd.
T1962.A8   Pictorial paper wrappers.

Grant, Douglas.
Mark Twain.
New York, (1962): Grove Press, Inc.
    Evergreen Pilot Book #EP20,
    price 95¢.
T1962.A8   Pictorial paper wrappers.

Graves, Charles.
Mark Twain: A See and Read Beginning to Read Biography.
New York, (1972): G.P. Putnam's Sons.
    Illustrated by Fermin Rocker.
TSI, p.373   Pictorial cloth.

Gregory, Ralph.
Mark Twain's First America: Florida, Missouri 1835-1840.
n.p., 1965: Privately published.
T1965.A3   Yellow wrappers.

Gregory, Ralph.
William Dean Howells Corrections, Suggestions and Questions on the English Manuscript of "Tom Sawyer."
Florida, Missouri, (July 1966): Mark Twain
    Memorial Shrine.
    One of 1000 copies.
TSI, p.358   Paper wrappers.

Gribben, Alan.
The Dispersal of Samuel L. Clemens' Library Books.
n.p., 1975: Resources for American Literary Study.
    Reprint from Volume 5, Number 2, Autum 1975.
TSI, p.389   Brown paper wrappers.

Gribben, Alan.
How Tom Sawyer Played Robin Hood "By The Book."
n.p., 1976: English Language Notes.
    Reprint from Volume 13, Number 3, March 1976.
TSI, p.401   Paper wrappers.

Gribben, Alan.
"It is Unsatisfactory to Read to One's Self": Mark Twain's Informal Readings.
n.p., 1976: The Quarterly Journal of Speech.
    Reprinted from Volume 62, Number 1, February 1976.
TSI, p.401   Paper wrappers.

Gribben, Alan.
Mark Twain's Library: A Reconstruction.
Boston, (1980): G.K. Hall & Co.
    Two volumes.
    Does not list works by Clemens, only those owned by him.
    Maroon cloth.

Gribben, Alan.
"The Master Hand of Old Malory": Mark Twain's Acquaintance with *Le Morte D'Arthur.*
n.p., 1978: English Language Notes.
    Reprint from Volume 16, Number 1, September 1976.
    Paper wrappers.

Gribben, Alan.
"A Splendor of Stars & Suns": Twain as a Reader of Browning's Poem.
New York, 1978: The Browning Institute and the University Center, CUNY.
    Reprinted from *Studies* Volume 6.
    Paper wrappers.

Harnsberger, Caroline Thomas.
Mark Twain Family Man.
New York, (1960): The Citadel Press.
T1960.A5   Black cloth: two copies.

Harnsberger, Caroline Thomas.
Mark Twain's Views of Religion.
Evanston, Ill., 1961: The Schori Press.
        #122 of 400, signed on the colophon by Ward K. Schori.
T1961.A8   Signed by the author. Pictorial cloth.

Henderson, Archibald.
Mark Twain.
New York, 1912: Frederick A. Stokes Company.
        With photographs by Alvin Langdon Coburn, two in autochrome.
T1911.A3   Green cloth.

Herford, Oliver.
Mark Twain: A Pipe Dream.
Avon, Conn., 1937: Avon Old Farms Press.
        Printed paper wrappers.

Hill, Hamlin.
The Composition and the Structure of Tom Sawyer.
n.p., 1961: American Literature.
        Reprint from Volume 32, Number 4, January 1961.
T1961.B35   Paper wrappers: two copies.

Hill, Hamlin.
Escol Sellers from Uncharted Space: A Footnote to *The Gilded Age.*
n.p., 1962: American Literature.
        Reprint from Volume 34, Number 1, March 1962.
T1962.B37   Paper wrappers.

Hill, Hamlin.
Mark Twain and Elisha Bliss.
Columbia, 1964: University of Missouri Press.
T1964.A4   Brown cloth with dustjacket.

Hill, Hamlin.
Mark Twain: Audience and Artistry.
n.p., n.d.: American Quarterly.
        Excerpted pages.

Hill, Hamlin.
Mark Twain: God's Fool.
New York, Evanston, San Francisco, London, (1973): Harper & Row, Publishers.
        Mustard cloth: two copies, one with
T1973.A5   dustjacket.

Hill, Hamlin.
Mark Twain's Book Sales, 1869-1879.
n.p., 1961: Bulletin of New York Public Library.
        Reprint from Volume 65, Number 6, June 1961.
T1961.B36   Paper wrappers.

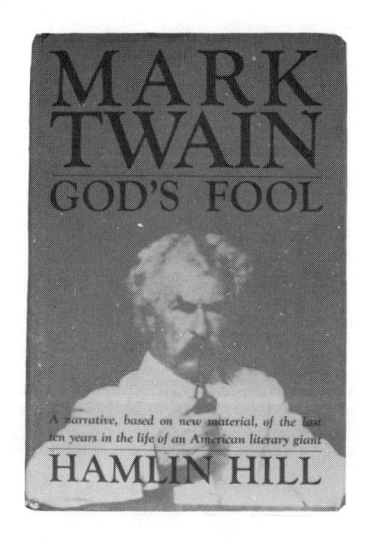

Hill, Hamlin.
Mark Twain's Brace of Brief Lectures on Science.
n.p., 1961: The New England Quarterly.
    Reprinted from Volume 34, Number 2, June 1961.
T1963.B43   Green paper wrappers.

Hill, Hamlin.
Mark Twain's Quarrels with Elisha Bliss.
n.p., 1962: American Literature.
    Reprint from Volume 33, Number 4, January 1962.
T1962.B38   Paper wrappers.

Hoffman, Michael J.
Huck's Ironic Circle.
n.p., 1969: The Georgia Review.
    Extracted pages from Volume 23, Number 3, Fall 1969.
T1969.B34   Paper wrappers.

Holbrook, Hal.
Mark Twain Tonight! An Actor's Portrait.
New York, (1959): Ives Washburn, Inc.
    Selections from Mark Twain edited adapted and arranged with a prologue.
T1959.A3   Blue cloth with dustjacket.

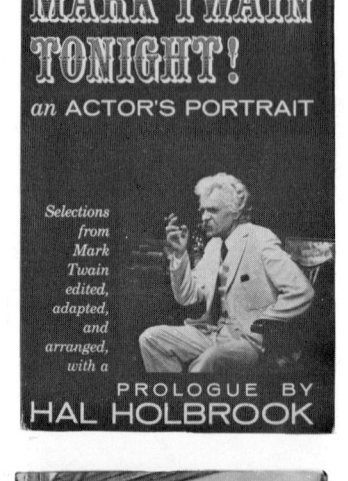

Howard, Joan.
The Story of Mark Twain.
New York, 1953: Grosset & Dunlap, Publishers.
    Illustrated by Donald McKay.
    Greygreen cloth: two copies, one with dustjacket.

Howells, W. D.
My Mark Twain.
New York and London, 1910: Harper & Brothers
Publishers.
Turquoise cloth stamped in red and
T1910.A3   gold: three copies.

James, George Wharton.
How Mark Twain Was Made.
n.p., 1911: National Magazine.
Reprinted from the issue of
February, 1911.
T1911.B13   Paper wrappers.

Jensen, Franklin.
Mark Twain's Comments on Books and Authors.
Emporia, Kansas, 1964: Emporia State Research
Studies.
Reprint from Volume 12, Number 4,
June 1864.
T1964.B63   Paper wrappers.

Jerome, Robert D. and Wisbey, Herbert A., Jr., eds.
Mark Twain in Elmira.
Elmira, N.Y., 1977: Mark Twain Society.
Red cloth: two copies, one signed by
TSII, pp.209-10   both editors.

Kahn, Sholom J.
Mark Twain's Mysterious Stranger: A Study of the Manuscript Texts.
Columbia and London, 1978: University of
Missouri Press.
TSII, p.216   Black cloth with dustjacket.

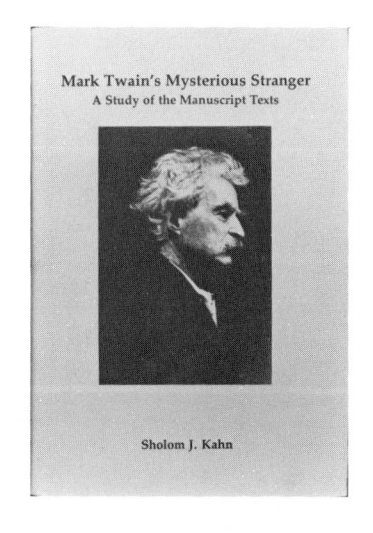

Kaplan, Justin, ed.
Mark Twain: A Profile.
New York, 1967: Hill and Wang.
T1967.A11   Grey cloth with dustjacket.

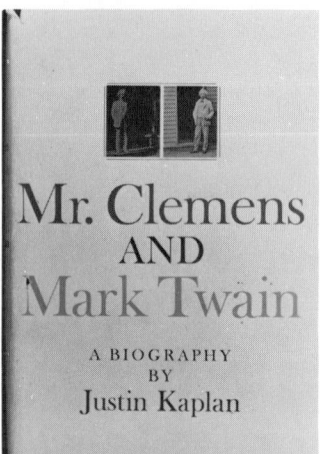

Kaplan, Justin.
Mr. Clemens and Mark Twain.
New York, 1966: Simon and Schuster.
             Black cloth with dustjacket: two first printings and one book club reprint. One first edition is signed by
T1966.A6   the author.

Kaplan, Justin.
Mr. Clemens and Mark Twain.
New York, 1968: Pocket Books, Inc.
             Pictorial paper wrappers.

Kipling, Rudyard.
"An Interview with Mark Twain"
New York, 1899: Doubleday and McClure.
             Excerpt from *From Sea to Sea: Letters*
T1899.B19   *of Travel.*

Krause, Sydney J.
Mark Twain as Critic.
Baltimore, (1967): The Johns Hopkins Press.
T1967.A13   Maroon cloth with dustjacket.

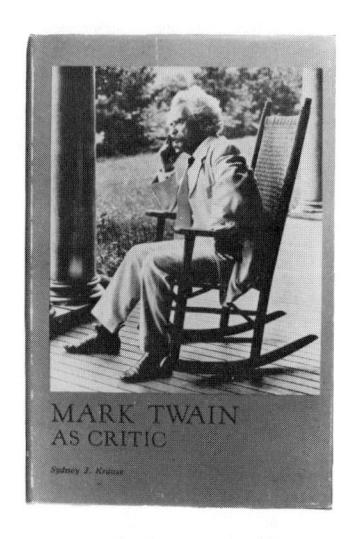

Kruse, Horst H.
Mark Twain and "Life on the Mississippi."
Amherst, (1981): The University of Massachusetts
            Press.
            Mustard cloth with dustjacket.

Langdon, Jervis, ed.
Samuel Langhorne Clemens: Some Reminisces and Some Excerpts from Letters and Unpublished Manuscripts.
n.p., n.d., (ca. 1938): no publisher.
TSI, p.342   Brown paper wrappers: three copies.

Langdon, Jervis.
Mark Twain and Elmira.
New York, 1935: Mark Twain Centennial Committee
            of New York.
TSII, p.187   Brown paper wrappers.

Langdon, Jervis.
Mark Twain in Elmira.
n.p., 1958: Chemung County Historical Society.
            A reprint of *Mark Twain and Elmira*
            (above).
            Pictorial wrappers: two copies.

Lawton, Mary.
A Lifetime with Mark Twain.
New York, 1925: Harcourt, Brace & Co.
            "The Memories of Kate Leary,
            for Thirty Years His Faithful and
            Devoted Servant."
T1925.A2   Brown-orange cloth: two copies.

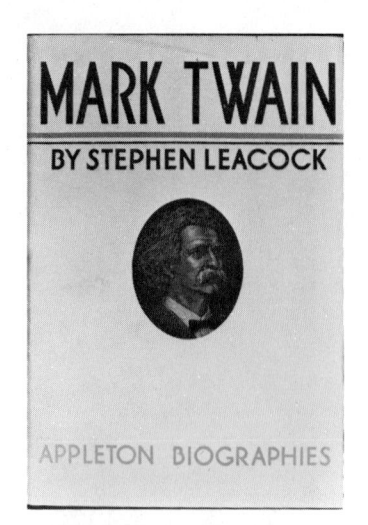

Leacock, Stephen.
Mark Twain.
New York, 1933: D. Appleton and Co.
T1932.A3   Black cloth with dustjacket.

Leary, Lewis, ed.
A Casebook on Mark Twain's Wound.
New York, (1962): Thomas Y. Crowell Company.
T1962.A10   Pictorial paper wrappers.

Leary, Lewis.
Mark Twain.
Minneapolis, (1960): University of Minnesota Press.
          "Pamphlet on American Writers
          No. 5, 65¢."
          Second printing 1960.
T1960.A6   Paper wrappers: two copies.

Lettis, Richard (&) McDonnell, Robert F.
(&) Morris, William E.
Huck Finn and His Critics.
New York, (1962): The Macmillian Company.
T1962.A11   Pictorial paper wrappers.

Long, E. Hudson.
Mark Twain Handbook.
New York, (1957): Hendricks House.
T1957.A3   Bluegreen cloth.

Lorch, Fred W.
The Trouble Begins at Eight: Mark Twain's Lecture Tours.
Ames, (1968): Iowa State University Press.
        Second printing 1969.
T1968.A2   Red cloth with dustjacket.

Lynn, Kenneth S.
Mark Twain and Southwestern Humor.
Boston and Toronto, (1958): Little, Brown and Company.
T1959.A4   Blue cloth

Mack, Effie Mona.
Mark Twain in Nevada.
New York, 1947: Charles Scribner's Sons.
        Red cloth: four copies, one with
T1947.A5   dustjacket.

Macnaughton, William R.
Mark Twain's Last Years as a Writer.
Columbus and London, 1979: University of Missouri Press.
        Grey cloth with dustjacket.

Masters, Edgar Lee.
Mark Twain: A Portrait.
New York and London, 1938: Charles Scribner's Sons.
T1938.A7   Orange cloth.

Mayfield, John S.
Mark Twain vs. The Street Railway Co.
n.p., 1926: Privately Printed.
BAL 3540   Introduction by Charles J. Finger.
T1926.A3   Paper wrappers.

Mark Twain: Samuel Langhorne Clemens: Notes on His Life and Works.
New York and London, 1928: Harper & Brothers.
    Major contributions by Henry VanDyke, Albert Bigelow Paine, and tributes by Joseph Conrad, Booth Tarkington, William Dean Howells, Kate Douglas Wiggin and others, quoted from their works. Red paper wrappers with label: five copies.

McKeithan, D.M.
Court Trails in Mark Twain and other essays.
(The Hague, Netherlands), 1958: Martinus Nijhoff.
T1958.A5   Light blue cloth with dustjacket.

Meltzer, Milton.
Mark Twain Himself: A Pictorial Biography.
New York, (1960): Thomas Y. Crowell Company.
T1960.A8   Tan cloth: four copies.

Miers, Earl Schenck.
Mark Twain on the Mississippi.
Cleveland and New York, 1957: The World Publishing Company.
    Illustrated by Robert Frankenberg.
T1957.A4   Pictorial cloth with dustjacket.

Miers, Earl Schenck.
Mark Twain on the Mississippi.
New York, (1963): Collier Books.
    Illustrated by Robert Frankenberger.
    "First Collier Books Edition 1963"
    Pictorial paper wrappers.

Miller, Albert G.
Mark Twain in Love.
New York, (1973): Harcourt Brace Jovanovich, Inc.
    Signed by the author.
    Blue cloth with dustjacket.

Moers, Ellen.
**Harriet Beecher Stowe and
American Literature.**
Hartford, 1978: The Stowe-Day Foundation.
        "With a Note on Mark Twain and
        Harriet Beecher Stowe."
        Wrappers: two copies.

Mutalik, Keshav.
Mark Twain in India.
Bombay, (1978): Noble Publishing House.
        Brown cloth with dustjacket.

Neider, Charles.
**Mark Twain and The Russians:
An Exchange of Views.**
New York, (1960): Hill and Wang.
        "An American Century Special 50¢"
T1960.A10   Printed paper wrappers: four copies.

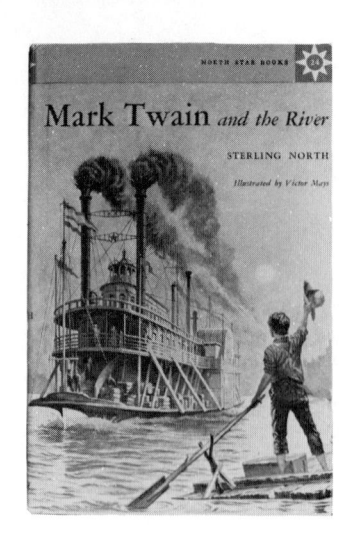

North, Sterling.
Mark Twain and the River.
Boston, 1961: Houghton, Mifflin Company.
          Illustrated by Victor Mays.
TSII, p.194   Tan pictorial cloth with dustjacket.

O'Connor, Laurel
Drinking with Mark Twain.
n.p., 1936: Frank Edward Kelsey.
          "Recollections of Mark Twain and his cronies as told to me Laurel
T1936.A4   O'Connor Raconteuse."
          White paper wrappers.

Paine, Albert Bigelow.
The Boy's Life of Mark Twain.
New York and London, (1926): Harper & Brothers Publishers.
          "The Story of a Man Who Made the World Laugh and Love Him."
          Blue cloth with dustjacket, a reprint.
          Second copy: "Fourteenth printing,
T1916.A1   March, 1929."

Paine, Albert Bigelow.
The Adventures of Mark Twain.
New York, (1944): Grosset & Dunlap Publishers.
          A reprint of *A Boy's Life of Mark Twain* to coincide with the motion picture of "The Adventures of Mark Twain" starring Frederic March and Alexis Smith.
          Tan cloth with dustjacket showing stills from the movie.

Paine, Albert Bigelow.
Mark Twain: A Biography.
New York and London, 1912: Harper & Brothers
              Publishers.
              "The Personal and Literary Life of
              Samuel Langhorne Clemens . . .
              with letters, comments and inciden-
              tal writings hitherto unpublished;
              also new episodes, anecdotes, etc."
              Three volumes.
              Copyright page date codes: Volume
              I: H-M, Volumes II & III: I-M.
              Red cloth matching that of
T1912.A3   *The $30,000 Bequest,* etc.

Paine, Albert Bigelow.
Mark Twain: A Biography.
New York and London, 1912: Harper & Brothers
              Publishers.
              Three volumes.
              Second issue with I-M date code on
              copyright page of each volume.
T1912.A3   Red cloth, different style than above.

Paine, Albert.
Mark Twain: A Biography.
New York and London, 1912: Harper & Brothers
              Publishers.
              Four volumes.
              Third issue with I-M date code on
              copyright page of each volume,
              but lacking "Published
              September 1912."
              Green cloth.

Paine, Albert Bigelow.
Mark Twain: A Biography.
New York, (1928): Harper & Brothers Publishers.
              Three volumes.
              K-C date code on copyright page.
              Blue cloth.

Paine, Albert Bigelow.
Mark Twain: A Biography.
New York, 1929: Harper & Brothers.
              Volumes 30, 31, 32 & 33 of
              The Stormfield Edition of
              The Writings of Mark Twain.
              Set #212 of 1024. Blue cloth stamped in gold.

Paine, Albert Bigelow.
A Short Life of Mark Twain.
Garden City, N.Y., 1925: Garden City Publishing Co.
              Brown-orange cloth.
              Reprint abridged from *Mark Twain:*
T1920.A4   *A Biography.*

Pellowe, William C.S.
Mark Twain: Pilgrim from Hannibal.
New York, 1945: The Hobson Book Press.
    Blue cloth with dustjacket:
T1946.A5   three copies.

Proudfit, Isabel.
River-Boy, The Story of Mark Twain.
New York, 1957: Julian Messner, Inc.
    Illustrated by W.C. Nims.
T1940.A5   Grey cloth with dustjacket.

Quick, Dorothy.
Enchantment: A Little Girl's Friendship with Mark Twain.
Norman, (1961): University of Oklahoma Press.
    Brown cloth with dustjacket:
    three copies, plus a set of unbound
T1961.A14   gatherings.

Regan, Robert.
Unpromising Heroes: Mark Twain and His Characters.
Berkeley and Los Angeles, 1966: University of California Press.
T1966.A8   Tan cloth with dustjacket.

Rikhoff, Jean.
Writing about the Frontier: Mark Twain.
Chicago, 1961: Kingston House.
Bookshelf for Young Americans. Illustrated by Richard Mlodock. Paper over boards with cloth shelf-
TSII, p.194   back and dustjacket: two copies.

Salomon, Roger B.
Twain and the Image of History.
New Haven, 1961: Yale University Press.
T1961.A16   Purple cloth with dustjacket.

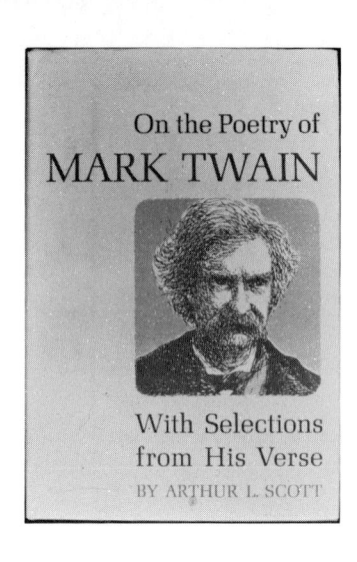

Scott, Arthur L.
On the Poetry of Mark Twain with selections from his verse.
Urbana and London, 1966: University of
    Illinois Press.
T1966.A9   Green cloth with dustjacket.
    two copies.

Seelye, John.
The True Adventures of Huckleberry Finn.
Evanston, 1970: Northwestern University Press.
T1970.A9   Paper over boards with dustjacket.

Seelye, John.
Mark Twain in the Movies: A Meditation with Pictures.
New York, (1977): The Viking Press.
    Paper over boards with cloth
    shelfback and dustjacket: two
TSII, p.212   copies.

Selby, P.O., compiler.
Theses on Mark Twain 1910-1967.
Kirksville, Mo., 1969: Missouriana Library,
    Northeast Missouri State College.

Simpson, Alan.
Mark Twain Goes Back To Vassar.
n.p., 1977: Vassar College.
    "An introduction to the
    Jean Webster McKinney Family
    Papers, published for the dedication
    of the Francis Fitz Randolph Rare
    Book Room in the Helen D.
    Lockwood Library, May 6, 1977."
TSII, p.213   Printed wrappers: two copies.

Smith, Henry Nash.
Mark Twain: A Collection of Critical Essays.
Englewood Cliffs, N.J., 1963: Prentice-Hall Inc.
T1963.A5   Paper wrappers: two copies.

Smith, Henry Nash.
Mark Twain: The Development of a Writer.
Cambridge, Mass., 1962: The Belknap Press of Harvard University Press.
Black cloth with dustjacket:
T1962.A15   two copies.

Smith, U.S.
Up a Tree with Mark Twain.
Quincy, Ill., 1978: Shondo-Shando Press.
"An oracular opus exposing a literary hoax so horrendous May God Have Mercy on the 1st Amendent."
Paper wrappers: two copies.

Spengemann, William C.
Mark Twain and the Backwoods Angel.
Kent, Ohio, (1966): Kent State University Press.
"The Matter of Innocence in the Works of Samuel L. Clemens."
T1966.A10   Brown cloth with dustjacket.

Stearns, Monroe.
Mark Twain.
New York, (1965): Franklin, Watts, Inc.
Pictorial cloth.
T1965.A9   Second printing.

Stern, Madeline B.
Mark Twain Had His Head Examined.
n.p., 1969: American Literature.
Reprint from Volume 41, Number 2, May 1969.
T1969.B71   Paper wrappers.

Stone, Albert E., Jr.
The Innocent Eye: Childhood in Mark Twain's Imagination.
New Haven, 1961: Yale University Press.
T1961.A18   Red cloth with dustjacket.

Stong, Phil.
Mississippi Pilot. With Mark Twain on the Great River.
Garden City, 1954: Doubleday & Company, Inc.
T1954.A4   Terra-cotta cloth with dustjacket: two copies.

Tuckey, John S.
Mark Twain and Little Satan: The Writing of The Mysterious Stranger.
West Lafayette, Ind., 1963: Purdue University Press.
T1963.A9   Pictorial paper wrappers: two copies.

Turner, Arlin.
Mark Twain, Cable and "A Professional Newspaper Liar."
n.p., 1955: The New England Quarterly.
     Reprint from Volume 28, Number 1, March 1955.
T1955.B49   Paper wrappers.

Turner, Arlin.
Notes on Mark Twain in New Orleans.
n.p., 1954: McNeese Review.
     Reprint from Volume 6, 1954.
T1954.B46   Paper wrappers.

Wagenknecht, Edward.
Mark Twain. The Man and His Work.
New Haven, 1935: Yale University Press.
T1935.A16   Red cloth: two copies, both second printings.

Wagenknecht, Edward.
Mark Twain. The Man and His Work.
Norman, (1961): University of Oklahoma Press.
T1961.A9   New and revised edition, first printing. Red cloth.

Walker, I. M.
Mark Twain.
London, (1970): Routledge & Kegan Paul.
T1970.A11   Blue cloth with dustjacket.

Wallace, Elizabeth.
Mark Twain and the Happy Island.
Chicago, 1913: A.C. McClurg & Co.
T1913.A1   Brown cloth: three copies.

Wecter, Dixon.
Sam Clemens of Hannibal.
Boston, 1952: Houghton Mifflin and Co.
T1952.A2   Paper over boards with cloth shelfback and dustjacket: four copies: two first edition, two reprints.

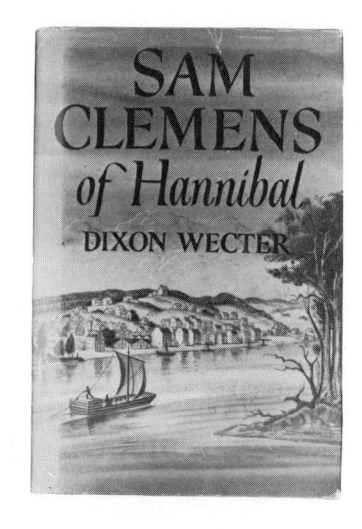

Welland, Dennis.
Mark Twain in England.
London, 1978: Chatto & Windus.
    Brown cloth with dustjacket.

Welland, Dennis.
Mark Twain's Last Travel Book.
n.p., 1965: Bulletin of the New York Public Library.
    Reprint from Volume 69, Number 1, January 1965.
T1965.B96   Paper wrappers.

Welland, Dennis.
A Note on Some Early Reviews of Tom Sawyer.
n.p., n.d.: Journal of American Studies.
    Reprint from Volume I, Number 1, 99-103.
T1967.B116   Paper wrappers.

Wiggins, Robert A.
Mark Twain: Jackleg Novelist.
Seattle, 1964: University of Washington Press.
T1964.A7   Brown cloth with dustjacket.

Winkler, John A.
Mark Twain's Hannibal: Guide and Biography.
(Hannibal, ca. 1950): Becky Thatcher Bookshop.
    Green pictorial wrappers.
T1951.B62*   * — revised and retitled as above.

A List of Mark Twain Primary Items not in the Collections.

In the interest of completeness, this section lists all primary BAL items by Mark Twain not elsewhere included in the Bibliography.

These listings are arranged in BAL chronological order and list the full title of the item if by Clemens or the item by Clemens included in another work. Inclusions are in italics, full titles of all works in bold face type. Binding descriptions from BAL are noted except where none was listed by BAL.

This section's information, titles, BAL numbers and publishers are not indexed elsewhere in this book.

The Play of Ingomar in California. in:
Fun for Three Months.
New York. (c.1864): T.W. Strong.
BAL 3308	Wrappers.

Lick House State Banquet Given by Messrs. Clemens and Pierson . . .
San Francisco, 1868: no publisher.
BAL 3312	Menu.

The Public to Mark Twain. Correspondence . . . New Mercantile Library . . . Thursday evening, July 2, 1868.
(San Francisco, 1868): no publisher.
BAL 3313	Single sheet.

Woman. in:
Marsh's Manual of Reformed Phonetic Short-Hand: Being a Complete Guide to the Best System of Phonography and Verbatim Reporting.
San Francisco, 1868: H.H. Bancrift & Company.
BAL 3314	Pictorial boards or wrappers.

Mark Twain's Description of the Azore Islands. in:
The California Scrap-Book . . . Compiled by Oscar T. Shuck.
San Francisco, 1869: H.H. Bancroft & Company.
BAL 3315	No binding description in BAL.

Jim Wolfe and the Cats. in:
Beckwith's Almanac. by George Beckwith.
New Haven, (n.d. 1869): Peck & Coan, etc.
BAL 3317	Self-wrappers.

Mark Twain on the Mental Photograph Album.
Not located by BAL.
BAL 3318	No binding description.

Mark Twain's Celebrated Jumping Frog of Calaveras County and Other Sketches.
London, 1870: George Routledge and Sons.
BAL 3319	No binding description.

My Watch. An Instructive Little Tale. in:
The National Watch Co's (Elgin,) Illustrated Almanac, 1871.
Chicago and New York, (1870): The National Watch Co.
BAL 3321	Pictorial Wrappers.

Office "Express" Printing Co.
Boston, 1870: Boston Lyceum Bureau.
BAL 3322	Letter reprinted.

The Story of a Good Little Boy Who Did Not Prosper. Wit-Inspirations of the Two-Year-Olds. The Late Benjamin Franklin. Higgins. Hogwash. in:
The Piccadilly Annual of Entertaining Literature.
London, (1870): John Camden Hotten.
BAL 3323	Printed wrappers.

Hon. Thomas Fitch.
(Boston, 1870): Redpath & Fall, Boston Lyceum Bureau.
BAL 3324	Single leaf, folded.

A New Specimen. in:
Christmas Fun.
New York, (n.d., c. 1870): 214 Centre Street.
BAL 3325	Printed wrappers.

Mark Twain's Memoranda. From the Galaxy.
Toronto, 1871: The Canadian News and Publishing Company.
BAL 3327	Black or blue cloth.

Our Guide in Genoa and Rome. My First Interview with Artemus Ward. The Great Beef-Contract. in:
Public and Parlor Readings . . . Humorous.
Boston, 1871: Lee and Shepard, Publishers.
BAL 3328	No binding description.

Mark Twain's (Burlesque) Autobiography . . . Medieval Romance . . . On Children.
London, (n.d. 1871): John Camden Hotten.
BAL 3329	Pictorial wrappers.

Eye Openers . . . by Mark Twain.
London, (n.d. 1871): John Camden Hotten.
BAL 3331	Pictorial wrappers or cloth.

The Late Benjamin Franklin. Advice to Little Girls. in:
Th: Nast's Illustrated Almanac for 1872.
(New York, 1871: Harper & Brothers.
BAL 3332	Pictorial wrappers.

Baker's Cat. About Barbers. (several other attributed pieces were disclaimed by Clemens). in:
Screamers. A Gathering of Scraps of Humour.
London, (n.d. 1871): John Camden Hotten.
BAL 3333	Pictorial wrappers or cloth.

Mark Twain's Celebrated Jumping Frog of Calaveras County, and Other Sketches. With the Burlesque Autobiography and First Romance.
London, (n.d. 1872): George Routledge and Sons.
BAL 3338	Pictorial wrappers.

Concerning a Bear. in:
The Pellet. A Record of the Massachusetts Homeopathic Hospital Fair.
Boston, 1872: Published by the Fair.
BAL 3339	No binding description.

Mark Twain's Sketches.
London, 1872: George Routledge & Sons.
BAL 3341	Pictorial boards.

Rigging the Market. Mark Twain's First Literary Venture. Mark Twain's Office Bore. About That Dog. Results of Kindness to a Cockroach. That Book Agent. An Enoch Arden Mormon. Mark Twain's Fine Old Man. in:
Practical Jokes with Artemus Ward Including the Story of the Man Who Fought Cats by Mark Twain and Other Humorists.
London, (n.d. 1872): John Camden Hotten.
BAL 3342	Pictorial wrappers or cloth.

The Innocents Abroad.
London, (1872): George Routledge & Sons.
BAL 3343   Pictorial Wrappers.

The New Pilgrims' Progress.
London, (1872): George Routledge & Sons.
BAL 3344   Pictorial wrappers.

Putting Up Stoves. in:
One Hundred Choice Selections No. 5.
Philadelphia & Chicago, 1872: P. Garrett & Co.
BAL 3345   Cloth or printed wrappers.

The Story of a Good Little Boy Who Did Not Prosper. in:
Th: Nast's Illustrated Almanac for 1873.
(New York), 1872: Harper & Brothers.
BAL 3346   Pictorial wrappers.

The Public to Mark Twain.
Mark Twain in New York. His Speech at The Aldine Dinner. in:
The Buyer's Manual and Business Guide . . . of the Pacific Coast.
San Francisco, 1872: Francis & Valentine.
BAL 3348   No binding description.

The Sandwich Islands. in:
New-York Tribune. — Lectures and Letters.
(New York, 1873): New York Tribune.
BAL 3349   Four-page supplement.

Information Wanted.
Mark Twain As George Washington.
How I Secured a Berth. in:
The Choice Humorous Works of Mark Twain. Now First Collected .
London, (n.d. 1873): John Camden Hotten.
BAL 3351   No binding description.

A Curious Dream.
My Late Senatorial Secretaryship.
The New Crime.
Back from 'Yurrup.'
More Distinction. in:
A Book for an Hour, Containing Choice Reading and Character Sketches.
A Curious Dream and Other Sketches, Revised and Selected for This Work by the Author Mark Twain.
New York, 1873: (B.J. Such).
BAL 3352   Printed wrappers.

Livingstone Lost and Found, or Africa and Its Explorers Compiled by Rev. Josiah Tyler.
Hartford, 1873: Mutual Publishing Company.
BAL 3353   Various bindings, none described.

Mark Twain's Letter to the New York Tribune.
(Boston, n.d., 1873): Cunard Line.
BAL 3354   Printed wrappers.

A Deception. in:
Th: Nast's Illustrated Almanac for 1874.
(New York), 1873: Harper & Brothers.
BAL 3355   Pictorial wrappers.

White's Portable Folding Fly and Musketo Net Frame.
(Dayton, Ohio, 1873): no publisher.
BAL 3356   Pamphlet.

Life As I Find It. in:
Agricultural Almanac, for . . . 1874.
Lancaster, (n.d. 1873): John Baer's Sons.
BAL 3358   Self-wrapper.

The Gilded Age . . . in Three Volumes.
London, 1874: George Routledge and Sons.
BAL 3359   No binding description.

An Introduction.
That Dog of Jim Smiley's.
The Celebrated Jumping Frog, etc. in:
Beecher's Recitations and Readings.
New York, (1874): Dick & Fitzgerald.
BAL 3361   Printed boards.

Mark Twain's Speech on Accident Insurance.
(Hartford, n.d. 1874): Hartford Accident Insurance Company.
BAL 3362   No binding description.

An Encounter with an Interviewer. in:
Lotos Leaves.
Boston, 1875: William F. Gill and Company.
BAL 3363   Cloth or leather.

(Mark Twain and the Jubilee Singers)
(1875)
BAL 3365   Not located by BAL.

Old Times on the Mississippi.
Toronto, 1876: Belford Brothers, Publishers.
BAL 3366B   No binding description.

A Literary Nightmare. in:
Centennial Fun.
(New York, n.d. 1876: Frank Leslie.)
BAL 3366C   Pictorial wrapper.

A Literary Nightmare. in:
The Quarterly Elocutionist.
New York, 1877: Anna Randall-Diehl.
BAL 3366D   Printed wrappers.

Punch, Brothers, Punch! and Other Sketches.
New York, (1878): Slote, Woodman & Co.
BAL 3366E   No binding description.

Punch, Brothers, Punch! Horse-Car Song.
Boston, 1876: Oliver Ditson & Co.
BAL 3366F   No binding description.

Mark Twain's Prologue to 'Our Best Society.' in:
Our Best Society: Being an Adaptation of the Potiphar Papers . . .
New York, 1876: Samuel French & Son.
BAL 3371   Printed wrapper.

Mark Twain on the Weather. in:
One Hundred Choice Selections No. 13.
Philadelphia & Chicago, 1877: P. Garrett & Co.
BAL 3372   Cloth or printed wrappers.

The Echo That Didn't Answer. A Story with a Lawsuit. in:
Beeton's Christmas Annual. Eighteenth Season.
London, (n.d. 1877): Ward, Lock and Co.
BAL 3374   Printed wrappers.

That Burial Lot.
Mark Twain's War Experiences. in:
Dick's Recitations and Readings No. 6.
New York, (1877): Dick & Fitzgerald, Publishers.
BAL 3375   Cloth or printed wrappers.

Mark Twain on St. Patrick. in:
Parlor Table Companion. A Home Treasury. . .
New York, 1877: G.W. Carleton & Co.
BAL 3376   No Binding description.

Tale of Rats. in:
The Log of an Ancient Mariner. Being the Life and Adventures of Captain Edgar Wakeman.
San Francisco, 1878: A.L.Bancroft & Co.
BAL 3379   No binding description.

Mark Twain's Amusing Sequels to Several Anecdotes. in:
Entertaining Anecdotes from Every Available Source.
Chicago, 1879: Rhodes & McClure.
BAL 3380   No binding description.

The Babies. in:
A: **Gen Grant's Reception at Chicago.**
Chicago, (1879?): Frank Roehr, Printer and Publisher.
          Printed wrappers.
B: **The Grant Reception Monograph.**
Chicago, 1879: L.E.Adams, Publisher.
          No binding description.
C: **Report of the Proceedings of the Society of the Army of the Tennessee, at the Thirteenth Annual Meeting.**
Cincinnati, 1879: F.W.Freeman.
          Printed wrappers
D: **Scrap-Book Recitation Series, No. 1.**
Chicago, (1879): T.S.Denison.
          Cloth or printed wrappers.
BAL 3382   (All four above, same BAL number).

Mark Twain on Babies.
(London, n.d.): George B. Hatfield.
BAL 3383   Single leaf, folded.

Sketches by Mark Twain.
Toronto, 1879: Belford, Clarke & Co.
BAL 3384   No binding description.

Mark Twain's Explanation. in:
The Atlantic Monthly Supplement. The Holmes Breakfast.
n.p., n.d. (Boston, 1880): Atlantic Monthly.
BAL 3385   Self-wrapper.

A Boy's Adventure. in:
Bazar Budget No. 4
Hartford, 1880: Union for Home Work.
BAL 3387   Newspaper format.

1601. Conversation As It Was by the Social Fireside, in the Time of the Tudors.
(n.p., n.d., possibly Cleveland, 1880: Alexander Gunn).
BAL 3388   Self-wrapper.

The Postal Order Business. in:
Gus Williams' World of Humor.
New York, 1880: Henry J. Wehman.
BAL 3389   Pictorial wrappers.

Starting a Paper. in:
Some Funny Things. etc.
New York, (1880): Frank Harrison & Co.
BAL 3390   Printed wrappers.

Edward Mills and George Benton.
Mrs. McWilliams and the Lightning.
A Telephonic Conversation. in:
Some Funny Things by Mark Twain. etc.
Toronto, (n.d. 1880?): W.G. Gibson.
BAL 3391   Printed wrapper.

Mrs. McWilliams and the Lightning. in:
One Hundred Choice Selections No. 19.
Philadelphia & Chicago, 1881: P. Garrett & Co.
BAL 3392   Cloth or printed wrapper.

Address of Mark Twain. in:
The Society of the Army of the Potomac. Report of the Twelfth Annual Re-Union, at Hartford, Connecticut, June 8, 1881.
New York, 1881: Macgowan & Slipper.
BAL 3393   Printed wrapper.

After Dinner Speech by Mark Twain. in:
Dick's Recitations and Readings No. 13.
New York, (1881): Dick & Fitzgerald.
BAL 3394   Cloth or printed wrapper.

A Curious Experience.
Toronto, (n.d., 1881): W.G. Gibson.
BAL 3395   Printed wrappers.

Mark Twain's Sketches. The Only Publication Containing Sketches Written Up to January, 1881.
Toronto, 1881: J. Ross Robertson.
BAL 3398   Printed wrapper.

Mark Twain's Duel. in:
Jolly Jokes for Jolly People.
New York, n.d., (between 1881 and 1889): M.J. Ivers & Co.
BAL 3399   Printed wrapper.

The Difficulty about That Dog. in:
Laugh and Be Happy. etc.
New York, n.d. (between 1881 and 1889): M.J. Ivers & Co.
BAL 3400   Printed wrapper.

Mark Twain's General Reply. in:
Authors and Authorship.
New York, 1882: G.P. Putnam's Sons.
BAL 3401   No binding description.

The McWilliamses and the Burglar Alarm. in:
Harper's Christmas Pictures & Papers.
New York, (1882): Harper & Brothers.
BAL 3405   Pictorial wrapper.

Speech (Plymouth Rock and the Pilgrims). in:
First Annual Festival of the New England Society of Pennsylvania.
(Philadelphia, 1882?: Times Printing House).
BAL 3406   Printed wrapper.

Date 1601. Conversation, As It Was by the Social Fireside, in the Time of the Tudors.
(West Point, New York, 1882): Ye Academie Presse.
BAL 3407   7 single leaves.

Speech on Woman. in:
Seventy-Seventh Anniversary Celebration of the New-England Society in the City of New York at Delmonico's, Dec. 22, 1882.
(New York, 1883): no publisher.
BAL 3408   Printed wrapper.

Statement. in:
Study and Stimulants.
Manchester & London, 1883: Abel Heywood and Son & Simpkin, Marshall, and Co.
BAL 3409   No binding description.

464

A Telephonic Conversation. in:
The Elocutionist's Annual Number 11.
Philadelphia, 1883: National School of
    Elocution and Oratory.
BAL 3413   Cloth or printed wrappers.

Mark Twain's Sketches of Henry Ward Beecher. Mark Twain's Remarkable Gold Mines. in:
Phunny Phellows. etc.
Chicago, 1885: Rhodes & McClure.
BAL 3416   Printed wrapper.

Col. Sellers as a Scientist. A Comedy.
(n.p., n.d., about 1885)
BAL 3417   Two sheets.

Letter and Speech. in:
Annual Dinner of the Typothetae of New York, in Honor of the Birthday of Benjamin Franklin at Delmonico's Monday January 18, 1886.
(New York, 1886): No publisher.
BAL 3418   Printed wrapper.

Statement. in:
In the Senate of the United States. May 21, 1886. Report.
(Washington, D.C., 1886: Government Printing Office.)
BAL 3419   Self wrapper.

General Grant's English. in:
Elocutionary Studies and New Recitations.
New York, 1887: Edgar S. Werner.
BAL 3421   Flexible cloth.

Speech. in:
The Shrew's Centenary. etc.
(New York), 1887: no publisher.
BAL 3422   Printed wrapper.

Opening Remarks in Mark Twain's Lecture. in:
The Fun Library. etc.
Boston, (n.d., about 1887): J.H.&A.K. Brigham.
BAL 3423   Printed wrapper.

Copy of a Letter Written in Answer to Inquiries Made by a Personal Friend.
(n.p., Hartford, n.d., about 1887): no publisher.
BAL 3424   Single leaf.

Forty-Three Days in an Open Boat. in:
Library of Universal Adventure by Sea and Land.
New York, 1888: Harper & Brothers.
BAL 3426   No binding description.

Statement. in:
What American Authors Think About International Copyright.
New York, 1888: American Copyright League.
BAL 3427   Printed wrapper.

Mark Twain on the 19th Century. in:
Dick's Comic and Dialect Recitations.
New York, (1888): Dick and Fitzgerald.
BAL 3428   Printed wrapper.

Contribution. in:
The Art of Authorship.
London, 1890: James Clarke & Co.
BAL 3430   No binding description.

Contribution. in:
The Art of Authorship.
New York, 1890: D. Appleton and Company.
BAL 3431   No binding description.

Facts for Mark Twain's Memory Builder.
New York, 1891: Charles L. Webster & Co.
BAL 3432   Self-wrapper.

How I Was Sold.
A Ghost Story. in:
Werner's Readings and Recitations. No. 5.
New York, 1891: Edgar S. Werner.
BAL 3433   Cloth or printed wrapper.

Pudd'nhead Wilson A. Tale.
London, 1894: Chatto & Windus.
BAL 3441   Red cloth stamped in gold.

Speech and Remarks, in:
A Brief History of the Lotos Club.
New York, (1895): Club House.
BAL 3443   Cloth or leather.

Mark Twain's Talk About Twins. in:
The Frank Leslie Christmas Book.
New York, (1895): Frank Leslie's Publishing House.
BAL 3444   Pictorial boards.

Mark Twain's Love Song (Inspired by a Sojourn at a European Health Resort). in:
The Medical Muse Grave and Gay.
New York, 1896: I.E. Booth.
BAL 3445   Cloth or wrappers.

Speech at the Authors' Club, June 12, 1889 (extracts). in:
Kipligiana.
New York, (1899): M.F. Mansfield & A. Wessels.
BAL 3454   No binding description.

Extracts from the Autobiography. in:
Prospectus for 1899-1900. The Century Illustrated Monthly Magazine.
New York, 1899: The Century Co.
BAL 3455   Printed wrapper.

The Pains of Lowly Life.
(London, 1900: London Anti-Vivisection Society.
BAL 3457   Red or green wrappers.

Two speeches and a letter. in:
Eccentricities of Genius.
New York, (1900): G.W. Dillingham Company.
BAL 3461   No binding description.

A Salutation Speech from the Nineteenth Century to the Twentieth Taken Down in Shorthand by Mark Twain.
(n.p., n.d.), 1900: no publisher.
BAL 3463   Printed card.

Extracts from Christian Science and the Book of Mrs. Eddy. in:
Christian Science and Kindred Superstitions.
London, New York, Montreal. (1900): The Abbey Press Publishers.
BAL 3464   No binding description.

To the American People Broadside No. 15.
Boston, (n.d. about 1900): New-England Anti-Imperialist League.
BAL 3466   Broadside.

Edmund Burke on Croker & Tammany by Mark Twain.
(New York, n.d., 1901: Economist Press.
BAL 3468   Printed grey wrapper.

At the Dinner in His Honor, November 10, 1900. in:
Speeches at the Lotos Club Arranged by John Elderkin, Chester S. Lord, Horatio N. Fraser.
New York, 1901: Privately printed.
BAL 3469   Cloth or leather.

A Double-Barrelled Detective Story.
Leipzig, 1902: Bernhard Tauchnitz.
BAL 3472   Printed wrapper.

New Ideas on Farming. in:
Masterpieces of Wit and Humor with Stories and an Introduction by Robert J. Burdette.
(n.p.), 1902: E.J. Long.
BAL 3473   No binding description.

Directions: Telephone Address: 150 Kings Bridge.
(n.p., n.d., New York, 1902): no publisher.
BAL 3474   Card.

Extract from a Letter of "Mark Twain" to Frederick W. Peabody. Riverdale, New York City.
(n.p., n.d., Boston 1902?): no publisher.
BAL 3475   Single Leaf.

Speech. in:
Mark Twain's Birthday Report of the Celebration of the Sixty-Seventh Thereof at the Metropolitan Club, New York November 28th 1902.
(New York, 1903: Privately printed).
BAL 3478   No binding description.

To Whom This Shall Come.
Florence, Italy, June 1904: no publisher.
BAL 3481   Mourning stationery.

Mark Twain's Cats. in:
Cat Stories Retold from St. Nicholas.
New York, 1904: The Century Co.
BAL 3482   No binding description.

Remarks. in:
Two Hundred and Fiftieth Anniversary of the Town August 5, 1902.
York, Maine, 1904: Old York Historical and Improvement Society.
BAL 3484   Printed wrapper.

Mark Twain on Vivisection Used by Permission of the Author.
Boston, (n.d.): New England Anti-vivisection Society.
BAL 3486A   Single Leaf.

Mark Twain on Vivisection.
New York, (n.d.): New York Anti-Vivisection Society.
BAL 3486B   Single leaf.

Mark Twain's Seventieth Birthday. Record of a Dinner Given in His Honor.
New York, (1905, i.e. 1906): Harper & Brothers, Publishers.
BAL 3487   Flexible grey boards.

Chapters from My Autobiography.
(n.p.), 1906: Harper & Brothers.
BAL 3491   Printed wrappers, 25 parts.

Mark Twain on Simplified Spelling, etc.
(New York, 1906: The Simplified Spelling Board).
BAL 3493   Single Leaf, folded.

Arguments before the Committees on Patents of the Senate and House of Representatives, Conjointly, on the Bills S. 6330 and H.R. 19853.
Washington, 1906: Government Printing Office.
BAL 3494   Printed wrapper.

A Birthplace Worth Saving.
(n.p., n.d., 1906): The Lincoln Farm Association.
BAL 3495   Single sheet.

Mark Twain Endorses Mr. Wright's Manuscript. in:
How Rev. Wiggin Rewrote Mrs. Eddy's Book or the Peculiar Chapter in Christian Science by Livingston Wright.
Brookline, Mass., 1906?: New York World.
BAL 3496   Printed wrapper.

Mark Twain's Own Account. in:
The Savage Club.
London, 1907: T. Fisher Unwin.
BAL 3498   Cloth or vellum.

The Only True and Reliable Account of the Great Prize Fight; The Evidence in the Case of Smith vs. Jones; Nevada Sketches. in:
The Wit and Humor of America. Volume V.
Indianapolis, (1907): The Bobbs-Merrill Company.
BAL 3499   No binding description.

Mark Twain Recalls an Incident of Carson Days. in:
The American Press Humorists' Book.
Los Angeles, 1907: Frank Thompson Searight.
BAL 3501   Cloth.

The Day We Celebrate. in:
The American Society in London.
(n.p., n.d., London, 1907?): no publisher.
BAL 3502   Printed boards.

Twain on Fulton (extract). in:
Extracts from the Minutes and Report of the Robert Fulton Monument Association.
(New York, 1907): no publisher.
BAL 3503   Printed wrapper.

Speech. in:
Dinner in Honor of the Honorable Whitelaw Reid...
(New York, 1908): no publisher.
BAL 3504   Printed wrapper.

Mark Twain on Three Weeks.
(n.p., n.d., likely London, 1908): Mrs. Glyn.
BAL 3505   Printed wrapper.

To My Guests Greeting and Salutation and Prosperity! And Therewith, Length of Days. Listen . . .
Redding, Conn., 1908: "Stormfield."
BAL 3506   Single leaf.

(The Educational Theatre.)
(likely New York, 1909).
BAL 3507   Not located by BAL.

Letter to Hon. Collier's Weekly. in:
Letters of a Japanese Schoolboy by Wallace Irwin.
New York, (1909): Doubleday, Page & Company.
BAL 3508   Self-wrapper.

Letter on John Camden Hotten. in:
The Lectures of Bret Harte . . .
Brooklyn, 1909: Charles Meeker Kozlay.
BAL 3510   Various editions and bindings.

Twain on Fulton. in:
New York at the Jamestown Exposition . . .
Albany, N.Y., 1909: J.B. Lyon Company.
BAL 3512   No binding description.

Mark Twain's London Lecture Notes.
n.p., 1910: Charles Meeker Kozlay.
BAL 3515 Single leaf.

Mark Twain and Fairhaven.
Fairhaven, Mass. (n.d., 1913): The Millicent Library.
BAL 3518 Paper wrappers.

Samuel Langhorne Clemens.
(n. p., n. d., likely Worcester, Mass., 1916: Davis Press.)
BAL 3521 Self-wrapper.

Mark Twain's Marjorie by Leon M. Green.
San Francisco, n.d.): Collection of James Tufts.
BAL 3522 No binding description.

A Message from Mark Twain. in:
The Bulletin Book.
(San Francisco, 1917: The Bulletin).
BAL 3526 Boards with label.

Letter (extract). in:
Books by E. W. Howe Sold at Johnson's Book Store. Atchison. Kansas. (n.d., about 1919): no publisher.
BAL 3528 Leaflet.

The Sandwich Islands.
New York, 1920: no publisher.
BAL 3530 Three-quarter morocco?

(The Mammoth Cod.)
(n.p., n.d., New York, about 1920): no publisher.
BAL 3531 Wrapper or single leaf.

A Prose Poem on Hawaii.
Honolulu, n.d. about 1920: Mercantile Press).
BAL 3532 Single sheet, folded.

S.L.C. to C.T. *(Charlotte Teller).*
(n.p., New York, 1925): no publisher.
BAL 3538 self-wrappers.

A Boy's Adventure . . .
(n.p., n.d., New York, 1928): no publisher.
BAL 3545 Single leaf, folded.

The Suppressed Chapter of Following the Equator.
(n.p., New York, 1928): Privately printed.
BAL 3546 Unbound pages.

A Letter from Mark Twain to His Publishers, Chatto & Windus of London, Calling Their Attention to Certain Indiscretions of the Proof Readers of Messrs. Spottiswoode & Co. . . .
San Francisco, 1929: The Penguin Press.
BAL 3547 Printed wrapper.

Innocence At Home Redding Connecticut Sept. 17/08. Dear Mr. Norris.
(n.p., n.d., 1929): no publisher.
BAL 3548 Single leaf.

The Dandy Frightening the Squatter. in:
Tall Tales of the Southwest.
New York, 1930: Alfred A. Knopf.
BAL 3550 No binding description.

Private Habits of Horace Greeley. in:
Sins of America as "Exposed" by the Police Gazette . . .
New York, 1931: Frederick A. Stokes Company.
BAL 3552 No binding description.

Mark Twain's Good-Bye...Music by Paul Rottmann.
Hannibal, Mo., (1935): Davis Studio.
BAL 3557 Sheet music.

Republican Letters.
Webster Groves, Mo., 1941: International Mark Twain Society.
BAL 3566 Red cloth.

Mark Twain's Letters to Will Bowen.
Austin, 1941: The University of Texas.
BAL 3567 Paper wrappers.

An Unpublished Mark Twain Letter by Lawrence Clark Powell.
(n.p., 1942: American Literature).
BAL 3568 Single leaf, folded.

Mark Twain and Hawaii by Walter Francis Frear.
Chicago, 1947: Privately printed, The Lakeside Press.
BAL 3576 No binding description.

Mark Twain to Uncle Remus 1881-1885,
Atlanta, Ga., 1953: Emory University.
BAL 3583. Red printed wrapper.

An Open Letter to, Commodore Vanderbilt.
(Boston, 1956): no publisher.
BAL 3584 Paper wrapper.

Mark Twain outside the houses of Parliament, 1907.

Index of Titles.

Abroad with Mark Twain and Eugene Field (Fisher) *439*
Address to . . . Alexander II *424*
Adventures of Huckleberry Finn *92ff.*
Adventures of Mark Twain (Allen) *428*
Adventures of Mark Twain (Paine) *452*
Adventures of Thomas Jefferson Snodgrass *265*
Adventures of Tom Sawyer *40ff.*
Ah Sin: A Dramatic Work *316*
Als Lotse auf dem Mississippi *55*
American Claimant *134ff.*
American First Editions (Johnson/Blanck) *94*
America's Own Mark Twain (Eaton) *437*
Amusing Answers to Correspondents *257*
Ancestry of Samual Clemens, Grandfather of Mark Twain (Bell) *429*
Art, Humor and Humanity of Mark Twain *309*
Author's Soldiering, The *418*
Autobiography, (Burlesque) First Romance and Memoranda *17*
Autobiography of Mark Twain *255*
Aventuras de Huck Finn *121*
Aventuras de Tom Sawyer *53*
Aventure de Tom Sawyer Detective *188*
Aventures de Huck Finn *120*
Aventures de Tom Sawyer *51ff.*
Avonturen van Tom Sawyer *50ff.*
Avventure di Tom Sawyer *52*

Basilopoulo Kai Zetranopoulo *78*
Beadle's Dime No. 3 *415*
Be Good, Be Good *268*
Bibliography of American Literature (Blanck) *94*
Bibliography of the Works of Mark Twain (Johnson) *94*
Boy's Life of Mark Twain (Paine) *452*
Buffalo's Mark Twain (Bingham) *429*

Californian's Tale *418*
Camden's Compliment to Walt Whitman *417*
Carpet-Bag, The *414*
Casebook of Mark Twain's Wound (Leary) *448*
Celebrated Jumping Frog of Calaveras County *2ff.*
Champagne Cocktail and a Catastrophe *267*
Choice Selections in Poetry and Prose no. 6 *416*
Christian Science, etc. *228ff.*
Clemens of the Call (Branch) *430*
Comic Mark Twain Reader *355*
Coming Out *250*
Complete Essays of Mark Twain *324*
Complete Humorous Sketches and Tales of Mark Twain *317*
Complete Novels of Mark Twain *326*
Complete Short Stories and Famous Essays of Mark Twain *282*
Complete Short Stories of Mark Twain *306*
Complete Story of Tom Sawyer *48*
Composition and Structure of Tom Sawyer (Hill) *443*
Concerning Cats *310*
Connecticut Yankee in King Arthur's Court *124ff.*
Cope's Tobacco Leaves for the Smoking Room *416*
Court Trials in Mark Twain (McKeithan) *450*
Curious Dream *27*
Curious Experience *259*
Curious Republic of Gondour *246*
Curtain Lecture Concerning Skating, etc. *332*

Dandy Frightening the Squatter *414*
Death-Disk *239*
Dictionary and Mark Twain (Coard) *435*
Discounts of an Author *418*
Dispersal of Samuel L. Clemens Library Books (Gribben) *442*
Dog's Tale *216*
Double Barrelled Detective Story *210*
Dozivljajai Haklberi Fina *119*
Drinking with Mark Twain (O'Connor) *452*

469

Early Tales and Sketches *358ff.*
Editorial Wild Oats *219*
Enchantment: A Little Girl's Friendship with Mark Twain (Quick) *454*
English As She is Spoke *256*
English As She is Taught *208*
Equisses Americaines de Mark Twain *38*
Escape Motif in the American Novel (Bluefarb) *430*
Escol Sellers from Uncharted Space (Hill) *443*
Europe and Elsewhere *253*
Everyone's Mark Twain *345*
Eve's Diary *220ff.*
Extract from Captain Stromfield's Visit to Heaven *234*
Extracts from Adams' Diary *241ff.*

Family Mark Twain *273*
Favorite Works of Mark Twain *273*
First Book of the Authors Club *418*
Following the Equator *192ff.*
Forgotten Writings of Mark Twain *325*
Fortifications of Paris *423*
Fragmentos del Diario de Adan y Diario de Eva *215*
Friendship of Helen Keller and Mark Twain (Chambliss) *433*

Gilded Age *28ff.*
Gold Rush Days with Mark Twain (Gillis) *441*
Great Short Works of Mark Twain *330*

Harriet Beecher Stowe and American Literature (Moers) *451*
Haunted Book: A Further Exploration Concerning Huckleberry Finn (Underill) *94*
Higher Animals, The *351*
History of the Big Bonanza *416*
Hombre Que Corrompio A Una Ciudad *206*
Horse's Tale *232*
How I Escaped Being Killed in a Duel *416*
How Mark Twain Was Made (James) *445*
How Tom Sawyer Played Robin Hood (Gribben) *442*
How to Tell a Story and Other Essays *190ff.*
Huck Finn and His Critics (Lettis, et al) *448*
Huck Finn at Phelps Farm (Beck) *429*
Huckleberry Finn (German) *120*
Huckleberry Finn (Hebrew) *121*
Huckleberry Finn: A Descriptive Bibliography of the Collection at the Buffalo Public Library (Adams) *95*
Huckleberry Finn Again (Clarke) *95*
Huckleberry Finn Aventyr *121*
Huck's Ironic Circle (Hoffman) *444*
Humorous Fables *260*
Humorous Sketches *258*

Idle Excursion, An *56*
Image and the Woman in the Life and Writings of Mark Twain (Goad) *441*
Improvement in Adjustable Detachable Straps for Garments *422*
Influence of the Nevada Frontier on Mark Twain (Carter) *432*
Influence of William Dean Howells Upon Mark Twain's Social Satire (Carter) *432*
Information Wanted and Other Sketches *54*
In Memoriam *425*
Innocent Eye: Childhood in Mark Twain's Imagination (Stone) *457*
Innocents Abroad *6ff.*
Innocents at Home *26*
Inquiry into Huckleberry Finn (Underhill) *95*
Interview with Mark Twain (Kipling) *446*
Introduction (1883) *416*
Introductory (1876) *416*
Is Shakespeare Dead? *233*
It is Unsatisfactory to Read to One's Self (Gribben) *442*

Jim Wolf and the Cats *360*
Journalism in Tennessee, etc. *261*
Jumping Frog in English, The *212*

King Leopold's Soliloquy *218*
Kraljevic I Prosjak *78*

Letters from the Earth *320*
Letters from Honolulu *280*
Letters from the Sandwich Islands *277*
Letters of Quintus Curtius Snodgrass *290*
Life on the Mississippi *84ff.*
Lifetime with Mark Twain, A (Lawton) *447*
Literary Essays *241*
Lost og Sast *38*
Love Letters of Mark Twain *296*

Mammoth Cod, The *354*
Man is the Only Animal That Blushes or Needs to *339*
Man That Corrupted Hadleyburg *200ff.*
Mark Twain (Burlingame) *294*
Mark Twain (Grant) *441*
Mark Twain (Henderson) *443*
Mark Twain (Leacock) *448*
Mark Twain (Leary) *448*
Mark Twain (Stearns) *457*
Mark Twain (Walker) *459*
Mark Twain: A Biography (Paine) *453*
Mark Twain Able Yachtsman *249*
Mark Twain Abroad: The Cruise of the "Quaker City" (Ganzel) *440*
Mark Twain: A Collection of Critical Essays (Smith) *456*
Mark Twain: A Cure for the Blues *327*
Mark Twain: A Laurel Reader *311*
Mark Twain: American Author (Frederick) *439*
Mark Twain: An American Voice (Frevert) *440*
Mark Twain: An American Prophet (Geismar) *440*
Mark Twain and Bret Harte (Duckett) *436*
Mark Twain and Education (Black) *429*
Mark Twain and Elisha Bliss (Hill) *443*
Mark Twain and Fairhaven *352*
Mark Twain and Harry S. Truman (Cyril Clemens) *434*
Mark Twain and Huck Finn (Blair) *95, 429*
Mark Twain and John F. Kennedy (Cyril Clemens) *434*
Mark Twain and Life on the Mississippi (Kruse) *446*
Mark Twain and Little Satan (Tuckey) *458*
Mark Twain and Mussolini (Cyril Clemens) *434*
Mark Twain and Richard M. Nixon (Cyril Clemens) *434*
Mark Twain and Southwestern Humor (Lynn) *449*
Mark Twain and the American Labor Movement (Carter) *432*
Mark Twain and the Backwoods Angel (Spengemann) *457*
Mark Twain and the Bible (Ensor) *437*
Mark Twain and the Community (Blues) *430*
Mark Twain and the Dictionary (Babcock) *428*
Mark Twain and the Gilded Age (French) *439*
Mark Twain and the Happy Island (Wallace) *459*
Mark Twain and the River (North) *452*
Mark Twain and the Russians (Neider) *451*
Mark Twain and the Three R's *347*
Mark Twain Anecdotes (Cyril Clemens) *434*
Mark Twain: An Introduction and Interpretation (Baldanza) *428*
Mark Twain: A Pipe Dream (Herford) *443*
Mark Twain: A Portrait (Masters) *449*
Mark Twain: A Profile (Kaplan) *446*
Mark Twain: A Reference Guide (Tenney) *427*
Mark Twain as Critic (Kruse) *447*
Mark Twain: A See and Read Biography (Graves) *441*

Mark Twain as Literary Artist (Bellamy) *429*
Mark Twain at Work (DeVoto) *436*
Mark Twain at Your Fingertips *293*
Mark Twain: Audience and Artistry (Hill) *443*
Mark Twain, Businessman *288*
Mark Twain, Cable and a Professional Newspaper Liar (Turner) *458*
Mark Twain Describes a San Francisco Earthquake (Carter) *432*
Mark Twain Family Man (Harnsberger) *443*
Mark Twain for Young People *302*
Mark Twain: God's Fool (Hill) *444*
Mark Twain Goes Back to Vassar (Simpson) *456*
Mark Twain Handbook (Long) *448*
Mark Twain Himself (Meltzer) *450*
Mark Twain: His Life and Work (Will Clemens) *435*
Mark Twain-Howells Letters *312*
Mark Twain in England (Welland) *460*
Mark Twain in Elmira (Jerome & Wisbey) *445*
Mark Twain in Elmira (Langdon) *447*
Mark Twain in Eruption *284*
Mark Twain in Hartford (Darbee) *435*
Mark Twain in India (Mutalik) *451*
Mark Twain in Love (Miller) *450*
Mark Twain in Nevada (Mack) *449*
Mark Twain in the Movies (Seelye) *456*
Mark Twain in Three Moods *292*
Mark Twain in Virginia City (Fatout) *437*
Mark Twain: Jackleg Novelist (Wiggins) *460*
Mark Twain: Life As I Find It *315*
Mark Twain: Man and Legend (Ferguson) *438*
Mark Twain Material in the New York Weekly Review (Carter) *433*
Mark Twain: Moralist in Disguise (Carter) *433*
Mark Twain of the Enterprise *304*
Mark Twain on Fritz Smythe's Horse *415*
Mark Twain on Juvenile Pugilists *416*
Mark Twain on Man and Beast *343*
Mark Twain on the Damned Human Race *318*
Mark Twain on the Lecture Circuit (Fatout) *438*
Mark Twain on the Mississippi (Miers) *450*
Mark Twain: Pilgrim from Hannibal (Pellowe) *454*
Mark Twain's America and Mark Twain at Work (DeVoto) *436*
Mark Twain: Samuel Langhorne Clemens: Notes on His Life and Works *450*
Mark Twain San Francisco Territorial Enterprise Correspondent *305*
Mark Twain's Autobiography *254ff.*
Mark Twain's Best *319*
Mark Twain's Book Sales 1869-1879 (Hill) *443*
Mark Twain's Brace of Brief Lectures on Science (Hill) *443*
Mark Twain's (Burlesque) Autobiography and First Romance *16ff.*
Mark Twain's Comments on Books and Authors (Jensen) *445*
Mark Twain's Correspondence with Henry Huddleston Rogers *336*
Mark Twain's Date — 1601 *68ff.*
Mark Twain's Early Writings in Hannibal Missouri Papers *267*
Mark Twain's Fable of Man *342*
Mark Twain's First American (Gregory) *441*
Mark Twain's First Story *301*
Mark Twain's First Year in Hartford (Day) *436*
Mark Twain's Hannibal (Winkler) *460*
Mark Twain's Hannibal Huck and Tom *338*
Mark Twain's House (Darbee) *435*
Mark Twain's Huck Finn: Race Class and Society (Egan) *437*
Mark Twain's Jest Book *307*
Mark Twain's Last Travel Book (Welland) *460*
Mark Twain's Last Years as a Writer (Macnaughton) *449*
Mark Twain's Letters *244ff.*
Mark Twain's Letters from Hawaii *303*
Mark Twain's Letters in the Muscatine Journal *285*

Mark Twain's Letters to His Publishers 1867-1894 *335*
Mark Twain's Letters to Mary *314*
Mark Twain's Letters to the Rogers Family *340*
Mark Twain's Letter to William Bowen *279*
Mark Twain's Library: A Reconstruction (Gribben) *442*
Mark Twain's Library of Humor *122ff.*
Mark Twain's Mysterious Stranger: A Study of the Manuscript Texts (Kahn) *445*
Mark Twain's Mysterious Stranger Manuscripts *337*
Mark Twain's Nightmare *57*
Mark Twain's Notebook *276*
Mark Twain's Notebooks and Journals *348ff.*
Mark Twain Social Critic (Foner) *439*
Mark Twain: Social Critic for the 80's *361*
Mark Twain Son of Missouri (Brashear) *431*
Mark Twain's Patent Scrapbook *420*
Mark Twain Speaking *356*
Mark Twain Speaks for Himself *357*
Mark Twain's Quarrels with Elisha Bliss (Hill) *444*
Mark Twain's San Francisco *322*
Mark Twain's Satires and Burlesques *333*
Mark Twain's 1601 *68ff.*
Mark Twain's Sketches *34*
Mark Twain's Sketches, New and Old *35ff.*
Mark Twain's Speeches *252*
Mark Twain's The Adventures of Huckleberry Finn (Butrym) *431*
Mark Twain's The Man That Corrupted Hadleyburg (Play) *205*
Mark Twain's Travels with Mr. Brown *283*
Mark Twain's View on Religion (Harnsberger) *442*
Mark Twain Tells About a Pipe *416*
Mark Twain: The Development of a Writer (Smith) *457*
Mark Twain: The Fate of Humor (Cox) *435*
Mark Twain The Letter Writer *270*
Mark Twain: The Man and His Work (Wagenknecht) *459*
Mark Twain: The Philosopher Who Laughed at the World (Finger) *439*
Mark Twain to Mrs. Fairbanks *295*
Mark Twain Tonight! (Holbrook) *444*
Mark Twain Turnover, A *344*
Mark Twain Wit and Wisdom *272*
Mark Twain Wit and Wisecracks *313*
Master Hand of Old Malory (Gribben) *442*
Masterpieces of American Eloquence *418*
Memories of Mark Twain and Steve Gillis (Gillis) *441*
Merry Tales *156*
£1,000,000 Bank Note *158ff.*
Mississippi Pilot: With Mark Twain on the Great River (Stong) *458*
Mr. Clemens and Mark Twain (Kaplan) *446*
Modern Eloquence *418*
Moments with Mark Twain *248*
More Maxims of Mark *263*
More Tramps Abroad *199*
Morgan Manuscript of Mark Twain's Pudd'nhead Wilson *173*
My Cousin Mark Twain (Cyril Clemens) *434*
Murder, A Mystery and a Marriage, A *287*
My Father, Mark Twain (Clemens) *433*
My Mark Twain (Howells) *445*
Mysterious Stranger and Other Stories *251*
Mysterious Stranger. A Romance. *242*

New Guide of the Conversation in Portuguese *416*
Niagara Book *160*
Note on Some Early Reviews of Tom Sawyer (Welland) *460*

Notes on Mark Twain in New Orleans (Turner) 458
Nuevos Cuentos 38

Old Times on the Mississippi 55
Olivia Clemens Edits Following the Equator (Carter) 433
On the Poetry of Mark Twain (Scott) 456
Ordeal of Mark Twain (Brooks) 431

Panama Railroad, The 418
Pen Warmed-up in Hell 346
Peripeteies tou Tom Soler, Oi 52
Personal Recollections of Joan of Arc 178ff.
Portable Mark Twain 289
Prigkipas kia O Phtochos, O 78
Princas Ir Elgeta 78
Prince and the Pauper, The 70ff.
Prince et le Pauvre 78
Principe E Il Povero 79
Przygody Huck'a 121
Pudd'nhead Wilson 171ff.
Pudd'nhead Wilson and Pudd'nhead Wilson's Calendar 173
Pudd'nhead Wilson and Those Extraordinary Twins 171ff.
Pudd'nhead Wilson's Calendar for 1894 168ff.
Punch, Brothers, Punch! 59
Pustolovine Haklberi Fina 119
Pustolovine Toma Sojera 50

Quaker City Hold Land Excursion 264
Queen Victoria's Jubilee 236

Renaissance of Mark Twain's House (Faude) 438
Report from Paradise 300
Revived Remarks on Mark Twain (Ade) 428
River-Boy: The Story of Mark Twain (Proudfit) 454
Roughing It. 18ff.

Saint Joan of Arc 247
Sam Clemens of Hannibal (Wecter) 459
Samuel Langhorne Clemens: Some Reminisces, etc. (Langdon) 447
Samuel L. Clemens: First Editions and Values (Potter) 94
Selected Mark Twain-Howells Letters 312
Selected Shorter Writings of Mark Twain 321
Short Life of Mark Twain, A (Paine) 453
Short Stories of Mark Twain 329
Simon Wheeler, Detective 323
"1601" 68ff.
Sixty and Six Chips from Literary Workshops 418
Sketches 36
Sketches of the Sixties 262
Sketches, New and Old 37ff.
Slovenly Peter 274
Some Notes on the First Editions of Mark Twain (Meine) 95
Some Thoughts on the Science of Onanism 299
Southward Currents under Huck Finn's Raft (Budd) 431
Special Performance of Hansel & Gretel 418
Speech (1901) 418
Splendor of Stars and Suns (Gribben) 442
Stolen White Elephant 80ff.
Story of Mark Twain (Howard) 444
Supplement to "A Bibliography of Mark Twain" (Blanck) 94
Suppressed Chapter of "Life on the Mississippi" 240
Susy and Mark Twain 328

Tempest in a Teapot or Notes on Huckleberry Finn (Underhill) 94
Testimonial (1906) 418
Theses on Mark Twain 1910-1967 (Selby) 456

$30,000 Bequest, The 224ff.
Three Aces 266
Tom Eventyr 50
Tom Hood's Comic Annual for 1873 416
Tom Sawyer (French) 51
Tom Sawyer (Hebrew) 52
Tom Sawyer (Marvel Comics) 49
Tom Sawyer (Spanish) 53
Tom Sawyer (Turkish) 53
Tom Sawyer Abenteuer 52
Tom Sawyer Abroad 162ff.
Tom Sawyer Abroad, Tom Sawyer Detective and Other Stories 164ff.
Tom Sawyer: A Drama 48
Tom Sawyer Anak Amerika 52
Tom Sawyer, Detective 186ff.
Tom Sawyer, En El Extranjero 188
Tom Sawyer En Skol Pjkhistoria 53
Tom Sawyer to Read Aloud 49
Tom Soler Astynomikos 52
To the Person Sitting in Darkness 209
Tragedy of Pudd'nhead Wilson and The Comedy of those Extraordinary Twins 170
Tramp Abroad, A 60ff.
Travelling with the Innocents Abroad 308
Travels at Home 237
Treasury of Mark Twain 331
Trouble Begins at Eight (Lorch) 449
True Adventures of Huckleberry Finn (Seelye) 456
True Story of the Recent Carnival of Crime 58
Turn West, Turn East (Canby) 432
Twain (Grant) 441
Twain and the Image of History (Salomon) 455
Twain, Howells and the Boston Nihilists (Budd) 431
Twainiana Notes from Walter Bliss 430
Twins of Genius (Cardwell) 432
Two Interesting Letters Pertaining to Huckleberry Finn (Underhill) 94

Unabridged Mark Twain 353
Unexpected Acquaintance, An 217
Unpromising Heroes: Mark Twain and His Characters (Regan) 455
Up a Tree with Mark Twain (Smith) 457

War Prayer, The 341
Washington in 1868 286
Washoe Giant in San Francisco 278
What is Man? 222
When Huck Finn Went Highbrow (DeCasseres) 436
Which Was The Dream? 334
Who Was Sarah Findlay? 243
William Dean Howells' Corrections of "Tom Sawyer" (Gregory) 441
Writing about The Frontier: Mark Twain (Rikhoff) 455

Yankee in the Court of King Arthur 128

Index of Authors, Editors, Compilers, Translators & Commentators other than Mark Twain.

This index lists anyone other than Mark Twain who wrote material included in his works or in works about him. The various categories of contributors are editors, translators, commentators, compilers, co-authors, biographers, critics, and writers of prefaces, introductions, afterwords, forewords, sketches and so forth. Also listed here are famous people who have been linked with Mark Twain in titles of books about him.

Adams, Lucille *94ff.*
Ade, George *428*
Akabia, A. *52,79*
Alden, Henry Mills *220*
Alfaro, Maria *53,188*
Allen, Jerry *428*
Anderson, Frederick *173,202,304-5,310,312,316*
Andreoposlos, Th. *52*
Armstrong, C.J. *267*

Babcock, C. Merton *428*
Baedner, Paul *24*
Baldanza, Frank *428*
Barrie, J.M. *243*
Barry, Emily Fanning *76*
Beatty, Richmond Croom *118*
Beck, Warren *429*
Bell, Raymond Martin *429*
Bellamy, Gladys Carmen *429*
Bennett, James O'Donnell *265*
Bernadete, Doris *313*
Billings, David Lane *126*
Bingham, Robert H. *429*
Blair, Walter *49,94ff.,429*
Blanck, Jacob *42,48,94ff.*
Blemont, Emile *38*
Bliss, Elisha *444*
Bliss, Walter *49,94ff.,202,321,430*
Bluefarb, Sam *430*
Blues, Thomas *430*
Bochynski, Kevin J.
Boehler, Wolfgang *66*
Bonner, Paul Hyde *126*
Bradley, Sculley *118*
Branch, Edgar Marquess *430*
Brashear, Minnie M. *267,309,431*
Braybrooke, Patrick *434*
Brooks, Cleanth *119*
Brooks, Van Wyck *431*
Brownell, George Hiram *428*
Browning, Elizabeth Barrett *442*
Browning, Robert Pack *442*
Bruner, Herbert B. *76*
Budd, Louis J. *431*
Burlingame, C. Charles *294*
Butrym, Alexander J. *118,431*
Byrd, Richard E. *165*

Cable, George W. *432,458*
Caille, P.F. *51*
Canby, Henry Seidel *432*
Cardwell, Guy A. *432*
Carrington, Ulrich Steindorff *66*
Carter, Paul J. Jr. *432-433*
Chambliss, Amy *433*
Chatzopolou, Poulas *78*
Chesterton, G.K. *434*
Chubb, Percival *237*
Clarke, Norman *94ff.*
Clemens, Clara *279,433*
Clemens, Cyril *270,272,286,302,307,434,441*
Clemens, Olivia *433*
Clemens, Will M. *435*
Coard, Robert L. *435*
Cocchi, Brunella *79*
Collier, Edmund *49*
Conrad, Joseph *450*
Cox, James M. *435*
Cutter, Bloodgood *6*

Dane, G. Ezra *277,283*
Darbee, Henry *435*
Day, A. Grove *303*
Day, Katharine Seymour *436*
DeCasseres, Benjamin *436*
deGail, Francois *52,188*
DeLautrec, Gabriel *5*
DeVoto, Bernard *48,284,289,320,436*
DeZeeuw, P. *50*
Duckett, Margaret *436*

473

Duschnes, Philip C. *263*
Duskis, Henry *325*

Eaton, Jeanette *437*
Edwards, Francis M. *430*
Egan, Michael *437*
Eliot, T.S. *116*
Elliott, George P. *48*
Ensor, Allison *437*
Eppe, Gisela *52*

Fatout, Paul *437-438*
Faude, Wilson H. *438*
Fayet, Marie-Madeleine *78*
Ferguson, DeLancey *76,438*
Field, Eugene *439*
Finger, Charles J. *439,449*
Fisher, Henry W. *439*
Fishkin, A. *121*
Fitzpatrick, Lucy Mabry *76,132*
Foner, Philip S. *439*
Frederick, John T. *439*
French, Bryant Morey *439*
Frevert, Patricia Dendtler *440*
Fuller, Edmund *311*

Galsworthy, John *434*
Ganzel, Dewey *440*
Geismar, Maxwell *318*
Gemme, Francis R. *173*
Gibson, William M. *251,312*
Gillis, Steve *441*
Gillis, William R. *441*
Goad, Mary Ellen *441*
Goldberger, Morris *319*
Gordon, Edward J. *118*
Graham, Eleanor *49*
Grant, Douglas *441*
Graves, Charles *441*
Gregory, Ralph *441*
Grete, Anna *66*
Gribben, Alan *442*
Gultekin, Vahdet *53*

Haas, Irvin *69*
Haldeman-Julius, E. *56,257*
Halperich, A. *121*
Harnsberger, Caroline Thomas *293,442-443*
Harris, Richard W. *205*
Harte, Bret *262,316,436*
Henderson, Archibald *443*
Herford, Oliver *443*
Hill, Hamlin *118,132,443-444*
Hilton, James *302*
Hingston, Edward P. *8*
Hoffman, Heinrich *274*
Hogan, Frank J. *48*
Hoggett, W.J. *53*
Holbrook, Hal *444*
Honce, Charles *265*
Hoover, Herbert *434*
Howard, Joan *444*
Howells, William Dean *122,160,220,235,252, 312,431-432,441,445,450*
Hughes, Langston *173*
Hugues, William L. *51*

Jacobs, W.W. *286*
James, George Wharton *445*
James, Henry *432*
Jensen, Franklin *445*
Jerome, Robert D. *445*
Johnson, Louis *434*
Johnson, Merle *6,94ff.,162,249,255*
Johnsson, Herald *121*
Jovanovic, Slobodan A. *78*

Kahn, Sholom J. *445*
Kaplan, Justin *32,330,446*
Kazin, Alfred *14*
Keller, Helen *433*

Kennedy, John F. *434*
Kipling, Rudyard *446*
Kirkland, Frederick R. *202*
Kloten, Edgar L. *205*
Kohn, John Van E. *107*
Kriegel, Leonard *24,90*
Krause, Sydney J. *447*
Kruse, Horst H. *446*

Langdon, Jervis *447*
Lans, Matthew Irving *208,256*
Lawton, Mary *447*
Leacock, Stephen *272,448*
Leary, Kate *447*
Leary, Lewis *314,448*
Leisy, Ernest E. *290*
Lettis, Richard *448*
Lewis, R.W.B. *119*
Lipmanson, L. *53*
Long, E. Hudson *118,448*
Lorch, Fred W. *449*
Lucas, E.V. *14,23,32,38,46,66,76,131,166,198,227, 231,235,245,251,252,255*
Lynn, Kenneth S. *449*
Lyon, Isabel Van Kleeck *255*

Mack, Effie Mona *449*
Macnaughton, William R. *449*
Malinverni, T. *79*
Malory, Thomas *442*
Manegat, Julio *53*
Mann, Max *66*
Masefield, John *434*
Masters, Edgar Lee *449*
Matthews, Brander *11,253*
Mayfield, John S. *449*
McClintock, Ragsdale *337*
McCutcheon, John T. *428*
McKeithan, Daniel Morley *173,308,450*
Meine, Franklin J. *68-69,301*
Meltzer, Milton *450*
Mensing, Wilhelm *159*
Miers, Earl Schenck *450*
Milicevis, Niak *50*
Miller, Albert G. *450*
Mirlas, Leon *206,215*
Moeis, Abdoel *52*
Moers, Ellen *451*
Moffett, Samuel E. *241*
Monfried, Lucia *132*
Morioka, Sakae *4*
Morse, Willard S. *103,267*
Mota, Francisco M. *53*
Mussolini, Benito *434*
Mutalik, Keshav *451*

Nast, F.A. *235*
Neider, Charles *132,255,306,315,317,324,326,451*
Netillard, Suzanne *120*
Nixon, Richard M. *434*
North, Sterling *452*

O'Connor, Laurel *452*
Orsi, T. *52*

Paine, Albert Bigelow *14,23,32,38,46,66,76,131, 137,166,227,231,235,244-245,248,251-255,264,273, 276,450,452-453*
Paul, John pseudy. *2*
Paul, Rodman W. *23*
Pellowe, William C.S. *454*
Potter, John K. *94ff.*
Powers, Verne E. *210*
Proudfit, Isabel *454*

Quick, Dorothy *454*
Quintana, Maria Teresa *53*

Ranolle, B.C. *52*
Regan, Robert *455*

474

Reiss, Edmund *251*
Rikhoff, Jean *455*
Rogers, Franklin R. *24,323*
Ros, Amando Lazaro *121*
Rowland, Beryl *166*

St. Clair, Robert *210*
Salamo, Lin *4*
Salomon, Roger B. *455*
Salsbury, Edith Colegate *328*
Sandburg, Carl *307*
Sanderson, Kenneth
Santanines, Simon *188*
Scott, Arthur L. *456*
Seelye, John *182,456*
Selby, P.O. *456*
Shakespeare, Geoffrey *434*
Shaler, Nathaniel S. *160*
Shapiro, Irwin *49*
Shorter, Clement *243*
Simpson, Alan *456*
Siwicka, Zofia *90*
Smedley, W.T. *216*
Smith, Henry Nash *132,304-305,312,320,456-457*
Smith, Janet *318*
Smith, U.S. *457*
Spalatin, Leonardo *14*
Spengemann, William C. *457*
Sphaellou, K.A. *52*
Starrett, Vincent *265*
Stearns, Monroe *457*
Steenstrup, Poul *50*
Stein, Bernard L. *132*
Stern, Madeleine B. *457*
Stone, Albert E., Jr. *457*
Stone, Phil *458*
Stowe, Harriet Beecher *451*
Strack, Ramon *53*
Surleau, Yolande & Rene *120*

Taft, William Howard *434*
Taper, Bernard *322*
Tarkington, Booth *450*
Tarsoule, Georgias *78*
Teacher, Lawrence
Townsend, Frank H. *49*
Truman, Harry S. *434*
Tuckey, John S. *458*
Turner, Arlin *458*

Underhill, Irving S. *94ff.*

Vandercook, John W. *280*
VanDoren, Carl *131*
VanDyke, Henry *450*
Vonnegut, Kurt Jr. *353*

Wagenkencht, Edward *4,66,89-90,173,309,459*
Wager, Willis *89*
Walker, Franklin *278,283*
Walker, I.M. *459*
Wallace, Elizabeth *459*
Warner, Charles Dudley *12,28*
Warren, Robert Penn *119*
Webb, Charles Henry *2*
Webster, Samuel Charles *288*
Wecter, Dixon *295-296,300,459*
Welland, Dennis *460*
Wiggin, Kate Douglas *450*
Wiggins, Robert A. *460*
Wilck, Otto *55*
Willoughby, John *90*
Winkler, John A. *460*
Wisbey, Herbert A., Jr. *445*
Wister, Owen *273*
Wood, Charles Erskine Scott *68,292*

Mark Twain in 1907.

Index of Publishers & Printers.

Aguilar (Madrid) *53,121*
Airmont Publishing Co. (New York) *76,90,166,173*
American News Company (New York) *34*
American Publishing Company (Hartford) *6-12 18-22,28,30,31,35-37,40,42,44,45,60,61,64,65,74,87, 88,114,129,130,164,170,171,180,190-192,194-196,227, 228,230,416*
American Literature (n.p.) *433,443,444,457*
American Quarterly *443*
Anti-Imperialist League (New York) *269*
Appleton, D., and Co. (New York) *448*
Appleton-Century (New York) *303*
Apollon Papademetriou & Siou (Athens) *78*
Archives des Lettres Modernes (Paris) *429*
Ashmead, D. (Philadelphia) *8,18,21*
AT Press (San Francisco) *361*
Authors Club, The (New York) *418*
Avon Old Farms Press (Avon, Conn.) *443*

Baldwin, Ralph (Denver) *332*
Bancroft, A.L., & Co. (San Francisco) *60*
Bancroft, H.H., and Company (San Francisco) *6-8*
Banner, The (Sonora, Calif.) *441*
Bantam Books (New York) *14,90,306*
Barnes, A.S., & Co. (South Brunswick, N.J. & New York) *345*
Barnes & Noble, Inc. (New York) *428*
Beadle and Company (New York) *415*
Becky Thatcher Bookshop (Hannibal, Mo.) *460*
Beechurst Press (New York) *294*
Belford & Co. (Toronto) *63*
Belford Brothers, Publishers (Toronto) *44,45*
Belknap Press of Harvard University (Cambridge, Mass.) *312,457*
Berlag von G. Freytag (Leipzig) *66*
Biblio Tou Paidiou (Greece) *78*
Bibliographical Society of America (n.p.) *433*
Bigger Press, The (New York) *294*
Black Cat Press (Chicago) *69*
Bliss & Co. (Newark, N.J.) *6-8*
Bliss, R.W., & Co. (Toledo, Ohio) *6-7*
Bliss, W.E. (Toledo, Ohio) *18,21*
Bobbs-Merrill Company, The (Indianapolis and New York) *347,438*
Boni, Albert & Charles (New York) *441*
Boni & Liveright (New York) *246*
Book Club of California, The (San Francisco) *279,305,310,316*
Books, Inc. (New York) *76*
Britnell, Albert (Toronto) *73*
Brown, Nicholas L. (New York) *439*
Browning Institute and the University Center, CUNY (New York) *442*
Buffalo Historical Society (Buffalo, N.Y.) *429*
Bulletin of the New York Public Library (New York) *443*
Butts, Henry (Dawson's Landing, Mo.) *168*

Campbell, James, & Son (Toronto) *17*
Carpet-Bag, The (Boston) *414*
Casa Editrice Marzocco (Firenze) *52*
Century Company, The (New York) *168-169*
Chandler Publishing Company (San Francisco) *118,132,173*
Chatto & Windus (London) *9,43,60-62,64,66,72,82, 86,113,123,128,135,159,163,179,186,199,202,460*
Chemung County Historical Society (Elmira, N.Y.) *447*
Christian Herald, The (New York) *418*
Citadel Press, The (New York) *325,443*
Clemens Publishing Company (San Francisco) *435*
Collier Books (New York) *76,450*
Collier, P.F. & Son (New York) *165,282*
Colt Press, The (San Francisco) *310*
Columbia University Press (New York) *314*
Cope's Tobacco Plant (Liverpool) *416*
Covici, Pascal (Chicago) *265*
Creative Education, Inc. (Mankato, Minn.) *440*
Cresset Press (London) *116*
Crowell, Thomas Y., Company (New York) *351,448, 450*
Czytelnik (Warsaw) *90*

This index lists publishers of Mark Twain's works and publishers of books about him and his works.

Davis, A.M., Co. (Boston) *208*
Dawson Brothers (Montreal) *73,87,113*
Dell Publishing Co. (New York) *48,166,311*
DeVinne Press (New York) *222*
DeWitt & Snelling (Oakland, Calif.) *238*
Dinas Penerbitan Balai Pustaka (Djakarta) *52*
Dolphin Books (Garden City, N.Y.) *117,166*
Doubleday & Company (Garden City, N.Y.) *324,326,355,458*
Doubleday and McClure (New York) *195,446*
Douglass & Myers (New York) *30*
Duschnes, Philip C. (New York) *4*
Dutton, E.P., & Co. (New York) *431*

Earth Publishing Company (n.p.) *68*
Edition European Places of Culture (Heidelberg) *66*
Editions Gallimard (Paris) *78,188, see also* Gallimard
Editorial Atlantida (Buenos Aires) *121*
Editorial Gente Nueva (Havana) *53*
Editorial Mateu (Barcelona) *188*
Editrice Boschi (Milan) *79*
Edizioni Capitol (Bologna) *79*
Eihosha Ltd., The (China) *4,14*
Eldredge Publishing Co. (Franklin, Ohio) *205*
Emporia State Research Studies (Emporia, Kan.) *441,445*
English Language Notes (n.p.) *442*
Ensslin & Laiblin (Reutlingen) *120*
Espasa-Calpe (Madrid) *38,206,215*
Espasa-Calpe Argentine (Buenos Aires) *188,206,215*
Exdoseis L.S. Blessa Odos Miltiadou (Athens) *52*

Farrar Straus and Cudahy (New York) *118*
Fawcett Publications (New York) *320*
Fields, George (San Francisco) *278*
Filter Press (Palmer Lake, Col.) *4*
Fischer, W. (Gottlingen) *52*
Franklin Library, The (Franklin Center, Pa.) *118*
Franklin, Watts, Inc. (New York) *457*
Friends of the Huntington Library (San Marino, Calif.) *292*
Funk & Wagnalls (New York) *329*
Fun Office, The (London) *416*

Gallimard(Paris)*52, 120, see also* Editions Gallimard
Garden City Publishing (Garden City, N.Y.) *453*
Garrett, P. & Co. (Philadelphia) *416*
Georgia Review, The (n.p.) *433,444*
Gilberton Company (New York) *48,76,118*
Gilman, F.G., & Co. (Chicago) *6-8,18,21,28,30*
Golden Hind Press (New York) *300*
Goldsmith Publishing Co. (Chicago) *49*
Goodspeed, J.W. (New Orleans) *8,21*
Grabhorn Press (San Francisco) *68,277,310*
Grosset & Dunlap (New York) *47-48,116,444,452*
Grove Press, Inc. (New York) *173,441*
Gyldenhal (Copenhagen) *50*

Hachette (Paris) *51,120*
Halcyon-Commonwealth Foundation (New York) *416*
Haldeman-Julius Company (Girard, Kan.) *56,83,256-261,439*
Hall, G.K., & Co. (Boston) *442*
Hallmark Editions (Kansas City, Mo.) *331*
Hanover House (Garden City, N.Y.) *306,315,317*
Harcourt, Brace &Co. (New York) *447*
Harcourt Brace Jovanovich (New York) *450*
Harper & Brothers (New York and London) *12-13, 22-23,31-32,37-38,45-47,65,75-76,88-89,114-116,130-131,136-137,164-165,171-173,178,180-182,190-191, 196-197,200,204-205,211-212,214-217,219-221,224, 226,230-235,237,241,245,247-248,251-255,273-274, 276,284,296,300,433,445,450,452-453*
Harper & Row (New York) *320,328,330,341,346,444*
Hart Publishing Company (New York) *123*
Harvard University Press (Cambridge, Mass.) *436*
Hendricks House (New York) *448*
Heritage Press, The (Avon, Conn.) *118*

Heritage Press, The (New York) *4,47,66,90,116,131,173*
Hill, Lawrence, & Co. (New York) *343*
Hill and Wang (New York) *132,318,446,451*
Hillside Press, The (Buffalo) *360*
Hobby Shop, The (Hartford) *430*
Hobson Book Press, The (New York) *454*
Hotten, John Camden (London) *8*
Houghton Mifflin Company (Boston) *49,117,321,432,436,440,452*
Howell, John (San Francisco) *262*
Huntington Library (San Marino, Calif.) *295*
Hutchinson, F.A., & Co. (St. Louis) *6-7*

Indiana University Press (Bloomington, Ind.) *437-438*
International Mark Twain Society (Webster Groves, Mo.) *286,434*
International Publishers (New York) *439*
Iowa State University Press (Ames) *449*
Isreel Publishing House, Ltd. (Tel Aviv) *79*
Izdavacko Preduzece veselin Maslesa (Sarajevo) *119*
Izdavako Knjizarske Produzece (Zagreb) *78*
Izreel Publishing House, Ltd. (Tel Aviv) *52,121*

Johns Hopkins Press (Baltimore) *447*

Kelsey, Frank Edward (n.p.) *452*
Kent State University Press (Kent, Ohio) *457*
Kingston House (Chicago) *455*
Knopf, Alfred A. (New York) *283*

Lancer Books (New York) *90,166*
Laurie, T. Werner, Ltd. (London) *434*
Lazarus (Northhampton, Mass.) *69*
Limited Editions Club (New York) *48,89,274*
Little, Brown and Company (Boston) *288,428,449*

Macmillan Company, The (New York) *448*
MacVicars, Robin & Marian (Westport, Conn.) *266*
Madigan, Thomas F., Inc. (New York) *437*
Maledicta, Inc. (Milwaukee) *354*
Manuscript House (New York) *287*
Marchbanks Press (New York) *250*
Mark Twain Association of America (Chicago) *285*
Mark Twain Centennial Committee of New York (New York) *447*
Mark Twain Journal (Kirkwood, Mo.) *307, 434*
Mark Twain Library & Memorial Commission (Hartford) *435*
Mark Twain Memorial (Hartford) *435*
Mark Twain Memorial Shrine (Florida, Mo.) *15*
Mark Twain Society (Chicago) *8*
Mark Twain Society (Elmira, N.Y.) *445*
Martinus Nijhoff (The Hague) *450*
Marvel Classics Comics (New York) *49*
Massmann, Robert E. (New Britain, Conn.) *344*
Matica Hrvatska (Zagreb) *14*
Mazenod, Lucien, Edition d'Art (Paris) *51*
McClurg, A.C., & Co. (Chicago) *459*
McGraw-Hill Book Co. (New York) *322*
McKay, David, Publisher (Philadelphia) *417*
McKinley Publishing (n.p.) *429*
McNeese Review (n.p.) *458*
Meador Publishing Company (Boston) *270*
Mercure de France (n.p.) *5*
Merriam, G.&C. (Springfield, Mass.) *428,435*
Messner, Julian, Inc. (New York) *454*
Metropolitan Opera House (New York) *418*
Michigan State College Press (Lansing) *432*
Millicent Library, The (Fairhaven, Mass.) *340,352*
Mississippi Valley Historical Review (Cedar Rapids, Ia.) *431*
Missouriana Library, Northeast Missouri State College (Kirksville) *456*
Modern Language Association of America (n.p.) *432*
Monarch Press (New York) *118*
Morris, John D., & Co. (Philadelphia) *418*

Morrow, William, & Company (New York) *437*
Mutual Book Company (Boston) *208*

National Magazine (n.p.) *445*
Nesrivat Anonim Siketi (Istanbul) *53*
Nettleton & Co. (Cincinnati) *6-8,18,21*
New American Library (New York) *24,90,251*
New York Public Library (New York) *323*
Nickerson, Thomas (Honolulu) *280*
Nijhoff, Martinus (The Hague) *450*
Noble Publishing House (Bombay) *451*
Northwestern University on the air (Chicago) *439*
Northwestern University Press (Evanston) *456*
Norton, W.W., & Company (New York) *118*

Obunsha Library (n.p.) *50*
Ohio State University Press (Columbus) *430*
Oliver & Boyd (Edinburgh and London) *441*
Ollendorff, P. (Paris) *38*
Osgood, James R. and Company (Boston) *58,70-72,80-81,83-85,416*

Papademetriou, Al. and E. (Athens) *52*
Penguin Books Ltd. (Harmondsworth, England) *49*
Peter Pauper Press (Larchmont, N.Y.) *17*
Peter Pauper Press (Mount Vernon, N.Y.) *4,313*
Pocket Books, Inc. (New York) *117,131,446*
Ponsa, A.G. (Barcelona) *53*
Prentice-Hall, Inc. (Englewood Cliffs, N.J.) *456*
Princeton University Press (Princeton, N.J.) *435*
Purdue University Press (West Lafayette, Ind.) *357,458*
Putnam's, G.P., Sons (New York) *441*

Quarterly Journal of Speech (n.p.) *442*
Queens House (Larchmont, N.Y.) *438*

Rand, McNally & Company (Chicago) *48*
Random House (New York) *339*
Resources for American Literary Study (n.p.) *442*
Reynolds-DeWalt Printing Co. (New Bedford, Mass.) *340*
Rinehart & Co. (New York) *23*
Ritchie, Ward, Press (San Francisco) *292*
Rizzoli, Editore (Milan) *5*
Rodale Press (Emmaus, Pa.) *434*
Roman, A., & Co. (San Francisco) *8,18,21,40*
Rose, G.M., & Sons (Toronto) *129*
Rose-Belford Publishing (Toronto) *44, 56, 73*
Routledge & Kegan Paul (London) *459*
Routledge, George, and Sons (London) *20-21,26-27,54*
Row, Peterson & Co. (Evanston, Ill.) *210*
Running Press (Philadelphia) *353*

St. Crispin Press (New York) *341*
Salvat Editores (n.p.) *53*
Schermerhorn, J.W., & Co. (New York) *415*
Scholastic Book Services (New York) *319*
Schoningh, Ferdinand (Harstelling) *159*
Schori Press (Evanston, Ill.) *442*
Schubothes, J.H. Boghandels (Copenhagen) *38*
Scribner's, Charles, Sons (New York) *449*
Seligman, Jos. (Stockholm) *53*
Seligman, Jos., & Chs. (Stockholm) *66*
Sheldon & Company (New York) *16-17*
Shondo-Shando Press (Quincy, Ill.) *457*
Shorter, Clement (London) *243*
Signet (New York) *48*
Simon & Schuster (New York) *446*
Slemin & Higgins (Toronto) *36*
Slote, Woodman & Co. (New York) *59*
Smith, Geirge M., & Co. (Boston) *18*
Southern Methodist University Press (Dallas) *439*
Sportska Knjiga (Boegrad) *119*
S/R Books (New York) *118*
Stanyan Books (New York) *339*

Stokes, Frederick A., Company (New York) *272,443*
Stowe-Day Foundation (Hartford) *182,451*
Stuart, Lyle (New York) *69*
Sussex University Press (London) *437*
Svensk Lararetignings (Stockholm) *121*

TAB Books (New York) *76*
Tauchnitz, Bernhard (Leipzig) *9,64,114,171*
Thor Publications (New York) *431*
Three Asterisks (n.p.) *68*
Three Sirens Press (New York) *47*
Trident Press (New York) *32*
Tuttle, Charles, Co. (Rutland, Vt.) *327*

Ueberreuter, Carl (Wein) *55*
Uitheverij V.A. Kramers-'s-Gravenhage (The Hague) *51*
Underhill & Nichols (Buffalo) *160*
University of California (Berkeley and Los Angeles) *24,132,251,304,333-338,342,348-350,359,429-430,455*
University of Chicago Press (Chicago) *440*
University of Colorado Studies (n.p.) *432-433*
University of Illinois Press (Urbana) *456*
University of Iowa Press (Iowa City) *356*
University of Kentucky Press (Lexington) *437*
University of Massachusetts Press (Amherst) *446*
University of Minnesota Press (Minneapolis) *448*
University of Missouri Press (Columbia) *443,445,449*
University of North Carolina Press (Chapel Hill) *431*
University of Oklahoma Press (Norman) *308,429,436,454*
University of Washington Press (Seattle)
University Press of Kentucky (Lexington) *430*
University Press/Southern Methodist University (Dallas) *290*
Unwin, T. Fisher (London) *208*

Van Goorzonen's, G.B. ('s-Gravenhage & Djakarta) *50*
Vassar College (n.p.) *456*
Verlag Ullstein (Frankfort) *66*
Veselin Maslesa (Sarajevo) *50*
Viking Press (New York) *289,456*
Vokietijos Krasto Valdybos (Leidinys, Czech.) *78*

Waldman, I., & Son (New York) *132*
Ward, Lock & Co. (London) *57*
Warren, P.R., Co. (Boston) *218*
Washington Square Press (New York) *255*
Watson Gill (Syracuse, N.Y.) *37,44*
Watts & Co. (London) *222*
Watts, Franklin (New York) *4*
Webb, C.H. (New York) *2,4*
Webster, Charles L., & Co. (New York) *74,83,92,111-112,114,122-126,129,134,156,158*
Werner, Edgar S. (New York) *239*
Western Humanities Review (n.p.) *432*
West Virginia Pulp and Paper Co. (n.p.) *4*
Whittier Books (New York) *302*
Winston, John C., Co. (Chicago) *47*
Wolfe, M.O. (Petersburg & Moscow) *50*
Wonder Books (New York) *49*
World Publishing Co. (Cleveland & New York) *450*

Yale University Press (New Haven) *455,457*
Yoseloff, Thomas, Ltd. (London) *345*

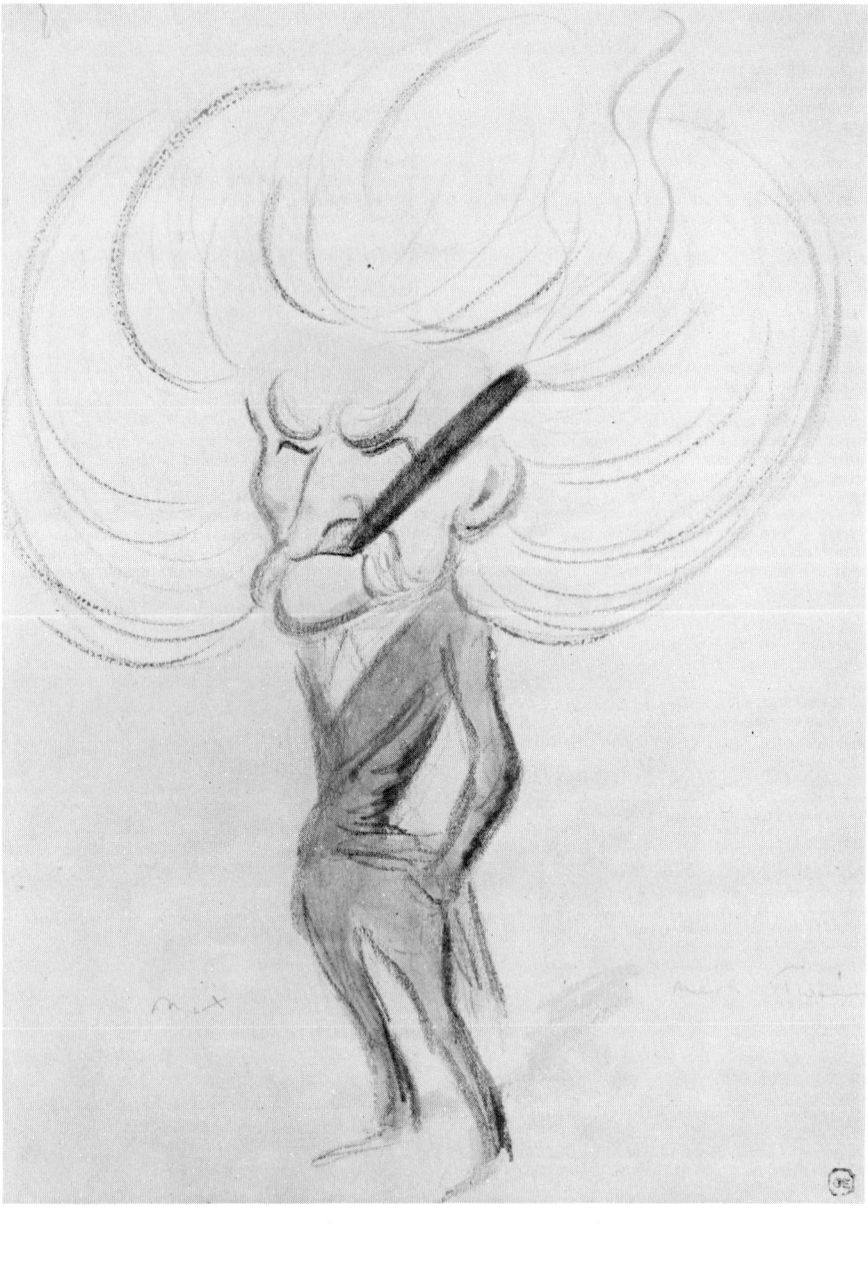

Index of Illustrators, Designers & Photographers.

This index lists illustrators, photographers and designers who contributed to the works of Mark Twain and to books about him.

Aptosliou, Bur. *52*

Baldi, F. *79*
Balic, Husnija *50*
Ballantyne, Dale *301*
Barret, G. *51*
Baskin, Leonard *330*
Beard, Dan *124, 126, 128, 134-135, 162, 163.*
Beck, Charles *76*
Benton, Thomas Hart *48,89-90*
Berson, Harold *4*
Blachon, Roger *5*
Brehm, Worth *47,115-116*

Coburn, Alvin Langdon *443*
Couratin, Patrick *78*
Cruz, E.R. *49*
Cutts, G.B. *182*

Dalmate, Marlaritas *52*
Dean, Mallette *316*
Dean, Vivien *316*
DuMond, F.Y. *178.*
Dwiggins, W.A. *283*

Faorzi, F. *52*
Farinas *188*
Fenn, Harry *160.*
Fisher, Leonard Everett *437*
Frankenberger, Robert *450*
Fraser, F.A. *21*
Frost, A.B. *57,164*

Gallagher, M.J. *436*
Gautier, Rene-Georges *120*
Gerhardt, Karl *106*
Gimenez, Miriam Gonzalez *53*
Glintenkamp, H. *441*
Grabhorn, Edwin *262*
Groth, John *173*
Grover, Dorothy *277*
Guilbeau *131*

Hampton, Blake *166*
Heron, Bernhard *188*
Heron, Jean Oliver *52*
Hitchcock, Lucius *202, 210, 232.*
Hoff, Lloyd *278*
Hoffman, Bill *329*
Hogarth, Paul *188*
Howard, Kathryn *294*
Hurd, Peter *47*
Hurst, Hal *135*

Kemble, E.W. *103,117,122-123*
Knight, David *66*
Koukake, N. *78*
Kovac, Anica *119*
Kredel, Fritz *274*
Krouwel, Coby C.M. *51*

LaPointe, Claude *52,120*
Leiner, Al *132*
Lemmi, R. *52,79*
Levering, Albert *234*
Lisa *121*
Locke, Charles *300*
Low, Joseph *4*

Martin, Henry R. *313*
Mays, Victor *452*
McIntyre, Kevin *76*
McKay, Donald *4,48,444*
Minton, Harold *51,117*
Moser, Barry *69*

Nielsen, Jon *49*
Nims, W.C. *454*

Opper, F. *219*

Paulide, P. *78*
Petersen, Bernhard *50*
Pitz, Henry *131*
Pyle, Howard *247*

Ralph, Lester *220*
Rockwell, Norman *47,50,52,116*
Rodriguez, Jose Gonzalez *53*
Rogers, Richard *47*
Roothciv *50*
Roth, Herb *17*
Roth, Richard *68*

Sambourne, Linley *57*
Schmischke, Kurt *52*
Silfverhjelm, Per *121*
Smith, Lawrence Beall *166*
Sperry, R.T. *34*
Stojnic, Mirko *119*
Strothman, F. *212,214,219*

Thompson, Bradbury *4*
Toffolo, G. *79*
Trier, Walter *53*
Tripp, von F.J. *55*
Twain, Mark *317,324*

Vanista, Josip *78*
Viby, Robert *50*

Williams, True *48*
Wilson, Adrian *304*
Winkler, H.H. *68*
Winter, Milo *48*
Wyeth, N.C. *242*

Mark Twain in 1907.

Index of Letters, including Recipients & Persons Mentioned in Inscriptions by Mark Twain.

This index lists recipients of letters, from Mark Twain, and people mentioned in inscriptions by Mark Twain in various of his works shown in this book.

Bartlett *9*
Beecher, Julia J. *72*
Bennett, Sir John *7*
Bishop, William Henry *409*
Bissell, George P. & Co. *372-374-375*
Bliss, Elisha Jr. *64,365,410*
Bliss, Frank E. *11,22,64,196,368,379,395,397*
Booth, Hattie *367*
Briggs, Mr. *245*
Brown, John G. *45*
Bunce, Edward *394*
Burdette, Robert J. *71*
Burton, H.C. *30*
Burton, Richard E. *411*

Carey, William *10,198*
Caulfield, E.B. *402*
Cheney, Frank Woodbridge *374*
Cheney, Mary Bushnell *403*
Clark, Charles Hopkins *410*
Clark, Ida *7*
Clemens, Clara *393,403,405-407*
Clemens, Jean Lampton *12,122,369,407*
Clemens, Olivia Langdon *374-374,378,385,388,401*
Clemens, Olivia Susan *369*
Clemens, Orion *367*
Coe family, the *409*
Coe, Mai Rogers *406-407, 409, 412*
Coe, William R. *405,409*
Collamore, Harry Bacon *43*
Colt, Elizabeth Hart *392*
Crane, Susan Langdon *383,389,405*
Crane, Theodore *367*

Day, Alice Hooker *391*
Day, John Calvin *371*
Dow, Commander *88*
Dunham, Austin Cornelius *412*

Enders, Harriet Whitmore *407*
Everitt, C.P. *126,387*

Fenn, Linus Tryon *382*
Ford, Eunice Langdon *368-369*
Frisbie, T.F. *37,196*
Fuller, Frank *365*

Garrett, Edmund H. *87*
Gillette, William *402*
Goodwin, Josephine Lippincott *400*
Griffin, George *377*

Hall, Elizabeth *412*
Hamersley, William *411*
Haney, *368*
Hewins, Matthew A. *378*
Hooker, Isabella Beecher *379*
Hurst, Mr. *395*

Jacob, Swinton *179*
Jenkins, Elizabeth Foote *382*
Jones, Eliza S.W. *72*

Keith, Dora Wheeler *382*
Kinney, J.C. *381,385*
Krause, R. Howard *195*

Langdon, Charles Jervis *368,374-375,389,394, 400,402,405,407*
Langdon, Ida Clark *178,216,391,398-399*
Langdon, Jervis *111,365,367,378,388*
Langdon, Olivia Lewis *368-369,371,375,377-378, 382-385,387*
Lawrence, Herbert M. *377*
Lewis, John T. *36*
Lowell, Abbott Lawrence *70*

McCook, John James *383,387,405*

Opper, Frederick Burr *37*

Paige, James W. *381*
Parker, E.P. *111*
Parker, Louis P. *111*
Perkins, Charles E. *371-374,377-378,410-412*
Potter, Edward Tuckerman *371*

Raymond, John T. *371*
Robinson, Henry *411*
Rogers, Henry Huddleston *391,393-395, 398-400,405-406,409,412*
Rogers, Mrs. Harry *221*
Routledge & Company *373*
Russell, T.W. *381*

Schonstadt, A. *398*
Shipman, Mary Caroline *377*
Slote, Daniel *368*
Smillie, Charles F. *111*
Spalding, Mr. *202*
Stanley, Robert N. *398*
Stone, Mr. *410*
Stowe, Harriet Beecher *71*
Stowe, Lyman Beecher *71*

Taft, Cincinnatus A. *379*
Taft, Ellen Teresa Clark *71,378-379*
Taft, Laura *83*
Trumbull, Annie Elliott *125,405*

Warner, Charles Dudley *12*
Warner, George H. *377,381,388,392*
Warner, Lilly (Elizabeth Gillette) *36*
Warner, Margaret *74*
Welch, Ellen Bunce *383-384*
Whitmore, Franklin G. *112,125,228,377,382-385, 387-389,391-392,394-395,397-401,403,405-406, 409-410,412*
Whitmore, Harriet Goulder, *61,81,221,401,407, 409*
Williams, Thomas W. *388*

BAL Index

3309 *415*	3514 *236*	
3310 *2*	3516 *238*	
3311 *424*	3519 *240*	
3316 *6*	3520 *242*	
3320 *423*	3523 *243*	
3326 *16*	3524 *222*	
3330 *415*	3525 *244*	
3334 *17*	3527 *246*	
3335 *20*	3529 *249*	
3336 *26*	3533 *250*	
3337 *18*	3534 *251*	
3340 *27*	3535 *252*	
3347 *416*	3536 *253*	
3350 *27*	3537 *254*	
3357 *28*	3539 *262*	
3360 *34*	3541 *262*	
3364 *35*	3542 *263*	
3366A *426*	3543 *264*	
3367 *43*	3544 *265*	
3368 *55*	3549 *266*	
3369 *40*	3551 *267*	
3370 *416*	3553 *268*	
3373 *58*	3554 *270*	
3377 *56*	3555 *274*	
3378 *59*	3556 *276*	
3381 *9*	3558 *277*	
3386 *60*	3559 *278*	
3396 *72*	3560 *279*	
3397 *73*	3561 *280*	This is a list of BAL items pictured in this book. Items not listed here may be found in the list of primary items by Mark Twain which are not owned by the Mark Twain Memorial or the Stowe-Day Foundation. See pages 461-464.
3402 *70*	3562 *48*	
3403 *82*	3563 *283*	
3404 *80*	3564 *284*	
3410 *86*	3565 *48*	
3411 *84*	3569 *285*	
3412 *416*	3570 *286*	
3414 *113*	3571 *89*	
3415 *92*	3572 *287*	
3420 *208*	3573 *288*	
3425 *122*	3574 *289*	
3429 *124*	3575 *290*	
3434 *134*	3577 *292*	
3435 *156*	3578 *295*	
3436 *158*	3579 *296*	
3437 *160*	3580 *299*	
3438 *418*	3581 *300*	
3439 *168*	3582 *301*	
3440 *162*	3590 *8*	
3442 *170*	3608 *54*	
3446 *178*	3609 *44*	
3447 *162*	3618 *57*	
3448 *186*	3622 *64*	
3449 *190*	3624 *36*	
3450 *425*	3629 *73*	
3451 *194, 196*	3645 *208*	
3452 *418*	3651 *37*	
3453 *199*	3664 *217*	
3456 *	3665 *219*	
3458 *190*	3670 *	
3459 *200*	3673 *237*	
3460 *202*	3676 *239*	
3462 *418*	3683 *247*	
3465 *208*	3686 *248*	
3467 *418*	3688 *248*	
3470 *209*	3688 *256*	
3471 *210*	3693 *257*	
3476 *211*	3694 *260*	
3477 *212*	3695 *261*	
3479 *216*	3696 *83*	
3480 *214*	3697 *259*	
3483 *216*	3698 *209*	
3485 *218*	3704 *273*	
3488 *220*	3707 *432*	
3489 *220*		
3490 *222*		
3492 *224*	*Items 3456 and 3670 are sets of the works of Mark Twain. The titles contained in them are listed throughout the text under the individual volume title.*	
3497 *228*		
3500 *232*		
3509 *233*	*BAL 3456 is the* Autograph Edition *of the Writings of Mark Twain (Hartford, 1899-1907). BAL 3670 is the* Hillcrest Edition *of the Writings of Mark Twain (New York and London, 1906-1907).*	
3511 *234*		
3513 *235*		

485

One thousand copies of this book are specially bound and each is numbered. This is copy number

820

Fifty-two copies, lettered A to Z and AA to ZZ, are reserved for the use of the publisher.

Fifteen hundred copies have been bound for the trade and are unnumbered.

This book is set in Century Old Style by **Printype** of Bristol, Connecticut.

The books were photographed by **Dudley Whittelsey** of Avon, Connecticut.

The photographs were processed by **The Color & Design Exchange** of Newington, Connecticut.

The black-and-white photographs were printed for reproduction by **Matthew Murphy** of West Hartford, Connecticut.

The mechanicals were prepared by **Jennifer Rogers** of Burlington, Connecticut.

The book was printed by **Burch Incorporated**, 300 Riverview Drive, Benton Harbor, Michigan 49022.

The book was designed by **Bill McBride.**

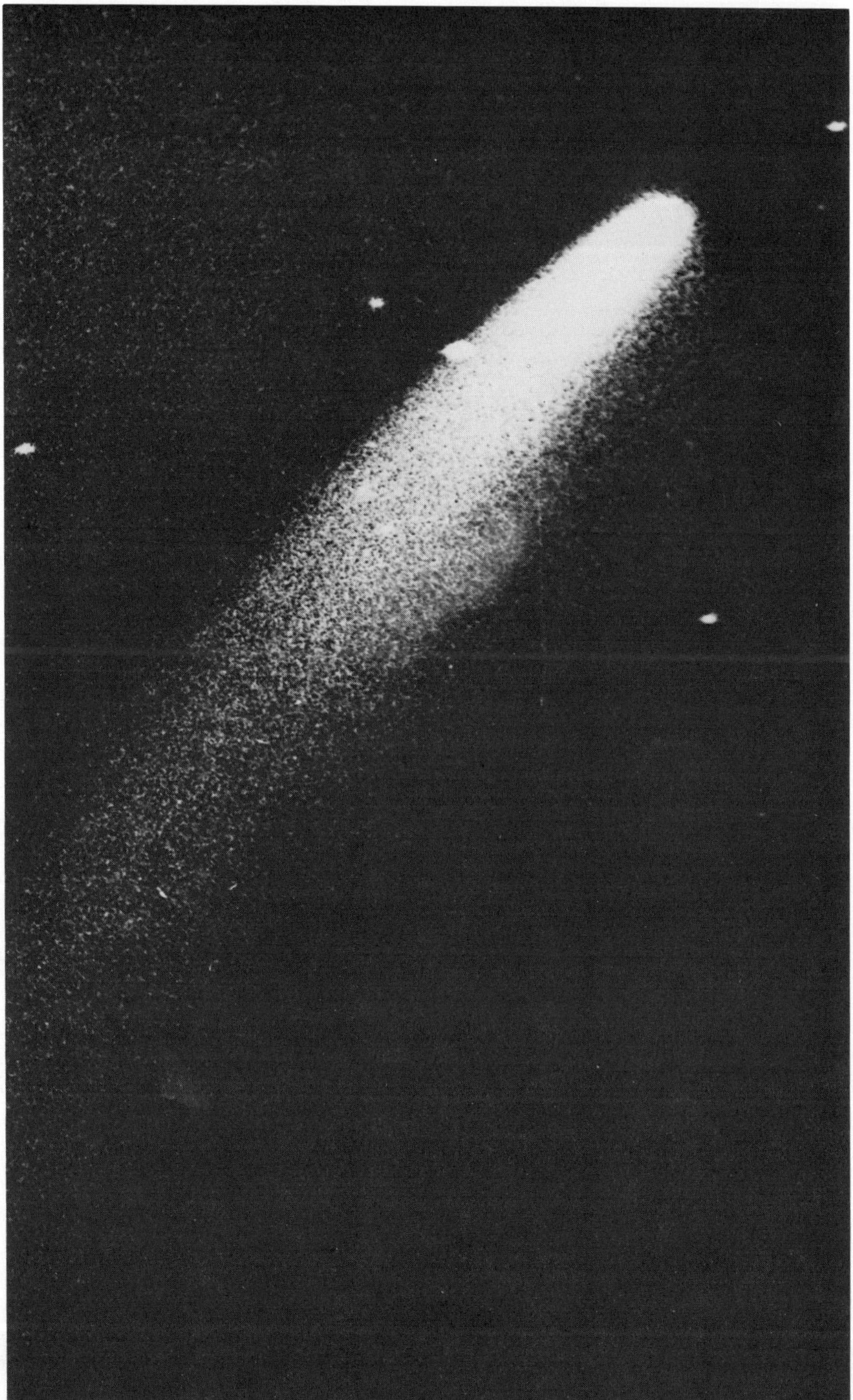